OUR AGING
SOCIETY

OUR AGING SOCIETY

Paradox and Promise

Edited by Alan Pifer and Lydia Bronte

W·W·NORTON & COMPANY
New York · London

First Edition

Library of Congress Cataloging-in-Publication Data
Main entry under title:
Our aging society.
    1. Aging—United States—Social conditions—
Addresses, essays, lectures. 2. Aging—United States—
Economic conditions—Addresses, essays, lectures.
3. Aging—United States—Family relationships—Addresses,
essays, lectures. 4. Age distribution (Demography)—
United States—Addresses, essays, lectures. 5. Aging—
Medical care—United States—Addresses, essays, lectures.
I. Pifer, Alan J. II. Bronte, Lydia.
HQ1064,U5O94 1986   305.2'6'0973 85—31979

ISBN 0-393-02299-4

ISBN 0-393-30334-9 (pbk.)

W. W. Norton & Company, Inc., 500 Fifth Avenue, New York, N.Y. 10110
W. W. Norton & Company Ltd., 37 Great Russell Street, London WC1B 3NU

1 2 3 4 5 6 7 8 9 0

Contents

v

Preface

THIS BOOK HAS ITS ORIGINS in an examination of population aging in America, undertaken by The Aging Society Project, an enterprise funded by Carnegie Corporation of New York. The Project, which came into being in 1982, is, we believe, the first of its kind to explore in breadth the social, economic, political, and ethical implications of this major demographic phenomenon that will, over the next half century and beyond, profoundly affect every one of our nation's institutions and individuals.

In the course of this study it became apparent that, while there has been (and is) a growing awareness of the problems and issues associated with the aging of *individuals*, there was little recognition or understanding by the general public of the focus of our study, the aging of our *society*. Nor had a major work appeared on this subject. It was then that the Project commissioned top experts in a wide range of disciplines to write about societal aging from the perspectives of their particular areas of competence and experience, in order to open up the subject in as comprehensive a manner as possible.

The eighteen essays that appear in this volume, then, represent original and individual thinking; opinions of the authors are not always identical. We think that this contributes to the strength of the book, helping to make it the mind-stretcher that we hoped from its inception it would be.

To our great delight, the American Academy of Arts and Sciences became our collaborator in the Project by agreeing to publish a large portion of this material in the Winter 1986 issue of its prestigious journal, *Daedalus*, and we are grateful to its editor, Stephen Graubard, for his valuable help in shaping this work.

We are also thankful to W. W. Norton & Company for publishing both a hardcover and paperback edition of this book, thereby helping us to reach as large a reading public as possible.

Our warmest thanks go to Carnegie Corporation of New York for making possible both the Aging Society Project and the book.

Finally, we appreciate the help of the book's special advisors: Constance H. Buchanan, Carol Gilligan, Kathleen Woodward, and Michael Teitelbaum.

Alan Pifer and Lydia Bronte

OUR AGING SOCIETY

Alan Pifer and Lydia Bronte

Introduction: Squaring the Pyramid

F EW AMERICANS REALIZE that their country is in the midst of
a demographic revolution that, sooner or later, will affect every
individual and every institution in the society. This revolution
is the inexorable aging of our population. By the middle of the next
century, when this revolution has run its course, the impact will have
been at least as powerful as that of any of the great economic and
social movements of the past: movements such as the conquest and
subsequent closing of the frontier, the successive waves of European
immigration, and the development of our great cities; or, from more
recent times, the post–World War II baby boom, the civil rights and
women's movements, the massive influx of women into the paid
labor force, the revolution in sexual mores, and the decay of many of
our large urban centers. All these developments have had a profound
effect on our nation, but the aging of the population will certainly
have equal, if not greater, impact, if some startling but quite possible
demographic projections materialize.

Population aging is a phenomenon totally unlike the aging of an
individual. An individual ages from the moment of birth to the
moment of death. In the absence of accident or illness, death comes
at the end of the natural life span as the result of physiological
decline. Population aging, however, is not inevitable. Populations can
become younger or older, depending on shifts in the proportions of
people at various age levels. Thus, during periods when relatively
large numbers of children are being born but few people live to older
ages, the median age of the population will fall, and the population
can be said to be getting "younger." Conversely, in periods when

3

relatively few children are being born but large numbers of people are reaching older ages, the median age will rise, and the population can be said to be "aging." The main factors that affect a population's general "youth" or "age" are changes in the fertility rate (the average number of children born to women in their childbearing years), changes in the infant-mortality rate, and changes in life expectancy at older ages.

The aging of America is not a new phenomenon. Our population has been growing older for a long time—since at least 1800. At that time, we were still a very young nation, in the sense that every second person was under the age of sixteen, and very few people lived beyond the age of sixty—a configuration not unlike that of many Third World countries, such as Mexico and Nigeria, today. Since 1800, the population has aged steadily, except for a brief period after World War II when a huge rise in the fertility rate—producing the baby boom—temporarily arrested the aging process.

What is startling about the aging trend today is the rapid pace at which it is proceeding. Two separate and simultaneous developments account for this. The first is the speed with which the numbers of older and very old people are growing. An increasing number of those born in the years before the end of World War I have been reaching their sixty-fifth birthdays. Moreover, since 1900—less than a century ago—our life expectancy has increased by twenty-eight years, from forty-seven to seventy-five. Just since 1950, the ranks of Americans sixty-five years of age and over have more than doubled. Americans in this age group now number some 28 million—more than the entire population of Canada. Within the same period, the number of individuals over age eighty-five has more than quadrupled, to a total of 2.6 million. Measuring population aging another way: the proportion of our people sixty-five and over has grown from 8 to 12 percent during the past thirty-five years, and is expected to reach 17 percent in the next thirty-five years. Ten years after that, in about the year 2035, every fifth, and possibly every fourth, American will be "elderly"—if sixty-five and over continues to be the definition of that term. By the middle of the next century there will be some 16 million people over the age of eighty-five!

Equally arresting has been the decline in the proportion of young people. At an earlier period of our history, as we have seen, over half the population was made up of children under the age of sixteen. By

1900, this group had declined to 35 percent of the population. It dropped further to 25 percent in 1940, rose temporarily to 31 percent in 1960, and has now receded to about 22 percent. In all probability, it will decline further in the decades ahead. Relatively speaking, we will then be on our way to becoming a "childless society."

The United States is not alone in experiencing this transformation in the profile of its population. All of the developed nations of the world are aging, and many of those in Western Europe are "older" than we are. What is distinctive about our situation, however, is the enormous bulge in the population caused by the postwar baby boom. Most other nations had baby booms too, but ours was unique in its size and duration. In the two decades from 1945 to 1964, we added 76 million children to our numbers (one third of today's total population and the equivalent of our entire population in 1900) as the total fertility rate climbed to a high, in 1957, of 3.7 (as discussed by Jacob Siegel and Cynthia Taeuber in this volume).

After 1964, however, the total fertility rate began to plummet, reaching a low of 1.7 in 1976, a figure that was below the replacement rate of the population. This resulted in the relatively small "baby dearth" annual cohorts of the past two decades. It is the advance onward through ensuing decades of this demographic twist—baby boom followed by baby bust—that is cause for so much unease. Our concern will be especially warranted if the fertility rate remains low, or if, as well may be the case, it falls even lower, with very few annual births becoming the long-term norm. But regardless of the level of the fertility rate, it will be well past the middle of the next century before we return to a more balanced population structure. Meanwhile, major changes in both public and private policy will be needed to cope with the effects of the interim skewed structure—especially after about the year 2010, when the first of the baby boomers, now approximately twenty to forty in age, start to retire. During the twenty years from 2010 to 2030, the survivors among the 76 million members of the baby boom will pass their sixty-fifth birthdays and will then range in age from sixty-five to eighty-five. Together with the many individuals over the age of eighty-five, they will form an *enormous* dependent group in the population. Providing for their support, their health care, and their housing will be as great a challenge as any the nation has ever faced.

"Squaring the Pyramid," the title of this introduction, is derived from a graphic representation of traditional population structure, which typically takes the form of a pyramid. Since each age group loses some of its members as the years go by, the pyramid is broad at its base in the first years of life, and narrows more or less steadily until it reaches its apex in a tiny group of people aged somewhere between one hundred and 110, the present limit of natural life. With the tremendous increase in life expectancy in the United States, due principally to the elimination of the killer diseases of childhood but also to the decline of mortality rates at older ages, the pyramid of our population structure is gradually turning into something approaching a square, or, more precisely, a rectangle. In theory, one can visualize a society in which the population maintains itself just at replacement rate and everyone who is born lives out his or her natural life span— making for a perfect rectangle. One could even imagine a more remote possibility, a structure looking something like an inverted pyramid, if the fertility rate were to decline progressively over a period of time to zero. But that eventuality would be tantamount to national suicide!

In fact, the Census Bureau predicts for the year 2030 a population structure for the United States that *is* an almost perfect rectangle up to the age of seventy. At that point, close to 6 percent of the population will be in the age group sixty-five to sixty-nine, about the same percentage as for children under the age of six and similar quinquennial groupings all the way up the ladder to age sixty-five.

This squaring of the pyramid, although it has been going on for a considerable length of time, has now gathered such momentum that it has produced unprecedented situations in many important areas of our national life. As one peers into the future, it becomes obvious that further population aging is going to have even more profound implications. This volume seeks to examine these implications for such institutions as the family, the economy, the labor force, the educational system, the health-care system, and for particular population groups, especially women, children, blacks, and Hispanics. The book is also about changes in societal attitudes and values, changes that are already becoming evident and which can be expected to accelerate as we move into the early decades of the next century.

The essays that follow are oriented to both the present and the medium-term future of our aging society. Relating to the present, they deal with economic and social phenomena that are already reality. Relating to the medium-term future, they deal with both reality and probability. Those Americans who will have the heaviest impact on the demography of that period have already been born. But if we extrapolate from current trends, we can anticipate further increases in life expectancy, based on socioeconomic developments and medical advances, along with the likelihood of continued low, or even lower, fertility. Together, reality and probability imply more and more old people and, relative to the entire population, fewer and fewer children.

Anticipating the longer range future—say, the middle of the next century—becomes, of course, far more problematic and speculative. Nonetheless, the implications of radical changes in population structure in the intervening decades are so staggering that it is instructive to examine some of the more extreme—*though possible*—extrapolations of current demographic trends in order to see what sorts of scenarios they paint. The most extreme scenario described in this collection is set forth by Siegel and Taeuber. They depict for the year 2050 a population with a life expectancy of one hundred, compared with today's seventy-five; a median age of fifty-three, as against the present thirty-one; a median age of death past the age of one hundred, compared with seventy-three today; 36 percent of the population age sixty-five or over, in contrast with today's 12 percent; 16 percent below the age of twenty, as against today's 31 percent; and almost four persons over sixty-five to every five persons of prime working age (twenty to sixty-four), or a gerontic dependency ratio four times our present one!

Would such a society, or anything approaching it, be viable? What adjustments would have to be made in our institutions, in our attitudes, perhaps in our ethical standards, if a population structure this far removed from previous demographic experience were to become a reality? And what if, as a result of the spectacular advances in molecular biology that some scientists consider possible, there occurs a gradual lengthening of the natural life span to the age of, say, 115, 120, or even 130? The implications of that possibility exceed the imagination.

The aging of our society is, in a sense, as broad a subject as society itself. Nevertheless, out of the subject's enormous expanse and its apparent diffuseness, six principal themes emerge in this volume. The first of these is clearly the overriding importance of children in a society characterized both by a decline in their absolute numbers and, more important, by the diminished size of the group of children as a proportion of the total population. In an aging society, it is inevitable that there will be fewer households with children. Today, fewer than 38 percent of households nationwide contain anyone under eighteen years of age, compared with nearly 50 percent in 1960. In a situation where so few adults feel any direct personal stake in the quality, or even the availability, of essential services for children, it is all too easy for those services to atrophy and decline.

But there is an additional factor that makes the present situation even more compelling and urgent. A growing proportion of children being born in the United States are of minority background, chiefly black and Hispanic. Because these children come from families that are less likely to share equally in the nation's affluence, they are less likely to receive the support they need—principally, good nutrition, health care, education, and the opportunity to live in decent housing in a safe neighborhood. Hidden away in deteriorating inner-city areas out of the sight of the average middle-class voter, these minority children may seem to be of little importance to the larger society. It may well seem preferable to the middle-class voter to keep taxes down, rather than investing in such children. Yet we *must* invest in our children—all of them. Poor nutrition, health care, and schooling, and housing in dangerous, run-down neighborhoods can only diminish a child's chances to develop into a strong, effective adult capable of playing a part in governing the nation, maintaining its security, and keeping its economy strong. Regardless of their racial or language background or their families' economic status, *all* of the nation's children belong to *all* of us—and each and every one of them will be needed. Together, and more so than ever in our aging society, they form the collective future of our country.

A second theme of this book is that population aging, although it affects everyone in the society, does not affect all groups equally or in the same way. First, there is the special situation of women, who considerably outnumber men at older ages, who are much more likely to be living alone, and whose economic situation is substantially worse than that of men. As a result of their greater longevity, women today outnumber men by three to two in the over-65 age group and almost two to one in the over-75 group. Only half as many women as men over age sixty-five are married. Among persons sixty-five and over living alone, some 80 percent are women, and they constitute about two-fifths of all women in that age range. The median annual income for men over sixty-five in 1983 was $9800, while for women it was only $5600—57 percent of that for men. Seventeen percent of these women were living in poverty, as opposed to 10 percent of men, and among black and Hispanic elderly females the poverty rates were, respectively, 42 percent and 24 percent. Clearly, along with declining numbers of children, a growing body of older citizens is the most prominent feature of our aging society. A substantial part of this group is composed of single females, living alone and in actual poverty, or close to it. Any consideration of policies affecting the elderly must, therefore, always be informed by a sensitive awareness of just who the elderly are.

Americans of black and Hispanic background are two other groups whose situation in our aging society is quite special. Because blacks, on the average, do not live as long as do whites, they gain less benefit from Social Security retirement provisions, while making the same contribution through the payroll tax as other workers. Hispanics, because they are generally a young population group with a strong interest in programs for children, find themselves in direct competition with the elderly for public expenditure. Separate essays in this volume examine the particular situations of each of these groups.

Finally, the rate of population aging is very different for different areas of the country, depending on such factors as fertility rates and net in-and-out migration both of young people and the elderly. The northeastern and Great Plains states have the oldest populations, and the western states, including Alaska and Hawaii, the youngest; the southern and western states are aging the most rapidly. Florida, already the oldest state with nearly 18 percent of its population age sixty-five and older, continues to age rapidly. These discrepancies have significant implications for severe economic, social, and political tensions among the regions.

A third theme of this volume addresses the nature of the relationship between the generations in an aging society. When the popular press has taken an interest in population aging, it has focused on the question of intergenerational equity and competition for resources among the various age groups—generally posed in terms of the old versus the young, or, more dramatically, "the war between the generations." It is, of course, almost inevitable that in an aging society increasing amounts of both public and private resources will have to be allocated to the elderly, simply because they are ever more numerous and are living to more advanced ages at which their needs for health care and other services are likely to be greater. Where resources are in limited supply, as is usually the case, it is also likely that more dollars for the elderly will mean less for other age groups— which raises both an equity issue and the searching question of what constitutes a wise distribution of resources in the light of the overall needs of the society. As we have seen, short-changing children poses great dangers for the future of the nation.

The issue of equity is a difficult one to judge. Has the generation now in retirement, or close to it, so managed the nation's affairs that its own members have greatly benefited themselves by passing along a heavy burden to the young? Some young people are making that claim. But does such an equity issue really exist? All generations make their contributions to the national welfare during their prime years according to their assessments of the needs of the times. Thus, for example, some generations are obliged to fight in wars and meet the attendant costs, while others face different burdens. In this situation, who is to say where justice lies?

The wise distribution of resources, however, is not a theoretical issue. It is real, and cannot be avoided in a complex society such as ours where the demands on tax dollars are seemingly endless. The question of age versus need as the basis for determining benefits for the elderly follows directly from this broader issue. It is a question that is already on the national agenda and one that will become ever more pressing—and emotional—as the population continues to age. However that question is ultimately settled, we must see to it that a destructive competition among the several age groups for the resources required to meet their most essential needs is avoided. Such a competition, though possible and even likely, would be scandalous in a nation that can well afford to see that everyone is properly cared for.

Many of the contributors to this volume, however, envision a *positive* outcome to population aging, rather than the negative outcome of intergenerational competition. What they see is the prospect of interdependence among the generations, the notion that the several age groups—children, young adults, the middle aged, the young-old, and even the old-old—all have something to contribute to the society, need each other, have reciprocal responsibilities, and together constitute a united and therefore viable national community. This is a constructive and exciting idea, because it leads us to consider what each age group can contribute and to examine the changes in policy and structures that need to be made to enable each group to make that contribution. It provides a framework for thinking about what the very young and the very old can give to each other and stimulates thinking about ways to bring these two groups into closer contact. It also suggests that the baby-boomers have a responsibility to provide generously for the education and welfare of the small baby-dearth cohorts following them in exchange for the latter's support two to three decades from now, when the baby-boomers begin to enter the dependent stage of their own lives.

A fourth theme, brought out in several chapters, relates to the constant change in the meaning, or significance, of given ages. Thus, while there are many more people past the age of, say, sixty-five in the aging society, what it means to *be* that age differs markedly from the norms of earlier periods. Most men and women over sixty-five today are vigorous, healthy, mentally alert, and still young in outlook. In short, today's so-called elderly are not at all the same people as the elderly of previous eras, even of two or three decades ago. And when the enterprising, aggressive, well-educated baby-boom cohorts reach their "golden years," societal notions of the meaning of that time of life will change still further. Thus, old age in the aging society is a fluid concept invested with meaning, not by past expectations and norms, but by the characteristics of each generation as it reaches that stage of life.

This tremendously important idea leads to an equally important fifth theme—the notion that age sixty-five has become obsolete as a basis for life-course policy. A more realistic basis for policy might be a new concept we call the "third quarter of life," the years from about fifty to about seventy-five—the lower age selected because it is a time of change for many people, and the upper because it is only after age seventy-five that many people begin to decline physically and mentally. Since the majority of Americans at the age of fifty today still have a third to a half of their life spans ahead of them, and since people between the ages of fifty and seventy-five will soon constitute nearly a third of the population, the third-quarter concept assumes that one's fifties and early sixties need not and should not be a period of gradual withdrawal and decline toward an inevitable cut-off point of age sixty-five. Instead, these years should constitute a period of rebirth, with the awakening of new interests and enthusiasm for life, and new possibilities for being productive—defined not necessarily as full-time paid employment but, more flexibly, to include part-time paid work and full- or part-time volunteer work. More and more, an aging society will need the contributions its older citizens can make, and, with long lives stretching ahead of them, they, in turn, will have an urgent need to stay productive.

We need, then, new attitudes and new policies in both the public and private spheres of our national life, geared to novel demographic patterns and the fundamental changes that have taken place in the field of human development. As change in both these areas has raced ahead, the nation has been left with a set of prevailing attitudes and policies that are not only anachronistic, but inhumane and inefficient as well.

A sixth and final theme that informs much of the volume is the emergence of a huge new area of moral uncertainty in our national life having to do with medical care of the elderly, especially the very old. Always there implicitly, this problem, because of rapid growth in the numbers of old people, has undergone a change in degree sufficient to make of it a change in kind. New therapies based on new biomedical knowledge and advances in medical technology have made it possible to keep people alive long after the quality of their lives has so deteriorated as to raise serious questions about the ethics of denying them a merciful death. Additional techniques for prolonging life undoubtedly lie ahead, which will simply exacerbate the problem. Sooner or later new procedures and standards will have to be established that, on the one hand, protect a person's right to life but, on the other, his or her right to die with dignity and without the unnecessary expediture of large sums of money to little or no purpose.

There is also the issue that is sure to become more intense as the numbers of old people grow of whether very expensive forms of treatment or therapies that are in short supply should be made available to the elderly. In Britain, for example, kidney dialysis is generally not provided for patients who have passed the age of fifty. Is there, however, any ethical basis for denying treatment to someone *solely* on the basis of age?

Nevertheless, per capita health-care expenditure on the elderly is nearly four times that of the rest of the population, and the fact of their growing numbers is one of the driving forces behind the nation's mounting health-care bill. These realities are sure to create pressures—indeed, they already are—to limit spending on the elderly. At bottom, there is the question of what health care is: is it a basic human right for everyone, an investment in human resource development, or simply a consumer good available to those who can afford it? The answer to this difficult question profoundly affects the decision the United States must soon make about how much it is to spend on the health of the elderly.

The purpose of this volume is to convey to the American people a sense of urgency about the effects population aging is having, and increasingly will have in the years ahead—effects on children, on women and minorities, on the family, on relations between the generations, on the labor force, on the health-care system, on the nature and meaning of stages of the life course, on the political system, on the nation's ethical standards, and on many other institutions and facets of our national life. If these effects are considered *now*, they can become the basis for beneficial new public and private policies. If they are ignored, they will cause severe social tensions in the years ahead and possibly even shatter that minimal sense of community that makes a nation viable.

The future is not preordained. Population aging holds within it the promise of a much better society for all of us or, paradoxically, a far worse one. The choice is clearly there, and it is ours to make.

W. Andrew Achenbaum

The Aging of
"The First New Nation"

WRITERS OFTEN USE THE MYTHS and images of youth and age that are commonplace in descriptions of human development to describe historical circumstances; for more than two centuries, this language of aging has been invoked to interpret American history. Hence, America was a "virgin land," a bold experiment that the "Old World" could admire but never quite emulate.[1] Chroniclers have praised and criticized America as an eternally "young Republic," a land of boundless energy and promise, with a capacity for appraising its own strengths, foibles, and ambiguities.

Americans have long taken pride in their self-proclaimed status as a "chosen" people who dared to avoid—and often defy—the very forces of history that ultimately drove other nations into decline. The belief that the frailties of the human condition could be surmounted as the country inexorably moved toward its "manifest destiny" was extolled as a self-evident truth. Today, demographic realities and dislocation in the political economy belie this kind of confidence in America's capacity to prolong the growth and achievements of its early years. The median age of citizens in the "first new nation" is over thirty. Some observers fear that the United States may be passing through a "grand climacteric" *because* it is an aging society.

And yet, today's specter of sclerotic decline may be as illusory as the hope that was earlier placed in this country's youthful vitality. Can we really reconstruct our past and forecast our collective destiny on the basis of a metaphor of individual aging? Despite the analogy's seductive (and ominous) appeal, there are ways in which societal development does not conform to the human life course.

Aspects of human aging, for instance, have no obvious parallels in the evolution of nations. The biblical "three-score-and-ten" roughly approximates the average life expectancy at birth in most contemporary Western societies, including ours. Most scientists stress the finite limits of human existence. What, in contrast, is a society's "natural" life span? Neither classical nor medieval civilization in the West or East gives any firm guideline. When, after all, does Roman history begin and end? When did "Japan" become Japan? There may not have been a sufficient passage of time to permit us to measure how long "modern" independent countries can reasonably expect to endure, or how many stages of development they might pass through. Most of the countries that belong to the United Nations are less than two hundred years old. "The American Century" will probably not last a hundred years. We simply have no basis for assuming that societal aging conforms to the dictates of some biological time-clock or to any other mechanistic measurement of duration.

Individual aging, moreover, implies an element of maturation, even if people do not invariably grow wiser or "better." Biomedical researchers have demonstrated that senescence involves changes in physiological and psychological functions that result from nothing more profound than the mere passage of time. Given the plasticity of the human organism, some of the deleterious processes of growing older can be delayed, compensated for, and even reversed. Can the same be said of societal development? If so, what are the manifest indications of "youth" and the telltale signs of "age"? Can we devise a measure of economic, political, social, or cultural growth that is not context-bound? Without such a trans-temporal instrument, any measure of societal "progress," much less regression, is a biased one.

Finally, societal aging is not "organic." Babies are born with all the parts and potential they ever will possess, yet societies' natural endowments are not all present at creation. Hence, China is an "ancient" country with a "young" population. Similarly, our country's heritage was not made, nor is it shared, only by those whose forebears were here in 1776. The basis of community in a nation of immigrants cannot be the proprietary domain of a select few.

Yet we must not minimize the social and cultural significance of those myths and images of age and aging that pervade our visions and interpretations of the American experience. Our existence as a nation depends in large measure on the ways that Americans translate our deepest longings into common symbols and collective beliefs.[2] A national ethos helps informed citizens make choices about how to conduct public affairs; it signals enduring and widely held modes of thought and behavior that might guide us as we cope with an ever-changing world.

If the basic premise of this volume is correct—that a distinctive set of demographic, political, economic, and social trends has converged, necessitating a shift in relationships among various age groups, a shift that will in turn undoubtedly have profound societal consequences— then it is essential to know something about the roots and the functioning of the images and myths of America as an aging society. Are there certain clusters of ideas associated with "youth" and "age," "growth" and "decline," that writers have seized on to describe the American experience? Do they resemble European notions? Will our current national symbols support or frustrate our efforts to acknowledge that we are in fact an aging society? Should we create new myths and images that will give greater prominence to the sorts of values and meanings that we need in the future?

II

The Founding Fathers realized that neither their conception of natural law nor their various interpretations of history justified hopes for their infant republic's inevitable, unlimited societal progress. After all, writers since Seneca and Florus had drawn analogies between the human life course and the parabolic histories of nations. The theme of societal "decline"—not only political, but moral, religious, economic, social, cultural, and cosmic—was well known.[3] So it was that in the early years of the republic, defenders of the American experiment invoked the metaphor of age to disarm their European critics and reinforce their conviction that a *novus ordo seclorum*—a new order of the ages—was possible.

Americans were quite sensitive to a late eighteenth-century dispute over the effect of the environment on human health and social development in the New World. French intellectuals cited reports by explorers, missionaries, and settlers indicating that Native Americans were intellectually and physically inferior, lacked sexual ardor and moral rectitude, and had shorter life expectancies than Europeans. Such evidence, they claimed, incontrovertibly proved that the American environment degenerated all living forms, including humans.[4] Others disagreed. Dom Antoine-Joseph Pernety, for instance, argued in his *Dissertation sur l'Amérique et les Américains* (1770) that the new land's rich soil, pure water, and temperate climate were conducive to growth. Americans joined the fray. When an Englishman once tried to persuade Benjamin Franklin that Americans were short-lived, Franklin retorted, "That is not ascertained, for the children of the first settlers are not yet dead!"[5]

Proponents and opponents alike concurred that life expectancy was a valid measure of the impact on health of civil as well as natural environment. "There is an indissoluble union," the eminent Philadelphia physician and patriot Benjamin Rush declared, "between moral, political and physical health."[6] Republican ideologues contended that good political and social institutions fostered long and fruitful lives. Corrupt governments oppressed citizens and shortened their lives. Survival to relatively old age therefore bespoke a virtuous political order. Such data were universally accepted. As J.P. Brissot de Warville remarked in 1788: "Tables of longevity may be everywhere considered the touchstones of governments; the scale on which may be measured their excellencies and their defects, the perfection or degradation of the human species."[7]

Americans gathered bills of mortality, combed church registers, and searched through other vital records to estimate the probability that people in the New World enjoyed a life expectancy that was at least comparable, if not superior, to that experienced in the Old. In an extended essay he prepared for the American Philosophical Society in 1791, William Barton claimed that "the probabilities of life, in *all its stages,* from its commencement to the utmost possible verge of its duration, are higher in these United States, than in such European countries as are esteemed the most favorable to life."[8] Isaac Bickerstaff's *New-England Almanack,* Robert B. Thomas's *Farmer's Almanack,* and the editor of *Cramer's Pittsburgh Almanack* entertained their readers with examples of long life. Hezekiah Niles, the editor of the most widely circulated and authoritative weekly magazine during the first quarter of the nineteenth century, recorded examples of "longevity" as a source of national pride. By 1823, Niles reported only cases of centenarians, pointing out that such evidence provided sufficient proof that the New World's propitious physical environment sustained republicanism. One of the *Resources of the United States of America* (1818), argued John Bristed, was that "the aggregate salubrity of the United States surpasses that of Europe. . . . The Americans average a longer life than the people in Europe."[9]

But did a comparative advantage in relative numbers of older people necessarily mean that the American experiment would prove successful in the long run? Many took to heart an ironical theory of societal development postulated by Edward Gibbon in his magisterial *Decline and Fall of the Roman Empire* (1776–88): "It was scarcely possible that the eyes of contemporaries should discover in the public felicity the latent causes of decay and corruption."[10] Gibbon was referring to a period in which Romans assiduously cultivated constitutional principles of frugality, industry, and prudence for the sake of the commonwealth's prosperity—virtues that the Founding Fathers sought to nurture on American soil.[11] How could those hallmarks of civic life that guaranteed growth and comity be instilled in a way that did not simultaneously contribute to the fledgling republic's premature aging and demise, as had been the case with classical Rome?

The way to defy the course of history, some believed, was to create a distinctive political economy that would not succumb to the vices and corruption that were endemic in European society. "For America in her infancy to adopt the maxims of the Old World," warned Noah Webster in his popular spelling book, "would be to stamp the wrinkles of old age upon the bloom of youth, and to plant the seed of decay in a vigorous constitution." Webster urged his fellow citizens to invent their own traditions: "Begin with the infant in the cradle . . . let the first words he lisps be 'Washington.' "[12] But even traditions worthy of Washington's imprimatur needed some time-tested anchor. The Founding Fathers believed that they had to animate their New-World order with sound, "venerable" principles appropriate for a daring venture in nation-building. As James Madison observed in Federalist Paper no. 49, "When the examples which fortify opinion are *ancient* as well as *numerous,* they are known to have a double effect."[13]

Thus Americans between 1780 and 1820 cultivated a *republican* political economy. They rejected British mercantilist principles, hoping to keep manufacturing interests ancillary to the prevailing agrarian order. "Those who labour in the earth are the chosen people of

God," declared Thomas Jefferson. "Corruption of morals in the mass of cultivators is a phaenomenon of which no age nor nation has furnished an example."[14] But Jefferson and his contemporaries were far from waxing nostalgic for some bucolic, pre-industrial elysium. Rather, they hoped to avoid the excesses usually associated with the shift from a simpler to a more complex economy by building on the tremendous potential that lay before Americans thanks to their vast western land reserves. Expanding commercial agriculture, they believed, would promote widespread equality of opportunity. If so, the United States might be able to avoid the artificial class distinctions that fueled conflict and envy and divided populations elsewhere. America could capitalize on individual self-interest to provide a level of material well-being that all citizens could enjoy.

The creators of the new nation also instituted an elaborate set of governmental processes to prevent the abuse of power. They took steps to ensure that the rising generation possessed the intellectual capacities and the work skills necessary to sustain growth. Leaders were drawn from the "natural aristoi." Fusing a commitment to the twin ideals of liberal, democratic capitalism and evangelical Protestantism, they hoped, would enable their offspring to avoid the mistakes and excesses that had reduced the Mother Country into "an old, wrinkled, withered, worn-out hag."[15]

The Founding Fathers thus bid for a prolonged social youth by exploiting natural resources and profiting from the lessons of the past. They forged national symbols that embodied this bold strategy, even if these bore faint relationship to "reality." There are surely more valid reasons for making the wild turkey rather than the bald eagle our national bird, but the latter flies more gracefully. And as the eagle soars, so too could Americans' faith in their ability to sustain their vitality by expanding their physical space from sea to sea. Similarly, despite Abigail Adam's plea to her husband "to remember the ladies," women were hardly accorded full legal protection and economic opportunity in the early years of the republic; yet Minerva, the goddess of wisdom, dressed in armor, became the prototype for Columbia.

Nor should it be altogether surprising that an old man with long white hair and chin whiskers came to be the symbol for a new land in which the median age of the population was around sixteen.[16] Dressed in red-and-white-striped pantaloons and a blue coat bespangled with stars, and sporting an unabashedly old-fashioned plug hat, "Uncle Sam" personified the belief that the young republic could act wisely beyond its years: Americans could transcend the circumstances that made Europe corrupt, overcrowded, and superannuated.

III

In the 1890s, a profound malaise gripped intellectuals on both sides of the Atlantic. Politicians and social critics in Paris feared that a declining birth rate would make France weak and aged, a scenario that fed the nation's concern over Germany's imperialistic designs.[17] A sense of decadence and *fin-de-siècle* melancholy pervaded other major capitals on the Continent. The threat of mass political movements and the dislocations wrought by heavy industrialism were raising doubts about the inevitability of progress and the supremacy of rationality in human behavior. "Anxiety, impotence, a heightened awareness of the brutality of social existence: these features assumed new centrality in a social climate where the creed of liberalism was being shattered by events."[18]

Similar sentiments were expressed in the United States. "We are the first Americans," observed Woodrow Wilson in 1885, "to entertain any serious doubts about the superiority of our own institutions as compared with the systems of Europe."[19] Recoiling against labor unrest and urban corruption, Mark Twain, Stephen Crane, and Theodore Dreiser focused on the dark side of human nature. Literary giants imbued their humor, realism, and naturalism with fatalistic overtones.

And yet, as the historian John Higham has rightly noted, pessimism and anxiety here was neither as profound nor as pervasive as it was in Europe. While the keenest minds in Europe reveled in the culture of despair, Americans struggled against it. Brooks Adams, for example, predicted the decline of Western civilization in his *Law of Civilization and Decay* (1895). But three years later, Adams believed that America's involvement in the Spanish-American War disproved his theories: "I am for the new world—the new America, the new empire . . . we are the people of destiny."[20]

Not all doubters and dissenters joined Adams in shifting suddenly from pessimism to jingoism about the invincibility of the American enterprise. The attack on the effete features of the reigning "genteel tradition" was genuine. An intellectual revolt against formalism culminated in new ways of conceiving of the law and the social sciences. Edward Bellamy and Henry George pressed for "utopian" solutions to urban-industrial disorder. Populism briefly became a potent force in politics. Americans perceived themselves to be in the midst of a profound rite of passage. In all areas of life, people struggled to find a voice and a style that reflected their new realities.

Prevailing images of age were transvalued in the process of redefining cultural values and norms. "She starts old, old, wrinkled and writhing in an old skin," observed D.H. Lawrence. "And there is a gradual sloughing of the old skin, towards a new youth. It is the myth of America."[21] Rather than create additional national symbols that embodied the wisdom of years, native writers coined epithets—fuddy-duddy, geezer, sissy, stuffed shirt, cold feet—that suggested a new uneasiness with decorum, gentility, and the propriety one expects from older people.[22] Americans were not prepared to abandon essential virtues, but they did not see any reason to insist on slavish conformity to old-fashioned middle-class values. The times demanded vigor and, above all, a new accent on youth.

In popular culture, the New England town green and Central Park still served important aesthetic and civic functions, but the masses increasingly flocked to Coney Island, a new locus of amusement. Here people could find a respite from convention and freedom from the restraints of regulated social behavior: "The haughty dowager, the exquisite maid, the formal-minded matron, the pompous buck, the pretty dandy, don with their unconstricting garb of bath-flannels, a devil-may-care disregard for the modes and conventions of fashion."[23] Coney Island's carnival-like spirit, of course, merely sustained the illusion of anarchic freedom. By throwing people off balance, literally and imaginatively, its promoters had designed a leisure-time activity that depended heavily on the latest technology and gimmickry while offering a temporary escape from routine and drudgery.

The World's Columbian Exposition, staged in Chicago to coincide with the four-hundredth anniversary of the discovery of the New World, was probably the most ambitious attempt to demonstrate the full promise of American life. "We celebrate the emancipation of man," declared Senator Chauncy M. Depew.[24] The four hundred buildings, broad avenues, and elegant canals that made up the fair were conceived in a monumental, neoclassical style. At once imitative of European taste and yet inspired by a nation coming of age, the fair was no less a play on illusions than Coney Island. The "White City" was designed to evoke a commitment to public harmony and civic virtue. It was a showcase displaying every "modern" convenience. All the world could come and see that America truly represented a new order that hewed to its original promise.

It was fitting that a young historian unveil a fresh interpretation of the American experience at the exposition. Well after midnight on July 12, 1893, at the end of a long session of the fledgling American Historical Association, Frederick Jackson Turner argued that although "the frontier was gone, and with its going has closed the first period of American history," there were new challenges and opportunities ahead.[25] Settling a vast continent had been the major force that shaped democracy. Now, America had to reorient itself toward the future, to guide a rising generation with new frontiers to conquer.

For the rest of his career, Turner elaborated variations on this theme. "Let us hold to our attitude of faith and courage, and creative zeal. Let us dream as our fathers dreamt and let us make our dreams come true."[26] Like Tennyson's "Ulysses"—a poem he frequently quoted—Turner envisioned America devoting its energies to achieving noble goals enunciated long ago. Repeating the words of Harriet Martineau, he appealed to Americans to "cherish their high democratic hope, their faith in man. The older they grow the more they must reverence the dreams of their youth."[27] America could stay vital as it aged if it saw new possibilities in its abiding dreams. By sloughing off the old, it could embrace the promise of its youth.

Maturing, yet not quite mature, and blessed with sufficient energy to realize its full potential—this was America's self-image at the end of the nineteenth century. While social theorists such as G. Stanley Hall probed the significance of "adolescence" as a new stage of life (itself the by-product of an emerging urban middle-class lifestyle), the nation was swept into a celebration of virility and youth. The best-sellers of the day—Jack London's exciting stories set in the Klondike and Owen Wister's tales of the West—extolled "the strenuous life" that Theodore Roosevelt characterized as essential to the American way: "It is only through strife, through hard and dangerous endeavor, that we shall ultimately win the goal of true national greatness."[28] Vigor counted everywhere. On campuses, young people such as Frank Merriwell's fictional Dink Stover were winning honors for God, country, and Yale. America's athletes demonstrated their prowess by setting most of the "world records" and capturing a lion's share of the medals in the first two Olympics.

There were limits, however, to this country's vaunted competitive spirit and its willingness to win the good fight. Americans were capable of beating the Europeans at their own games, but they were not prepared to assume the full responsibilities of participating in the world community. The skirmish with the Spanish in 1898 was a "lovely little war," but efforts to control the Philippines genuinely shocked the nation with insights into the ugly side of imperialism. Awed by the growth of big business and eager to capitalize on the energy unleashed by new technologies, Americans were oblivious to the plight of Southern blacks, fearful of the growing numbers of new immigrants, and innocent of developments abroad.

In this posture, too, the myth of America as an adolescent seems to have reflected—and possibly inspired—a familiar approach to important matters. Generation after generation has bemoaned its loss of "innocence," conveniently forgetting a legacy of racism and rapaciousness that dates back to the colonial period. Innocence perpetually lost, however, rarely regenerates itself into virtue. As George Santayana presciently remarked, "Such is youth 'til from that summer's trance we wake to find Despair before us, Vanity behind."[29]

IV

The year 1976 was not an auspicious time to celebrate America's bicentennial. After more than two decades of extraordinary prosperity, the country was experiencing a marked slowdown in economic growth. Abuses and scandals reported in morning papers and evening newscasts added to the national post–Vietnam-and-Watergate distemper. Pollsters recorded a striking erosion of confidence in major institutions and leaders. Malaise was far more pervasive than it had been in 1876.[30] "Western civilization's decline will coincide with the decline of the United States," declared Jean Gimpel, who excoriated the nation for its complacency and for the loss of its technological initiatives.[31]

Some critics charged that "bicentennial schlock" revealed the intellectual exhaustion of a nation that was showing its age in hard times. Across the land, civic groups tried mightily to produce the biggest and the best ephemera for a day in which indulging in superlatives was appropriately all-American. Beer companies, jewelers, and other manufacturers designed new lines of plastic and disposable products to cash in on patriotism. Wondrous images linger from the festivities—of 212 ships from thirty-four nations sailing into New York's harbor, of crowds cheering and howitzers booming through the finale of Tchaikovsky's "1812 Overture" as fireworks lit the skies—but they did not uplift spirits for long.[32]

In the past, images of age had comforted Americans in times of stress. "Uncle Sam" used to be the military's best recruiter. Fighting men called Andrew Jackson "Old Hickory," Ulysses S. Grant "Old Three-Stars," and George Patton "Old Blood and Guts."[33] "Old" familiarities do not sustain us today. Rehearsing facts of population aging, to be sure, has become standard fare in assessments of the state of the nation.[34] Everybody comments on the sheer growth in the number of older people. Few deny the broadening scope and magnitude of public and private bureaucracies that respond to the elderly's needs. All large social and economic institutions rely on chronological age as a criterion for making bureaucratic decisions. But, without discounting the importance of such trends, it must be observed that we have not spent much time thinking about the ramifications of characterizing America as an aging society. Nor have we created any symbols that might inspire us as we contemplate new frontiers in robotics, bio-ethics, international relations, and space.

But should we create such symbols? To ask this is to confront anew issues raised at the beginning of this chapter. What traits characterize an "aging" society? Does an increase in relative numbers of older people challenge the belief that America is still a relatively young country? Americans may be more age-conscious than ever before, but are we clearer about how demography affects destiny?

Some of us equate the liabilities of physical aging with the problems associated with an aging society. While the "greening" of America was celebrated in the late 1960s, the country's "graying" causes alarm. Neoconservatives are not the only people who charge that satisfying the needs of our elders is "busting" the federal budget. The specter of intergenerational rivalry colors much of the debate over national priorities. "Put bluntly, the old have come to insist the young not only hold them blameless for their past profligacy, but sacrifice their own prosperity to pay for it," a journalist under thirty recently declared. "As the government's generosity becomes further limited, the old promise to become even more militant in advancing their claims of generational privilege. Unless the young join in this grubby competition for equity, they will find their birthright mortgaged even more."[35] In this scenario, expenditures on the elderly are not worth as much as protecting the rights of the baby-boom generation or investing in their children. Even those who do not accept such a radical stance are troubled by the unfortunate age bias that exists in many federal policies. Public spending on the young, when compared to outlays for the old, has been less effective in meeting real needs and in accomplishing "official" purposes.

Others see little point in worrying about the relative status of the aged in an aging society, because they know that American culture encourages people to make the problems of age "invisible." No one has discovered the "fountain of youth," but the producers of Clairol and Grecian Formula make profits by guaranteeing that no one has to be visibly gray. And while there is something pathetic about watching baseball's Old Timers getting trounced by relatively unknown rookies, Arnold Palmer now contentedly (and profitably) plays the senior circuit; perhaps it is better for aging athletes to stay active and not be discouraged from doing things they could do easily earlier in their lives. Applying the same logic, this camp suggests that America can avoid a societal identity crisis the same way that many successful middle-aged citizens manage to do it.

The *graying* of America cannot be reversed; it is a function of long-term declining fertility rates. But Americans should not discount their superior advantages simply because the country is getting a little older. The immigrants who throng our shores—including those who daily cross our borders illegally—risk all for a dream: the United States still affords seemingly boundless opportunities to those with enough skill, luck, and perseverance to take advantage of its resources. Thus, just as advertisers have difficulty reaching the over-49 market because the people in it are so much a part of the mainstream,[36] America seems "old" only when defeatist attitudes prevail, and the public thinks we cannot compete with other nations. At such times, age alone is not the real issue.

Others go a step further and deny that America is getting older. "We stand on the threshold of a great ability to produce more, do more, be more," observed Ronald Reagan, who celebrated his seventy-fourth birthday as he delivered his fifth State of the Union address. "Our economy is not getting older and weaker, it's getting younger and stronger; it doesn't need rest and supervision, it needs new challenge and greater freedom."[37] The President did not challenge conventional images of an aging society. He simply refused to believe that America had to abandon "dreams we can make come true."

In short, Americans contemplate their societal aging with fear, ambivalence, avoidance, and denial. These reactions are understandable, but none is wholly satisfactory. They do not facilitate our ability to plan for the future. Still, these responses do not exhaust the possibilities. The time has come, I believe, for us to be more precise in talking about individual and societal images of age in America today.

V

This chapter began with the proposition that societal development may not necessarily conform to the stages of the human life course. Yet our survey of two centuries of American and European images suggests that such metaphorical associations have long enjoyed currency, even if they have no empirical basis in reality. "Old" societies are consistently viewed negatively; they are perceived as nations in decline, seemingly incapable of renewal and growth. "Young" countries, in contrast, can position themselves at the cutting edge of change. No wonder, then, that Americans chafe at the notion that the U.S. is getting on in years. Insofar as we view ourselves as a society that is constantly growing better, not older, as a nation we welcome challenges, confident that we are capable of absorbing change and flourishing on it.

But how can we get around ambiguous and conflicting feelings about America as an aging society? Let's face it: more is involved than demographic trends. Our institutions are evolving as our population ages, albeit in different ways. For this reason, a thoughtful *myth* of aging can serve a critical function.

The historical record suggests several myths we might embrace. Reagan's tack of denying societal aging, for instance, has an impressive pedigree. From the start, Americans have defied conventional wisdom by proclaiming a unique role in world history. We began by inventing a myth of "young America" that melded classical republicanism with Enlightenment liberalism. The whole process of "Americanization," fostered by late nineteenth-century educational, political, and social institutions, embodies a myth that perceived the country in all of its youthful glory. It resonated with our restless energy and a strain of optimism that counterbalanced doubt and dissent. And in the twentieth century, for all of the convergence of political economies, we have differed in at least one important respect from other aging Western societies: the two world wars devastated Europe physically and psychologically in ways unimaginable here. We looked upon the ruins cocksure that we had the military might, the organizational know-how, and the right stuff to build a better world. Unlike our comrades in Europe, the best was yet to come.

Not only can we renew our status as the "first new nation" on historical grounds, but we might take comfort in our comparative "youth." Being a nation of immigrants serves us well. We always are and always will be younger than the European countries from which so many of us originated. Although our newest citizens—who hail from Asia, Africa, the Middle East, and Hispanic America—come from cultures older than ours, they themselves are generally young and hopeful.

Furthermore, I must confess to considerable uneasiness with myths of aging that rest on stereotypic images of age. To claim that "young" nations are inevitably vital and "old" ones sclerotic strikes me as ahistorical and wrong-headed. After all, our chief competitor not only in computers but also in other areas of technology is Japan, an old civilization with a modern polity and a youthful culture. And in space, we have only one deadly rival, a very old state with a gerontocratic bureaucracy.

Perhaps the way out of an age-vs.-youth set of alternatives is for this country to rejoice in its relative maturity. A "mature" self-image might foster a more sophisticated approach to the problems we are likely to face, a keener appreciation of the ironies of the human condition, and a stoic response to the inevitable conflicts of societal development that will persist. Yet adopting this approach clearly requires us to assume a different orientation toward those myths of aging that resonate with long-standing American traditions.

We have unwittingly reduced our ability to find a myth of aging that can bind the nation together. In the past, honing the distinction between age and aging was not vitally important. When we were a new republic, few mistook boasts of precocity for signs of premature senility. Now we need to establish a collective frame of mind that can help us to understand and accept our place as the world's oldest democracy. We need a myth that can direct attention to what is shared in our diverse and pluralistic society. Such a myth need not have anything to do with age per se: It could build on visions of constantly new frontiers. But aging is an experience everyone shares. Contemplating a new myth on aging that builds on enduring historical truths might fill the bill better than any alternative.

We should begin rather than end with the notion that an aging society spans generational interests all the days of our lives. In this view, all age groups have certain basic rights and responsibilities, and all face common problems. The sense of community that such interdependence implies is fragile. It requires that we look forward and gaze backward as we deal with present-day opportunities and challenges. It forces us to acknowledge our lifelong stake in the American enterprise despite all the forces that induce us to go our own atomistic ways. But it is primarily through appreciating the fragility of "America" as a collective ideal that we can grasp why a myth of aging succeeds insofar as it draws young and old to contemplate the new by honoring America's venerable, but not ancient, traditions.

In terms of domestic policy, living up to a reformulated myth of aging would require us to re-form our major welfare programs. Social Security, which observed its fiftieth birthday in 1985, is perceived as an old-folk's institution, in part because it constitutes the elderly's single most important source of economic support. Medicare, Medicaid, and the Older Americans Act, enacted twenty years ago as essential features of Lyndon Johnson's vision of a Great Society, address the societal risks associated with the end of the life course. Leaving aside budgetary considerations and partisan politics, might not their greatest deficiency be that they provide health-care and social services that younger people are still not entitled to receive?

The question makes sense in a world in which "youth" and "age" must compete for limited resources. From a "mature" perspective, however, the question appears grossly misleading, for it presumes that the age-specific policies designed for one segment of the population benefit only that group. Roughly one out of eight Social

Security recipients is under the age of eighteen. From the start, the program's architects stressed that by addressing the problem of old-age dependency, they would relieve some of the burdens that would otherwise fall on the middle-aged. Yet one of Social Security's paradoxes is that it has become broader in the scope of the services it underwrites, yet narrower in the way it fulfills its institutional purposes.[38] Lawmakers have been reluctant to coordinate a set of policies that would embrace the total range of risks that people face at each stage of their lives. From this perspective, by relying on age-specific criteria, we may have lost sight of factors that wreak havoc on the family and threaten the passage of generations. If this is true, then we must rethink the meaning of "age" in an aging society.

Similarly, in the international arena, a new myth of aging would force us to exercise more care in enunciating our priorities and more caution before involving ourselves in other people's affairs. A mature society understands that it needs to cooperate with the rest of the world in allocating natural and human resources. As a mature society, we perforce will be less reckless in competing in an arms race and less adolescent in presuming that the world will be deterred from evil by an arrogant display of muscle and power.

A new myth of America as an aging society is no less self-interested than the ones it replaces. Yet it invokes a fresh sense of interdependence across geopolitical boundaries that transcends parochial concerns. It builds on a sense of community that fulfills the needs and inspires the noblest sentiments of a brave new age.

ENDNOTES

[1] For an elegant elaboration of some of these themes, see C. Vann Woodward, "The Aging of America," *American Historical Review*, June 1977, pp. 583–94, as well as the comments immediately following by Leo Marx and Ernest R. May.

[2] Stephen B. Oakes, *Abraham Lincoln: The Man Behind the Myth* (New York: Harper & Row, 1984), pp. 4, 16–17.

[3] Peter Burke, "The Idea of Decline," *Daedalus*, Summer 1976, pp. 138–42.

[4] Antonello Gerbi, *The Dispute of the New World* (Pittsburgh: University of Pittsburgh Press, 1973); Henry Steele Commager and Elmo Giordanetti, *Was America A Mistake?* (New York: Harper & Row, 1967).

[5] Quoted in *Niles Register*, Feb. 2, 1822, p. 356.

[6] Quoted in George Rosen, "Political Order and Human Health in Jeffersonian Thought," *Bulletin of the History of Medicine*, Jan.–Feb. 1952, p. 34.

[7]Quoted in James H. Cassedy, *Demography in Early America* (Cambridge, MA: Harvard University Press, 1969), p. 263.

[8]William Barton, "Observations on the Probabilities of the Duration of Life and the Progress of Population, in the United States of America," (Philadelphia: Aitken, 1791), p. 26.

[9]John Bristed, *Resources of the United States of America* (New York: James Eastburn and Co, 1818), pp. 20, 453.

[10]Edward Gibbon, *The Decline and Fall of the Roman Empire,* ed. Dero A. Saunders (New York: Penguin English Library, 1983), p. 81.

[11]Gordon Wood, *The Creation of the American Republic* (Chapel Hill, N.C.: University of North Carolina Press, 1969); Garry Wills, *Explaining America* (New York: Penguin Books, 1981).

[12]Quoted in Carl Kaestle, *Pillars of the Republic* (New York: Hill & Wang, 1983), p. 6.

[13]*The Federalist Papers* (New York: New American Library, 1961), p. 315. For British examples of constructing "ancient" traditions, see Eric Hobsbawm and Terence Ranger, eds., *The Invention of Tradition* (Cambridge: Cambridge University Press, 1983).

[14]Thomas Jefferson, *Notes on the State of Virginia,* ed. William Peden (Chapel Hill, N.C.: University of North Carolina Press, 1958), pp. 164–65.

[15]Drew R. McCoy, *The Elusive Republic* (New York: W.W. Norton, 1980), chap. 2; the characterization of England appears on p. 60. See also Jan Lewis, *The Pursuit of Happiness* (New York: Cambridge University Press, 1982) and Joyce Appleby, *Capitalism and a New Social Order* (New York: New York University Press, 1984).

[16]Some scholars claim that the character was inspired by a certain Samuel Wilson of Troy, New York, who served as an inspector of provisions for the U.S. Army during the War of 1812. See Mitford M. Mathews, *A Dictionary of Americanism on Historical Principles,* 2 vols. (Chicago: University of Chicago Press, 1951). vol. 2, p. 1793; *Encyclopedia Americana,* s.v. "Samuel Wilson."

[17]Alfred Sauvy, *Zero Growth?* (New York: Praeger, 1975); John C. Hunter, "The Problem of the French Birth Rate on the Eve of World War I." *French Historical Studies,* Fall 1962, pp. 490–503; and Michael S. Teitlebaum's contribution to this volume.

[18]Carl E. Schorske, *Fin-de-Siècle Vienna* (New York: Alfred A. Knopf, 1980), p. 6.

[19]Woodrow Wilson, *Congressional Government* (Boston: Houghton-Mifflin, 1885), p. 5.

[20]Quoted in John Higham, *Writing American History* (Bloomington: Indiana University Press, 1970), p. 94. Higham's essay, "American Culture in the 1890s" served as a wellspring of sources and ideas developed here.

[21]D.H. Lawrence, *Studies in Classic American Literature* (New York: The Viking Press, 1923), p. 54. Lawrence was criticizing J. Fenimore Cooper's *Leatherstocking Saga,* yet his remark applies equally well to American self-images at the turn of the century.

[22]Mathews, op. cit.

[23]This description is from the August 1892 edition of *Illustrated American Magazine,* quoted in John F. Kasson, *Amusing the Million: Coney Island at the Turn of the Century* (New York: Hill & Wang, 1978), p. 45.

[24]Quoted in Alan Trachtenberg, *The Incorporation of America* (New York: Hill & Wang, 1982), p. 208.

[25]Frederick Jackson Turner, "The Significance of the Frontier in American History," in *The Frontier in American History* (New York: Holt, Rinehart and Winston, 1962), p. 38.

[26]Frederick Jackson Turner, "The West and American Ideals" (1914), op. cit., pp. 300–301.

[27]Frederick Jackson Turner, "Middle Western Pioneer Democracy" (1918), op. cit., p. 339.

[28]Theodore Roosevelt, *The Strenuous Life: Essays and Addresses* (New York: The Century Company, 1900), pp. 20–21.

[29]Quoted in H.R. Moody, "The Spectre of Decline: Fear of an Aging Society," unpublished paper (1983).

[30]The nation's centennial, it is worth recalling, coincided with a recession. The 1876 presidential election was not resolved until compromises were made that had tragic consequences for reconstructing the South and improving race relations. Bloody railroad strikes the following year ushered in a new era of labor tensions.

[31]Jean Gimpel, "The Greying of America," *National Review*, Nov. 26, 1976, p. 1284. Not everyone expressed such pessimism, of course. See "The Score: Rome 1500, U.S. 200," *Time*, Aug. 23, 1976, p. 59. See also Harrison E. Salisbury, "Travels Through America," *Esquire*, Feb. 1976, pp. 29–50; Barbara Tuchman, "On Our Birthday—America as Idea," *Newsweek*, July 12, 1976, p. 9; and the July and Nov. 1976 issues of the *Annals* of the American Academy of Political and Social Science.

[32]For highlights of the festivities, see "Oh, What a Lovely Party!" *Time*, July 19, 1976, p. 8; see also Jesse Lemisch, "Bicentennial Schlock," *The New Republic*, Nov. 6, 1976, p. 23.

[33]Stuart Berg Flexner, *Listening to America* (New York: Simon and Schuster, 1982), pp. 217–18.

[34]See, for instance, U.S. Senate, Special Committee on Aging, *Developments in Aging: 1983* (Washington, D.C.: U.S. Government Printing Office, 1984), pp. 1–2; W. Andrew Achenbaum, *Shades of Gray* (Boston: Little, Brown and Company, 1983), especially chaps. 5–6.

[35]Philip Longman, "Taking America to the Cleaners," *Washington Monthly*, Nov. 1982, pp. 24, 30. See also Robert J. Samuelson, "Busting the Budget: The Graying of America," *National Journal*, Feb. 18, 1982, pp. 256–60; and Samuel H. Preston, "Children and the Elderly in the U.S.," *Scientific American*, Dec. 1984, pp. 44–49. The chapters in this volume by Alan Pifer, Matilda White and John Riley, and Bernice and Dail Neugarten present a counter-hypothesis about the opportunities of an aging society.

[36]Rena Bartos, "Over 49: The Invisible Consumer Market," *Harvard Business Review*, Jan.–Feb. 1980, pp. 140–148.

[37]"Text of the President's State of the Union Address to Congress." *New York Times*, Feb. 7, 1985, p. 13.

[38]I develop this theme in my forthcoming Twentieth Century Fund Report, *Social Security: Visions and Revisions*.

Bernice L. Neugarten and Dail A. Neugarten

Changing Meanings of Age
in the Aging Society

A GE IS A MAJOR DIMENSION of social organization, as well as a major touchstone by which individuals organize their experiences throughout their lives. For both the society and the individual, new questions are arising regarding the social meanings of age. In many ways, the significance of age is clearly decreasing, but in other ways, it may be increasing.

The aging of the population has brought with it, also, new concerns about the relations among age groups and the possibility of age divisiveness in the political arena. There is little evidence, however, that such political divisiveness is actually occurring in the United States, nor even that it is likely to occur. Furthermore, if public policy–making is to match the social realities, programs based on age might better be played down rather than played up.

In effect, the aging society provides not only a new context but a new opportunity to rethink our traditional views of age in ways that may prove constructive to us as individuals and to the society as a whole.

THE CHANGING SOCIAL MEANINGS OF AGE

Our society is changing in many ways that relate to age. Perceptions of the periods of life are being altered, as well as role transitions, social competencies, and the ages that mark their boundaries. New inconsistencies with regard to age-appropriate behavior are appearing in informal age norms as well as in the norms codified in law.

33

Some of these changes are occurring because of increasing longevity; others are taking place because of the rising educational demands of a technological society, alterations in family structure, changes in the economy and in the composition of the labor force, and changes in formal systems of health and social services.

Periods of the Life Cycle

In all societies, lifetime is divided into socially relevant units, and biological time is translated into social time. The social systems that emerge are based in a general way on functional age; that is, as the individual's competencies change over lifetime, those competencies are nurtured and utilized in the interests of society. Social age distinctions are created and systematized, and responsibilities and rights are differentially distributed according to social age.

Even the simplest societies define at least three periods of life: childhood, adulthood, and old age. In more complex societies, the periods of life become more numerous as they reflect other forms of social change. Different patterns of age distinctions are created in different areas of life, such as in education, the family, and the work force. Chronological age becomes an expedient index of social age.

Historians have described the ways in which life periods became increasingly demarcated in Western societies over the past few hundred years. In the sixteenth and seventeenth centuries, with the appearance of industrialization, a middle class, and formally organized schools, childhood became a clearly discernible period of life, identified by special needs and particular characteristics. Adolescence took on its present meaning in the late nineteenth century and became a widespread concept in the twentieth, as the period of formal education lengthened and the transition to adulthood was increasingly delayed. A stage called youth was delineated only a few decades ago, as growing numbers of young people, after leaving high school and before marrying or making their occupational choices, opted for a period of exploring life roles.

It was only a few decades ago, too, that middle age became identified, largely as a reflection of the historically changing rhythm of events in the family cycle. With fewer children per family, and with births spaced closer together, the time when children grow up and leave the parental home was described as the major marker of middle age. In turn, old age came to be regarded as the time following retirement, and it was usually perceived as a distinct and separable period marked by declining physical and intellectual vigor, chronic illness, social disengagement, and often by isolation and desolation. Life periods became closely associated with chronological age, even though age lines were seldom sharply drawn.[1]

The Blurring of Life Periods

The old distinctions between life periods are blurring in today's society. The clearest evidence for this is the appearance of the young-old.[2] It is a new historical phenomenon that a very large group of retirees and their spouses are healthy and vigorous, relatively well-off financially, well integrated into the lives of their families and communities, and politically active. The term "young-old" has become part of everyday parlance, and it needs little elaboration here other than to point out that the concept was originally based, not on chronological age, but on health and social characteristics. Thus, a young-old person might be fifty-five or eighty-five. The term represents the social reality that the line between middle age and old age is no longer clear. What was once considered old age is now recognized to be pertinent only to that minority of persons who are the old-old, that particularly vulnerable group in need of special care.

When, then, does old age now begin?[3] The societal view has been that it starts at sixty-five, when most people retire from the labor force. But in the United States today, most people retire before that age. The majority begin to take their Social Security benefits at age sixty-two or sixty-three, and at ages fifty-five to sixty-four fewer than three of every four men are presently in the labor force. At the same time, with continued good health some persons are staying at work full-time or part-time until their eighties. So, age sixty-five and the event of retirement are no longer clear markers between middle age and old age.

Alternatively, old age is often said to begin when a person requires special health care because of frailty or chronic disease, or when health creates a major limitation on the activities of everyday life. Yet half of all persons who are now seventy-five to eighty-four report no such health limitations. Even in the very oldest group, those above eighty-five, more than one-third report no limitations due to health; about one-third report some limitations, and one-third are unable to carry out everyday activities.[4] Thus, health status is also becoming a poor age marker.

It is not only in the second half of life that the blurring of life periods is occurring. Adults of all ages are experiencing changes in the traditional rhythm and timing of events of the life cycle. More men and women marry, divorce, remarry, and redivorce up through their seventies. More stay single; more women have their first child when they are fourteen or fifteen, and more have their first child at thirty-five or forty. This produces first-time grandparenthood for persons who range in age from thirty-five to seventy-five. There are more women, but also increasing numbers of men, who raise children consecutively in two-parent, then one-parent, and then two-parent households. More women, but increasing numbers of men as well, exit and re-enter our educational institutions, enter and re-enter the labor force, change jobs, and undertake second and third careers up through their seventies. It therefore becomes more difficult to distinguish the young, the middle-aged, and the young-old either in terms of major life events or of the ages at which those events occur.

The line between adolescence and adulthood is also becoming obscured. The role transitions that traditionally marked entry into adulthood and the social competencies they implied—full-time jobs, marriage, and parenthood—are disappearing as markers of social age. For some men and women, the entry into an occupation or profession is being delayed to age thirty as education is being extended. For others, entry into the labor force occurs at ages sixteen and seventeen. And not only are there more teen-age pregnancies; there are more teen-age women who are mothering their children. All this adds up to what has been aptly called "the fluid life cycle."[5]

This is not to deny that our society still recognizes differences between adolescents, young people, and old people, and that persons still relate to each other accordingly. Yet we are less sure where to put the punctuation marks in the life line, what should be the nature of those punctuation marks, and therefore how we should draw boundaries between the periods of life. All across adulthood, age has become a poor predictor of the timing of life events, as well as a poor predictor of a person's health, work status, family status, and therefore, also, of a person's interests, preoccupations, and needs. We have multiple images of persons of the same age: there is the seventy-year-old in a wheelchair and the seventy-year-old on the tennis court; there is the eighteen-year-old who is married and supporting a family and the eighteen-year-old college student who brings his laundry home to his mother each week.

Differences among individuals, multiple images of age groups, and inconsistencies in age norms were surely present in earlier periods of our history, but as our society has become more complex, the differences are becoming more evident. It is the irregularities that are becoming the social reality.

These trends are mirrored also in public perceptions. Although systematic research is sparse, there are a few studies that show a diminishing public consensus about the periods of life and their markers. In the early 1960s, for instance, a group of middle-class, middle-aged persons were asked their opinions about the "best" ages for major life transitions to occur (such as completing school, marrying, retiring), or the ages they associated with such phrases as "a young man," "an old woman," and "when a man (or woman) has the most responsibilities." When the same questions were asked of a similar group of people two decades later, consensus had dropped regarding every item of the questionnaire. In the earlier study, nearly 90 percent of the respondents replied that the best age for a woman to marry was between nineteen and twenty-four; in the repeat study, only 40 percent chose this brief period of years. In the first study, "a young man" was said to be a man between eighteen and twenty-two; in the repeat study, "a young man" was anywhere from eighteen to forty. These findings are based on very small study populations, but they serve to illustrate how public views are changing in line with the social realities.[6]

Childhood and Adulthood

In some respects, the line between childhood and adulthood is also fading. It is a common thesis now that childhood is disappearing. Styles of dress, language forms, games, preferred television programs—all are becoming the same for both children and adults. Children have more knowledge of once-taboo topics such as sex, drugs, alcoholism, suicide, and nuclear war. They also engage in more adult-like sexual behavior, and in more adult-like crime. At the same time, with the pressures for achievement we have witnessed the advent of "the hurried child" and "the harried child."[7]

We also have become familiar with the many descriptions of today's adults as the "me" generation: narcissistic, self-interested, and self-indulgent. There are fewer lasting marriages, fewer lasting commitments to work roles, more uncontrolled expressions of emotion, more frequent expressions of a sense of powerlessness—in short, more childlike behavior among adults.

This description may be overdrawn. In a wide range of formal and informal settings, both children and adults are continually exhorted to "act your age," and they seldom misunderstand what is meant. Yet there is something real in the argument that the expectations of appropriate behavior for children and adults are becoming less differentiated. We are less sure of what intellectual and social competencies to expect of children—not only because some children are teaching their teachers how to use computers, but also because so many children are streetwise by age eight, and so many others are the confidantes of their parents by age twelve.

Some observers attribute the blurring of childhood and adulthood primarily to the effects of television, which exposes the total culture and which reveals the secrets that adults have traditionally withheld from children. But it is not only television that accounts for the differences in socialization. One example may serve to underline the fact that children are being socialized in different ways today by parents, schools, churches, and peer groups as well:

The Girl Scouts of America recently announced that it had spent much effort in the last ten years studying its role in the society. Among many other changes, the decision was made to admit five-year-olds. The national executive director said, "Girl Scouts are not just campfire and cookie sales anymore . . . career education is part of the program for Brownies as young as six . . . The decision to admit five-year-olds reflects the changes in the American labor market. Women are working for part or all of their adult lives now. . . . The possibilities are limitless, but you need to prepare. So we think six is not too early to learn about career opportunities, and we also think that girls need to learn about making decisions. When you're five, you're not too young. . . ."[8]

All this is not to say that age norms are disappearing altogether. The person who moves to the Sun Belt to lead a life of leisure is approved of if he is seventy, but not if he is thirty. An unmarried mother meets with greater disapproval if she is fifteen than if she is thirty-five. At some levels, our society still distributes rights and responsibilities in traditional ways. But age distinctions and age norms operate inconsistently in a complex society.

Age Distinctions and the Law

The inconsistencies are nowhere better illustrated than in the norms that are formally codified into law. Laws establishing age distinctions pervade most areas of life: education, family, housing, entry and exit from various occupations, the allocation of public resources, the extension and denial of benefits, the imposition and the relaxation of legal responsibilities. At both state and federal levels, scores of statutes refer to age.

Age is used in the law just as it is used in other social institutions, as a proxy for a wide range of characteristics: intellectual and emotional maturity (for example, minimum ages for entering school), readiness to assume adult responsibilities (minimum ages for voting, drinking, driving, and marrying), physical strength or speed of response (maximum ages for policemen, bus drivers, or airline pilots), economic productivity (age of eligibility for various occupational licensing or age of retirement), and various types of debility (ages of eligibility for federally subsidized medical and social services).

Perhaps the use of age as a proxy is indispensable in a society like ours. It renders decision-making easier, not only for employers, but for lawmakers. It is less costly than using individualized assessments of competency. The major disadvantage is that the validity of using age as a proxy depends on how well age corresponds with the characteristic for which it stands. And the presumed correspondence is often based, not on good evidence, but on age stereotypes.

Laws change over time, and as might well be anticipated, they reflect some of the present incongruencies in the wider society regarding the significance of age. One pair of examples demonstrates recent changes in legal definitions of maturity. A California law passed a few years ago, known as the Emancipation of Minors Act, was designed to help teenagers who have fled intolerable family situations. The law specifies that if they are at least fourteen and are living away from home and supporting themselves, they can be declared independent of their parents and, for most legal purposes, can be treated as adults. In this instance, the individual's social competency is assessed by the court, and age (after fourteen) is not used as its proxy. Some dozen states have now passed similar laws.

In contrast, many states, faced with the problem of drunk driving and with the fact that more highway accidents involve drunk teenagers than drunk adults, are raising the age at which it is legal to purchase alcohol. In this instance, age is being used as the proxy for social responsibility. Despite the fact that only a small minority of eighteen-year-olds are drunk drivers, the laws apply to all eighteen-year-olds as an age class. In the first example, then, the law is saying that all fourteen-year-olds are not alike; but in the second example, it is saying that all eighteen-year-olds are alike.

At the same time that we are generating age-based laws, age discrimination is becoming a matter of societal concern. With reference to both the young and the old, age rights constitute a new focus in the arena of civil rights. One example is the recent legislation passed by Congress that abolishes age as the basis for retirement until age seventy in the private sector, and that removes the mandatory retirement age altogether for most federal employees. In this case, age is not treated as entirely irrelevant, but the law is nevertheless a step in that direction. Another example is the recent Age Discrimination Act, which applies across the age spectrum to both young and old, and prohibits discrimination on the basis of age in any program that receives federal support (for example, community mental health centers) unless that program was specifically aimed at a particular age group (e.g., Medicare). While the regulations allow for major exceptions that have the effect of watering down its strength, the Age Discrimination Act is nevertheless a formal step toward making age equality a civil right, and toward treating age as an irrelevant characteristic in the distribution of public goods and services.[9]

The problems of deciding what constitutes age discrimination are enormous, and perhaps will become even more so. Is it discriminatory towards younger people when special benefit programs like Medicare are created only for older people? At the state level, is it just to require a sixty-five-year-old—but not a sixty-four-year-old—to pass a vision test before obtaining a driver's license? At the local level, is it discriminatory to bar children from age-segregated housing—especially when that housing is subsidized by public funds? Such distinctions are presently legal, but they may come to be regarded as unjust if public consciousness rises regarding age distinctions and age rights.[10]

The Significance of Age to the Individual

The changing meanings of age are both causes and effects of the ways people lead their lives, and it is therefore artificial to think about individuals as separate from the society in which they live. Yet there is another dimension of social reality that applies directly to individuals. As they reach adolescence, most persons develop concepts of normal, expectable life sequences, and anticipations that major transitions in education, work, and family will occur at relatively predictable times. They internalize social clocks that tell them whether they are on time. Being on time or off time is a compelling basis for self-assessment as people compare themselves with others in deciding whether they are doing well or poorly for their age.

In many ways, social timetables in today's society do not lead to the regularities so often anticipated by adolescents or young adults. We have noted the ways in which timetables are losing their cogency, yet in other contexts some of those timetables may be more compelling than before. A young man feels he will be a failure if he does not "make it" in his corporation by the time he is thirty-five. Or an older business executive is invited to retire just when he thinks of himself as at the peak of his competencies. A young woman delays marriage because of her career, and then hurries to catch up with parenthood because of the biological imperative. The same young woman might feel pressed to marry, bear a child, and establish herself in a career, all within a five-year period. And this, even though she recognizes that she is likely to live to be eighty-five.

Sometimes new perspectives sit uneasily with traditional views, even in the mind of the same individual. A young woman who deliberately delays marriage may be the same woman who worries that she has lost status because she is not married by twenty-five. A middle-aged man who starts a second family feels compelled to explain that he has not behaved inappropriately, for he expects to live to see his new children reach adulthood. Or an old person reports that because he did not expect to live so long, he is now unprepared to take on the "new ways" of his age peers. Some people live in new ways, but continue to think in old ways.

Given such complications, shall we say that individuals are paying less or more attention to age as a prod or a brake upon their behavior? That age consciousness is decreasing or increasing? Whether or not historical change is occurring, it is fair to say that one's own age remains highly salient to the individual all the way from early childhood through advanced old age. A person uses age as a guide in accommodating to the behavior of others, in forming and re-forming the self-image, in giving meaning to the life course, and in contemplating the time that is past and the time that is left ahead.

All of this gives us an outline of the multiple levels of social and psychological reality that are based on social age, and, in modern societies, on calendar age as the marker of social age. The complexities are no fewer for the individual than they are for the society at large.

RELATIONS AMONG AGE GROUPS

At the societal level, the relations among age groups are influenced by changing perceptions of the periods of life and changing age norms, as well as by the relative numbers of young, middle-aged, and old. Policymakers and journalists frequently comment that an aging society may bring with it age polarization or age-divisiveness. The issue is often posed in terms of intergenerational conflict, reminiscent of the ways in which the so-called generation gap was described during the 1960s. Now, as then, the phenomenon may be more image than reality.

Many social scientists discovered during the late 1960s that it was difficult to find evidence of a generation gap. While some college students were demonstrating against the United States participation in the war in Vietnam, others of similar age, both in and out of college, were strongly supporting it. Further, a number of studies showed that college students shared the political views of their parents more often than not; and that although the forms of their behavior might be different from those of their parents, most left-wing students had left-wing parents, and most right-wing students right-wing parents.

Today, many observers are expressing concern about the possibility of so-called intergenerational conflict between the working-age and the retired; they fear the conflict will center on economic issues, specifically on the Social Security program, and on whether workers will rebel against paying increases in Social Security taxes to support the growing proportion of retirees. The aging society does face real problems of resource distribution that are complicated by demographic changes in the population. But is it true that different age groups perceive the solutions to those problems so differently?

First, it would be well to frame the issues in terms of age groups, not generations, for the two terms are by no means synonymous. If the issues were truly intergenerational, they might drop from public attention entirely, for there are adhesives between generations in the family that appear to be as strong today as they were in earlier periods of our history. A wide range of research shows that, as long as they live, parents remain invested in the welfare of their offspring, and that ties of obligation, whether or not they are also ties of affection, remain strong in offspring. The fragility of horizontal family ties is not paralleled in vertical family ties, particularly those between grandmothers, mothers, and children. Despite the shifts of financial responsibility to the government, the evidence is clear that the family remains the major social support of older people, just as it is for children.[11]

It appears that people's views of their own intergenerational relations become intertwined with, or projected onto, their views of age groups. So far as the evidence goes, workers in the United States are not protesting the rise in Social Security taxes. Repeated surveys show this to be the case.[12] One reason is that most people prefer a strong Social Security system to the alternative of placing the financial responsibility for older people back on the family.

The evidence also shows that it was not older people who were responsible for the passage of the Social Security Act in the 1930s, but younger and middle-aged workers. And throughout the postwar period, it has been labor unions, by and large, not the organized advocacy groups for older people, that have been the major advocates of expanded Social Security benefits.[13] The reason is that public policy for older people is usually also a public policy that benefits younger people, today as well as tomorrow.

Some young people now believe they will not enjoy as high a material standard of living as their parents, and some point to the federal budget deficits and to demographic changes to support their assertions that they will not receive as much in Social Security benefits when they grow old. But there is no evidence that young people are blaming old people for what they perceive as this deplorable state of affairs. One reason might be that "the older generation" often refers to their own parents, whose wealth they have the valid expectation of inheriting.[14] The few studies presently available indicate that during the lifetimes of parental generations, a larger amount of financial assistance flows down the family ladder than flows up that ladder, even though we would benefit from more data on what that trickle-down effect amounts to.[15] How many parents or grandparents are providing the down payments on homes for young-adult children? How many are providing funds to help divorced daughters who have young children to support?

Neither have we yet seen any movement on the part of older people that might be regarded as the expression of age-group conflict. Although it is true that there are more elderly voters than before and that a higher proportion of older people than younger people are exercising the franchise, older voters will remain a minority of voters for the foreseeable future. Further, the continuing agreement among political scientists is that no politics of age is developing in the United States, nor is there evidence of an old-age "bloc," largely because older persons are very heterogeneous in social, political, and economic terms.[16] It appears to be the case that, in old age, people continue to vote more in accord with their economic status than with the number of their birthdays. Nor is there evidence that when, in a given locality, older people vote against school bonds, they are voting against children rather than voting against increased taxes.

There are still other reasons to be cautious about using the phrase "intergenerational conflict." Some observers, concerned over conflict or equity among age groups, pose the issue in terms of a zero-sum game in which, if federal expenditures for the old were reduced, more funds for children would automatically be available.[17] It is undeniable that the increasing number of poor children is a disgrace to the affluent society, and that the implications are calamitous.[18] But the problem is part of a larger and more complex one: what proportion of federal resources should go to social programs, and how should those resources be allocated to the various subgroups who need assistance? This question, too, is more complex than it appears from examining federal expenditures. For one thing, although the data are not easily summarized, state government expenditures for children are probably equal to or higher than federal allocations. But even all government expenditures together constitute only one of two major components in the total system of economic transfers, for the family remains by far the major economic support for children.

To refer to the issue as age-group equity rather than age-group conflict may serve only to make it more murky. How is equity to be assessed in the context of the life cycle? Most public programs are future-oriented in the sense that an expenditure today is intended to affect, not only the present, but the future of those who are the beneficiaries. To help today's old is to help today's young, and presumably therefore to help those young when they are old tomorrow. But few policymakers are intrepid enough to predict tomorrow's value of today's outlays, whether that value be reckoned in economic or social terms. And how is equity to be assessed along another time line, that of successive birth cohorts? If outlays for old people are today nearly 30 percent of the federal budget, but a decade ago were only 20 percent, is the society therefore more generous to old people today, even when reckoned on a per-capita basis? And when we talk about saddling future generations with today's large federal deficits, is it really young persons we will be saddling, or all persons, young or old, who will constitute tomorrow's society?

Until philosophers as well as economists can shed more light on such questions, it is doubtful that we are much aided in facing the problems before us by framing the issues in terms of equity among age groups.[19]

AGE AND SOCIAL POLICY

From the policy perspective, there is another and more radical framework within which to consider the relations among age groups and the goal—implied whenever the issue is raised at all—of maintaining an age-integrated society. Is it more constructive for society to create policies designed for age groups, or instead, policies for persons who, irrespective of age, share a problem or a life condition that calls for intervention by a public or private agency?[20]

Despite the fact that age is becoming a less relevant basis for assessing adult competencies and needs, and even as traditional age norms and conceptions of age groups are becoming blurred, we are witnessing a proliferation of public and private policy decisions in which the basis for defining target groups is age. The trend is most evident when we look at older people. At federal, state, and local levels of government, programs are created that provide elderly persons with income, health services, social services, transportation, housing, and special tax benefits.[21] Private civic, educational, and religious bodies create special programs in health care, education, recreation, and other community services. For the past few decades, we have been engaged in what might be said to be a wide range of affirmative-action programs for older people. There is little doubt that the economic and social situation of older people as a group has been dramatically improved.

Despite these large outlays, there remain sizable sub-groups of very poor elderly people. And when all federal programs are considered together—the direct payments, the in-kind transfers, the tax benefits—it is evident that most of the benefits are going to those older people who are in the top third of the income distribution. Further, if these programs continue in their present direction, they will not only maintain the present inequalities, they will create even further disadvantage for those older persons who are poor.[22]

Age-based policies present still other problems. Some observers believe that to create programs directed at older people is to encourage the stereotype that older people are themselves a problem group, and is to add inadvertently to age separation and age segregation. Given that the proportion of poor among persons over sixty-five is now lower than in other age groups, others believe that older persons are becoming an advantaged rather than disadvantaged group. Some commentators are concerned by what they regard as the possibly divisive political power of older voters; others fear a possible political backlash in which older people will become the scapegoats in an attempt to contain federal expenditures.[23] Such positions often reflect the kind of distortions that arise whenever "the old" are described as a homogeneous group. The opinions diverge even more sharply when the debate focuses directly on age-targeted vs. age-neutral programs. Some point out that until age-targeted federal programs were established, older people failed to receive adequate attention because of ageist attitudes in the society at large, and that to abandon or even to alter age-targeted programs would jeopardize the great progress older people have realized over the past few decades.

Although the "age or need" issue may become more salient in the next few years and the political debate more heated, the policy issues are, in truth, more complex. In practice, they do not usually take the form of simple either/or decisions, but involve complicated combinations of age and need. It is not always an easy matter to disentangle the issue of age-irrelevancy. One example relates again to Social Security.

While their programs differ one from the next, all industrialized countries have some system of public pensions based on age-eligibility. Whether or not the present Social Security system in the United States is changed in major or minor ways, we are not likely to abandon public programs of income maintenance for older people. In the latest amendments to the Social Security Act, age has been manipulated as a major variable, with the age of eligibility for full benefits to be slowly raised from age sixty-five to age sixty-seven. For the first time, however, the income levels of the beneficiaries are also to be considered. For those older persons whose incomes surpass a given dollar level, half their Social Security benefits will be taxable. Thus, both age and need have become relevant. From the broader perspective, however, should we concentrate first on providing a guaranteed minimum income for persons of all ages, and only then shape the Social Security programs to fit that wider framework? And how shall we think about children, whose needs have not yet attracted the same degree of public attention?

Unlike the situation for older people, we have not shifted much of the responsibility for children away from the family and the voluntary organization to the federal government.[24] The inescapable fact that government can assist children only indirectly, and mainly through the family, complicates the issues enormously, for there is no public consensus today regarding the principle, let alone the method, of government support for families. But if government does begin to take a greater role, how shall we deal with the problem of poverty among children? Shall we create programs targeted towards children as a group? Or towards poor children? Or towards poor people, whatever their age? And will we continue to act on the conviction that programs for the poor must necessarily be poor programs, and that income-tested programs must necessarily be demeaning to the beneficiaries? Or will we be willing to reexamine that conviction, and to find ways of offering support that are not stigmatizing?

As we look ahead, it seems clear that some of the policy issues regarding age will be less troublesome than others. It is probably not controversial to suggest that the aging society will need a broader definition of productivity than the one that is current today, a definition that goes beyond participation in the labor force and extends to non-paid roles. These would include not only those that are attached to formally organized voluntary associations, but also to services that individuals provide to family members both inside and outside the household, services to neighbors and friends, and self-care activities.[25] The need is to seek out and nurture the potential for social productivity, in this broad sense, wherever it is to be found—not only among the young-old, but among younger people as well.

Along the same lines, it is probably not controversial to observe that in an aging society it will be increasingly important to remove the irrelevant age constraints that now exist for the young as well as for the young-old in various areas of employment, housing, education, and community participation.

But many of the problems that an aging society will pose will be much more difficult, for they will involve fundamental ethical as well as political questions. Some will raise issues that have not yet been clearly articulated. If, for instance, there is growing recognition that rising health costs are due less to the rising numbers of old people than to the rising costs of high-technology medicine and rising levels of reimbursement to health-care professionals, will we be able to deal directly with these problems? Difficult though it may be, it will probably be easier to reach consensus that the quality of life should take precedence over the length of life. But as questions of health-care rationing take new forms, will society be willing to ration this care on an age-neutral basis?[26] To push that question a step further: it has been suggested that high-technology medicine might be reserved for those persons who can be expected to have five to ten more years of a decent quality of life.[27] Shall we be willing to apply that standard, not only to old persons, but to the young as well—to withhold high-technology treatment from those infants and children whose futures show no such promise? Shall we weigh the value of lifetime, not on the basis of years since birth, but on the basis of years of decent life that lie ahead? Will we ever agree that an extra five years of good life have as much value to society when they are produced for a seventy-year-old as for a seven-year-old? Or shall we, instead, first give young people a chance to live at least to the age of average life expectancy? Is it likely that a society of such diverse social, ethical, and religious values as our own can reach consensus on such difficult questions?

Baffling as they are, questions like these are likely to become more compelling as the aging of the population becomes even more dramatic in the decades ahead. Can we use today's aging society as an appropriate context for rethinking our traditional views of age and age distinctions? Perhaps the most constructive ways of adapting to an aging society will emerge by focusing, not on age at all, but on more relevant dimensions of human needs, human competencies, and human diversity.

ENDNOTES

[1] For a fuller treatment of the historical appearance of childhood, adolescence, and youth, see Philippe Aries, *Centuries of Childhood* (New York: Random House, 1962); John Demos and Virginia Demos, "Adolescence in Historical Perspective," *Journal of Marriage and Family,* Nov. 1969, pp. 632–38; John R. Gillis, *Youth and History* (New York: Academic Press, 1974); Kenneth Keniston, "Youth as a Stage of Life," *American Scholar,* Autumn 1970, pp. 631–54; Panel on Youth, President's Science Advisory Committee, *Youth: Transition to Adulthood* (Washington, D.C.: U.S. Government Printing Office, 1973). The book edited by Erik Erikson, *Adulthood* (New York: W.W. Norton & Co., 1978), asks whether the historical obsession with childhood and adolescence may now be giving way to "the century of the adult."

[2] Bernice L. Neugarten, "Age Groups in American Society and the Rise of the Young-old," *Annals of the American Academy of Political and Social Science,* Sept. 1974, pp. 187–98.

[3] For a differently focused discussion of this issue, see *How Old is "Old?" The Effects of Aging on Learning and Working.* Hearing before the Senate Special Committee on Aging, 96th Congress, 2nd Session (Washington, D.C.: U.S. Government Printing Office, 1980).

[4] Lewis H. Butler and Paul W. Newacheck, "Health and Social Factors Relevant to Long Term Care Policy," in Judith Meltzer, Harold Richman, and Frank Farrow, eds., *Policy Options in Long Term Care* (Chicago: University of Chicago Press, 1981).

[5] Larry Hirschhorn, "Social Policy and the Life Cycle: A Developmental Perspective," *Social Service Review,* Sept. 1977, pp. 434–50.

[6] B.L. Neugarten, Joan Moore, and John Lowe, "Age Norms, Age Constraints, and Adult Socialization," *American Journal of Sociology,* May 1965, pp. 710–17; and Patricia Passuth, David Maines, and B.L. Neugarten, "Age Norms and Age Constraints Twenty Years Later," paper presented at the Midwest Sociological Society meetings, Chicago, April 1984.

[7]Among the growing number of publications on the changing nature of childhood, see David Elkind, *The Hurried Child: Growing Up Too Fast Too Soon.* (Reading, MA: Addison-Wesley, 1981); John Holt, *Escape from Childhood* (New York: Dutton, 1974); Joshua Meyrowitz, "The Blurring of Childhood and Adulthood," chap. 13 in *No Sense of Place* (New York: Oxford University Press, 1985). (An essay drawn from that chapter was published in *Daedalus,* Summer 1984, under the title, "The Adultlike Child and the Childlike Adult: Socialization in an Electronic Age.") See also Neil Postman, *The Disappearance of Childhood* (New York: Delacorte Press, 1982); and Marie Winn, *Children Without Childhood* (New York: Pantheon, 1983).

[8]Reported in the *New York Times,* Oct. 28, 1984.

[9]The two federal laws being referred to are the Age Discrimination in Employment Act of 1967, as amended (29 U.S. Code Sections 621–634); and the Age Discrimination Act of 1975, as amended (42 U.S. Code Sections 6101–6107).

[10]For an analysis of the legal issues related to age distinctions and age discrimination, see Howard Eglit, "Age and the Law," chap. 18 in the *Handbook of Aging and the Social Sciences,* Robert H. Binstock and Ethel Shanas, eds. (New York: Van Nostrand Reinhold, 1985).

[11]See, for instance, Elaine Brody, "Parent Care as a Normative Family Stress," *The Gerontologist,* Feb. 1985, pp. 19–29; and Shanas, "Social Myth as Hypothesis: The Case of the Family Relations of Old People." *The Gerontologist,* Feb. 1979, pp. 1–9.

[12]This fact has often emerged from newspaper polls and other public opinion polls. For a fuller context, see the two surveys published by the National Council on the Aging, *The Myth and Reality of Aging in America,* and *Aging in the Eighties: America in Transition.* (Washington, D.C.: National Council on the Aging, 1975 and 1981).

[13]For an analysis of the role of old-age advocacy groups, see Henry J. Pratt, *The Gray Lobby* (Chicago: University of Chicago Press, 1976) and "The 'Gray Lobby' Revisited," *National Forum,* Fall 1982, pp. 31–33.

[14]For an analysis of family inheritance patterns, see Marvin Sussman, Judith Cates, and David Smith, *The Family and Inheritance* (New York: Russell Sage Foundation, 1970).

[15]In summarizing one major set of studies on this topic, James M. Morgan, an economist, reports that in the general picture of who helps whom, relatively little regular financial assistance goes to family members who live outside the household, but that the amount expended in offering emergency help—in the form of time or money—is considerable. The middle-aged do most of the giving, but the receiving appears to be mostly by the young (18 to 35) rather than by the old (65 and over). James M. Morgan, "The Redistribution of Income by Families and Institutions and Emergency Help Patterns," in *Five Thousand Families—Patterns of Economic Progress,* vol. X, ed. by Greg J. Duncan and James N. Morgan (Ann Arbor, MI: Institute for Social Research, 1983), and by the same author, "Time in the Measurement of Transfers and Well-being," in Marilyn Moon, ed., *Economic Transfers in the United States* (Chicago: The University of Chicago Press, 1984).

[16]In the most recent review of research on political orientations, values and ideologies, party attachments, voting, and other forms of political behavior, the authors conclude—as have other reviewers—that older persons are more notable for their similarities to other age groups than for their differences. This

results from the heterogeneity that exists within all age groups. The authors point also to the general absence of policy-relevant age-consciousness. Robert B. Hudson and John Strate, "Aging and Political Systems," chap. 19 in Binstock and Shanas, eds., op. cit.

[17]See, for example, Samuel H. Preston, "Children and the Elderly in the United States," *Scientific American*, Dec. 1984.

[18]A recent report of the Congressional Research Office and the Congressional Budget Office shows that in 1983, the latest year for which the data are complete, over 22 percent of children under age 18 were living below the poverty level. This is the highest figure since the mid-1960s. (*New York Times*, May 23, 1985, p. 1.)

[19]For a philosopher's approach to these issues, see Norman Daniels, "Justice Between Age Groups: Am I My Parents' Keeper?" *Milbank Memorial Fund Quarterly/Health and Society*, Summer 1983, pp. 489–522. The economist Marilyn Moon comments that a recurrent and controversial issue is how to define meaningful time periods in studying economic transfers; she further observes that estimating intergenerational equity remains a relatively unexplored area. See Moon, ed., op. cit., , p. 6.

[20]B.L. Neugarten, ed., *Age or Need? Public Policies for Older People* (Beverly Hills, CA: Sage Publications, 1982).

[21]See, for example, Elizabeth A. Kutza, *The Benefits of Old Age* (Chicago: University of Chicago Press, 1981) for an analysis of federal programs; and for a critique of how many of those programs are failing older people, see Carol L. Estes, *The Aging Enterprise* (San Francisco: Jossey-Bass Publishers, 1979).

[22]See, for instance, Gary M. Nelson, "Social Class and Public Policy for the Elderly," *Social Service Review*, March 1982, pp. 85–107 (reprinted in B.L. Neugarten, *Age or Need?* op. cit.).

[23]Binstock, "The Aged as Scapegoat," in *The Gerontologist*, April 1983, pp. 136–43; and by the same author, "The Oldest Old: A Fresh Perspective or Compassionate Ageism Revisited?" *Milbank Memorial Fund Quarterly/Health and Society*, Spring 1985.

[24]See the chapter by Richman and Stagner in this volume.

[25]See the report, *Productive Roles in an Aging Society*, prepared by the Committee on an Aging Society of the National Academy of Sciences, Feb. 1986.

[26]See, for example, Henry J. Aaron and William B. Schwartz, *The Painful Prescription: Rationing Hospital Care* (Washington, D.C.: The Brookings Institution, 1984).

[27]See the chapter by Daniel Callahan in this volume.

Matilda White Riley and John W. Riley, Jr.

Longevity and Social Structure: The Potential of the Added Years

W HAT IS THE CONTOUR OF the lives of individuals when, for the first time in human history, the great majority survive to old age? What is life like in a society in which the entire structure is changing as the proportion of the population over age sixty-five is increasing, and the proportion of young children is declining?[1]

The answers to these questions are only barely discernible, for entirely new patterns are currently emerging. As longevity increases, the complex processes of aging from birth to death—biological, psychological, and social—are continally being shaped and reshaped by ongoing changes in social structure and social roles. Meanwhile, as the life course is modified, pressures are generated for still further changes—in social structures, institutions, beliefs, norms, and values. In turn, these societal changes influence the nature of the life course. Thus, there is a continuing dialectic between the processes of aging and changing social structures.[2] People who are growing up and growing old today differ from their predecessors in the markedly increased length of their lives, as well as in many other ways. Lives have been changing, but our society's compensatory structural changes lag behind, producing strains both on individuals and on society as a whole.

This essay will touch first on the nature of longevity, which is transforming the life course of individuals. It will then describe the uneasy relation between the aging of individuals and the changes in society, an imbalance that results in the current structural lag. For

53

purposes of illustration, we shall select a few of the changes that are emerging in the later life course and the problematic future outcomes of these changes. Three themes run throughout this discussion:

(*1*) The actual and potential capacities and strengths of long-lived people;

(*2*) The actual and potential roles in this aging society and its institutions that are capable of utilizing the capacities of these increasingly long lives;

(*3*) The imbalance that currently exists between a population of increasingly long-lived people and the decreasing opportunities for them to participate in the society.

These problematics of the individual life course in an aging society require deeper scientific understanding and wider public recognition so that they may form the basis for improved public policy and professional practice.

THE ADDED YEARS

The U.S. Census estimates that, among babies born in 1980, 77 percent can look forward to reaching age sixty-five.[3] This is an unprecedented statistic. Even for persons surviving to the older ages, there have been increases since the turn of the century in the estimated average number of years of life remaining at age sixty-five, from 11.9 in 1900 to 16.4 in 1980, with even more rapid recent increases at age eighty-five (see the essay in this volume by Jacob S. Siegel and Cynthia M. Taeuber). According to one estimate, about half the dramatic increase between 1960 and 1980 in the number of people age sixty-five and over can be attributed to the unusually large size of these cohorts at birth, and about half to the unexpected spurt in life expectancy at the older ages.[4] As longevity permeates the population, the full life course takes on new meaning, for death is no longer largely adventitious, and few lives are now "truncated before the major stages of education, work and family building are completed."[5]

Such revolutionary change is difficult to comprehend because we are in the midst of it: Samuel Preston has estimated that over two-thirds of the improvement in longevity in the entire world, from prehistoric times until the present, has taken place in the brief period since 1900.[6] Americans are living longer today than was anticipated even a decade ago. For the future, we still do not have answers to the haunting questions of just how far the average length of life will be extended, and just how healthy and capable people will be if ever-increasing proportions survive past infancy and young adulthood and into their eighties and nineties.

From the perspective of individuals, longevity—however abstract the demographic concept may be—is of major importance, affecting the number of years of life that lie behind as well as ahead, both for individuals and their relatives and significant others. Also affecting individuals is the age composition of the population of the total society in which they are growing older, although longevity and the aging of the population are distinct phenomena. Longevity in a society depends on life-course patterns of mortality, and is not necessarily coincident with an increasing proportion of old people in the population: such a proportion is influenced in the long term more by fertility than by mortality. Thus, toward the middle of the twenty-first century, when the baby-boom cohorts are replaced in the oldest age strata by their less populous successors, the United States population will predictably grow "younger." At that point, longevity may remain high even though the portion of old people declines. Conversely, even while the society is aging, increases in longevity might be prevented by outbreaks of new diseases, or by a rise in cancer resulting from environmental pollution.

The implications posed by the added years for the nature of the individual's life course are only now beginning to be apprehended. In general, it is clear that increased longevity: *(1)* prolongs the opportunity for accumulating social, psychological, and biological experiences;[7] *(2)* maximizes a person's opportunities to complete or to change the role assignments of early and middle life—for example, to change jobs, marriage partners, or educational plans, and to take on new roles in the later years; *(3)* prolongs a person's relationships to others—to spouse, parents, offsprings, friends—whose lives are also extended; and *(4)* increases the potential structural complexity of a person's social networks—for example, of kinship, friendship, community—as all members survive longer. All these consequences of longevity mean that people now have unprecedented opportunity to accumulate experience, to exercise new and expanded options, to respond to social change, and to influence it.

SOCIAL CHANGE AND AGING OVER THE LIFE COURSE

As lives lengthen, what are the dynamic processes by which social changes shape the course of individual lives, while the course of the collective lives of many individuals contributes to further social change? New "stages" emerge as new age-graded roles are added and become more specialized. Over the past century, with the increased complexity of social structures, the life course has become even more differentiated, gradually eliciting both scientific and popular recognition of such "stages" as adolescence (early and late), young adulthood, late middle age, and old age (with distinctions among "young-old," "old-old," and, most recently, "oldest-old"—those eighty-five and over).

The definition of life-course stages vary widely, but exist in some form or other in all societies. The extraordinary range of variability, widely documented through historical and cross-cultural analyses, is quickly suggested by comparing our own society with a pre-modern society in which male children from an early age help herd the cattle, young adult males are considered warriors and are not supposed to marry, and women are monopolized as wives for the polygynous elders who hold the power. Stages are sometimes defined by years of age, and sometimes by biological or social life-source markers (such as puberty, the acquisition of property, attainment of adult stature, the father's retirement, or marriage of the youngest child). Stages are partly—but only partly—determined by biology. Very old people are not expected to engage in contact sports, for example, or pre-school children to manage large organizations, nor can an arbitrary age criterion specify natural motherhood before or after a woman is in the reproductive years. But the "right age" to have children may be determined less by biology than by the many social and political considerations that confront the mother, the father, the family, and the perceptions of future opportunities for the child.

Thus, chronological age or life-course markers are features not only of individuals and populations, but also of the role structures through which people pass as they grow older. Age affects which roles are open or closed to an individual, and which social networks and cultural norms will offer certain opportunities or impose certain demands. Age is built into the changing organization of institutions and roles through formal or informal criteria for entry and exit, through expectations of how roles are to be performed, and through sanctions for role performance.

How, then, can the shaping and re-shaping of the life course be understood as an interplay between individuals who are growing older and changes in the age-graded roles and cultural expectations of social structures? As years are added to the life course, and the society continues to age, how can alterations in the life course come about? How do particular life stages develop and change? Despite the persistent centrality of this question, there are few answers yet available. It may be useful to examine this question in light of the dialectical nature of change. Our observations are as follows:

(*1*) In response to social change, people engage in new age-typical patterns and regularities of behavior (change in the way the aging process occurs);

(*2*) As these behavior patterns become commonplace, they are defined as age-appropriate norms and rules, are reinforced by "authorities," and are thereby institutionalized in the role structure of society (change in the social structure);

(*3*) In turn, these changes in age norms and social structures re-direct or otherwise alter a panoply of age-related behaviors (further changes in the aging process); and so on.

Most problematic in this dialectic is that new age norms seem to be formed not only by direct action of the state or other organizations, but also by the indirect influence of cohort members—that is, culturally prescribed age criteria develop as bases for role assignment and role performance in social structures, and for the definition of life stages. A brief review of many studies suggests some ways in which age regularities in behavior become translated into age norms and are finally institutionalized in social roles and social structures:

(*1*) Sometimes, modal patterns of behavior are created as age is written into law (as Bismarck, for example, set the legal age for retirement a century ago in accordance with the mortality conditions of his own time);

(2) Sometimes, new age-norms are formed by the emphases of social movements (such as organizations promoting the rights of children or the elderly); or by the "need" for social control (formal schooling designed, in part, to contain and monitor disruptive youths); or by influential writers (from popular purveyors of age-linked "passages" to biological reductionists who assert—often erroneously—that the stages of later life bring inevitable and universal physiological decline);

(3) Perhaps the most widespread means of converting behavioral regularities into normative criteria that define new age strata or life stages is the process of "cohort norm formation."[8] As members of the same cohort respond to shared experiences, they gradually and subtly develop common patterns of response, common definitions, and common beliefs, all of which crystallize into shared norms about what is appropriate, proper, or true. For example, many young women in the period following World War II responded to common social changes by making separate but similar personal "decisions" to have several children, rather than just one or two, extending the stage of child-rearing, and creating the norm of full-time motherhood.[9] Such collective decisions not only reversed the long-term decline in fertility, but created the baby boom, with its momentous ramifications on the structure and mores of society.

To the extent that members of each cohort make common decisions, they exert a collective force as they move through the age-stratified society, pressing for normative adjustments in social roles and social values, and changing the shape of the age structure of society and hence of the stages of the life course. The question at issue in this chapter is how this dialectical process will operate under today's conditions of long life, an aging population, and a society subjected to rapid social, economic, and cultural change. Since social institutions are lagging behind the people who inhabit them, will a new balance be struck between the claims and capacities of aging individuals and the shifting demands of society?

With this brief theoretical introduction, we will now turn to some of the social consequences of the years that have been added to the life course. As society ages and as more and more people survive into their later years, new role structures are called for. What the shape and nature of these roles might be, and how they affect the uneasy balance between people and roles, provides a complex agenda for research efforts and policymaking. This agenda touches on every age: on infants as they embark on daycare or on pre-school learning, or as they are no longer believed to be entirely programmed by their early-life experiences; on today's youth, who may be growing up faster than their parents in bodily development and sexual experience, but more slowly in emotional or judgmental maturity; on adults as they become involved in changing family forms or shifting political climates; and so on. In this brief essay, we have chosen to focus on the older ages, discussing just three pressure points in the relation between social structure and the extended lives of older people: *(1)* the continuing capacity for performance in a society where role opportunities are scarce, particularly for men; *(2)* some sign that women, in a society where the oldest age strata are made up largely of women, can have influence in changing social structures; and *(3)* the context of dying and its human meaning in a society where the process of dying is increasingly under medical and social control, and where new norms and new contexts for the dying person are needed. To anticipate the analysis, let us note that there has been serious miscalculation of the significance of the added years for effective functioning of individuals, for the future role of women, and for the sensibilities of those who are at the end of the life course, and of their caretakers.

POTENTIALS FOR CONTINUING PERFORMANCE

Perhaps the most striking area in which social and cultural structures lag behind increasing longevity is in work for men. Over the century, the labor force participation of both old and young has been eroding, and the competence of older workers for productive performance has been consistently underrated. Today, on the average, people find they are spending one-quarter of their adult lifetime in retirement![10] What processes in the social structure and in the lives of individuals produce this phenomenon? Where might these processes lead?

The Background
At the turn of the century, one-quarter of boys age ten to fifteen were gainfully employed, and most men did not retire at sixty-five but

continued to work. Since 1900, the general trend has been toward increasing concentration of economic activity in the early and middle adult years. In general (with the exception of spot reversals of the trend, as occurred during World War II or, most recently, in 1983), the average age of entry into the labor force rose, and the proportions of older people remaining in the labor force fell.[11] In 1900, two-thirds of men age sixty-five and over were still in the labor force, a fraction that has declined dramatically to the current figure of only one-fifth. After 1930, the United States Census, when compiling labor force statistics, stopped counting children under fourteen, and in 1967 it stopped counting children under sixteen—facts that further document the changing age criteria for role entry.

These drastic changes in the age structure of economic roles for men—changes paralleled in most industrial countries—offer dramatic evidence that retirement norms, like the shape of the life course, are highly mutable. The long-term societal trends in age of employment have been associated with a complex of factors including massive secular declines in both agriculture and self-employment, extension of formal education, steadily increasing proportions of women in the labor force, establishment of age requirements for starting or discontinuing a job, and extension of public and private pension plans that afford alternative sources of income and often specify mandatory ages of retirement. There is ample evidence that when middle-aged workers lose their jobs or seek to change them, they find it more difficult than younger workers to find new employment; and despite legislative attempts to prevent age discrimination, various practices by employers can make it difficult for older workers to keep their current jobs.

As work opportunities become constricted, pressures mount for socially rewarding roles in retirement. To be sure, numerous studies show that retirement is now widely accepted as an entitlement, that only selected types of workers regret relinquishing their former involvement in work, and that—at least in the short run—little negative impact on health is detectable when workers retire. Yet there are structural problems of retirement in an aging society deriving in large part from the failure of popular attitudes and public policy to address the question: what is retirement a transition *to?* People entering the role of retiree often have little comprehension of what the absence of work entails. They lack direction for finding new roles that could provide substitute gratifications. Unpaid volunteer work has become an alternative activity for only a minority of old people. Expensive leisure pursuits are widely prohibited by income that is reduced with lengthening retirement. For the disabled elderly, medical care is costly and inadequate. There are relatively few organizations for "senior citizens." Retirement has perhaps correctly been called a "roleless role," lacking content and sure rewards. For some old people, this lack of content is an advantage, permitting them to escape hated jobs, to spend more time on activities they have always enjoyed, or to fashion new roles consonant with their energies, interests, and financial resources. For others, retirement is marked by lowered self-esteem, and a lack of stimulation that can lead to apathy or depression, jeopardizing vigor and effective functioning. In an aging society, where status attainment and material success are still valued, most opportunities for these rewards become scarce (at least to male members of society) as age advances.

Potentials for Performance

A considerable amount of attention has been devoted in this country to questions of how to protect willing older workers against exploitation, or how to provide long-term care for the sick and disabled elderly. But since only a minority of older people are unable to perform major activities, and only a very small minority require nursing-home care, it is imperative that some scientific and popular attention be directed to ways of maintaining health and effective functioning among that great majority of middle-aged and older people whose potential is still high.

There has been a pervasive belief in this country that all older workers should retire because they are no longer able to be productive, and that longevity simply prolongs their uselessness. However, these beliefs are now being challenged. It has been demonstrated as a general principle that declines accompanying aging, including biological declines, are neither entirely inevitable nor universal, since growing old is a set of processes in which biological aging continually interacts with social and psychological aging. In respect to performance, cohort studies show that many of the deficits of today's older people can be explained, not by aging, but by differences in cohort experiences (as new cohorts may be comparatively better educated, healthier, etc., than earlier ones); and by experimental studies that demonstrate that, by correcting defective aspects of social structure, old-age deficits can often be reduced or prevented. In short, the potential strengths of older people are currently underrated.

To illustrate this potential, we shall describe a series of studies on just one topic, intellectual functioning, that shows *improvement* with aging under certain conditions: if life situations are challenging, if people continue to use their skills, and if the social environment provides incentives and opportunities for learning. This research centers primarily on the work of Warner Schaie and Paul Baltes.[12]

The first study is a follow-up by Schaie at four successive seven-year intervals of adults of all ages who are members of a Seattle health maintenance organization. Among its many findings was the unexpected relationship to age of most types of intelligence. Contrary to conventional wisdom, scarcely any individuals up to age sixty, and less than half of individuals even at age eighty, showed reliable decrements in cognitive-test performance over a seven-year period. Among individuals at the oldest ages, there was wide variation, and this prompted Schaie to look for explanations. In this first study, he traced the differences partly to cardiovascular and other diseases, and partly also to economic status and to the intellectual stimulation of the environment. Thus, in this early study Schaie repudiates the notion of inevitable and universal intellectual decline with aging and begins the search for possible ways to prevent or modify those declines that do occur. Despite numerous challenges, many of his findings and explanations are being supported by other investigators. For example, John L. Horn and Gary Donaldson show that, with daily life opportunities for practice, specific types of cognitive performance—"crystallized" intelligence—clearly remain stable or even improve in later adulthood.[13]

The second set of studies, building on Schaie's work, uses experiments conducted by Paul B. Baltes and Sherry L. Willis to explore the modifiability of performance on intelligence tests. These experiments involve people with a mean age of seventy who are living in the community. They focus on those intellectual skills—spatial orientation and inductive reasoning—in which elderly persons have been most likely to show declines in test performance. And indeed the results do demonstrate that performance improves markedly when the social environment affords both incentives and opportunities for practice. Even though these experimental interventions were brief and short-term—far different from the massive educational exposures of younger people—the magnitude of improvement is at least large enough to recover the previous aging decline observed in longitudinal studies from age sixty to age eighty. Over three-fourths of the subjects show improvement following training, and training effects last for at least six months and transfer to other tests of similar types. These findings are of considerable practical importance for the present, as well as of enormous potential significance for the future. Other related experiments currently in progress are designed to replicate this important finding of improved performance among the elderly. The experiments examine the mechanisms—such as attention, reduced anxiety, or motivation—that may affect memory and mental performance; they probe further into other potentially related changes. How, for example, does enhanced intellectual performance affect one's sense of personal efficacy? How does it relate to the accomplishment of such real-life tasks as reading medicine-bottle labels, shopping wisely, interpreting time schedules, or understanding the news?

The third study, by Schaie and Willis, also attempted to replicate the earlier finding of the modifiability of older people's intellectual performance through training.[14] But this study added to the earlier design by conducting the experiments on the very subjects whose earlier intellectual histories are known from their participation in Schaie's original Seattle longitudinal study many years earlier. Consider what that means: if these investigators also find improvement through training, they can then begin to tell how much of the improvement is merely *relearning*—reversing the aging losses—and how much is entirely *new* learning that transcends the levels attained earlier in life. The findings from this third study will address the question of older people's potential ability, not only to avoid declines, but perhaps also to reach new heights of cognitive skill.

In the fourth study (only now beginning), Schaie is going back to his initial twenty-one-year longitudinal study in order to follow the seven hundred survivors for still another seven years, and he is adding a fifth wave of persons, ranging in age from twenty-two to ninety-eight. This cohort-longitudinal design achieves the scientific power of research that not only examines longitudinally the aging patterns of members of a single cohort, but also compares the aging patterns of successive cohorts as these may be influenced by social change. In following up several new clues from the earlier studies, this research therefore asks about the future: will the *lower* levels of high-school performance widely reported among students in recent decades persist into later life as these new cohorts of young people grow older?[15] Previously, successive cohorts of young adults had started with higher and higher levels of education, giving them a great advantage over the old. Schaie's new research can explore whether or not educational advantages may continue to differentiate cohorts in the future. Will the real-life performances of the future young be reduced to the current levels of the very old? Or can the performance levels of both young and old be raised as life-long education and training become a reality? These four studies are just one body of research that points to the potential of the old to maintain their intellectual functioning.

Longevity may quite possibly bring its own unique assets. Most of the standard measures of intellectual functioning have been designed for the young, for use in schools or in entry jobs. Yet there may be other components of intelligence that develop in middle or later life, such as experience-based decision making, interpersonal competence, or "wisdom"—the faculty of evaluating alternative actions, setting priorities, and knowing what responses a situation requires.[16] Clues from many other areas of research suggest how to sustain well-being, vigorous health, physical functioning, and productivity into the middle and later years, and how to postpone disability and lack of independence until the last years of the extended life course.[17]

Incipient Changes

As members of successive cohorts retire at young ages and are better educated and perhaps healthier than their predecessors, it seems predictable that pressures from old people and from the public at large will modify the existing work and retirement roles. Scattered changes are already underway to offset the lag of social structures behind the potential strengths of long-lived people. For example, older adults now drop in and out of the educational system, retraining for medicine or law, preparing for new careers, pursuing leisure in the Aristotelian sense. Certain structural features of work are used to discourage early retirement; some businesses are arranging regular educational leaves, phased retirement, or pension plans that offer pre-retirement cultural or travel benefits; many retirees continue to work part-time; and some retirees (one-sixth of one national sample) are now becoming former retirees. As people actually begin to comprehend how much of the adult lifetime is now spent in retirement, study after study suggests that the need for involvement and participation in the larger society does not end with formal retirement—that retirement itself is not a single and irreversible event, but a process involving successive decisions. Yet the needs still outstrip the incipient opportunities.

Our emerging knowledge of aging is marked by two dramatic discoveries. First, we have been grossly underestimating the strengths and potentials of the added years. Second, we are only now beginning to understand that productive and rewarding roles might be provided for many longevitous people in our society. For the future, one inference seems inescapable: the presence of increasing numbers of capable people living in a society that offers them few meaningful roles is bound to bring about changes, either in the people or in the role structures. Capable people and empty role structures cannot co-exist for long.

WOMEN AS INNOVATORS

In considering how structures and norms may take new shape in response to increasing longevity, it is important to assess the influence of women. Women live longer than men; the aging society is increasingly becoming a society of older women. Many women have had experiences in complex roles. Collectively, they have introduced significant societal innovations. What does their influence portend for the resolution of the growing strains between social structures and long-lived people?

Life expectancy at birth in the United States in 1978 was set at sixty-nine for men and seventy-nine for women, and given the surprising recent declines in mortality, some estimates of the comparable figures for 2003 run as high as seventy-four and eighty-four—levels never attained in any nation.[18] Because longevity in the past has increased faster for women than for men, at the oldest ages women are the most numerous members of society in all industrial countries today.[19] In the United States, by the year 2000, there will be only an estimated 64.5 men for every one hundred women age sixty-five and over, and an estimated 37.2 men for every hundred women age eighty-five and over.[20] Role structures and opportunities for these older women are slow to develop. Today, one-half of all women over age seventy-five live alone—and while most elderly men are still married, most elderly women are widows.[21] For these cohorts of women, for whom marriage and keeping house was the major activity, many have lost their traditional places in society.

Capacity to Cope

Many studies attest to the resilience of older women in the face of adversity. Women who live alone do not give evidence of excessive unhappiness; nor do they fail to eat nutritious meals. On the average, women are less likely than men to die following the death of a spouse.[22]

The stereotype of the "lonely widow" is challenged in a study by Herbert Hyman.[23] Hyman is impressed by two potential flaws in much of the research to date. First, the data have been collected from widows *as* widows. Thus, the first questions often asked of respondents are: how long have you been widowed? What did your husband die of? The respondent is thus labeled as a widow and presumably answers within that context. The second problem has been designing appropriate control groups for comparison. Hyman's solution to both problems is to rely entirely on a secondary analysis of data that were not collected for the purpose of studying widows. He makes systematic use of two large data sets that provide measures of such dependent variables as "outlook on life," "social involvement," "feeling tone," and "health status." In effect, he constructs a "double blind" research design: the respondents were not asked about widowhood, nor did Hyman have any voice in selecting the items included in the questionnaires. He uses the data to "purify" and "refine" three categories of the independent variable: widows, married, divorced/separated. To avoid the problem that, when the bereaved have also died, they are underrepresented in the cross-sectional studies, longitudinal data are analyzed to compare the "persistently widowed," the "persistently married," and the "recently widowed." Hyman concludes that, though many widows do, of course, grieve and some die following the death of their husbands, on the average widowhood does not ordinarily produce the massive and enduring negative effects that have typically been reported.

This analysis, which flies in the face of many earlier beliefs about widowhood, is all the more provocative in view of the objective disadvantages—for example, in income or housing—of widowed, as contrasted with still married, older women.

Incipient Change

Hyman's study indicates many of the subtle consequences of social change for women. Not only are new roles for women envisioned for the future, they have already been manifested. Women have provided evidence of the process of cohort-norm formation, as many women in the young-adult cohorts have responded to common social changes by making separate but similar personal "decisions" to move in new directions—to continue their education, to combine marriage and child care with participation in the labor force, to structure their families in innovative ways. In the United States, such decisions initially affected only selected segments of society; they were only gradually translated into new age norms. As gender roles at work and in the family are subtly beginning to change at every age, these norms are becoming institutionalized. If, as many have hoped, the life course can be modified to intersperse periods of education and work with periods of leisure and recreation, it is women who are paving the way for such reforms. They are performing traditional roles in the home, and at the same time forging new ones in the work place. They are striking delicate balances between the demands of family and the pressures of a job, often in the face of social criticism. No similar course in socialization has been offered to men, many of whom seem to be lagging behind. Only the most recent cohorts of fathers are beginning to participate in child care.[24] To be sure, substantial minorities of women reject the changes, and older working women today still face pervasive discrimination.

Yet one thing is certain. If the transformation in gender-role attitudes and behavior continues, it will affect every facet of American life: housing, child rearing, care of frail elderly parents, business practices, taxation, recreation, and leisure. We must ask whether our social institutions can change rapidly enough to accommodate the trend toward gender equality through such adaptations as neo-families, communal living, job sharing, and changed work schedules that enable fathers to participate more fully in child rearing. However far the changes go, many women are growing old in new roles and new social situations. As many middle-aged women today are enacting more roles than men, they will reach old age with ever greater role flexibility and practice in coping with complex and changing roles.

Women of the Future

As future cohorts of women reach the later years of their lives, will they perhaps influence other members of society to assume greater flexibility in the phases of the life course?[25] Will they find a way to keep their flexibility from being exploited, as it is in the current practice of leaving to old women the care of their frail or disabled very old parents? Will they set a special stamp on social norms and social structures, emphasizing those characteristics that are currently regarded as distinctively feminine? Will they invent new forms of lay care (social, mental, and spiritual, as well as physical) to supplement the high-technology cures now applied to the care of both children and elderly parents? Will they be able to introduce more humane standards into political or economic life, or to bring their expressive talents into the retirement role? Will they introduce a new stage in family life of "husband retirement," in which the typically younger and more longevitous wife continues to work after the husband retires? The clearest images of older women of the future must be drawn from the knowledge we have about these women now while they are young, from research findings, and from the frequently overlooked fact that the cohort that sparked the women's movement will soon be entering old age. For the foreseeable future, the number of older women will far exceed the supply of socially valued roles open to them. Social structure changes slowly. The challenge to older women will be to continue voicing the legitimacy of their demands, and to continue creating new and valued roles.

Dilemmas of Dying

Every known society has rules and norms for defining death as the ultimate rite of passage and has social structures for dealing with its consequences. During the twentieth century, the phenomenon of death and its social meanings have been transformed, with most deaths now occurring, not among the young, but among the old. In the United States, three-fourths of all deaths now occur among people sixty-five and over.[26] In place of the earlier rapidity of death from pneumonia or other acute diseases, the process of dying today—from chronic diseases affecting old people—is often prolonged, involving care in hospitals or nursing homes. While the rate of dying from heart diseases has recently been reduced, heart diseases remain a major cause of death. The long search for a cure for cancer continues, and there is great interest now in cures for Alzheimer disease. Moreover, the timing and circumstances of death are increasingly under medical control, as technological advances produce respirators, transplanted or artificial organs, kidney machines, and the like.[27] Dying, thus postponed and potentially controlled, has given new meanings not only to individual lives, but also to death itself.

As this dramatic postponement of death has occurred with such rapidity, it is not surprising that popular interest in death and popular confusion about its meaning have increased dramatically, and that social norms and social structures related to dying have lagged behind. Over the past two decades, a massive and often confusing literature, both scholarly and quasi-popular, has been produced by historians, philosophers, theologians, social critics, journalists, nurses, ethicists, thanatologists, psychologists, and sociologists.[28] Out of this have come several noteworthy observations relevant to the lengthening life course, concerned with the changing meanings of death, dying as a social process, the social contexts of dying, and the problematic character of new norm formation.

Changing Meanings of Death

A number of studies of social attitudes show that, contrary to widespread belief, fear is not necessarily the outstanding feature in the anticipation of death. As J.C. Diggory and D.Z. Rothman suggested over twenty years ago, when persons do fear their own death it is largely because death would eliminate the opportunity to achieve goals important to them.[29] As growing proportions of the population live into the later years, and predictable or "on-time" deaths tend to become the rule, increasing numbers of people are in a position to contemplate their own deaths. During the last twenty years or so, scholars have concerned themselves with questions related to the social meanings people in their everyday lives attach to death and to the process of dying: how salient is the topic of death?

What images of death do people carry in their heads? What preparations, if any, do people make in anticipation of death?[30]

The first national U.S. survey of attitudes towards death was conducted in the early 1960s.[31] This study, along with some additional questions, was repeated approximately ten years later. The research assessed the content of everyday thoughts about death and found that most Americans held non-threatening images of death ("death is sometimes a blessing," "death is not tragic for the person who dies, only for the survivors"), while only half agreed that "death always comes too soon," and only one-tenth that "to die is to suffer." Although few attitudinal changes were found to have developed in the ten years between the two studies, the research showed an increase in the extent to which thoughts about death intrude upon people's everyday lives. Asked how often they thought about the uncertainty of their own lives or about the death of someone close to them, one-third of the 1960s respondents answered "often," a proportion that rose ten years later to over 40 percent. More important, the salience of death as a topic of thought, while increasing among persons of all ages, rose especially among those who were in their later years. These data suggest that people have become less reluctant to confront the realities of the end of the life course.

Dying as a Social Process

Several studies provide insights into the dying process among those older patients who, under the conditions of an aging society, are sentient and aware of their own finitude. For example, the classic study by B.G. Glaser and A.L. Strauss asked whether people can die socially before they die biologically, and what this means for human relationships.[32] The essential distinction between social and biological death lies in one's awareness of an impending separation of self from others. Based on the behavior of dying patients and their caretakers, four types of awareness are identified: "closed"—the dying person does not recognize his or her impending death, even though others do; "suspected"—the dying person suspects what the others know and attempts to confirm or invalidate this suspicion; "mutual pretense"—each understands the significance but pretends that the other does not; and "open"—both are aware, and they act on this awareness relatively openly. In the first three types, there is little meaningful relation between the biological and the social status of the dying person, in contrast to the fourth type, where an "open awareness" of the impending death permits unfettered interaction between the dying person and the prospective survivors. In this situation, mutual support can develop and it becomes possible to negotiate the final phase of life. With family and friends, previously unspoken affirmations of appreciation and love can be expressed, financial arrangements for heirs can be cooperatively attended to, and old enmities can be ended. The dying and the surviving together may even make decisions about the conditions under which death will take place.

In another study, the psychiatrist E. Mansell Pattison examined the proposition that an interval of "living-dying" typically follows the crisis experienced by the self upon learning that the time of death will occur within a predicted number of hours, days, weeks, months, or even years.[33] Pattison identified the clinical prescriptions for dealing with the living-dying interval and for enabling the self to deal with such fears as loneliness, the loss of others, and the loss of identity. In calling for social-emotional support systems for the dying person, he suggests that the essential task is "to retain self-esteem and respect for the self until death."

Other studies of dying as a social process consider such topics as selfhood and the need for autonomy. For example, O. Pollak examines the capacities of older people for adaptation, relearning, and renewal in an era in which life has been lengthened by social change and technological advance.[34] Stressing the need for autonomy, Pollak says of terminal cases that "having had no autonomy over being born, at least they can exercise a measure of autonomy over dying. Simply turning to the wall or not cooperating with physicians, nurses, and aides can be exercise of this autonomy."

The Social Contexts

Another problematic issue for research reflects the social structural adjustments (or the lack of adjustments) that are occasioned by the trend toward postponement of death. Reflecting the structural lag, S. Levine and N.A. Scotch, in their analysis of "Dying as an Emerging Social Problem," provide an inventory of the insults often heaped upon the selfhood of dying patients in the interest of bureaucratic rules and efficiency: unnecessary prolongation of life after its quality has completely deteriorated; restriction options for therapy and treatment; stigmatization. As these researchers conclude, "the dying patient is often defined as "irresponsible.' It is tragic . . . with so little time left, that the very meaning of life—consciousness, self-control, decision-making—is taken away."[35] In their view, the modern hospital is not organized to deal with the subjective complexities of dying. Nevertheless, structural changes are underway. Because most contemporary hospitals are indeed highly technical organizations that are focused on cure rather than care, it is not surprising that alternatives to dying in hospitals are being developed and that programs specifically designed for the care of the terminally ill are receiving special attention.[36] Among the newly emerging programs is the "hospice"—an antithesis to hospital bureaucracy. In recent decades, the British have developed the hospice as a free-standing facility, while the hospice "movement," now active in every part of the United States, emphasizes care of the dying person in the home, with the unit of care consisting of the patient and the family. (The consequences of this arrangement for the family present another emerging issue.)

New Norm Formation

Social norms, like social structure, also reflect the postponement of death, the changing character of the dying process, and the heavy costs to families and to society at large. An example of changing medical attitudes toward death is to be found in the contrast between two studies of doctors who were treating patients with terminal cancer: in the early 1960s, most preferred not to present their patients with the facts; by 1979, nearly all said it was generally their policy to tell cancer patients the truth about their condition. This reversal over only two decades may reflect a better understanding of the needs of terminal patients, the emergence of patients' "rights," or the widespread doctrine of "informed consent" in medical research. Whatever the explanation, it has apparently become easier for physicians to present patients with realities, however harsh. In another study, one that questioned persons enrolled in a prepaid medical care group, over 70 percent in every age category agreed with the statement, "when a person is in the last stages of a terminal illness, the patient or his family should decide if further treatment should be continued."[37] And a national cross-section study shows a majority of respondents agreeing with the statement that "each person has the right to die with dignity" (95 percent), and that "if a patient is dying, a doctor ought to tell him" (67 percent); while only 26 percent agreed that "doctors should use any means for keeping a patient alive, even after the patient is no longer himself."[38]

At the forefront of ethical dilemmas in an aging society (second only to the potential of genetic engineering to modulate the evolution of the species), is the issue of prolongation of life. While two powerful professions, medicine and law, struggle to control decisions about life and death, conflicting pressures for change will likely give way to the creation of new norms. "Living wills" that state in advance a patient's wishes about medical care will be tested for legal acceptability. Hospital ethics committees will continue to multiply throughout the country. Many deaths will be negotiated in meetings among doctors, families, and often lawyers, a process the *New York Times* has described as "a kind of open national secret."[39] If, in the bizarre calculus of modern technology, life expectancy can be extended even after brain and body are dead, the ethical issues will have to be confronted. As we suggested nearly a decade ago, ". . . there might develop greater emphasis in the health professions on care of terminal patients rather than on hopeless cures, more open discussion of the good death and euthanasia, and the fact of death once again becoming a celebration of renewed solidarity in family and community."[40] Such issues call for both popular and scientific debate that can lead to new norms and new social structures.

THE PROBLEMATIC FUTURE

This essay has explored some of the social and cultural factors, both positive and negative, that help to shape the unprecedently long lives of contemporary Americans. It has illustrated, through selected examples, the interplay between aging processes and social structures. Thus, retirement is understood in the context of a time in which serious doubts are being cast on the inevitability of declining productivity at later ages, and when few socially rewarding roles are available to retirees. Women, those most often left alone in later life to create new roles for themselves, bring to this task a lifelong experience of combining family responsibilities with varied work, leisure, and community roles. And, as most deaths are now postponed to old age, entirely new social arrangements are evolving to care for the dying. In examining each of these topics, we have noted the pressures exerted by increasing longevity on existing social structures, norms, and beliefs and have tried to look past these to the future.

Two conclusions emerge from these discussions. First, there is the potential for a high degree of social control over the future shape of social structures and human lives in an aging society. Second, there is both urgency and risk in planning for this future. The potential for social control increases as new knowledge of aging provides a scientific base for public policy and professional practice. Older people's opportunities for performance are being influenced by concerted efforts to correct erroneous stereotypes of old-age decline, and improved opportunities can both enhance their functioning and employ the large reservoir of underutilized human resources. Women have already demonstrated the feasibility of breaking the rigid sequence of education, work, and leisure by interspersing them over the full life course. Modern medicine is improving its command over the timing of death, enabling dying persons and their caretakers to contemplate the event, and to prepare for it.

Yet interventions can have latent consequences. Every alteration in one phase of a person's life, whether deliberate or not, can have consequences both for that particular phase and for other phases; for the life of that particular person as well as for the lives of others, of every age. These consequences can be either positive or negative. Postponing education in youth can affect educational plans in middle or old age; women's entry into the labor force can affect the social roles of men as workers and as fathers; the massive allocation of public funds to care for the elderly can divert support from the care and education of children. Nowhere is the interdependence of human lives more apparent than in the effects of alterations in longevity itself. The same increased longevity that often causes problems for the elderly today has now largely dispelled the once major social problem of orphanhood. Compared with those born a century or so ago, today's children are almost completely protected against the premature death of a parent. Moreover, at no point in their lives will today's average working couple have more young children than they will have living parents.[41]

The consequences of interventions in any phase of the life course are extremely difficult to assess. The risks are great. Yet, whether or not we are aware of it, we are continually exerting such control. As policymakers, as professionals, and in our personal lives, we make daily decisions that affect the shape of the social structure, the course of our own lives, and the lives of others. Fortunately, a knowledge base is developing that can guide such decisions toward correcting the structural lag and enriching the prolonged life course. Fortunately, too, as members of an aging society we have been given not only added years, but also the privilege—too often taken for granted—of thinking about such problems and participating in the attempts to solve them.

ENDNOTES

The authors are deeply appreciative of editorial help on earlier versions of this manuscript from: Dale Dannefer, Anne Foner, Beth B. Hess, David Kertzer, Alice S. Rossi, Harris Schrank, Joan Waring, and other contributors to this volume who met at the American Academy of Arts and Sciences to discuss the Aging Society Project.

[1] Samuel H. Preston, "Children and the Elderly in the U.S.," *Scientific American,* 251(6) 1984, pp. 44–49.

[2] The dialectic between aging and social change was set forth in Matilda White Riley, "Aging, Social Change, and the Power of Ideas," *Daedalus,* Fall 1978, pp. 39–52. See also M.W. Riley, "Age Strata in Social Systems," in R.H. Binstock and E. Shanas, eds., *Handbook on Aging and the Social Sciences* (New York: Van Nostrand Reinhold, 1985).

[3] U.S. Bureau of the Census, current population reports, series P-23, no. 138, "Demographic and Socioeconomic Aspects of Aging in the United States" (Washington, D.C.: U.S. Government Printing Office, 1984).

[4] Preston, "Children and the Elderly: Divergent Paths for America's Dependents," *Demography,* 21(4) 1984, p. 435.

[5] See Talcott Parsons, "Death in American Society: A Brief Working Paper," *American Behavioral Scientist* (special issue, *Social Research and Life Insurance*), May 1963, pp. 61–65; and Preston, "Mortality Trends," *Annual Review of Sociology,* vol. 3 1977, pp. 163ff.

[6] See Preston, *Mortality Patterns in National Populations* (New York: Academic Press, 1976).

[7] In her 1978 *Daedalus* article (op. cit.), M.W. Riley wrote, ". . . the longer a person lives, the greater the chances of having acquired irreversible characteristics, such characteristics as a higher level of educational attainment or a chronic disease (if 'chronic' is defined as 'incurable')."

[8] Ibid.

[9] Alice S. Rossi, "Equality Between the Sexes: An Immodest Proposal," *Daedalus,* Spring 1964, pp. 607–652.

[10] Barbara Boyle Torrey, "The Lengthening of Retirement," in M.W. Riley, Ronald P. Abeles, and Michael Teitelbaum, eds., *Aging From Birth to Death, vol. II: Sociotemporal Perspectives* (Boulder, CO: Westview Press, 1982), pp. 181–96.

[11]Preston, "Children and Elderly: Divergent Paths," op. cit.

[12]Warner K. Schaie, ed., *Longitudinal Studies of Adult Psychological Development* (New York: Guilford Press, 1983); Paul B. Baltes and Sherry L. Willis, "Enhancement (Plasticity) of Intellectual Functioning in Old Age: Penn State's Adult Development and Enrichment Project (ADEPT)," in F.I.M. Craik and S.E. Trehub, eds., *Aging and the Cognitive Processes* (New York: Plenum, 1982).

[13]John L. Horn and Gary Donaldson, "Cognitive Development in Adulthood," in Orville G. Brim and Jerome Kagan, eds., *Constancy and Change in Human Development* (Cambridge, MA: Harvard University Press, 1980).

[14]Schaie, op. cit.

[15]Herbert J. Walberg, "Scientific Literacy and Economic Productivity in International Perspective," *Daedalus*, Spring 1983, pp. 1–27.

[16]See M.W. Riley, "Aging and Society: Notes on the Development on New Understandings," lecture at the University of Michigan, Ann Arbor, 1983.

[17]See K.G. Manton, "Changing Concepts of Morbidity and Mortality in the Elderly Population," *Milbank Memorial Fund Quarterly/Health and Society*, Spring 1982, pp. 183–244; Melvin Kohn and Carmi Schooler, *Work and Personality: An Inquiry into the Impact of Social Stratification* (Norwood, N.J.: Ablex Press, 1983); Jacob J. Feldman, "Work Ability of the Aged Under Conditions of Improving Mortality," *Milbank Memorial Fund Quarterly/Health and Society*, Summer 1983, pp. 430–444; M.W. Riley and Kathleen Bond, "Beyond Ageism: Postponing the Onset of Disability," in M.W. Riley, Beth B. Hess, and Bond, eds., *Aging in Society: Selected Reviews of Recent Research* (Hillsdale, N.J.: Lawrence Erlbaum, 1983), pp. 243–52.

[18]National Center for Health Statistics, *Vital and Health Statistics,* series 3, no. 23, DHHS pub. no. (P1-1s) 83-1407 (Washington, D.C.: U.S. Government Printing Office; 1983). The unexpected decreases in mortality at the later ages have led to a spate of revisions in the estimates of life expectancy, defined as the average number of years that a group of newborn infants would live if they were to experience throughout life the age-specific death rates prevailing in the calendar year of their births. Given varying assumptions for continuing mortality reduction, there is considerable debate over appropriate methods of estimation.

[19]United Nations, Secretary General, "First Review and Appraisal of the Implementation of the International Plan of Action in Aging," Vienna 1985, unpublished document.

[20]U.S. Bureau of the Census, op. cit.

[21]Jacob A. Brody and D.B. Brock, "Epidemiological and Statistical Characteristics of the United States Elderly Population," in C. Finch and E. Schneider, eds., *Handbook of the Biology of Aging* (New York: Van Nostrand Reinhold, 1985).

[22]K.J. Helsing and M. Szklo, "Mortality After Bereavement," *American Journal of Epidemiology*, (114) 1981, pp. 41–52.

[23]Herbert H. Hyman, *Of Time and Widowhood: Nationwide Studies of Enduring Effects* (Durham, N.C.: Duke University Press, 1983).

[24]B.B. Hess and M.B. Sussman, eds., *Women and the Family: Two Decades of Change* (New York: Haworth, 1984).

[25]M.W. Riley, "Men, Women, and the Lengthening Life Course," in Alice S. Rossi, ed., *Gender and the Lifecourse* (New York: Aldine Publishing Co., 1984).

[26]U.S. Bureau of the Census, op. cit.

[27]In her 1978 *Daedalus* article (op. cit.), M.W. Riley described the implications of secular declines in mortality. Earlier declines, which occurred at young ages, led

to control over fertility; recent declines, which occur at later ages, predictably lead to increased control over the process of dying.

[28] J.W. Riley, Jr., "Dying and the Meanings of Death: Sociological Inquiries," *Annual Review of Sociology*, vol. 3, 1983, pp. 191–216.

[29] J.C. Diggory and D.Z. Rothman, "Values Destroyed by Death," *Journal of Abnormal and Social Psychology* (63) 1961, pp. 205–10.

[30] J.W. Riley, "Death and Bereavement," in D.L. Sills, ed., *International Encyclopedia of the Social Sciences,* vol. 4 (N.J.: Macmillan Co. & Free Press, 1968), pp. 19–26.

[31] J.W. Riley, "What People Think About Death," in O.G. Brim, Jr., et al., eds., *The Dying Patient* (New York: Russell Sage Foundation, 1970), pp. 30–41.

[32] B.G. Glaser and A.L. Strauss, *Time for Dying* (Chicago: Aldine, 1968).

[33] E. Mansell Pattison, *The Experience of Dying* (Englewood Cliff, N.J.: Prentice-Hall, 1977).

[34] J.M. Pollack, "Correlates of Death Anxiety: A Review of Empirical Studies," *Omega*, vol. 10, no. 3, 1979–80, pp. 97–121.

[35] S. Levine and N.A. Scotch, "Dying as an Emerging Social Problem," in O.G. Brim, et al., eds., op. cit. pp. 211–24.

[36] See D. Crane, *The Sanctity of Social Life: Physicians' Treatment of Chronically Ill Patients* (New York: Russell Sage Foundation, 1975); and R.A. Kalish, *Death, Grief, and Caring Relationships* (Monterey, CA: Brooks/Cole, 1981).

[37] M. Haug, "Aging and the Right to Terminate Medical Treatment," *Journal of Gerontology*, 33(4) 1978, pp. 586–91.

[38] J.W. Riley, "What People Think About Death," op. cit.

[39] *The New York Times*, Dec. 30, 1984.

[40] M.W. Riley, "Aging, Social Change, and the Power of Ideas," loc. cit.

[41] Preston, "Children and the Elderly in the U.S.," loc. cit.

Jacob S. Siegel and Cynthia M. Taeuber

Demographic Dimensions of an Aging Population

T HE UNITED STATES HAS a rapidly growing older population
whose share of the total population is steadily rising. The
number of elderly (sixty-five years and over) has more than
doubled since 1950 to about 28 million in 1984, and the number of
the older aged (eighty-five years and over) has more than quadrupled
since 1950 to 2.6 million. From a mere 8 percent in 1950, the
percentage of elderly in the population climbed to 12 percent in 1984.
By 2020, about 17 percent of the total U.S. population will be elderly,
the same proportion as in the most "elderly" state today, Florida.

For the present essay, population aging will be defined simply as a
rise in the proportion of the population sixty-five years old and over.
Population aging is a characteristic of population groups and is
influenced by changes in mortality, migration, and, especially, fertility. In contrast, *individual aging,* measured for population aggregates
by a rise in life expectancy or survival rates, is a characteristic of
individuals summarized for populations. Individual aging is determined wholly by death rates at each age of life. In the United States,
population aging is associated with low and declining mortality, but
this relationship is not a necessary or intrinsic one.

The elderly population is a demographically heterogeneous group
that includes a wide range of ages and sharp variations in the
characteristics of the members of the component ages. In addition,
there is rapid turnover in this population, mortality rates being
relatively high: a younger group enters the "elderly" age range, and
each age group among the elderly moves up to occupy a new and

higher age category as the former occupants age or die. These new members may have quite different characteristics from those they replace. Variations also occur in the size of age (birth) cohorts, survival rates, and the share of immigrants in each cohort. As a result, substantial shifts take place in the characteristics of each constituent age group and of the elderly population as a whole. In fact, the shifts in numbers, age distribution, sex composition, health status, marital status, and economic characteristics may be considerable.

POPULATION AGING

U.S. Population Aging

The elderly population of the United States is growing much more rapidly than the population as a whole. The population sixty-five years and over increased by 28 percent in the decade of the 1970s, and the 85-and-over group increased by 59 percent compared with an 11 percent increase for the population as a whole. These growth rates can also be compared with an increase of 54 percent for those 30-to-34 years of age, the group in 1980 representing the first wave of the "baby-boom" cohorts. The older aged are currently, in fact, the fastest growing age segment of the U.S. population.

Past changes in the number of births are usually the most important influence on later changes in the numbers at each age in a population, although improvements in the chance of survival and shifts in the volume of net immigration play a part. The number of elderly persons in the United States has been growing rapidly in the past several decades, mainly because of the increases in the annual number of births before 1921, but also because of the greatly improved chance of survival to old age. Because the elderly of the future (at least for sixty-five years ahead) have already been born, it is now possible to anticipate the future size of the older population with much greater confidence than age groups still to be born.

From 1921 to 1945, the annual number of births was declining, or was low, in comparison with the years before 1921. This turnaround accounts for the fact that up to about the year 2010 we can expect a period of sustained but undramatic growth in the elderly population. Then, as the postwar baby-boom cohorts of 1946 to 1964 first begin to reach age sixty-five, the number of elderly persons and the ratio of elderly persons to younger persons will rise dramatically. From 2010 to 2030, according to the U.S. Census Bureau's middle series of projections, the population sixty-five and over will increase from 39 million to 65 million. (See table 1, next page.)

The growth of the overall elderly population, and particularly of the younger segment of the elderly population, will then decelerate beginning about 2030, as the persons born in the "baby-bust" period (1965 on) begin to reach age sixty-five. At the same time, the baby-boom group will swell the size of the 85-and-over population. Society will continue to feel the impact of the baby-boom cohorts from about 2030 to 2050 as they reach age eighty-five. In 2030, this older segment of the elderly population is expected to number nearly 9 million (middle series), and in just two additional decades could grow to 16 million. With greater reductions in mortality rates than now anticipated in the middle projections, even these figures would understate the size of the future older aged population.

The elderly population has grown steadily as a share of the total U.S. population. In 1920, every twenty-second American (4.6 percent) was sixty-five years or older; the proportion had increased to every twelfth person (8.1 percent) by 1950; and to every eighth to ninth person (11.8 percent) by 1984. By 2030, we can expect at least every fifth American to be elderly. (See table 1, next page.)

Changes in the percent age distribution of a population are also affected more by changes in fertility than by changes in mortality. Changes in the proportion of elderly are directly affected both by fluctuations in the number of births sixty-five or more years earlier and by trends in the birth rate in the intervening years. The number of births showed marked increases, or was relatively high, from 1946 to 1964; continued low birth rates, together with declines in death rates that are concentrated at the older ages, are projected for 1985 to 2030. This combination of conditions will lead to sharp increases in the proportion of elderly persons during the 2010–2030 period. Immigration will increase the numbers in the various age groups but will affect the age distribution very little. The larger the volume of immigration, the lower the proportion of elderly persons.

Even as the proportion of elderly persons has been rising, so the elderly population itself has been getting older, with an increasing share over age seventy-five. This trend is expected to continue, at least until the first decade of the next century. Once the baby-boom cohorts begin to

TABLE 1. Population 65+ and Annual Average Increase, 1950 to 2050, as of July 1 (Numbers in thousands)

Year	Population	Percent of population 65 and over	Average annual increase in preceding period	
			Amount	Percent
1950	12397	8.1	x	x
1965	18451	9.5	404	2.7
1984	28040	11.8	505	2.2
Middle series[1]				
1995	33887	13.1	532	1.7
2010	39196	13.8	354	1.0
2030	64580	21.2	1269	2.5
2050	67412	21.8	142	0.2
Highest series[2]				
1995	34618	12.9	598	1.9
2010	42067	13.6	497	1.3
2030	72587	19.6	1526	2.7
2050	82744	19.3	508	0.7
Lowest series[3]				
1995	33127	13.2	462	1.5
2010	36547	14.0	228	0.7
2030	58085	22.6	1077	2.3
2050	56336	24.3	-87	-0.2

SOURCE: Based on various *Current Population Reports* of the U.S. Census Bureau: series P-25, nos. 311, 519, 917, 952, and 965. The projections are presented in "Projections of the Population of the United States, by Age, Sex, and Race: 1983 to 2080," by Gregory Spencer, *Current Population Reports*, series P-25, no. 952, May 1984.   [1]Middle fertility, middle mortality, middle immigration.   [2]High fertility, low mortality, high immigration.   [3]Low fertility, high mortality, low immigration.

reach age sixty-five, the trend should reverse itself, until these cohorts reach age seventy-five. At its initial peak in 2005 or so, the share of the 65+ population that is seventy-five and over will be about 51 percent, compared with 41 percent today. At its second peak in 2050 or so, the share will exceed 55 percent. With the increases in the number of old people, chronic illnesses will probably become more prevalent, although much depends on lifestyle, technological developments, health-care delivery practices, and other factors.[1]

Societal Dependency Ratios

Public policy issues often arise with changing balances of numbers in different age groups. Broad changes in the age structure are reflected in the gerontic dependency ratio, which shows the number of persons sixty-five years and over per hundred persons of "prime working age" (twenty to sixty-four years). At present, there are about twenty persons sixty-five years and over for every hundred persons of prime working age. By 2030, after all the baby-boom cohorts have become members of the elderly group, this ratio is expected to nearly double. (See table 2, next page.) The neontic dependency ratio—the ratio of those under twenty years old to hundred persons age twenty to sixty-four—is expected to show only a moderate decline in this period, from fifty-one to forty-four. By 2050, the gerontic dependency ratio and the neontic dependency ratio may be approximately equal for the first time (40 vs. 42). The net effect of this rise in the gerontic dependency ratio and smaller decline in the neontic dependency ratio will be a substantial rise in total dependency by 2050.

Dependency ratios indicate the contribution of the age composition of a population to society's problem of economic dependency. Variations in the ratios also suggest the periods when the age distribution is likely to make a significant contribution to the problems of providing health and social services, Social Security benefits, adequate housing, and satisfying jobs for the elderly, and when the possible competition between the elderly and children for societal support will be greatest.[2]

International Perspective

Aging of the populations of the world's regions is nearly universal.[3] Yet the older population (sixty years and over) in some less developed regions will still be a relatively small proportion of the total popula-

TABLE 2. Societal and Familial Age Dependency Ratio, 1950 to 2050, as of July 1[1]

Year	Societal Dependency Ratios			Familial Dependency Ratios	
	Total[2]	Neontic[3]	Gerontic[4]	One elderly generation[5]	Two elderly generations[6]
1950	73	59	14	116	12
1965	95	77	18	135	17
1984	71	51	20	194	29
1995	70	48	22	142	42
2010	65	42	23	126	56
2030	83	44	39	242	47
2050	82	42	40	224	96

SOURCE: Based on various *Current Population Reports* of the U.S. Census Bureau: series P-25, nos. 311, 519, 917, 952, and 965. The projections are presented in "Projections of the Population of the United States, by Age, Sex, and Race: 1983 to 2080," by Gregory Spencer, *Current Population Reports*, series P-25, no. 952, May 1984.

[1]Figures include U.S. Armed Forces overseas. Projections are from the middle series.

[2] $\dfrac{\text{Population under 20 years} + \text{population 65 years and over}}{\text{Population 20 to 64 years}} \times 100$

[3] $\dfrac{\text{Population under 20 years}}{\text{Population 20 to 64 years}} \times 100$

[4] $\dfrac{\text{Population 65 years and over}}{\text{Population 20 to 64 years}} \times 100$

[5] $\dfrac{\text{Population 65 to 79 years old}}{\text{Population 45 to 49 years old}} \times 100$

[6] $\dfrac{\text{Population 85 years and over}}{\text{Population 65 to 69 years old}} \times 100$

tion in 2020 (e.g., 6 percent in Africa). In contrast, the proportions for Northern America and Europe (21 and 23 percent, respectively) will be quite high. The relative "youth" of the less developed regions is essentially a consequence of high fertility, offset in part by low survival to old age in most regions. The relative "agedness" of the more developed regions is associated with a pattern of continuing low fertility, past rises in the number of births, and low mortality characteristic of both the earlier and later stages of life.

Low fertility and mortality give rise to populations that are not growing ("zero population growth") and to age structures that are approaching stationarity (i.e., a fixed shape and zero population growth). Several countries in Western Europe are now losing population (e.g., West Germany, Denmark, Great Britain) and will soon reflect the higher percentages of elderly persons shown by stationary populations with high life expectancies (e.g., 17 percent above age sixty-five when life expectancy is seventy-four years).

Decreases in fertility, leading to declining numbers of births, mean that a smaller number of persons of working age will be available to provide the services the elderly need. This is already a problem in several more developed countries, such as West Germany and Japan.[4] In West Germany, the ratio of retired persons to workers is the highest in the world, and Japan is now experiencing the most dramatic increases in this regard. These countries face the prospect of allocating a much larger portion of their budget to Social Security benefits at a time when the population will be less able to save and invest and, hence, to support such programs.

Sex, Race, and Ethnic Composition

Elderly women in the United States now outnumber elderly men three to two (corresponding to a sex ratio of sixty-seven men per one hundred women). This represents a considerable change since 1930, when there were about an equal number of elderly men and women. The deficit of males grows steadily with advancing age, following an initial excess of boys among births and at the younger ages. The official estimates for 1984 show 105 boys for every 100 girls under age five, 99 men per 100 women aged 30 to 34, 81 men for every 100 women aged 65 to 69, and only 41 men for every 100 women aged 85 or over. If these sex ratios are adjusted for differences in the census coverage of males and females, the sexes cross the balance point at ages 40 to 44, rather than 30 to 34.

The low sex ratios in the older ages and their downward trend result from the fact that the survival rates of females exceed those of males throughout the age span, and that this advantage has been expanding for many decades. It is decelerating, however, and the relative difference in the numbers of elderly men and women has almost ceased growing. In fact, the sex ratios of the birth cohorts of 1980–1985 are expected to fall more slowly with advancing age than those observed in 1984, crossing a hundred, the balance point, at the ages of 45–49 instead of ages 40–44, as was the case in 1984. The massive excess of females at ages 65 and over, now numbering 5 1/2 million, is expected to grow, however, as the elderly population grows, nearly doubling by 2025.

Because most elderly persons, especially those over age seventy-five, are female, the health, social, and economic problems of the elderly may be viewed as mostly the problems of women. Aged women are often widowed, live alone, have difficulty in functioning independently because of chronic health conditions, and experience a disproportionate degree of poverty. On the other hand, men commonly have already made the "supreme sacrifice." From a philosophical and ethical viewpoint, we may also see this as an issue of treatment versus prevention, and the locus of the problem is a legitimate matter of debate.

The black population is much younger than the white population. Although the black elderly population is growing more rapidly than the white elderly population, a much smaller proportion of the black population is over sixty-five years of age (8 percent versus 13 percent in 1984). The higher fertility of blacks, associated with the higher mortality of blacks below age sixty-five, is the main factor in the difference in the proportion of white and black elderly persons. The difference has been increasing and is expected to continue to do so.

GEOGRAPHIC DISTRIBUTION AND RESIDENTIAL MOBILITY

The aging of the nation's population is pervasively reflected in the record of most states. Almost all the states have shown a steady rise in the proportion of elderly persons since 1960. As a result mainly of the influence of internal migration, many states are aging at an accelerated pace compared to the country as a whole.

Florida leads the other states by far in its proportion of elderly, with 17.5 percent age sixty-five and over in 1983. Many Midwestern farm-belt states—Iowa, Missouri, South Dakota, Nebraska, Kansas—as well as Maine, Massachusetts, Rhode Island, Pennsylvania, and Arkansas, show relatively high proportions of elderly (13.0 percent or more), as compared with the national average (11.7 percent). Several Western states—Utah, Wyoming, Colorado, Nevada, New Mexico—and the South—Texas, Louisiana, South Carolina, Georgia—as well as Alaska and Hawaii, show low proportions (below 10.0 percent). The high proportions tend to result from continuing large net out-migration of young adults (in the Midwest), continuing large net in-migration of older persons (to Florida), and low fertility (in Maine, Massachusetts, Pennsylvania, Rhode Island).

Low proportions of elderly tend to occur under the opposite conditions, principally in-migration of young adults—to Colorado, Nevada, Texas, Wyoming—and high fertility—in South Carolina, Georgia, New Mexico, Utah, Wyoming. Variation in mortality is not a significant factor in identifying states with high or low proportions of elderly. In recent years, the role of direct migration of the elderly as a factor in the aging of state populations may have increased as the economic status of the elderly has improved and retirement centers have become more widespread.

Some states have many counties with "elderly" populations. Apart from Florida, over one-quarter of the counties in Kansas and over one-fifth of the counties of Texas and Missouri had elderly proportions of 20 percent or more in 1980. These are usually "small" counties, that is, counties with no place over 25,000 inhabitants. In general, the proportion of elderly in a population tends to vary inversely with the size of the area. Non-metropolitan counties with only small places had the highest proportions, and the urban fringes of large metropolitan counties had the lowest proportions. From a simple numerical standpoint, the small rural counties of the Midwest potentially have the most serious problem in planning services for the elderly.

Old people mostly "stay put." Many live out their lives in small-town America or in certain sections of our large cities, especially the inner, deteriorated sections. Gerontic enclaves have long been evident in large cities, but concentrations of elderly people are now appearing in metropolitan suburbs, albeit in a more dispersed form, as residues of the large postwar migration to these areas.[5]

After "youth," the tendency to move drops steadily until old age, when migration rates are quite low. Among the elderly, however, mobility is greater for the younger segment (65 to 74 years) than for the older segment (75 years and over). Currently, only about 3 1/2 percent of the population sixty-five and over moves to a different house in the same county in a year, and only about 2 percent changes its county of residence in a year.[6] Of those who move, nearly half remain within the same metropolitan area. The level and age pattern of mobility rates have not changed much in the last few decades.

LONGEVITY AND HEALTH

Life expectancy at birth has increased tremendously since the beginning of the century, when it was about forty-nine years. It rose to sixty-eight years in 1949–1951, or by about nineteen years in the first half of the century. There was relatively little change thereafter until 1968, when life expectancy again began to advance steadily and briskly. The latest figure is 74.7 years for 1983. According to the life table for 1949–1951, only two-thirds of all babies would live to age sixty-five; now, nearly four out of five babies would live to this age. These figures on life expectancy and chances of survival understate greatly the actual prospects for persons born in the years indicated. Life expectancy for a child born in 1950 has been projected by the Social Security Administration (SSA) at 76 years, or eight years more than the figure for calendar year 1950, for example.[7]

The chance of surviving to the oldest ages has also increased, especially if one has already reached age sixty-five. Life expectancy at age sixty-five was twelve years in 1900–1902, fourteen years in 1949–1951, and seventeen years in 1983. The SSA projection for the birth cohort reaching age sixty-five in 1950 is 19 1/2 years, or 5 1/2 years more than the 1950 calendar-year figure. The proportion of persons surviving from age sixty-five to age eighty-five was 23 percent in 1950 and 38 percent in 1983. That is to say, for every hundred persons aged sixty-five, an additional fifteen persons survived to age eighty-five in this 33-year period. Compared with the improvements at the younger ages, the relative improvements at the older ages, whether measured in terms of survival rates or average years lived, have been markedly greater in this period, although the relative declines in age-specific death rates have been somewhat smaller. In the 1900–1950 period, mortality indicators were consistent in showing lesser gains at the older ages.

Even though life expectancy at birth has been steadily increasing, the human life span may be fixed at about 100 to 105 years. The curve of survivors, based on annual death rates, has become increasingly rectangular in shape.[8] When overall mortality was relatively high, death rates were much higher at the younger ages than now, and the curve of survivors sloped downward at roughly a 45-degree angle, as in the 1900–1902 curve. As death rates have fallen at the young and middle ages, the survival curve has become increasingly level over most of the age span and has fallen more and more sharply at the higher ages, as in the 1983 curve. At its theoretical limit, the curve would assume a 90-degree angle, with virtually every member of the cohort surviving to age one hundred and then dying within the short time span suggested by the above age range. Fries and Crapo have added the notion that the period of chronic morbidity in later life is also being compressed as life expectancy and life span merge.[9]

We can measure the progress toward this theoretical limit, i.e., the complete "squaring" of the survival curve, as follows: In 1900–1902, when life expectancy was forty-nine years, it fell short of its potential "maximum" of about one hundred years by fifty-one years. By 1983, the number (and percent) of years lost had been cut in half to twenty-six (i.e., 100 minus 74). For persons who reached age sixty-five, the corresponding figures are twenty-three years (i.e., 100 minus 77) for 1900–1902, and eighteen years (i.e., 100 minus 82) for 1983.

Both the rectangularization of the survival curve and the associated hypothesis on the compression of the period of morbidity have been questioned.[10] Complete rectangularization of the survival curve cannot be expected for many decades at best, since it would require much progress in the treatment of chronic illness. In the meantime, the human life span may be slowly rising and, according to Walford and others, there is a reasonable possibility of extending it in the next few decades by fifteen to thirty years.[11] The implications for our society of a life expectancy near one hundred, and a life span of 115 to 130 years, have yet to be thoroughly explored.

Sex and Race Differences

Life expectancy at birth differs substantially according to sex and race. The figures for males and females in 1983, 71.0 years and 78.3 years, indicate a massive difference of 7.3 years. The race difference, 5.6 years, is of somewhat lesser magnitude; whites can expect to live 75.2 years and blacks can expect to live 69.6 years at current death rates. (See table 3.)

The peak difference between the sexes, 7.8 years, was reached in 1979, and is perceptibly higher than the current difference, 7.3 years. Much of the difference in life expectancy at birth between the sexes is accounted for by differences in mortality *after* age sixty-five, but nearly all of the difference between the races is accounted for by differences in mortality *before* age sixty-five. According to the life table for 1983, a female who had lived to age sixty-five could expect to live an additional 18.6 years; a male, 14.2 years. A white who had lived to age sixty-five could expect to live an additional 16.6 years; a black, 15.1 years. The respective differences are 4.4 years for the sexes and 1.5 years for the races.

Males and females have not shared equally in the reduction of mortality in this century. In 1900–1902, white females had an advantage of less than three years in life expectancy at birth over white men, and only about one year at age sixty-five. Between 1900–1902 and 1983, expectation of life at birth increased nearly twenty-three years for white males and more than twenty-seven years for white females; hence, about four years were added to the original difference of almost three years, yielding a total difference of over seven years. Life expectancy at age sixty-five showed gains between 1900–1902 and 1983 of 2.9 years for white males, and 6.6 years for white females. As a result, the gap between the sexes for whites at age sixty-five is nearly five years today.

The relative contribution of genetic and environmental factors to the difference in the longevity of males and females is a matter of considerable debate. It is clear that both biological and environmental factors have an influence.[12] Cigarette smoking, for example, has been identified as a major contributor to the difference.[13] Generally, men are engaged in the more stressful, physically demanding, and dangerous occupations. With the narrowing of the difference in the environment, roles, and lifestyles of men and women, the longevity

TABLE 3. Life Expectancy by Race and Sex: 1929–1931 to 2050

Years	Life Expectancy				Years gained since previous date			
	At Birth		At age 65		At birth		At age 65	
	Male	*Female*	*Male*	*Female*	*Male*	*Female*	*Male*	*Female*
	White		*White*		*White*		*White*	
1929–1931	59.8	61.1	11.7	12.8	x	x	x	x
1949–1951	65.5	71.0	12.7	15.0	7.7	9.9	1.0	2.2
1983	76.0	78.3	14.5	18.8	5.5	7.3	1.8	3.8
2050[1]	75.5	83.6	17.4	23.1	4.5	5.3	2.9	4.3
	Black		*Black*		*Black*		*Black*	
1929–1931	60.9	48.4	12.3	11.6	x	x	x	x
1949–1951[2]	69.0	60.7	13.9	13.6	8.1	12.3	1.6	2.0
1983	75.2	69.6	16.9	15.4	6.2	8.9	3.0	1.8
2050[1]	79.8	78.2	20.3	20.0	4.6	8.6	3.4	4.6

SOURCE: Based on reports of the National Center for Health Statistics, U.S.P.H.S., or for 2050, the U.S. Bureau of the Census.
[1]Middle mortality assumption.
[2]Data designated "black" are for races other than white.

gap might be expected to diminish considerably. So far, however, this has not happened in the United States or in those European countries where there are sizable sex differences in longevity. There is no evidence that the increasing labor-force participation of women, the decreasing labor-force participation of men, and other approximations of the environment, roles, and lifestyles of men and women have brought male and female longevity significantly closer.[14]

There is also strong evidence for the role of biological factors in the male-female difference in the average length of life. Female mammals in general tend to be longer-lived. Fetal and infant mortality is substantially higher among males than among females. There is also evidence that the reproductive period plays a protective role in the health of women with respect to the clotting factor, hormonal balance, cholesterol metabolism, and the elasticity of the vascular system. With the virtual elimination of infective and parasitic diseases, the great reduction in maternal mortality, and the emergence of chronic degenerative diseases (heart disease, cancer, stroke, etc.) as the principal causes of death, the biological superiority of women has evidenced itself more strongly. Men fall victim and succumb more readily to these chronic, often fatal, diseases.

As suggested, a significant convergence of the death rates of males and females may not result merely from high or rising percentages of women working—although this may "help." Changes in smoking habits and other elements of lifestyle—such as eating habits, physical exercise, sleeping, automobile driving, and alcohol consumption—presumably could have a significant positive impact on the longevity of both sexes, especially males. Additional convergence could result if children's socialization became more similar and, particularly, if males and females were reared from infancy on to handle stress less differently. The processes of personality restructuring appear to have started, but they "take effect" slowly. Even with these changes, a biologically influenced part of the sex difference in mortality will tend to remain.

No serious student of the subject has projected an equalization of the life expectancies of the sexes in the foreseeable future. We first need to understand the male-female differences in death rates and to reduce the gap. Men would benefit from an aggressive preventive and therapeutic program that favors them (that is, an "Equal Health Opportunity" program) and that encourages them to give more attention to preventive health care. The consequences of the gap are immense. It is related in varying degrees to female widowhood, paternal orphanhood, solitary living of older women, sharply reduced income of women in later life, earlier and longer institutionalization and forced reentry into the labor force of older women, their need for special support from other family members or society, and other life-course changes, some clearly undesirable.

The massive mortality gap observed between the races in 1900 has been steadily narrowing. In 1929–1931 there was approximately a thirteen-year gap in life expectation at birth between whites and blacks; in 1983 there was a difference of six years. At age sixty-five, life expectancy of blacks and whites has been about the same for many decades. Much of the difference in the mortality of the races at the ages below sixty-five may be accounted for by differences in the socioeconomic status of the race groups.[15] Serious health problems remain for blacks because of their greater poverty, poorer housing, and lower educational attainment. Whether the difference can be completely eliminated is unclear.

Causes of Death

In the United States today, more than three out of four deaths of elderly persons result from heart disease, cancer, or stroke. In 1982, heart disease accounted for some 44 percent of elderly deaths, cancer for 22 percent, and stroke for 12 percent. Heart disease was the major cause of death of the elderly in 1950 and remains so today, even though there has been, since 1968, a spectacular decline in the death rate from this cause. Mortality among the elderly since 1968 has plunged, in fact, because of a marked reduction of deaths from heart disease, stroke, and other major causes, especially among females. Death rates from cancer, especially the death rate from lung cancer, have been increasing for several decades.

According to the death rates of 1978, a newborn child has a 41 percent chance of eventually dying from heart disease, a 19 percent chance of dying from cancer, and a 10 percent chance of dying from cerebrovascular disease.[16] These probabilities are not greatly different at age sixty-five. If cancer were entirely eliminated as a cause of death, life expectation at age sixty-five would be extended by two years under the assumption that the risks from different causes are independent. In fact, however, more persons would then die from heart disease and other causes as a result of the increase both in the population at risk and in the death rates for the other causes. Similarly, eliminating deaths from heart disease would add some seven years to life expectancy at age sixty-five under the assumption of independence. The degree to which the incidence of a particular cause of death would be affected by the elimination of some other cause depends in large part on the rank order and proximity of the median ages of the various causes, and on the relative magnitudes of the rates. With the elimination of cancer, few additional lives would be saved, even in the short run.[17]

The median age at death for persons dying from malignant neoplasms in 1979 was sixty-nine years; from major cardiovascular diseases, seventy-seven years; from "influenza and pneumonia," eighty years; from diabetes, seventy-three years; and from "bronchitis, emphysema, and asthma," seventy-two years. The median age at death was twice as high (seventy-two years) in 1979 as in 1900 (thirty-six years), when people died mainly from infectious and parasitic diseases and the population was much younger. The median age at death for all causes combined is a sensitive summary measure of an aging population with low mortality since it is dependent both on the age pattern of mortality rates and on the age distribution of the population.

Elderly men are more likely than elderly women to die from heart disease, cancer, "influenza and pneumonia," accidents, cirrhosis of the liver, "nephritis and nephrosis," and especially "bronchitis, emphysema, and asthma." In fact, for all of the ten leading causes of death at ages sixty-five and over, the rates for males sixty-five to eighty-four years are well above those for women of the same ages except for diabetes. After age eighty-five, the rates for men continue to be higher than those for women for all leading causes except cerebrovascular disease and diabetes.

Prospects for Increased Longevity

Life expectancy is expected to continue upward, though probably at a somewhat attenuated pace as compared with the experience of the last decade-and-a-half. If the average annual rates of decrease in age-specific death rates recorded in the years since 1968 continue to prevail in the coming sixty-five years (that is, to the year 2050), life expectancy at birth would approximate one hundred in that year.

This figure has possible implications for the extension of human life span, since the corresponding figure for total life expectancy (including years already lived) at age eighty-five is 108 years. Fries's theory of the rectangularization of the survival curve/compression of mortality would argue against any necessary extension of life span. None of the official projections of life expectancy at birth even roughly approximate the hundred-year mark. The three projections for 2050 of the Social Security Administration are eighty-four years (high), eighty years (medium), and seventy-seven years (low).[18] The high series implies a nearly 50-percent decline in age-specific death rates between 1982 and 2050. The Census Bureau's high series expectancy figure is eighty-three years. A rosier impression is secured from the SSA's high series figure for females at age sixty-five in 2050, namely twenty-seven years (implying a total life expectation at this age of ninety-two years), and from its projection of a 0.1 percent probability of survival to age 113 in 2050. Although the SSA claims that these projections rule out significant medical and technological breakthroughs in the treatment of the major chronic diseases, its implied figure for life span is clearly allowed to float upward.

A conservative evaluation of the prospects for the increase in longevity in the United States is given by a composite life table using the lowest death rates at each age currently observed in any country. Such a table, based mainly on rates for 1980, has an expectation of life at birth of 78 years (75 years for males and 81 years for females) and an expectation of life at age 65 of 18 years (16 years for males and 20 years for females). These figures are, respectively, only three years and one year above the 1983 levels for the United States. Japan's figures for 1982 nearly equal the "best-country composite," with 74.5 years for males and 80.2 years for females. Somewhat more favorable projections can be secured by constructing the table with the lowest age-specific death rates for endogenous causes only.[19]

Smoking, dietary habits, alcohol consumption, stress, exercise, and obesity have a proven effect on health, especially on the incidence of endogenous diseases.[20] The U.S. Public Health Service has estimated that lifestyle accounts for nearly two-fifths to more than one-half of the mortality from heart disease, cancer, cerebrovascular disease, and arteriosclerosis.[21] Personal habits and lifestyles of Americans are changing for the better. Will these changes continue and become more widespread? It seems reasonable to believe so, and to ask what would happen to life expectancy if the mortality caused by adverse lifestyle were eliminated. We estimate that seven years would be added to the life expectancy of females at birth and at age sixty-five. This change would add 3.6 years to the "best-country composite" at birth, and 5.5 years to the "best-country composite" at age sixty-five, bringing life expectancy for females to eighty-five years at birth and to twenty-five years at age sixty-five.

These and other gains could possibly be achieved by extending the application of present medical knowledge regarding prevention, diagnosis, and treatment of the major illnesses to the less educated and less affluent classes, and to the geographic areas now poorly serviced. Specific methods of closing these gaps include health-education efforts and changes in the financing and delivery of medical care. Programs to improve the competence of health personnel, reduce environmental pollution, and increase automobile and industrial safety should have an additional salutory effect.

We may assume that existing diagnostic and therapeutic procedures for specific diseases will be improved or new ones will be developed. There is also the possibility of devising and implementing techniques for slowing the aging process. The prospects for reducing death rates at the older ages, reshaping the survival curve, and extending the human life span remain a matter of debate.

Health Status

Clinical measures clearly indicate the decline of health status with age. The elderly are more likely to have a chronic condition that limits their activities, and they experience about twice as many days of restricted activity because of illness as the general population (almost forty days versus nineteen days in 1981). Those elderly who worked, however, do not experience a marked difference in the number of lost work days as compared with the younger working population—about four or five days a year, on the average, for both groups.[22] Arthritis, rheumatism, and heart conditions account for half of the conditions that cause limitations in the activities of the elderly.

Pronounced changes occur over the older age span in the area of health. For example, in 1979, only 5.7 percent of the non-institutional population aged sixty-five to seventy-four said they needed help with one or more home management activities, including shopping, doing routine household chores, preparing meals, or handling money, whereas 40 percent of persons aged eighty-five years and over reported needing such help. Furthermore, 5 percent and 35 percent of these two age groups, respectively, reported needing help with one or more basic physical activities. For example, just over a fourth of the non-institutional population eighty-five and over needed help walking, and nearly 4 percent needed help eating.[23] Not until age group eighty-five and over do about half of the non-institutional population report being unable to carry on a major activity because of chronic illness.

Since the turn of the century, there has been a significant shift in the principal causes of ill health, from the infectious and parasitic diseases to the chronic diseases. This so-called epidemiological transition parallels the changes in the causes of death. Although morbidity and mortality have both declined sharply since 1900, the improvement in morbidity has been much less than that in mortality.[24] The measures suggest that no major improvements in the health status of the elderly population occurred during the period 1965 to 1979. The proportion of individuals sixty-five years and over with limitations of activity— especially limitations associated with the leading chronic diseases—rose in this period. Paradoxically, then, it appears that during this period health conditions did not improve, or even deteriorated, while longevity steadily moved upward.[25] While total life expectancy has increased, so may have the years after the onset of chronic disease and disability (that is, "inactive life expectancy").[26]

While older males have higher death rates than older females, a higher percentage of elderly females report having one or more chronic conditions. Elderly females also have a higher incidence rate for acute conditions. The diseases that commonly affect elderly men predominate as causes of death (e.g., heart disease, cancer), while those that commonly affect elderly women predominate as causes of illness (e.g., arthritis, osteoporosis).[27]

MARITAL STATUS AND LIVING ARRANGEMENTS

The patterns of marital status and living arrangements shift considerably with advancing age. While the changes follow the same general course for elderly women and elderly men, they are much more dramatic for the former than for the latter. Elderly women are

more likely to be widowed than married, and a substantial proportion live alone. Elderly men, on the other hand, are much more likely
to be married than widowed; most, therefore, live in a family setting.
These differences are due to the higher death rates of elderly married
men than elderly married women (2½ times higher), the far higher
remarriage rates of elderly men than elderly women (seven times
higher), and the tendency of the elderly men who marry to marry
younger women as well as single, divorced, and widowed women
over sixty-five.

Marital Status

In 1984, four out of five men aged sixty-five to seventy-four years,
and two out of three men age seventy-five and over were married and
living with their wives.[28] Only half of the women aged sixty-five to
seventy-four were married and living with their husbands, and less
than one in four women seventy-five years and over lived with a
husband. At ages sixty-five to seventy-four, only one in eleven men
was widowed, as compared with two in five women. After age
seventy-five, about a fourth of the men were widowed as compared
with two-thirds of the women. Only 5 to 6 percent of elderly men and
women had never married, and 3 to 4 percent were divorced.

This general pattern applies to whites and blacks alike. Whites,
however, have a much higher probability of being married than
blacks, and black females have a much higher probability of being
widowed than white women. This pattern of black-white variation
applies in marked degree to ages seventy-five and over. In 1984,
nearly three-quarters of aged black women were widowed.

The gains in life expectancy have influenced not only the probability of a newborn child surviving to marriageable age, but also other
aspects of marriage, divorce, and widowhood. The experience of
recent and earlier cohorts is rather different. Men and women now in
their eighties and nineties were somewhat less likely to marry in their
lifetime than are those now in their mid-thirties and forties.[29] Women
and men in the early cohorts did not marry, on the average, until age
twenty-three and twenty-six, respectively. Until recently, the average
age at first marriage had been declining steadily (to twenty-one years
for women and twenty-three years for men). The rate of marital
dissolution has also sharply increased; 42 to 46 percent of current
marriages are expected to end in divorce, while about one in five

marriages of persons now over age eighty ended in divorce. Women born at or before the turn of the century experienced widowhood at younger ages than will be true for women born in the 1940s and 1950s, and were more likely to remarry. Women now in their thirties and forties can expect, on the average, to become widowed around age sixty-eight and live fifteen years as widows; only 8 percent of the members of these cohorts is expected to remarry once they are widowed if current patterns continue.

Living Arrangements

Associated with these marital changes have been pronounced changes in the living arrangements of elderly women. The most notable of these have been the sharp increase in the proportion of women living alone, and the sharp decline in the proportion of women living with other family members. There has been relatively little change in the proportion of elderly men living alone or with other family members.

Both in 1965 and 1984, about one in seven men lived alone, and more than four out of five elderly men lived with family members. In 1984, as compared with 1965, however, elderly men were much more likely to be living with a wife than to be widowed and living with other family members. Over two out of five women aged sixty-five and over lived alone in 1984, compared with less than one in three in 1965. Less than a fifth of the women sixty-five and over lived with relatives other than a husband in 1984, compared with a third in 1965. Over the last two decades, both women and men were much less inclined to live with other people if they no longer had a spouse. This was especially true among women seventy-five years and over; of all aged women, 30 percent lived alone in 1965, and 50 percent lived alone in 1984. Aged black women are much more likely than aged white women to live with other family members if they have no husband (39 percent versus 23 percent, respectively), but both groups have a high probability of living alone (51 percent for white women and 40 percent for black women) in 1984.

The increased tendency of older women, including older aged women, to live alone, is likely to continue. It is expected that by 1995, over 60 percent of the women seventy-five years and over will be living alone. The proportion of aged men living alone is not expected to change much. The U.S. Census Bureau projections suggest that in

1995, about 52 percent of the households maintained by persons seventy-five years and over will be maintained by women living alone or with non-relatives; the current proportion is about 46 percent.[30]

The trend towards independent living has come about partly as a result of improvements in the economic and health status of the elderly, partly from a desire not to be dependent on others, and partly, for some, from simple lack of alternative. Living alone is generally viewed negatively, not only compared to living with a spouse, but also compared to living with another relative or a non-relative. Yet sketchy evidence suggests that we may not properly understand the experience of many of the elderly who live alone. It may come as a surprise that those living alone are not necessarily lonely and may have more outside contacts than those living with others. Women living alone typically eat diets as nutritional as those eaten by married couples. Men do not; they may have a more difficult time living alone than women because many do not know how to cook.[31]

Changes in familial aged-dependency ratios reflect the way that the age composition of the population affects the balance between older persons and their children and suggest variations in the magnitude of the family support problem over time. Familial aged-dependency ratios, defined here as the ratio of persons aged 65–79 to persons aged 45–49 (one elderly generation); or the ratio of persons 85 and over to persons 65–69 (two elderly generations), show wide fluctuations because of the cyclical character of fluctuations in the number of births in the last several decades. (See table 2, page 84.) The familial dependency ratio with one elderly generation is falling and will reach a low point in 2010, while the ratio with two elderly generations is rising and will reach a high point in that year. The crunch will come first in 2030, when the "baby-boom" cohorts are just over age sixty-five, and again in 2050, when they will be just over age eighty-five and have relatively few (elderly) children to support them.

Formerly, parents were not as likely to survive to very old age as they are today; the phenomenon of large numbers of people, mostly women, reaching very old age is touching more and more families. In fact, it is new to human experience for a large majority of middle-aged women to have living mothers. Menken has estimated on the basis of the rates of fertility, mortality, and marriage for 1940 and 1980 that the proportion of 50-year-old women with living mothers jumped from 37 to 65 percent in this period.[32] In general, families today have more generations—between three and four—than families had earlier in this century, and by the year 2020 the typical family is expected to consist of four generations.

Institutional Population

Most elderly persons live in households, and the proportion of the elderly population in institutions is small. In 1980, about 5 percent of the population sixty-five years and over resided in institutions. The likelihood of institutional residence rises sharply with age. About 1.5 percent of the population 65 to 74 years old, 7 percent of the population 75 to 84 years old, and 22 percent of those 85 and over lived in nursing homes in 1980. There has been a marked increase over the last decade in the *number* of elderly persons who are institutionalized, but the *proportion* has remained about the same. In 1970, as in 1980, about 5 percent of the population sixty-five years and over resided in institutions; the proportion was only 3.4 percent in 1960.

Institutionalization has come at increasingly older ages over the last two decades. In 1963, the 65-to-74–year group made up about one-fifth of nursing home residents, the 75-to-84–year group made up almost half, and the group eighty-five and over made up a third. Now, out of every five residents, one is aged 65 to 74, two are 75 to 84, and two are 85 and over. In 1980, seven out of ten residents of nursing homes, and almost four out of five older-aged residents of nursing homes, were women. The increase in the number of elderly women in institutions has been much more marked than that of elderly men.

It has been estimated by life-table methods that an elderly individual's risk of institutionalization approaches, and may exceed, 50 percent.[33] While this may seem high, it should be recognized that most admissions are short-term. Liu and Manton estimate that one-third of admissions are for less than thirty days and three out of four are for less than a year.[34] About 17 percent of the residents die within the first year and another 19 percent die shortly after discharge. Clearly, many stays are not long-term, and nursing homes are much used for recuperative and terminal care.

There are factors that could lead us to expect that the number and proportion of institutionalized elderly will grow in the next few

TABLE 4. Demographic Parameters of the U.S. Population in the Year 2050 Under Various Assumptions of Fertility, Mortality, and Net Immigration (Numbers in thousands)

Parameter	Current data, 1982	High fertility High mortality High immigration	Middle fertility Middle mortality Middle immigration	Low fertility Low mortality Low immigration	Low-middle fertility[1] Extremely low mortality Middle immigration	Low fertility Extremely low mortality Low immigration
Total fertility rate	1831	2300	1900	1600	1750	1600
Life expectancy at birth	74.6	76.7	79.6	83.3	100.0	100.0
Net immigration (per year)	480	750	450	250	450	250
Population	232,057	402,687	309,488	253,603	331,972	287,960
Ages (percent)						
Total (all ages)	100.0	100.0	100.0	100.0	100.0[2]	100.0[2]
Under 20 years	30.7	29.5	23.3	18.1	18.4	16.1
20–44	38.6	33.2	30.9	27.7	26.2	24.8
45–64	19.2	21.7	24.0	24.9	22.5	22.9
65 and over	11.6	15.6	21.8	29.3	32.9	36.2
Median age	31	35	42	49	51	53
Dependency ratios						
Total[3]	73	83	82	90	105	110
Neontic[4]	53	54	42	34	38	34
Gerontic[5]	20	29	40	56	67	76

Net growth rate (per 1000)	+9.5	+6.2	0.0	-4.7	+2.0	-0.9
Birth rate	16.1	15.4	11.4	8.2	8.8	7.3
Death rate	8.6	11.1	12.8	13.9	8.2	9.1
Immigration rate	2.1	1.9	1.5	1.0	1.4	0.9
Net change	+2199	+2500	+10	-1198	+653	-265
Births	3731	6206	3517	2089	2917	2101
Deaths	1986	4455	3957	3537	2714	2615
Median age of deaths	73	77	84	91	ca. 102	ca. 105

SOURCE: Based on, or estimated from data in, reports of the U.S. Census Bureau, esp. *Current Population Reports*, series P-25, no. 952. Projections assuming "extremely low mortality," were prepared in collaboration with Gregory Spencer of the U.S. Census Bureau.

[1] Intermediate between middle and low fertility.

[2] Age distribution estimated by short-cut methods from available Census Bureau population projections.

[3] $\dfrac{\text{Population under 20 years and population 65 years and over}}{\text{Population 20 to 64 years}} \times 100$

[4] $\dfrac{\text{Population under 20 years}}{\text{Population 20 to 64 years}} \times 100$

[5] $\dfrac{\text{Population 65 years and over}}{\text{Population 20 to 64 years}} \times 100$

decades. One is the rapid increase in the size of the very old population, which will constitute a larger share of the total population and of the older population. The proportion of the population seventy-five years and over is expected to rise from about 5 percent in 1983 to 7 percent in 2010 and to double by 2030. Next, the prevalence of chronic disabling disease increases with age. Finally, middle-aged women have been the major source of family support for the very old but, more and more, they are in the labor force, preparing for their own old age, and hence are not as available for this task as earlier. On the other hand, medical advances and the extension of home care may reduce the need for institutionalization.

CONCLUDING NOTES

We conclude this essay with a series of demographic scenarios for the United States in the middle of the next century for comparison with the profile of today. Three of these scenarios correspond to three of the thirty projection series published by the U.S. Census Bureau in 1984; two others employ assumptions on mortality that are more extreme than those used in the Census Bureau's series. The latter two scenarios, in fact, imply a life expectancy of one hundred years in 2050. The scenarios are summarized in table 4 in terms of broad age distributions, median ages of the population, dependency ratios, and other parameters for the year 2050.

Inasmuch as the variation in the degree of aging depends principally on the fertility assumption, and in all series fertility is assumed to conform to lower levels than have been historically typical, in all series the population will continue to age. There is considerable agreement among demographers that the general long-term outlook for fertility in the United States is for low fertility.[35] In many of the projection series of the U.S. Census Bureau (including especially the low fertility series, and the middle fertility series with low or middle immigration), the population will reach "zero population growth" (ZPG) and then decline sometime in the next century—early in the century under low fertility, and about the middle of the century under middle fertility. Sharp future declines in mortality, such as those leading to a life expectancy of one hundred in the year 2050, will also contribute greatly to the aging of the population insofar as these declines will be concentrated at the older ages.

Some Demographic Scenarios for 2050

Under the most likely scenario for 2050, the "middle" series of the U.S. Census Bureau (assuming middle fertility, mortality, and immigration), the total population would grow to about 310 million and would then stop growing. The proportion over age sixty-five would be almost twice as great as today (22 percent vs. 12 percent), and the proportion under age twenty would be three-quarters as great as today (23 percent vs. 31 percent). The median age of the population would be forty-two years, and the median age at death would be eighty-four years, both eleven years higher than today. Eighty-three percent of deaths would occur after age sixty-five as compared with 68 percent today, and 43 percent of deaths would occur to persons over age eighty-five as compared with 18 percent today. The death rate, at 12.8 per thousand population, would be about 50 percent greater than it is today, and there would be twice as many deaths in a year as now, with a 12-percent excess of deaths over births. Deaths will occur at almost predictable occasions, mostly when people have "lived out" their full lives. Middle-aged couples will have had less than two children, fewer than they have living parents.

Among the 67 million people over age sixty-five, some 60 percent would be women, who would outnumber men by 13 1/2 million. The gerontic dependency ratio (ratio of persons 65 and over to persons 20 to 64) would be double its present level of 20, and the total dependency ratio would be 12 percent higher. On the assumption that there would be no major medical breakthroughs, but only sustained, gradual progress in health matters, the average age of onset of chronic illness would be unchanged, and the number of chronically ill persons in the population would be far greater than today. However, the number of persons limited in their activity as a result of chronic illness may not be greater than today because of progress in the management of the principal chronic illnesses.

Suppose, instead, that fertility, mortality, and net immigration fall to the "low" levels of the Census Bureau. Such a series would tend to "maximize" the proportion of elderly and "minimize" the proportion of children. This is the series labeled "low fertility, low mortality, and low immigration" in table 4. The population would reach ZPG at a somewhat earlier date than in the middle series, about 2023, then decline. In 2050, the median age of the population would be forty-nine years, about eighteen years higher than today. Some 29 percent of the population would be over age sixty-five, and only 18 percent would be below age twenty. The gerontic dependency ratio would be nearly three times its present level, but the total dependency ratio would be only one-quarter greater because of the decline of the child population. There would be nearly 45 percent fewer births and nearly 80 percent more deaths than today, so that death will be much more frequent than birth. If the average age of onset of chronic illness continues to remain unchanged, the number of chronically ill persons would be vastly increased over today's number. However, depending on progress in postponing the age of onset of limitation of activity as a result of chronic illness, the number of persons functionally disabled could be either more or less than today.

The other Census Bureau series presented in table 4 employs high fertility, high mortality, and high immigration and thereby tends to "minimize" both the rise in the proportion of elderly persons and the fall in the proportion of children. Some 16 percent of the population would be over age sixty-five, and the median age of the population would rise by only four years to thirty-five. The other demographic parameters would be modified accordingly.

Finally, we consider the two scenarios suggested by a population with a life expectancy of a hundred years in the year 2050. This assumption corresponds approximately to the level of mortality obtained by projecting death rates at each age at the rates of decline recorded in the last decade and a half. A life expectancy of one hundred could also be achieved by a reduction of some 70 percent in age-specific death rates below the best-country age-specific death rates for females on record in 1980. A life expectancy of a hundred is consistent with an extension of human life span to 115, 120, or even 130 years, but this is only a probable association, not a necessary one. If we assume a rectangularization of the "present" survival curve, the life span could remain around a hundred. In a population with a life span of, say, 125 years, the relationship of chronological age and functional age as we know it could be completely changed. Persons seventy-five years old may be able to function like the sixty-five-year-olds of today.

The first of these scenarios employs assumptions on fertility and net immigration corresponding to the recorded levels of recent years. It is labelled "low-middle fertility, extremely low mortality, and middle immigration" in table 4. The median age of the resulting population would be fifty-one years, and the median age at death would exceed a hundred. About 33 percent of the population would be over age sixty-five, and only 18 percent would be under age 20, as compared with 12 percent and 31 percent today. The gerontic dependency ratio would be 3 1/2 times its current level, and the overall dependency ratio would be nearly 50 percent greater.

The final scenario combines low fertility and low net immigration with the extremely low mortality assumption described. This set of assumptions identifies an extreme, albeit possible, course of population change, in which the median age would be fifty-three, and 36 percent of the population would be aged sixty-five or older! Only one out of six persons would be under age twenty—that is only half the proportion of today! In spite of the sharp decline in the share of children, the overall dependency ratio would be well over the current figure because of the nearly fourfold increase in the gerontic dependency ratio.

Implications

Under the demographic conditions assumed in the last two scenarios, the nature of American society in 2050 would differ vastly from the way it is today. Very high proportions of elderly persons and very high dependency ratios, accompanying continuing low fertility and very low mortality, could have profound social and economic consequences. Education, health care, housing, recreation, and work life could be affected by the changes in age structure described. There could be serious dislocations in the economy as it tries to adjust to changing needs for jobs, goods, and services. Societal aging calls for increasingly larger financial contributions to the federal treasury by workers on behalf of older non-workers. Tax rates could become oppressively high and serve as a disincentive to work. The productive capacity of the economy could be diminished as the proportion of persons of working age shrinks and vast expenditures have to be made for the "maintenance" of the burgeoning number of elderly persons. Much depends on the development of methods for sustaining or even increasing the productive vigor of older persons. Both major technological innovations and institutional adjustments will be required to deal with the population changes described.[36]

ENDNOTES

[1]Jacob A. Brody, "Prospects for an Aging Population," *Nature,* June 6, 1985, pp. 463–66.

[2]Samuel Preston, "Children and the Elderly: Divergent Paths for America's Dependents," *Demography,* Nov. 1984, pp. 435–57.

[3]Jacob S. Siegel and Sally Hoover, "Demographic Aspects of the Health of the Elderly to the Year 2000 and Beyond," *World Health Statistics Quarterly,* vol. 35, nos. 3/4, pp. 133–202, 1982.

[4]Bundesrepublik Deutschland, *Bericht über die Bevölkerungsentwicklung in der Bundesrepublik Deutschland,* teil 2 (Population Development in the Federal Republic of Germany, part 2), 1984. Toshio Kuroda, "Aging of the Population of Japan: Prospects and Challenges," in *Population Aging in Japan: Problems and Policy Issues in 21st Century,* International Symposium on An Aging Society: Strategies for 21st Century Japan, November 24–27, 1982.

[5]Kevin M. Fitzpatrick and John R. Logan, "The Aging of the Suburbs, 1960–1980," *American Sociological Review,* Feb. 1985, pp. 106–117. Donald Cowgill, "Residential Segregation by Age in American Metropolitan Areas," *Journal of Gerontology,* May 1978, pp. 446–53.

[6]U.S. Bureau of the Census, "Geographical Mobility: March 1982 to March 1983," *Current Population Reports,* Series P-20, no. 393, Oct. 1984. See also Stephen M. Golant, "Spatial Context of Residential Moves by Elderly Persons," *International Journal of Aging and Human Development,* vol. 8, no. 3, 1977–78, pp. 279–89.

[7]U.S. Office of the Actuary, Social Security Administration, *Life Tables for the United States: 1900–2050,* actuarial study no. 87, by Joseph F. Faber, Sept. 1982.

[8]The increasing rectangularization of the survival curve may be measured by the ratio of the slope of the curve after age seventy to the slope of the curve before age seventy.

[9]James F. Fries, "Aging, Natural Death, and the Compression of Morbidity," *New England Journal of Medicine,* July 17, 1980, pp. 130–35; Fries and Lawrence M. Crapo, *Vitality and Aging: Implications of the Rectangular Curve* (San Francisco: W.H. Freeman and Company, 1981), chap. 11.

[10]George C. Myers and Kenneth G. Manton, "Recent Changes in the U.S. Age at Death Distribution: Further Observations," *Gerontologist,* Dec. 1984, pp. 572–75. Myers and Manton, "The Compression of Morbidity: Myth or Reality?" *Gerontologist,* Aug. 1984, pp. 346–53. Edward L. Schneider and Brody, "Aging, Natural Death, and the Compression of Morbidity: Another View," *New England Journal of Medicine,* Oct. 6, 1983, pp. 854–56.

[11]Roy Walford, *Maximum Life Span* (New York: W.W. Norton and Co., 1983).

[12]Ingrid Waldron, "Sex Differences in Human Mortality: The Role of Genetic Factors," *Social Science Medicine,* vol. 17, no. 6, 1983, pp. 321–33.

[13]Robert D. Retherford, "Tobacco Smoking and the Sex Mortality Differentials," *Demography,* vol. 9, no. 2, 1972, pp. 203–216; Retherford, *The Changing Sex Differential in Mortality,* (Westport, CT.: Greenwood Press, 1975). Waldron, "The Contribution of Smoking to Sex Differences in Mortality," paper presented at the annual meeting of the Population Association of America, Boston, March 1985.

[14]See, in this connection, Lois M. Verbrugge and Jennifer H. Madans, "Social Roles and Health Trends of American Women," paper presented at the annual meeting of the Population Association of America, Boston, March 1985.

[15]Evelyn M. Kitagawa and Philip M. Hauser, *Differential Mortality in the United States: A Study in Socioeconomic Epidemiology* (Cambridge, MA: Harvard University Press, 1973), esp. pp. 11, 14, and 157.

[16]U.S. Bureau of the Census, "Demographic and Socioeconomic Aspects of Aging in the United States," by Jacob S. Siegel and Maria Davidson, *Current Population Reports*, series P-23, no. 138, 1984., tables 5–10 and 5–11.

[17]Nathan Keyfitz, "What Difference Would It Make if Cancer Were Eradicated? An Examination of the Taeuber Paradox," *Demography*, Nov. 1977, pp. 411–18.

[18]U.S. Social Security Administration, Actuary's Office, *Social Security Area Population Projections, 1983*, actuarial study no. 88, by John C. Wilkin, Aug. 1983, table 8a.

[19]Endogenous causes exclude infective and parasitic diseases, respiratory diseases, and accidents, poisonings, and violence.

[20]Elena Nightingale, "Prospects for Reducing Mortality in Developed Countries by Changes in Day-to-Day Behavior," pp. 207–33, and Mervyn Susser, "Industrialization, Urbanization, and Health, An Epidemiological View," in *International Population Conference, Manila 1981* (Liege, Belgium: International Union for the Scientific Study of Population, 1981). J.A. Wiley and T.C. Camacho, "Life Style and Future Health: Evidence from the Alameda County Study," *Preventive Medicine*, vol. 9, 1980, pp. 1–21.

[21]U.S. Public Health Service, Center for Disease Control, *Ten Leading Causes of Death in the United States, 1978.*

[22]U.S. Public Health Service, National Center for Health Statistics, "Current Estimates from the National Health Interview Survey, United States, 1981," by Barbara Bloom, *Vital and Health Statistics*, series 10, no. 141, table 12, p. 22.

[23]U.S. Public Health Service, National Center for Health Statistics, "Americans Needing Help to Function at Home," by Barbara Feller, *Vital and Health Statistics*, Advance Data, series 10, no. 92, Sept. 1983, tables 1, 2, and 3.

[24]Abdel R. Omran, "Epidemiological Transition in the United States: The Health Factor in Population Change," *Population Bulletin* (Washington, D.C.: Population Reference Bureau, May 1977).

[25]A. Colvez and M. Blanchet, "Disability Trends in the United States Population, 1966–76: Analysis of Reported Cases," *American Journal of Public Health*, May 1981, pp. 464–71. Lois M. Verbrugge, "Longer Life but Worsening Health? Trends in Health and Mortality of Middle-Aged and Older Persons," *Milbank Memorial Fund Quarterly/Health and Society*, Summer 1984, pp. 475–519. Jacob J. Feldman, "Work Ability of the Aged Under Conditions of Improving Mortality," *Milbank Memorial Fund Quarterly/Health and Society*, Summer 1983, pp. 430–44.

[26]For a measure of life expectancy, see Sidney Katz, et al., "Active Life Expectancy," *New England Journal of Medicine*, Nov. 17, 1983, pp. 1218–1224.

[27]Lois M. Verbrugge, "Sex Differentials in Morbidity and Mortality in the United States," *Social Biology*, Winter 1976, pp. 275–96; Verbrugge, "Women and Men: Mortality and Health of Older People," pp. 139–74, in M.W. Riley, B.B. Hess, and K. Bond, eds., *Aging in Society: Selected Reviews of Recent Research* (Hillsdale, N.J.: Lawrence Erlbaum Associates, 1983).

[28]U.S. Bureau of the Census, "Marital Status and Living Arrangements: March 1984," *Current Population Reports*, series P-20, no. 399.

[29]Robert Schoen, William Urton, Karen Woodrow, and John Baj, "Marriage and Divorce in Twentieth Century American Cohorts," *Demography*, Feb. 1985, pp. 101–114.

[30]U.S Bureau of the Census, "Projections of the Number of Households and Families: 1979 to 1995," *Current Population Reports*, series P-25, no. 805, esp. table 2.

[31]Riley, "Aging and Society: Notes on the Development of New Understandings," lecture at the University of Michigan, Dec. 12, 1983, p. 13.

[32]Jane Menken, "Age and Fertility: How Late Can You Wait?" presidential address delivered at the annual meeting of the Population Association of America, Boston, March 27–30, 1985.

[33]Charles E. McConnel, "A Note on the Lifetime Risk of Nursing Home Residency," *Gerontologist*, April 1984, pp. 193–98.

[34]K. Liu and Manton, "The Characteristics and Utilization Pattern of Admission Cohorts of Nursing Home Patients," *Gerontologist*, forthcoming.

[35]Charles F. Westoff, "Some Speculation on the Future of Marriage and Fertility," *Family Planning Perspectives*, March/April 1978, pp. 79–83. Deirdre Wulf, "Low Fertility in Europe: A Report from the IUSSP Meeting," *International Family Perspectives*, June 1982, pp. 63–69. Judith Treas, "The Great American Fertility Debate: Gerontological Balance and Support of the Aged," *Gerontologist*, Feb. 1981, pp. 98–103.

[36]William J. Serow, "Socioeconomic Implications of Changing Age Compositions of Low Fertility Countries. Empirical Evidence: An Assessment, in Particular, of its Practical Significance" pp. 271–84, and Joseph van den Boomen, "Age-Cost Profiles: A Common Denominator?" pp. 285–99, in *International Population Conference, Manila, 1981*, op. cit. Hilde Wander, "Short, Medium, and Long Term Implications of a Stationary or Declining Population on Education, Labour Force, Housing Needs, Social Security and Economic Development. *International Population Conference, Mexico City, 1977*, vol. 3 (Liege, Belgium: International Union for the Scientific Study of Population, 1977), pp. 95–112. Lincoln Day, *What will a ZPG Society Be Like?*, Population Bulletin, June 1978, Population Reference Bureau, Washington, D.C.

Alice S. Rossi

Sex and Gender in the Aging Society

T HE EXTENSION OF THE HUMAN life span that has taken place in developed societies is only the latest in a number of biosocial changes our species has undergone during the past century. We not only live longer, we are taller, healthier, heavier, more numerous, and more fertile for a longer span of years than our ancestors. Most people view these changes as indications of irreversible improvements in the human condition. Who would claim that it is not a good thing to be healthy and fertile, or to carry an attractive amount of flesh? And who does not believe that a longer life is not a great gift? It is possible, however, that valuing these attributes so highly reflects a perspective more appropriate to the past than to our late twentieth-century society. If we were still living in a hunting-gathering, an agricultural, or an early industrial society, the attributes we admire would be highly adaptive, since size, strength, and high fertility would facilitate our ability to labor long and hard, and to produce many children in order to assure our support in old age.

These same attributes may be out of joint with the social and physical world we inhabit in 1986, and they may be even more maladaptive in the world our children and grandchildren will inhabit in the twenty-first century. Our increased height is more appropriate to working on an open plain, riding a horse, and living in high-ceilinged rooms than it is to dwelling in a crowded city, driving a low-slung modern car, and inhabiting a small urban apartment. Our increased size means that we consume more food, yet the global acreage per person has declined from forty-two to seven in the past two centuries, and global arable land now verges on a decline. Our increased numbers means greatly increased population density: on a global scale, population density has increased from 549 per square mile in 1960 to 796 per square mile today.[1] The difficulties associated with population density will become even greater in the future, for the increasingly urban, global population will grow from 4.8 billion today to an estimated six billion by the turn of the twenty-first century.

Our greater physical strength and endurance far exceed that required by our increasingly mechanized and sedentary occupations, with the result that many people expend more of their energy on jogging, tennis, golf, and swimming than they do on productive labor at their jobs. The quickened pace of technological and social change puts a premium on human flexibility that may be more difficult for an aging population than for a youthful one to develop and sustain. And now that women begin to menstruate earlier and reach menopause later, and both sexes enjoy a longer life span, we are fertile for a much longer number of years, yet there is no social need—and, increasingly, no individual desire—for large families.

All of these changes involve physical characteristics—height, weight, health, fertility, and longevity—but they are phenotypic rather than genotypic changes, reflecting environmental influences at work over relatively short periods of historic times, and not genetic changes in the human organism. Thus, second-generation children, when compared with their immigrant parents, showed an average increase in height of a full inch, and the age at which girls begin to menstruate has dropped an average of six months per decade over the last half century, both trends that reflect the influence of the greatly improved quality and quantity of our food, and the better, more extensive, health care that is available in Western societies. Because these changes have come about in response to environmental change, they could reverse course in response to still other environmental changes; all future generations in developed societies may not necessarily live as well or as long as have recent generations. It is therefore only an optimistic faith in the persistence of improved diet and health that underlies the prediction that future generations in Western societies will be healthy, large, long-lived creatures, and that the age composition of societies will be increasingly tipped to an older population.

Just as a bio-evolutionary perspective is helpful in viewing increased longevity as only one among several phenotypic changes in Western societies and in alerting us to the possibility that such changes are reversible, so, too, a long-term historic perspective can help us assess the significance of changes that involve sex and gender. It is tempting, but misleading, to believe that the changes taking place in the social roles of men and women in recent years are unprecedented, irreversible, and largely the product of purposive political action or hidden market factors. This essay will attempt to correct this historical myopia by examining sex and gender in a bio-evolutionary framework, and by discussing what implications they have for changes in the characteristics of elderly men and women in the future compared to those alive today.

Fundamental to this analysis is the distinction between "sex" and "gender": by "sex" we refer to reproductive and sexual characteristics that differentiate the female from the male; by "gender" we refer to all the social and psychological attributes linked to the social roles of men and women. What the balance is between persistent, stable sex characteristics and more flexible, socially constructed gender characteristics is, of course, a matter of ongoing controversy. It is often claimed that the "only" difference between men and women is that women menstruate, lactate, and give birth, but it is the assumption of this essay that biological sex is not a minor fact, but one that carries profound significance for the social roles and the psychological attributes of men and women.

Indeed, it is because of this assumption that we shall begin by examining several unique sex characteristics of our species in a comparative bio-evolutionary framework. We do so for the explicit reason that, despite the very great changes that have taken place in human history in our mode of production, our cultural sophistication, and our ability to transcend the limitations of time and space, our genotype has undergone only modest changes since the early hominids branched away from the mammalian primate line. Whatever adaptations have taken place in the human species occurred during the 95 percent of human history that humans were hunters and gatherers.[2] The result has been genotypic sex differences in the human species which are unique and persistent, and they are important to keep in focus as we look ahead to aging societies of the future.

The second part of this essay considers those trends in Western societies over the past two hundred years that carry important implications for the degree to which men and women are differentially embedded in the social institutions of family, work, and politics. Again, we shall examine the trends in a broad historical framework, with an eye to their implications for the characteristics of elderly men and women in the future as compared with those alive today.

Last, we address the question of what difference it will make to the larger society when the majority of adults are men and women in middle and old age. One fundamental "gender gap" of a demographic nature in an aging society is the sex difference in longevity. The fact that women now live longer than men means that the larger the proportion of elderly in a population, the greater will be the tendency to a female majority in that population. This adds particular interest to our examination of gender differences in the second half of life. The social institutions we inherited from the past have been masculine in tone, not simply because men held the power to structure social institutions to their advantage, but because few adults survived beyond their reproductive years.[3] By contrast, in an aging society, a female majority, combined with the dramatic blurring of sex and gender differences in the second half of life, may well effect a change in the structure of social institutions, and in the values that become dominant in the society.

EVOLUTIONARY CHANGE AND SEXUAL DIMORPHISM

It is our enlarged cortex and our bipedalism that uniquely distinguish *homo sapiens* from the other primates. The simultaneous development of a shift to an upright, two-footed posture and a cranial capacity several times that of other primates posed a critical evolutionary dilemma: if the brain had enlarged too greatly, then the pelvis required for effective bipedalism might have enlarged to accommodate the increase, and we might have remained four-footed creatures. If the pelvis had expanded to handle the enlarged head, our gait would have been so ungainly that we could not have survived against swift predators. The evolutionary dilemma was resolved by postponing a considerable proportion of our brain growth until after birth. Consequently, all human babies are born premature, with very immature brains compared with other primates. The newborn chimpanzee, for example, is the developmental equivalent of a nine-month old human infant. At birth, the chimp already possesses a relatively well-developed cortex, and is endowed with social responsiveness and the capacity for independent mobility. The utter dependency of the human infant, requiring full-time care and supervision for several years, demanded novel social arrangements, including a social group that provided protection and help for pregnant, lactating females and their young, and cooperative feeding patterns. Humans are unique among mammals in providing food for their weaned young rather than leaving them to forage for themselves.[4]

Bipedalism had another important consequence. Four-footed creatures carry their fetuses in relative safety, hanging in a loose abdomen, while the carrying of a human fetus by an upright, two-footed female involves great pressure on the back and pelvis, and hence an increased risk of miscarriage, a risk that was reduced by the evolutionary increase in sex hormone levels in the human animal. This, in turn, contributed to the expansion of sexual activity to the non-ovulatory phases of the menstrual cycle. The effect was to alter the relationship between sex and reproduction in the human. In most species, sexual activity is a seasonal affair, with a marked contrast in social organization between the short period of courtship and mating, and the longer periods of time devoted to rearing the young. We humans are unique in the constancy of our sexual activity, subject only to minor seasonal variations and abstinence for a short period before and after births. In sum, sex is largely in the service of reproduction in other species, while in humans reproduction is only an occasional consequence of recreative rather than procreative sexual activity.

Hence humans are easily "turned-on" sexy animals in all seasons, and human females are the only animals with permanent, highly visible breasts and prominent, fatty buttocks.[5] The balance of fat to muscle tissue markedly contrasts the human male and female. Fifteen percent of the body weight of the human male is in adipose tissue, compared to 28 percent in the female, while the proportion devoted to muscle tissue is the reverse: 55 percent for the male, 40 percent for the female.[6] The fat deposits were critical for the human female to sustain feeding of the young during the prolonged nursing that characterized child rearing for most of human history—three to four years per infant—since it takes as many calories to nurse an infant as it does for human males to engage in very hard physical labor.[7]

Another important aspect of human sex differences concerns the relationship between sexual maturity and fecundity. Males are fecund very early in their sexual maturation, for sperm is present in the ejaculate long before the male has fully developed his secondary sex characteristics.[8] By contrast, females become fecund later, typically after a period of at least partial adolescent sterility for up to two years after the onset of menstruation.[9] The probable reason for this sex difference is the great toll of pregnancy and infant care upon the female, in contrast to the male, who undergoes no physiological changes as a consequence of inseminating the female. Consequently, most human females have been far more conservative in their sexual availability than males.

Echoes of this sex difference can still be seen in the sexual developmental profile of contemporary men and women. John Gagnon and William Simon suggest that males begin their sexual careers with a narrow focus on the simple release of sexual tension and slowly develop sociosexual skills and a capacity for intimacy, while females begin their sexual careers with a desire for social and romantic involvement rather than for the physical release of sexual tension, and slowly develop specifically sexual skills.[10] To be sure, there have been changes in sexual behavior in recent years, as more women follow the permissive male sexual script and engage in non-marital sex during adolescence and early adulthood. The longstanding sex difference may now be visible largely where extra-marital sex is concerned, with married men more likely to engage in casual sex than married women.

Although the evidence is not yet firm, it is also likely that the sexes differ in the ease with which they become attached to infants. Both sexes have the potential for equal investment in and attachment to infants, but males seem to require more experience than females in caring for the young,[11] a proposal that is supported by the finding that young men are much less apt than young women or older men to respond with interest to unfamiliar infants.[12] In a review of research in this area, B.R. Tinsley and Robert Parke conclude that compassion increased in a near-linear manner for men from single early adulthood to grandparenthood, while women showed more interest in and tenderness toward infants than men did at all stages of the life course except grandparenthood.[13] Tinsley and Parke interpret these findings as reflections of family roles, but they may also reflect maturational factors that are quite independent of whether or not adults are parents or grandparents. Hence, it remains a possibility that women are readily attracted to and become easily attached to both an opposite-sex adult and an infant, while men are more persistently focused on sexual attraction to adult women than they are on attraction to infants.

The shift from a hunting-gathering to a settled agricultural society had one profound impact on female reproductive functioning, which in turn triggered the growth of the human population. In hunter-gatherer societies, the effect of adults feeding at a low level of the food chain combined with the prolonged lactation that followed each birth was *lactational amenorrhea:* the hunter-gatherer woman did not ovulate for the three or four years she nursed each child, with the result that she gave birth on average to only four or five babies and was spared the physical and emotional stress associated with many closely spaced births. Over the course of the prime childbearing years, the hunter-gatherer woman ovulated and menstruated for an average of a mere four years. Contemporary women average thirty-five years of menstrual cyclicity, a nine-fold increase.[14]

With the shift to settled agriculture, the stage was set for a profound change in human fertility rates. An enriched diet meant more body fat, sufficient to stimulate ovulation despite nursing, and the availability of grain and milk from domesticated animals provided an alternative to human milk in the form of gruel for young babies. Both men and women were required to triple the amount of time they devoted to productive labor, from the less than twenty hours each week that were needed to sustain them in a hunter-gatherer society to the sixty or more hours that were demanded to produce a surplus crop in settled agricultural societies. With land to cultivate, to which children's labor could contribute, and with land to transmit to descendants, the stage was also set for both increased motivation and increased ability to bear and rear large numbers of children. With the interval between births narrowed, fertility increased and the human population grew.

Yet another consequence of improved nutrition in agricultural and industrial societies compared with hunter-gatherer societies was the enlargement of the span of fertile years among women. Instead of twenty-four years of potential fertility—from menarche at age sixteen to menopause at age forty—modern women are fertile for thirty-eight years—from an average of twelve years of age at menarche to fifty at menopause.[15]

There is a bitter irony in the fact that for the first time in history, the age-old objective of agrarian people to produce large families is being achieved by a majority of parents in many parts of the Third World, in an era when land shortage and economic development cannot absorb their high fertility. Among the Gusii people in Kenya, for example, infant mortality has dropped dramatically, but there has been little accompanying change in parental motivation to control fertility; as a consequence, Gusii women are now showing an average of 8.7 births at the end of their childbearing years.[16] Countless thousands of these children face starvation and death as a result of the combination of sheer population size, a shrinking base of tillable soil, deforestation, and drought.

For most of human history, there was no need for contraception or abortion to control fertility, not only because high fertility was socially valued, but because lactational amenorrhea and a shorter span of life precluded the possibility of older men impregnating younger women. Indeed, one consequence of the marked extension of the human life span in developed societies is a considerable sex difference in potential fertility. When people rarely lived beyond their fourth decade, men and women were fertile for roughly the same proportion of their life spans, but with average expected longevity now extending into the seventh and eighth decades of life, there is a decided contrast between the sexes in the average duration of potential fertility. Women in their thirties face a far more acute dilemma if they have not married or borne a child than men in their thirties do, since men are able to conceive a child for several decades longer than women.

This sex difference in the duration of human fertility was undoubtedly one reason marriage took on a predominant pattern in which husbands were older than their wives.[17] Given that small families are now both the goal and the reality for most young adults in developed societies, one might predict that the long-standing pattern of husbands being older than their wives will gradually give way to reduced age differences between husbands and wives, and to an increased incidence of women marrying men younger than themselves.

Indeed, such a development would be of greater relevance in an aging society than in a youthful society, since it would reduce the gender imbalance in the incidence of widowhood. That the elderly over seventy-five consist overwhelmingly of widows reflects the combined effect of women's greater longevity and their being on average younger than their husbands.[18]

The point that contemporary men have a much longer number of fertile years than women should not be exaggerated. For one thing, we have only recently begun to learn about the male's contribution to pregnancy outcome and the effect of age upon male fecundity. Recent research suggests a U-shaped pattern in semen quality: gradual improvement in quality up to age 25, a plateau from age 26 to 35, followed by a decline, with marked changes in the 41 to 45 age group that include low sperm count, blocked sperm ducts, and defective sperm.[19] Defective sperm are one cause of early miscarriages, and paternal age has been identified as more important than maternal age in at least one form of Down's syndrome.[20] That gene mutations in birth defects increase with the age of the father is probably due to a fundamental sex difference: sperm are produced continually throughout a man's life, while the oocytes from which an egg is formed each month are present in the female from birth. Hence, environmental contamination and the aging of the organism can more profoundly impair the male in this regard.[21] As more men become aware of the possibilities of their own contribution to impaired fertility and pregnancy outcome, they may come to share the concern only women now feel when they reach their thirties, so that both men and women will be eager to have children before the age of forty.

Another trend suggests that men and women have already begun to cope with their excess potential fertility: the highly significant increase over the past decade in voluntary sterilization on the part of married men and women. Indeed, it is startling to note how high the figures have become in this area. Among all currently married women between fifteen and forty-four years of age, only *half* are fecund; most of the non-fecund women are either themselves surgically sterile, or their husbands have been sterilized. Voluntary sterilization accounts for most of this low level of fecundity among married women over thirty, with only 12 percent due to impaired fecundity.[22] Sterilization is fast becoming the major birth control measure for married American men and women over thirty-five years of age.

This brief account of changes in the sexual and reproductive lives of men and women over the long history of our species suggests that a fundamental shift has taken place in the central meaning of being female or male. For women in a hunting-gathering society, life was short, sexual maturation was late, pregnancies were relatively few and far between, menstruation was an infrequent occurrence, and nursing was a major feature of their adult roles as mothers. The breast as a symbol of fertility is a major metaphor for femaleness in such societies, as one can see, for example, in African sculpture. In agricultural societies, it is the uterus that more often represents the central focus of reproductive life, for pregnancies were numerous, the intervals between births were short, and infants were weaned at an early age.

In contemporary Western societies the breast has become an erotic symbol, rather than one that represents fertility. Pregnancies are few, and only a very small proportion of a long life span is devoted to child rearing. With effective contraception available for use during adolescence and early adulthood, and the frequency of voluntary sterilization in the mid-thirties, a firm wedge is now potentially in place between sex and reproduction. We have already seen the effect of this protection against pregnancies in the rapid drop in the age of sexual initiation and in the increasing number of sexual partners both men and women choose prior to marriage. As a result of the greater reliance on sterilization, the same assurance in differentiating between procreative and recreative sex may lead in the future to an increased prevalence of extra-marital sex. While farmers and peasants boasted about fathering a large number of children, men in contemporary urban societies are more apt to boast about the number of women they have known sexually. It remains to be seen whether women will eventually indulge in boasting about their own sexual experiences before and after marriage.

The changes in effective fertility control and their associated impact on sexual behavior have been quite recent, and they have involved adults who are now in their early and middle adulthood. In the decades when today's elderly men and women grew up, sex before marriage was less prevalent and was more exclusively a male phenomenon. Women's premarital sex experience was usually either non-existent or restricted to the men they subsequently married. So too, childbearing and child rearing represented a far more central place in the expectations today's elderly brought to marriage. If they eventually had small-sized families, it was due less to intention than to the economic hardship of the Depression years of the 1930s. It is also doubtful that today's elderly expected to live as long as they are now doing, while today's youth can anticipate the kind of long life that they now observe among the older relatives in their families.

But this gets us a bit ahead of our analysis. We turn now to an overview of the demographic changes taking place in Western societies, and to their implications for gender differences in family, work, and politics.

DEMOGRAPHIC TRENDS IN WESTERN SOCIETIES

In the decades following World War II, social scientists were shocked and humbled by their failure to predict so many major societal developments: the sharp rise in the birth rate, the linear increase in the employment of married women, an escalating divorce rate, and the emergence of major social movements. Partially in reaction to having been taken by surprise, social scientists have increasingly tended to move away from seeking universal laws of human behavior, and instead are searching the past for a deeper understanding of contemporary trends and problems. Many longstanding theories about social change have undergone significant revisions as a result. A leading example of this is the discovery that the nuclear family *preceded* industrialization in Western societies, rather than emerging as a *consequence* of industrialization. This finding posed a significant challenge to the view that economic change is the exclusive source of changes in marriage, divorce, and fertility patterns. In recent years, historical demographers have looked elsewhere for clues to these demographic changes—in particular, to long-term shifts in fundamental social values and belief systems. In what follows, we sketch several of these new ideas, for they sensitize us to common factors in demographic trends in Western society that in turn contribute to an understanding of changes in the social, economic, and political roles of contemporary men and women.

A good starting place is the historical work of Philippe Aries, who opened the way to a new understanding of changes in family structure and the value of children in Western societies.[23] Aries pointed to a critical transformation in parental concerns from child *quantity* (the more hands the better in rural agricultural life) to child *quality* (the fewer the children, the better parents could equip them with the skills they would need in urban, industrial life). More recently, the Belgian demographer Ron Lesthaeghe has linked this redefinition of parental responsibilities not to industrialization and urbanization, but to the philosophers of the Enlightenment, in particular to their legitimization of the principle of individual freedom of choice as a central social value.[24] In Lesthaeghe's view, it has been this principle of individual freedom that has dominated the social, economic, and political transformations that have occurred in the past two centuries. Indeed, he considers the increased focus on individual choice "one of the most important legacies of the West."[25] The shift from child quantity to child quality, noted by Aries, was possible only by birth restriction, and Lesthaeghe points to the remarkable coincidence of the fact that the two countries that experienced revolutions premised on the ideals of the Enlightenment—France and the United States—were the same two countries where control of marital fertility began as early as the end of the eighteenth and the beginning of the nineteenth centuries, when both countries were predominantly rural and agricultural.

Lesthaeghe argues further that Western societies are now undergoing a second fundamental transformation of basic values, a shift from a child-centered culture to one that is self-centered. This transformation implies that Western people have become less firmly rooted in the traditional contexts of family, church, and community; instead, they have been showing a much stronger commitment to individual goal attainment, and to the right of individuals to define those goals unhampered by traditional obligations. In this view, Westerners are shifting from a concern for their children's futures to a self-orientation that gives priority to their own desires over the needs of even spouses and children.

The long-term trend in Western society that Lesthaeghe noted is also detailed in the work of Hans Peter Dreitzel.[26] Building on the work of Norbert Elias,[27] Dreitzel describes what he sees as new elements in Western social character structure, a "new flexibility of attachment and detachment with individuals and groups, and a corresponding ability for constantly changing identifications with new roles."[28] A number of trends in demographic data and national surveys lend support to Lesthaeghe and Dreitzel's view that Westerners are becoming "averse to long-term commitments" and increasingly focused on individual autonomy and detachment.

Age at Marriage

The age-specific marriage rate per thousand single women in eight European countries fell steadily during the 1960s and 1970s. In the United States, there has been a tripling of the proportion of women not married by their late twenties (when the education of even advanced degree-holders is largely completed), from 9 percent in 1967 to 30 percent in 1980. George Masnick and Mary Jo Bane predict that by 1990, half the men and well over a third of American women in their late twenties will still be unmarried.[29]

Additional evidence concerning these trends in marriage can be found in attitude research. In one broad national survey, first conducted in 1957 and then replicated in 1976, Jerome Veroff and Elizabeth Douvan show a dramatic reduction in the proportion of young respondents who hold negative views toward anyone who does not marry, from 46 percent in 1957 to only 22 percent in 1976.[30] More significantly, the proportion of young unmarried women who considered marriage "restrictive" *doubled* over the twenty-year period (from 33 percent in 1957 to 67 percent in 1976). Veroff and Douvan report that this increased tolerance of people who reject marriage as a way of life on the grounds of its restrictiveness is the most dramatic change recorded from 1957 to 1976 in their entire study.[31]

Divorce

Marriages are not only being viewed as restrictive and being postponed to later ages, they are also more fragile than ever. In Europe as in the United States, the divorce rate doubled from 1970 to 1978. When divorce rates first began to rise steeply, they were not interpreted as reflecting disenchantment with marriage per se, but only as disillusionment with specific marital partners, since divorce was typically followed within a few years by remarriage. This interpretation has been challenged by recent evidence of a drop in the remarriage rate among divorced adults, and of a high divorce rate among those who have remarried.

The combined trends toward later marriages, a smaller proportion of adults marrying overall, a high and rising divorce rate, a declining remarriage rate, and the increased tolerance toward those who never marry, led Kingsley Davis and Patricia van den Oever to suggest that marriage was "falling out of fashion."[32] Lesthaeghe might interpret the same trends as confirmation of his thesis that Westerners have become averse to long-term commitments, and Dreitzel that the trends show increasing detachment from customary social roles.

Fertility

Whether becoming a parent is also "falling out of fashion" is less certain. For one thing, the dissolution of a marriage leaves two individuals free to marry again or not, but parenthood continues beyond a divorce for at least one parent, typically the mother. Demographers have conducted numerous studies of fertility expectations in recent years, in an effort to determine whether the low fertility pattern that followed the baby boom of the 1950s would continue. Most demographers now agree with Charles Westoff that late marriage and low fertility will remain a stable characteristic of Western societies.[33] The lifetime birth expectations of young women in the United States are below replacement level for their birth cohort.[34] Estimates vary on the incidence of voluntary childlessness among those now in their childbearing years, from a low estimate of well under 10 percent to a high of between 20 and 30 percent.[35]

It may be premature to predict what the future level of childlessness will be, for a period of change in attitude may be needed before any significant proportion of adults remains childless by intention. It is a far easier thing for a young couple to contract their plans from four to two children than it is to shift from planning one child to planning none. A shift in public attitudes is suggested by Veroff and Douvan's report of a decline between 1957 and 1976 in the proportion of American adults who consider children a major source of happiness, and a similar drop in the reported degree of satisfaction with their own parenting role.[36] Joan Huber and Glenna Spitze report a considerable decline in the view that remaining childless is "selfish," from 70 percent in a survey in the early 1970s to only 21 percent in their 1978 sample.[37]

Another significant change in fertility behavior is its less secure confinement to marriage. The overall rate of out-of-wedlock births for women fifteen to forty-four years of age—29.4 per thousand women—is the highest rate ever recorded, and now represents 18 percent of all births in the United States. What is not known is what proportion of these out-of-wedlock births is motivated by the desire for a child but no desire for a spouse. Despite the availability of legal abortions, many young women are choosing to bear and rear children outside of marriage.

A trend worth watching in the years ahead is the incidence of artificial reproduction. So far, insemination by anonymous donors has been relied upon largely by married couples with fertility problems,[38] but there is scattered evidence that some proportion of current users of these services are women who want a child but do not wish to marry. One California clinic reports that one-third of its clients are composed of such women.[39] Our impression is that many well-educated women who have devoted their twenties to becoming established in their careers find themselves groping for a solution to the dilemma of wanting to have a child before their reproductive prime time runs out, but having no suitable spouse on the horizon.

To date, the number of out-of-wedlock births, whether accidental or purposely planned, pales beside the other major category of solo parenting—divorced women who head their own households and rear their children with little or no support from their ex-husbands. Single female-headed households have been the fastest-growing type of household in the United States in recent years, and all the evidence is that most divorced men do not provide support for their children beyond the first year following the divorce.

Two important observations are suggested by these trends. One is that childbearing and child rearing may undergo a gradual dissociation from marriage in the years ahead, much as there was a gradual dissociation of sex from marriage over the past sixty years. Second, Lesthaeghe's thesis concerning an increasing aversion to long-term commitments, and Dreitzel's thesis concerning an increasing detachment from traditional social roles, require the qualification that they apply more to men than they do to women, a possibility neither of these theorists even consider.

Employment of Women

In almost every industrial society in the world, the proportion of married women in the labor force has risen dramatically, a fact that is integrally related to the trends we have reviewed. Some social scientists have attributed this pattern to the feminist movement;

others claim it reflects the impact of women's increased education—
that women's time has become too valuable to be limited to domestic
labor, for example; still others have viewed rising female employment
rates as a phenomenon of family adaptation in a period of inflation.
None of these theories is adequate in light of the fact that the trend
in married women's employment has shown a linear increase since
1920, continuing right through the Great Depression of the 1930s,
the postwar years of affluence and high birth rates, the years of
anti-war activism, counterculture, and youth revolt, and on into the
inflationary years of the 1980s, with every indication that the trend
will persist in the years ahead.

Kingsley Davis suggests that this trend must be seen as part of a
much larger historical process, in which the period of 1860 to 1920,
when few married women were in the labor force, was the aberrant
era that demands special explanation, not the period since 1920.[40]
Davis characterizes the period from 1860 to 1920 as the "rise and fall
of the breadwinner system": a transitional period during which the
work of men and women was more highly differentiated than ever
before, with women remaining at home while men followed the shift
of productive labor from home to work place. In this perspective,
married women, who have been steadily moving into the labor force
since 1920, are not engaging in a revolutionary new phenomenon,
but are simply resuming the pattern of joint productive labor that
characterized all previous human history before 1860. Whether they
were wives in a hunting-gathering society or a rural agricultural
society, women almost always engaged in productive labor in addition to their domestic and child-rearing activities. What is new and
difficult for contemporary women is not productive labor per se, but
the fact that there is now spatial separation between home and work
place, and little flexibility in the occupational system to accommodate
that fact, since urban industrial jobs were designed for male workers
who were backed up by their women at home.

To perceive the period 1860–1920 as an historical aberration in
the role of married women in productive labor does not mean that
there is no need for further major structural change in women's
position in the labor force. To an extent we have only recently
realized, the American economy is overwhelmingly gender-stratified:
there is so much gender segregation by firm and by plant that most
jobs are held either largely by men or largely by women.[41] This fact

makes the doctrine of "equal pay for equal work" of far less relevance to narrowing the gap in earnings between men and women than the doctrine of "comparable worth," and it is on this latter ground that debate and political action will center in the decade ahead. It is not enough to open previously all-male jobs to women: we must also redress the wage inequities between jobs, so that, for example, surgical nurses with master's degrees are paid more, instead of less, than truck drivers who never completed high school.[42]

Removing the pay inequity between men and women would also go a long way towards solving a growing social problem in the United States: the sharp rise in the proportion of children and women who live in poverty. The single strongest predictor of children's living in poverty is the divorce of their parents. And the reason divorce has this impact on children is twofold: because, as we have noted, very few men provide for their children's support after a divorce, and because the jobs women hold pay so poorly.[43]

Household Composition

All the trends we have reviewed combine to effect one of the most dramatic demographic changes taking place in Western societies: a radical shift in the modal household from one headed by a marital pair rearing dependent-age children to a household headed by a single adult.[44] In 1960, the proportion of single adult–headed households in the United States was 25 percent, followed by an increase to 35 percent by 1975, and a projected 45 percent of all households by 1990. This pattern reflects the combined effect of young adults moving away from their parents' homes once schooling is completed; the later age at marriage, the increase in divorce, with its general aftermath of single female–headed households with children and of divorced men living alone; and the aging of the population, with widowhood resulting in an increasingly larger proportion of older women living by themselves. The long-term rise in economic affluence has given further impetus to this trend, since single-adult households are more costly than shared dwellings.

The trends we have reviewed pose important consequences for society. That only one in four American households now includes even one dependent-age child may mean a significant erosion of a major source of social integration, since parenting serves social functions by linking adults to the community.[45] Lydia O'Donnell found that parents in the active stages of child rearing are more involved in neighborhood and community affairs than childless and post-parental adults. Samuel Preston suggests that American society has already shown significant shifts in the population group that makes use of most of our national resources, a shift from children to the elderly.[46] An important contribution to this shift is the fact that only a minority of political constituents are rearing children today, thus undercutting the inclination of elected public officials to respond to the needs of the very young. By contrast, the needs of the elderly have become increasingly prominent in electoral campaigns and lobbying efforts on Congress, given their growing numbers, their much higher turnout in elections, and the rapid growth of voluntary associations and lobbies that represent their interests.

We have observed that an increasing proportion of both sexes now lives alone—unmarried, separated or divorced, widowed—and this suggests yet another, and unprecedented, social pattern, with implications for the social cohesion of Western society. It is women who remain responsible for children, while most unmarried and divorced men do not. A larger proportion of women than of men are therefore tied into communal activities and institutions. Further, men and women cope with stress and with being alone in quite different ways. When women are under stress, they turn their anxieties inward, while men tend to act out their anxieties, frequently resorting to aggressive, combative, or risk-taking behavior.[47] When women are alone, they tend to seek out other people; they form quasi-sisterly friendships with other women; and they turn to parents, adult children, and siblings to satisfy their social and emotional needs, all of which further reinforce their embeddedness in social institutions, a pattern men do not show to nearly the same extent.

This gender difference implies that men are more dependent than women on primary social relationships for enjoying social intimacy, maintaining responsible behavior, and sustaining psychological stability. This thesis is at radical odds with the view, fashionable nowadays, that family systems victimize and oppress women, for it suggests that a critical function of family systems is to bind men into the social collective. All the sociological literature on social deviance lends support to this interpretation, for young, unattached males predominate in sexual violence, alcohol and drug abuse, crime, and terrorism.[48]

It is ironic to note in this connection that the expansion of welfare programs has the effect of winnowing away male family responsibilities while simultaneously increasing female responsibilities. Men know that if they do not honor child support when they divorce, welfare programs will provide at least basic necessities. Unlike many other countries, divorced men's wages are not garnisheed in the United States. Consequently, divorce has the effect of increasing the standard of living of men while markedly decreasing that of women and their children. In a similar fashion, pension, disability, and social security programs reduce men's financial responsibility for their elderly parents, while these programs have no provisions to substitute for the personal care-giving that women traditionally have expended on their elderly parents.[49]

Social anthropologists have often argued that the "family of man" is a universal social unit in all societies, and that the bond between men and women and their children is the most treasured relationship of people everywhere. One of the social mechanisms that encouraged this pattern was nearly universal and continuous residence in family households: with parents until marriage; with spouse and children until the children left to form their own families; with grown children after the death of the spouse. The combined effect of the demographic trends we have charted here is to break this chain of continuous embeddedness in families at several points in the life course.

Whether other social institutions can substitute for the family in providing social relationships that can sustain social integration and cohesion is not clear. Some social theorists in the past, like Emile Durkheim, looked to occupations to provide meaningful social integration, but nothing we have learned in the decades since he published his *Division of Labor in Society* suggests that this is likely or even possible. Apart from the small stratum of professional and technical occupations that provide high levels of intrinsic gratification, most people in industrial and service jobs experience work that is deadening in its routine and in its only partial use of human capabilities. Almost all Western societies report steadily lowering ages of retirement,[50] despite the fact of rising inflation over the past decade. Rather than something to be dreaded, most Western workers seem to view retirement as a release from time and activity restraints.

One positive outcome of these changes may be greater adaptability to living alone on the part of future cohorts of the elderly, more of whom will have spent some significant portion of their earlier lives outside the family context. Many will have been single all their lives, more will never have had children, and many will have relied on friendships for social and intimate sustenance rather than on family members. And in light of the fact that women are more apt than men to form quasi-kin relationships, it is perhaps fortunate that it is elderly women rather than men who tend to outlive their spouses. With more continuous work histories behind them, and, one hopes, more equitable pay, elderly women in the future may also be less likely to lead penurious lives.

As a "new" nation, American society has been both more youthful and more masculine than other Western countries. Now we are entering an era in which America is becoming older and more feminine. What difference will this make to American society? Some clues to this future may be found in the sex and gender differences of the second half of life, to which we now turn.

SEX AND GENDER IN THE SECOND HALF OF LIFE

In a recent book on later life, Florine Livson retells a Moroccan parable that says, in effect, that at birth each boy is surrounded by one hundred devils and each girl by one hundred angels; with each year of life a devil is exchanged for an angel, so if men and women live to one hundred years of age, men end up surrounded by angels and women by devils.[51] The ready assumption in this Moroccan folktale—that men and women undergo significant changes as they age—has not been a congenial one to social scientists until quite recently, for developmental theory had long assumed that the most important aspects of human development took place during child-hood and adolescence. Like wound-up clocks, adults were perceived to be relatively stable, acting in conformity to the personalities and values they had internalized in their earlier years. By contrast, most social scientists today believe that it is change, not stability along the lifeline, that is the keynote of adult development.[52]

Nevertheless, there is little agreement on what the balance of factors is that explains changes along the life course. The penchant of sociologists and developmental psychologists is to interpret age-related change as reflections of cohort membership or of unusual historical events that had greater impact on one age group than another, rather than as responses to both internal biological and psychological factors and external social and historical factors. Purely social explanations are clearly sufficient to account for certain phenomena. For example, there is growing evidence that changes in gender-role behavior and in values have taken place far more dramatically among young American women than among older ones. A particularly persuasive example is found in the results of a longitudinal study of women who were first studied in 1962, when they were between fifteen and thirty-nine years of age, and then were re-interviewed in 1977, when they were between thirty and fifty-four years of age.[53] In 1962, the youngest women, then under twenty-four, were the most traditional in their gender-role views, while by 1977 they had shifted dramatically and were the *least* traditional. To account for this, Arland Thornton and Deborah Freedman suggest that the youngest women, who had not yet made critical life decisions, were free to be influenced by the widespread debate on gender issues stimulated by the feminist movement of the 1960s and 1970s, while older women, with considerable investment in their earlier choices of spouse, family size, and work, were less open to reexamining gender-related issues.[54] Another study reports that older people showed only moderate change from traditional gender-role attitudes, while younger respondents showed major shifts.[55]

If we turn our attention from specific attitudes in one domain of life to more global personal characteristics, we find growing evidence of an interesting developmental change in men and women in the second half of life. This is not the place to detail the whole range of evidence;[56] rather, we offer some suggestive examples from the research literature. Dorothy Eichorn and her associates traced personality changes in the same women and men from adolescence to their early fifties, and reported that over time, women become more analytic and assertive while men become more giving and expressive.[57] This was not because they lost earlier traits, but because they added new ones to their existing repertoire, so that the older men and women respectively developed supplementary qualities that are conventionally defined as appropriate to the opposite sex. In a similar vein, Bernice Neugarten and David Gutmann[58] have found that, compared with younger men, older men in four very different cultures became more dependent and expressive in old age, while women became less nurturant and more assertive.[59]

Because these gender- and age-linked developmental changes are being reported on the basis of samples derived from several different cultures and time periods, it is highly unlikely that they reflect changes that occurred as a result of either cohort membership or as a response to specific historical influences. Instead, the evidence suggests that the changes reflect a decline in sex and gender differences that takes place following the peak reproductive phase of the human life span. Hence, estrogen decline in women and testosterone decline in men from early middle-age on seem likely to play a contributing role in the personality changes taking place as men and women age. Even sexual responses differ in the human male from mid-life on, for men become more like women in their sexual behavior as they age, with a focus on sheer sensual touching and enriched fantasies; as Ruth Weg put it, older men engage in touch for its own sake rather than merely as a way station to intercourse.[60]

To implicate hormonal change as a component of developmental changes in personality as men and women age does not preclude social change as well. Gender characteristics are clearly modifiable under changed social circumstances, as men and women take on either greater or lesser similarity of roles and experiences. Indeed, most of the demographic trends we have charted will provide special biographic marks on future cohorts of older men and women, as suggested earlier. Political and economic pressures are now blurring traditional gender roles in the first half of life, as women resume equal responsibility with men for the support of themselves and their children. If the tendency of the human organism in the second half of life is towards more androgynous qualities in both sexes, then these recent political and economic changes in gender roles in early adulthood may make for a smoother passage through the transitional years of middle age. In an era marked by so much technological and political change, and by personal lives that are often fragmented by disparate and conflicting roles, with periods of loneliness, heartache, and isolation, there is comfort in the idea that more androgynous qualities may become stable characteristics of men and women throughout their lives.

For the present, however, realism dictates the sober reflection that it will take decades to effect changes in gender roles in the first half of life. There is personal turmoil in store for those whose lives will be affected by these changes, and much political effort necessary for those who take active roles in the institutional changes that are still to be secured. Few political tasks are more urgent than to rid Western societies of the pay inequities that now prevail between men and women, and to topple the barriers that restrict the aspirations and access of women to top professional and managerial occupations. It is improbable indeed that an equitable division in labor in home maintenance and child rearing will come about until wives' time is valued on a par with that of their husbands, a shift that is not likely to be widespread so long as women contribute only a third or less of the total family income.

In the interim, there are grounds for cautious optimism precisely because Western societies are becoming increasingly aging societies. For one, the androgynous qualities of men and women in the second half of life will be more dominant in the population. Second, women are a growing majority of the population in aging societies, which means that any gender gap in political views can become critical in close political contests, and will become even more important in the future as larger proportions of women gain political skills and experience. Since older people participate in elections to a much greater extent than young adults do, older women carry more electoral weight than their sheer numbers suggest. In the 1984 American national election, for example, there were 5.5 million more women than men voters. The rapid increase in the number of women in law and business that has been taking place over the past decade is also important, because these are the feeder occupations to both appointive and elective office-holding in politics.

Because political careers take many years to develop, it is too soon to see the full impact of women in politics. Geraldine Ferraro was important as a symbol of women's potential political prominence, but the full effect of women's presence is not yet visible on the national level. Nevertheless, as women enter the political arena in significant numbers, we can see signs of the kind of changes that may develop in the future. In 1984, the largest number of women ever were elected to state legislatures (939); this figure is still small as a proportion of state legislators, but it is triple what it had been a short decade-and-a-half ago. Even more impressive gains have been made at local levels, but the data that include the 1984 local election results are not yet available.

There is a good deal of evidence for the existence of a gender gap in political views: women are more opposed than men to corruption, war, political extremism, military expansion, and environmental and occupational hazards.[61] More women than men are opposed to conscription, nuclear weapons, racial discrimination, and capital punishment; and women are more sympathetic than men to a wide range of social welfare programs.[62] It is also the case that the better educated the voter, the greater the gender gap in these views. This implies that in the future, elderly men and women will differ on political issues even more than they do today because they will be better educated.[63]

On a national political level, women have constituted only a tiny minority of elective office-holders anywhere in the Western world, and one must thus be cautious in assuming that an increase in women's numerical presence in national politics will reflect the style and values either of women generally or of those women now active in local politics. The small minority of women who represent a pioneer spearhead in national politics tends to consist of exceptional individuals, highly self-selected and pressured to take on the characteristics of the male turf they have penetrated. Even when women hold half of the seats in Congress and key executive posts in government, the pressures inherent in geopolitical reality will affect the political decisions of women as they have of men. On the other hand, an equitable gender representation in political leadership will not be an isolated development; it will take place along with many other transformations in Western societies. As more women move from being marginal observers to becoming active participants in the circles of power in the work world and in politics, and as more men move from vicarious to active participation in the intimate world of family, one can envisage a far better balance in both men and women of those socially desirable attributes that are conventionally linked to gender.

The larger proportion of people in the second half of their lives may also contribute to this social transformation; young adults are more absorbed in personal and interpersonal issues, while older people bring much broader social concerns to their political partici-pation. An aging society therefore holds the promise of arresting and perhaps even reversing the propensity toward egotism and fragmen-tation that Lesthaeghe and Dreitzel have perceived in the current trends in Western societies. Just as their ideas require qualification because they do not take gender into account, so too do their perceptions require qualification because they focus too narrowly on the characteristics of youth rather than maturity. The future of Western societies seems far less dismal when these qualifications are made. Indeed, the prospect is bright that an aging and androgynous society holds the potential for becoming a society that is more humane and more caring than any Western nation yet has been.

ENDNOTES

[1] K. Davis, "Demographic Imbalance and International Conflict," paper presented at the Annual Meeting of the American Sociological Association in San Antonio, Texas, August 1984.

[2] R.B. Lee and I. DeVore, *Man the Hunter* (Chicago: Aldine, 1968).

[3] R. Hall, ed., *Sexual Dimorphism in Homo Sapiens* (New York: Praeger, 1982).

[4] G.L. Isaac, "The Food-sharing Behavior of Protohuman Hominids," *Scientific American,* April 1978, pp. 90–108; and A.L. Zihlman, "Women as Shapers of the Human Adaptation," in F. Dahlberg, ed., *Woman the Gatherer* (New Haven: Yale University Press, 1981), pp. 75–120.

[5] R. Huss-Ashmore, "Fat and Fertility: Demographic Implications of Differential Fat Storage," *Yearbook of Physical Anthropology,* 1980, pp. 65–91.

[6] J.B. Lancaster, "Sex and Gender in Evolutionary Perspective," in H. Katchadourian, ed., *Human Sexuality: A Comparative and Developmental Perspective* (Los Angeles: University of California Press, 1979), pp. 51–80; and Lancaster, "Evolutionary Perspectives on Sex Differences in the Higher Primates," in A.S. Rossi, ed., *Gender and the Life Course* (New York: Aldine, 1985), pp. 3–27.

[7] J.B. Lancaster, "Evolutionary Perspectives on Sex Differences," op. cit.

[8] D.W. Richardson and R.V. Short, "Time of Onset of Sperm Production in Boys," *Journal of Biosocial Science Supplement,* vol. 5, 1978, pp. 15–26.

[9] J.B. Lancaster, "Human Adolescence and Reproduction: An Evolutionary Perspective," in J.B. Lancaster and B.A. Hamburg, eds., *School-Age Pregnancy and Parenthood: Biosocial Dimensions* (New York: Aldine, forthcoming); and M.F. Montagu, *The Reproductive Development of the Female: A Study in the Comparative Physiology of the Adolescent Organism* (Littleton, MA: PSG Publishing, 1979).

[10] J.H. Gagnon and W. Simon, *Sexual Conduct: The Social Sources of Human Sexuality* (New York: Aldine, 1983); and Gagnon and Simon, "Psychosexual Development," in Gagnon and Simon, eds., *The Sexual Scene* (New York: Aldine, 1970), pp. 23–41.

[11] J.B. Lancaster and C.S. Lancaster, "Parental Investment: The Hominid Adaptation," in S.B. Ortner, ed., *How Humans Adapt: A Biosocial Odyssey* (Washington, D.C.: Smithsonian Institution Press, 1983), pp. 33–66; and Rossi, "Gender and Parenthood," *American Sociological Review,* Feb. 1984, pp. 1–19.

[12] S.S. Feldman, "Sex Differences in Responsiveness to Babies among Mature Adults," *Developmental Psychology,* July 1979, pp. 430–36; and Feldman, Z.C.

Birigen, and S.C. Nash, "Fluctuation of Sex-related Self-attributions as a Function of Stage of Family Life Cycle," *Developmental Psychology*, Jan. 1981, pp. 24–35.

[13]B.R. Tinsley and R.D. Parke, "Grandparents as Support and Socialization Agents," in M. Lewis, ed., *Beyond the Dyad* (New York: Plenum Press, 1984), pp. 161–93.

[14]W.A. Stini, "Adaptive Strategies of Human Populations under Nutritional Stress," in Stini, ed., *Physiological and Morphological Adaptation and Evolution* (Mouton: The Hague, 1979), pp. 387–407; and Stini, "Body Composition and Nutrient Reserves in Evolutionary Perspective," in D.N. Walcher and N. Kretchmer, eds., *Food, Nutrition, and Evolution* (New York: Masson, 1981), pp. 107–120.

[15]J.B. Lancaster, "Evolutionary Perspectives on Sex Differences," op. cit.; R.V. Short, "The Evolution of Human Reproduction," *Proceedings of the Royal Society*, B195 (1976), pp. 3–24; and Short, "Sexual Selection and its Component Parts, Somatic and Genital Selection, as illustrated by Man and the Greater Apes," *Advances in the Study of Behavior*, vol. 9, 1979, pp. 131–58.

[16]R.A. LeVine and S. LeVine, "Age, Gender, and the Demographic Transition: The Life Course in Agrarian Societies," in Rossi, ed., *Gender and the Life Course*, op. cit., pp. 29–42.

[17]This is the argument put forth by Davis and P. van Oever, "Demographic Foundations of New Sex Roles," *Population and Development Review*, Sept. 1982, pp. 495–511.

[18]S.H. Preston, "Children and the Elderly: Divergent Paths for America's Dependents," *Demography*, Nov. 1984, pp. 435–57.

[19]D. Nortman, "Parental Age as a Factor in Pregnancy Outcome and Child Development," *Reports on Population/Family Planning* (New York: The Population Council), Aug. 1974; and D. Schwartz, et al., "Semen Characteristics as a Function of Age in 833 Fertile Men," *Fertility and Sterility*, April 1983, pp. 530–35.

[20]Two useful reviews that cover research on male fecundity and fertility are P. Daniels and K. Weingarten, "A New Look at the Medical Risks in Late Childbearing," *Women and Health*, Spring 1979, pp. 5–36; and W.H. Baldwin and C.W. Nord, "Delayed Childbearing in the United States: Facts and Fictions," *Population Bulletin*, Nov. 1984, esp. pp. 27–28.

[21]This is at the heart of the Agent Orange controversy, in which veterans charge that their exposure to the defoliant in Vietnam has caused serious birth defects in their children.

[22]W. Mosher and W. Pratt, "Fecundity and Infertility in the United States, 1965–1982," *NCHS Advanced Data*, no. 104, (Washington, D.C.: U.S. Department of Health and Human Services, Feb. 11, 1985).

[23]P. Aries, *Centuries of Childhood* (Harmondsworth, England: Penguin, 1973); and Aries, "Two Successive Motivations for the Declining Birth Rate in the West," *Population and Development Review*, Dec. 1980, pp. 645–50.

[24]R. Lesthaeghe, "On the Social Control of Human Reproduction," *Population and Development Review*, Dec. 1980, pp. 527–48; and Lesthaeghe, "A Century of Demographic and Cultural Change in Western Europe: An Exploration of Underlying Dimensions," *Population and Development Review*, Sept. 1983, pp. 411–35.

[25]Lesthaeghe, "A Century of Demographic and Cultural Change," op. cit., p. 413.

[26]H.P. Dreitzel, "Generational Conflict from the Point of View of Civilization Theory," in V. Garms-Homolova, E.M. Hoerning, and D. Schaeffer, eds.,

Intergenerational Relationships (Lewiston, New York: C.J. Hogrefe, 1984), pp. 17–26.

[27]N. Elias, *The Civilizing Process,* vol. 1: *The History of Manners* (New York: Urizon Press, 1978), and vol. II: *Power and Civility* (New York: Urizon Press, 1982).

[28]Dreitzel, op. cit., p. 24.

[29]G. Masnick and M.J. Bane, *The Nation's Families: 1960 to 1990* (Cambridge, MA: Joint Center for Urban Studies, 1980).

[30]J. Veroff and E. Douvan, *The Inner American: A Self Portrait from 1957 to 1976* (New York: Basic Books, 1981).

[31]Ibid., p. 191.

[32]Davis and van den Oever, op. cit.

[33]C. Westoff, "Fertility Decline in the West: Causes and Prospects," *Population and Development Review,* March 1983, pp. 99–105.

[34]National Center for Health Statistics, "Advance Report on Final Natality Statistics," *Monthly Vital Statistics Report,* Nov. 30, 1982, Supplement.

[35]For an example of a demographer who predicts a high incidence of childlessness, see D. Bloom, "What's Happening to the Age at First Birth in the United States?", *Demography,* Aug. 1982, pp. 351–70.

[36]Veroff and Douvan, op. cit., p. 217. They also report that among college-educated adults, two-thirds of the men, and slightly more of the women held either neutral or positive views toward not having children.

[37]J. Huber and G. Spitze, *Sex Stratification: Children, Housework, and Jobs* (New York: Academic Press, 1983), pp. 135–37.

[38]R. Snowden, G.D. Mitchell, and E.M. Snowden, *Artificial Reproduction: A Social Investigation* (London: George Allen and Unwin, 1983).

[39]P. Bagne, "High Tech Breeding," *Mother Jones,* Aug. 7, 1983, pp. 23–29; 35.

[40]Davis, "Wives and Work: Consequences of the Sex Role Revolution," *Population and Development Review,* Sept. 1984, pp. 397–418.

[41]J.N. Baron and W.T. Bielby, "Organizational Barriers to Gender Equality: Sex Segregation of Jobs and Opportunities," in Rossi, ed., *Gender and the Life Course,* op. cit., pp. 233–51; and D.V. Treiman and H.I. Hartmann, eds., *Women, Work, and Wages: Equal Pay for Jobs of Equal Value* (Washington, D.C.: National Academy Press, 1981).

[42]Many large corporations, such as Westinghouse, have conducted detailed job assessments to classify jobs into labor grades, but then determined actual wage levels separately for those jobs held predominantly by men and predominantly by women. See R.L. Feldberg, "Comparable Worth: Toward Theory and Practice in the United States," *Signs: Journal of Women in Culture and Society,* Winter 1984, pp. 311–28.

[43]The Panel Study of Income Dynamics, conducted annually since 1968, has tracked the economic circumstances of a nationally representative sample of American families. The PSID longitudinal study has shown that over the course of ten years, one-quarter of the families studied were below the poverty line at some time, but the majority were poor only for one or two years out of the ten, and only one in ten were poor for at least eight years. A large proportion of this latter—the persistently poor—were widows, whose income undergoes a dramatic and irremedial decline following the death of their husbands. For an excellent overview of the PSID findings on women and poverty, see M. Corcoran, G.J. Duncan, and M.S. Hill, "The Economic Fortunes of Women and Children:

Lessons from the Panel Study of Income Dynamics," *Signs: Journal of Women in Culture and Society,* Winter 1984, pp. 232–48. This entire Winter 1984 issue of *Signs* is devoted to the topic of Women and Poverty.

[44]Masnick and Bane, op. cit.; F.E. Kobrin, "The Fall in Household Size and the Rise in the Primary Individual in the United States," *Demography,* May 1976, pp. 127–38; and J.A. Sweet, "Components of Change in the Number of Households: 1970–1980," *Demography,* May 1984, pp. 129–40.

[45]C. Fischer, R.M. Jackson, et al., *Networks and Places* (New York: Free Press, 1977); L. O'Donnell, "The Social World of Parents," *Marriage and Family Review,* Winter 1983, pp. 9–36; and O'Donnell, *The Unheralded Majority: Contemporary Women as Mothers* (Lexington, MA: D.C. Heath, 1985), esp. chaps. 7 and 8.

[46]Preston, op. cit.

[47]W.R. Gove, "The Effect of Age and Gender on Deviant Behavior: A Biopsycho-social Perspective," in Rossi, ed., *Gender and the Life Course,* op. cit., pp. 115–44; and M. Guttentag, S. Salasin, and D. Belle, *The Mental Health of Women* (New York: Academic Press, 1980).

[48]See Gove, op. cit., for an overview of research and theory on the age and gender linkage to social deviance.

[49]Studies of care giving to the elderly show that it is women who provide personal care to elderly husbands, parents, and even parents-in-law. See E.M. Brody, P.T. Johnsen, et al., "Women's Changing Roles and Help to Elderly Parents: Attitudes of Three Generations of Women," *Journal of Gerontology,* Sept. 1983, pp. 597–607; and L.R. Fischer and C. Hoffman, "Who Cares for the Elderly: The Dilemma of Family Support," in M. Lewis and J.L. Miller, eds., *Research in Social Problems and Public Policy,* (Greenwich, CN: JAI Press, 1984), pp. 169–216.

[50]For a recent overview from several Western countries, see R.F. Tomasson, "Government Old Age Pensions under Affluence and Austerity: West Germany, Sweden, the Netherlands, and the United States," in Lewis and Miller, op. cit., pp. 217–72.

[51]F.B. Livson, "Gender Identity: A Life-span view of Sex Role Development," in R.B. Weg, ed., *Sexuality in the Later Years: Roles and Behavior* (New York: Academic Press, 1983), pp. 105–127.

[52]O.G. Brim, Jr. and J. Kagan, eds., *Constancy and Change in Human Development* (Cambridge, MA: Harvard University Press, 1980).

[53]A. Thornton and D.S. Freedman, "Changes in the Sex Role Attitudes of Women, 1962–1977: Evidence from a Panel Study," *American Sociological Review,* Oct. 1979, pp. 831–42.

[54]Ibid, p. 837.

[55]K.O. Mason, J.L. Czajka, and S. Arber, "Change in U.S. Women's Sex Role Attitudes, 1964–1974," *American Sociological Review,* Aug. 1976, pp. 573–96.

[56]See Livson, op. cit., for a good review of gender identity development in a life span framework. For an interesting longitudinal study of personality change from adolescence to mid-life, see D.H. Eichorn, J.A. Clausen, et al., *Present and Past in Middle Life* (New York: Academic Press, 1981).

[57]Ibid.

[58]B.L. Neugarten and D. Gutmann, "Age-sex Roles and Personality in Middle Age: A Thematic Apperception Study," in Neugarten, ed., *Middle Age and Aging* (Chicago: University of Chicago Press, 1968), pp. 58–71; and Gutmann, "Par-enthood: A Key to the Comparative Study of the Life Cycle," in N. Datan and

L.H. Ginsberg, eds., *Life Span Development and Psychology: Normative Life Crisis* (New York: Academic Press, 1975), pp. 169–84.

[59]The Neugarten and Gutmann studies suggest a gender role reversal among elderly people, while the Eichorn study suggests merely the addition of opposite-sex qualities to existing ones. It may be that the Eichorn study captures a process of change still underway, since their subjects were only in their early fifties at the time of the study.

[60]Weg, "The Physiological Perspective," in Weg, ed., op. cit., pp. 40–80.

[61]S. Baxter and M. Lansing, *Women and Politics: The Invisible Majority* (Ann Arbor: University of Michigan Press, 1980).

[62]M. Githens and J.L. Prestage, eds., *A Portrait of Marginality: The Political Behavior of American Women* (New York: Longman, 1977); and Rossi, "Beyond the Gender Gap: Women's Bid for Political Power," *Social Science Quarterly*, Dec. 1983, pp. 718–33.

[63]E.C. Ladd, "The Brittle Mandate: Electoral Dealignment and the 1980 Presidential Election," *Political Science Quarterly*, Spring 1981, pp. 1–25. There was little overall gender difference in the voting in the 1984 election, although Sidney Sheldon points out that an analysis of the CBS poll showed a large gender gap in voting for Reagan among college educated voters. See S. Sheldon, "Women's Different Voice for Peace," *Radcliffe Quarterly*, March 1985, pp. 12–13.

Gunhild O. Hagestad

The Family: Women and Grandparents as Kin-Keepers

F AMILIES AND RELATIONSHIPS within them have been strongly affected by demographic change and by the wider societal changes that are often associated with population aging.

Decreased mortality, altered patterns of fertility, and the increasing imbalance in sex ratios during the second half of adulthood have had profound effects on families and on some key aspects of family life. As our aging society confronts the twenty-first century, families face a number of new challenges and opportunities as the result of recent demographic and cultural changes.

We shall be looking especially at three main trends in recent population change. The first is the increased general life expectancy and what demographers refer to as "the rectangularization of sur-vival curves"—that is, the fact that the majority of the population now survives into old age, and about three-fourths of all deaths occur among those over the age of sixty-five. The second trend is the decrease in family size and the smaller age difference that prevails today between a typical family's oldest and youngest child. Around the turn of the century, mothers bore, on the average, 3.9 children. The current estimate is about 1.8. The widened gap between the mortality rates of men and women, which has produced a seven-year difference in their general life expectancy, is the third major change. Together, they pose some often surprising challenges and possibilities for family life in the near future.

DEMOGRAPHIC CHANGE AND FAMILY LIFE

Altered Patterns of Family Deaths

... We place dying in what we take to be its logical position, which is at the close of a long life, whereas our ancestors accepted the futility of placing it in any position at all. In the midst of life we are in death, they said, and they meant it. To them it was a fact; to us it is a metaphor.[1]

The British author Ronald Blythe has captured the human realities behind the demographers' life tables. Less than a century ago, death was a normal experience in all phases of family life; only in the last few decades has it become associated more with advanced age.

Recent work on turning points in the course of human lives has emphasized the need for predictability—the craving to know what lies ahead.[2] Those life changes that we regard as normal, and thus expect, do not typically become crises, but unanticipated or untimely events sometimes do. When events come at a "scheduled" time, they are less likely to catch us unprepared than when they are unscheduled or come too early. Life changes are also easier when they occur "on schedule" because the individuals who are experiencing them may enjoy the comfort of others who are "in the same boat."

Recent changes in mortality have made the time of death more predictable and have clarified the meaning of the term "untimely death." Today, the death of parents before their child has reached midlife, and the death of their children—at any age—would be assigned that label. Because such events are not expected, they may be more traumatic now than they were in the past, for they catch us in the vulnerability of unpreparedness. They are also likely to be lonely transitions, neither shared nor fully understood by peers.

Among children born in 1910 who survived to their fifteenth birthday, more than one-half had experienced the death of a parent or a sibling by their early teens.[3] Today, the loss of parents is not expected until the second half of adulthood. For current generations of young women, the death of the mother may come close to the daughter's retirement age.[4]

At the beginning of this century, parents with an average number of children had a .62 chance of experiencing the death of a young child. In the late 1970s, the probability was only .04. The loss of a child has ceased to be a normal, anticipated part of family life.

For a growing number of adults, the loss of a grandparent is their first encounter with family deaths. We now anticipate that grandparents will not die until our early adulthood, but until quite recently most grandparents did not live long enough to know their grandchildren well.[5]

Concern is growing over the strain experienced by families who provide care for their ill or impaired elderly members. It is frequently argued that families in an aging society must be prepared to assume more of a care load than was the case for families in the past. We do not really have the historical data to judge if such statements are accurate, but it is important to keep in mind that before improved living conditions and medical advances produced rectangular survival curves, illness and death were encountered in all phases of family life—and at a time when there were far fewer outside institutional facilities and programs to alleviate their pressures. Families have always been expected to experience and absorb the shocks of illness and bereavement. The main difference between today's families and those of the past is not likely to be in the total *amount* of care and concern they expend, but the *focus* of them.

Infants and young children have always been regarded as vulnerable and dependent. But now, after childhood, these attributes are linked nearly exclusively with old age. Never before in human history has the experience of human frailty and the loss of a family member been so clearly linked to one group: the old. Perhaps part of the sense of burden associated with their care stems from the fact that the illness and loss are represented by *parents*—individuals who for decades were perceived as pillars of strength and support.

Durable Bonds

The Rileys, in their contribution to this volume, discuss how today's increased longevity provides new opportunities for individuals to accumulate a variety of experiences and skills. The same theme emerges when we consider decades of joint survival in family relationships across generations. Parents and children may accrue half a century of interwoven biographies, shared experiences, and memories. For the majority of life years shared by parents and children, the child is not *chronologically* a child. As we were growing up, most of us heard our parents say: "Some day you will understand," or "When you are a parent yourself . . . ." Research on adults, particularly on mothers and daughters, bears out the folk wisdom: there seems to be new rapport and empathy between parents and children once the children become parents themselves.

In an aging society, a growing proportion of parents and children will share such key experiences of adulthood as work, parenthood, and even retirement and widowhood. In the grandparent-grandchild relationship, the grandparent may survive to experience many years of the grandchild's adulthood.

There is little doubt that altered mortality and fertility patterns have created a new climate for the building and maintenance of family relationships. Historians and demographers have suggested that under conditions of high mortality, people were reluctant to form strong attachments to particular individuals, knowing that such ties could not be counted upon to endure. Instead, they invested in the security of the family as a group. Today, most people not only take long-term family bonds for granted and invest accordingly in them, but because of reduced fertility rates, there are also fewer individuals within each generation to invest in. As a result, intergenerational relationships are not only more *extensive* now, but they may also have become more *intensive*. Such "intensification of family life" may have gained even further momentum because of the weakening ties between family and community.[6]

A New Uniformity in Childhood Experiences?

We have noted that in recent decades, average family size has declined, as has the age difference between the oldest child and youngest child in the family. In some of my own work, I have used Norwegian census material to examine the types of families that firstborns grew up in during various decades of this century. Among Norwegian children born during the 1920s, nearly one-half grew up in families of five or more children, and close to one-third were sixteen or older when their youngest sibling was born. Among firstborns from the 1950s, only one in seven ended up with four or more siblings, and less than one-tenth of this group have sixteen years or more between them and their youngest sibling. The proportion of firstborns who grew up with one or two siblings went from one-third in the 1920s group to nearly two-thirds in the 1950s group. These changes suggest an increasing uniformity in childhood experiences and in parent-child relationships as well.

Over the last century, successive generations of children have become more similar in terms of birth order, and the very meaning of sibling position may have changed. Among children born in 1870, one-third were either first or second children in their families. For children born in 1930, this proportion had nearly doubled.[7]

Psychology offers a sizeable literature on the effects of sibling position on individual development. Many of these generalizations regarding birth order may not hold true when siblings are less than five years apart and come to think of themselves as peers once they reach adulthood. This is in sharp contrast to siblings from families in which the mother bore children throughout her fertile years, and firstborns were adults and parents themselves before the youngest sibling was born. In such cases, common until very recently, oldest and youngest siblings grew up in different families and encountered their parents in strikingly different life phases. Furthermore, the experience of parental death was also likely to occur in quite different phases of life for the first- and last-born individuals, and they grew up with different "kin galleries." Firstborns had a much greater chance to know their grandparents than did their younger siblings.

As a growing proportion of children grow up in small families, other differences in their early life experiences are becoming reduced. There is strong evidence to suggest that small and large families constitute qualitatively different developmental contexts. Children in small families receive more attention from parents than do children with a number of siblings, and recent research has linked such differences to intellectual development and school performance.[8]

The Changing Age Structure of Kin Networks

Not only do the size and age-structure of nuclear families change in the process of population aging, but kin networks also take new forms. Multi-generational families are becoming more common; families are increasingly "top heavy"; family members have a growing number of vertical, intergenerational relationships, while relationships *within* generations are decreasing in number; and generational demarcations are becoming clearer.

Currently, about one-half of all individuals over sixty-five are great-grandparents—that is, members of four-generation families. We have no good estimates of how common five-generation families are, but they, too, have most likely increased over the last few decades. The number of generations in a family lineage gives us an indication of the web of relationships it contains. In a four-generation family there are three sets of parent-child connections, two sets of grandparent-grandchild ties, and members of two generations who occupy the roles of both parents and children. Individuals in a multi-generational family line relate in a much more complex set of family identities than is the case in a lineage with only two generations, those of parent and child. Under earlier demographic conditions, individuals were likely to have a variety of intragenerational, that is, horizontal, family ties. Under current conditions, a variety of relationships are *vertical,* crossing generational lines. An extreme illustration of such change would be China's recent one-child policy. If it succeeds and continues, Chinese in the twenty-first century will have *only* vertical family relationships outside the marital role, as they will have no siblings and no cousins.

Because of changes in fertility and mortality, the relative balance between old and young has shifted—in society as well as family. The demographer Samuel Preston reminds us that this is the first time in history that the average married couple has more parents than children.[9] There is little doubt that the age composition of family reunions is strikingly different now from the way it was at around the turn of the century. Then, it was not unusual to find families in which children and grandchildren were the same age, and aunts and uncles were younger than their nieces and nephews. With the period of childbearing now concentrated in a shorter span of women's adult years, and the age difference between first- and last-born children reduced, generational demarcations have become clearer. Active involvement in the day-to-day demands of child rearing is also now likely to be over by the time women are grandmothers. The extent to which this has made grandmotherhood a more distinct role has not been fully explored, but it may mean that grandparents will increasingly emerge as a major stabilizing force in families, a point to which we shall return.

Both these trends—distinct generational demarcations and the clearer sequencing of parenthood and grandparenthood—are more typical of women's family lines than they are for paternal lines. Because of trends in age at first marriage and remarriage, and the growing number of "second families," men are more likely than women to have families whose age composition is characteristic of families early in this century.

Effects of "The Mortality Gap"

Women in the United States currently outlive men by about seven to eight years. The world of the very old is a world of women, both in society and within families. Men and women also spend the latter part of their lives in differing living arrangements and relationships. Most older women are widows living alone; most older men live with their wives. For example, among individuals over the age of seventy-five, two-thirds of the men are living with a spouse, while less than one-fifth of the women are.

These contrasts between older men and women have strong implications for the rest of their family members. First of all, the oldest members of a family are likely to be women. Women are also more likely to have great- and great-great-grandchildren. In societies where historical events have made sex ratios even more imbalanced than in this country, the three oldest generations may be populated only by women. For example, a German study found that many five-generation families contained three generations of widows.[10]

Differences in widowhood and remarriage mean that men tend to maintain a significant horizontal, intragenerational relationship until the end of their lives; women do not. Consequently, women draw more on their intergenerational relationships for help and support in old age. At the time when men face serious impairment, they are likely to have a wife to care for them, while frail and ill older women are typically widows who turn to younger generations for help. This may be one reason why women, throughout their adulthood, invest more time and energy in intergenerational ties than men do.

Of course, the lives of men and women have been affected by complex social and cultural processes that range far beyond demographic change. The extent to which this has intensified the differences between the genders will be explored in a later section, but let us first consider some social changes that are associated with aging societies, and how they have affected family life.

THE IMPACT OF WIDER SOCIETAL CHANGE

The Lack of Cultural Rules

Demographic change may have been so rapid and so dramatic that we have experienced "cultural lags" (see the essay by Riley and

Riley). Some of us find ourselves in life stages for which our society has no clear culturally shared expectations, and family members often face each other in relationships for which there is no historical precedence, and therefore minimal cultural guidance on which to rely. Such themes are very clear in recent discussions of grandparent-hood. Studies of grandparenting styles find a great deal of variety, and when a student and I analyzed popular magazine descriptions of grandparents in the 1880s and in the 1970s, we found current magazines to reflect a new uncertainty. Members of several genera-tions expressed confusion over what grandparents are supposed to do. What are their rights and obligations? In a society where grandparents range from twenty-five-year-olds to centenarians, and where grandchildren run the spectrum from infants to retirees, we should not be surprised to find that cultural images of grandparent-hood harbor both variety and uncertainty.[11]

New Forms of Interdependence

Closely related to the issue of what people expect of one another in family relationships is the question of what holds them together. Over the last century, economic needs have given way to emotional needs as the main family "glue," especially in relationships among adults. Over the same time period, we have seen a shift in emphasis from the needs of the family as a group to the needs and wishes of individuals. Individual choices, such as decisions about when to marry and leave the family, were once guided by the needs of the family unit as a whole. The twentieth century, with its pension and health-care plans, has "freed" generations from many of these economic interdependencies.[12] It is commonly argued that, as a result, family ties have become more *voluntary* in nature.[13] Kin connections are seen as a latent potential, from which active and viable relationships may or may not develop.

Even though we have a good deal of cultural ambiguity regarding relationships between young and old in the family, members of our society still share some key values and norms about family respon-sibilities and interconnections.[14] Surveys that have compared the attitudes and expectations of parents and children have often found that children are more ready than parents to state that the younger generation should provide help to needy elderly parents. It has also been found that the old are the most receptive to formal, non-family services, while the young are those most in favor of family-provided help. Researchers attribute such contrasts to "youthful idealism" on the part of the young. The middle-aged and the old, on the other hand, are often responding on the basis of actual care-taking experiences. Recently, a number of writers have argued that with the growth of societal supports for the old, an increasingly important function of the family will be to serve as mediators between bureaucracies and the aged,[15] and that modern families not only meet needs, they identify needs, so that other institutions can address them.

While pension systems and health plans have lightened the economic pressures for most families, there is still a steady flow of intergenerational support, and the majority of the states have enacted so-called "family responsibility" laws, statutes that establish relatives' responsibility for family members who are indigent, needy, or dependent. But recent research and public debate indicate that enormous complexity still remains in sorting out rights and obligations among family members in an aging society.

EMERGING ISSUES

Who Has the Right to be Old?

The recent German study of five-generation families revealed that high levels of role ambiguity and strain confront the contemporary multigenerational family. Nearly 90 percent of the oldest generation were living in private households, and among these great-great-grandparents 50 percent lived with a daughter who herself was in advanced old age. The families expressed a good deal of confusion about who had the right to some of the privileges of old age, and whose duty it was to provide them. The interviews often reflected a strong sense of jealousy in the two generations below the oldest, where members felt that they were missing out on some returns from their earlier family investments. The investigators warn that we may see increased rates of illness among young-old women in such families, both because of the stress of caring for the very old, and because of the possible benefits derived from the sick role, since the anticipated rewards of old age are not being realized. Perhaps more than any other society, Japan illustrates the potential ambiguity and strain produced by demographic change. Traditionally, the oldest son and his parents have maintained a pattern of co-residence within the Japanese stem family. With dramatic increases in life expectancy, the average duration of such co-residence nearly doubled between 1930 and 1950.[16] In today's Japan, an increasing number of families find themselves with two gray-haired and retired generations under one roof, both of whom expect support and deference.

In the United States, as in most Western industrialized societies, a good deal of debate has centered on families as units of care giving. A focal point in such discussions has been the role of women in family networks and in intergenerational patterns of support.

Kin-keeping and its Costs

There is a rather extensive literature showing that women are kin-keepers, and that their preparation for this role starts early in life. Kin-keeping tasks include maintaining communication, facilitating contact and the exchange of goods and services, and monitoring family relationships. These functions are often performed for the husband's kin as well as for the women's own family line. Even when they are not the initiators and orchestrators of family get-togethers, old women may nevertheless facilitate family contact by serving as the "excuse" for bringing kin together. The mother-daughter connection has emerged as the pivotal link, both in the maintenance of family contact and in the flow of support.

Daughters have been found to be the linchpin of widows' support systems. When aging parents live with offspring, eight out of ten are mothers, and two-thirds of them are living with a daughter. It is estimated that when older family members are in need of constant care, 80 percent of such care is provided by kin, usually by wives and daughters.[17] It is interesting to note that the same clear trends, identifying women as carrying an extensive and complex load of family caring, have emerged in studies of welfare states. Although Norway eliminated family-responsibility laws following the introduction of a "law for comprehensive care" which covered the young as well as the old, the care provided by Norwegian women has been described as "the hidden welfare state."[18]

It has been common, especially in the popular press, to suggest that women's involvement in the world of work will make them spend less time and effort on kin-tending. There is little evidence to support such a claim. Indeed, there are indications that an opposite trend is occurring. A growing number of women may be adjusting their work plans and work schedules to accommodate the needs of elderly parents[19]—much as they formerly planned around the needs of their children. Recent research found that employment significantly reduced care-giving to aging parents among sons, but this was *not* a statistically significant trend for daughters.[20]

There seems to be good reason to worry about what Betty Friedan has called "the superwoman squeeze"—the overload experienced by middle-generation women who provide support for both children and parents, in addition to facing the demands of the workaday world.[21] A growing number of writers express concern that our current social expectations regarding family help to the elderly are unrealistic—even dysfunctional, given recent demographic and social change. One asks: "At what point does the expectation of filial responsibility become social irresponsibility?"[22]

It is quite possible that as a result of dramatic and rapid demographic change—particularly the enormous increase in the proportion of people who survive to advanced old age and face chronic health problems—we are finding that old attitudes and expectations about family care for impaired members simply do not work. The main casualties of this situation are likely to be middle-aged and young-old women, who face unmanageable burdens or strong feelings of guilt. It is important, however, to regard to such conclusions cautiously; in devoting so much attention to the sick and the needy old, we may go too far in equating "old" with "needy."

The Old as Resources

Television, newspapers, and popular magazines portray the old as a frail, dependent group that represents a drain on national and family resources. Yet there is a striking lack of perception of the old as *constituting a resource,* a lack that ignores economic as well as psychological realities. With regard to the family realm, few systematic efforts have been made to map the flow of material support from older generations to the young, even though "It is clear that the family is by far the most important welfare or redistributional mechanism even in an advanced industrial country like the U.S."[23] Available research evidence indicates that, overall, the old in Western industrialized societies tend to give more economic assistance than they receive.[24]

We may have overlooked some critical "safety-valve" functions performed by older generations. When families make plans, for example, regarding major purchases, they often count on the older generation as a potential back-up if a crisis should intervene. Most older people own property, while it is becoming increasingly difficult for the young to do so. Often, the young may not actually end up turning to their elders, but their choices and behavior would have been more restrained if the older generation were not there as potential support. Such functions of the older generations may constitute an important and much neglected aspect of modern grandparenthood.

Evidence shows that grandparents may serve as indirect "stabilizers" of family life. As a result of the clearer separation between parenthood and grandparenthood in the life of women, mothers may become more of a supportive force for their daughter's mothering.[25] Grandparents may help to render parents more understandable to their children, may function as arbitrators in conflicts between them, or may serve as confidants in difficult times. *How often* such mediation and arbitration occurs may not be the right question to ask; rather, we might inquire as to what extent families perceive grandparents as a potential "safety valve." Writers have pointed to two particular current social trends that are likely to activate grandparents as stress-buffers: the growing number of single adolescent parents and the high rates of divorce. In these cases, grandparents may take over some of the tasks of parenting. How often divorce leads to three-generational living, and how often grandparents provide substantial financial support to grandchildren following divorce, is not known, but a current study of divorce and grandparenthood shows grandparents on the "custodial side" to be significant factors in post-divorce adjustment.[26]

The Effects of Divorce and Remarriage

Many aging societies are, like the United States, divorcing societies. The historian Philippe Aries has suggested that this may be inevitable, because modern longevity makes marriage a much more long-term commitment than it was in the past. At the end of the nineteenth century, the average length of marriage until the time when one spouse died was about twenty-eight years. In the late 1970s, it was over forty-three years.[27] In the typical nineteenth-century family, one spouse was deceased before all the children were raised.

Nineteen hundred and seventy-four was the first year that more marriages in the U.S. were terminated by divorce than they were by death.[28] Nearly half of recent marriages will end in divorce. Trends in divorce and remarriage are shaping the life courses and kin networks of men, women, and children, and each of these groups faces somewhat different challenges as a result of marital disruption and family reconstitution.

Studies of the differences between men's and women's divorce experiences paint a picture of severe financial losses for women, and of weakened family networks for men. There is little doubt that for many women, divorce brings a severe reduction in standard of living and an uncertain financial future. This has ripple effects for children, who not only face reduced material resources, but who also have a mother who bears the strain of economic worries. In a study of college students whose parents had recently divorced, my colleagues and I found that nearly all said they worried about their mother's future. There is also good reason to think that divorce puts new stress on the parents of those divorcing, but they have tended to be the forgotten people in divorce research. For example, we do not know how often substantial financial aid is contributed to divorced children, especially daughters, nor do we know how often plans for retirement are postponed or otherwise altered as a result of children's marital break-ups. In cases of divorce after the age of forty, parents may find that their expectations regarding support from children, especially from daughters, are left unmet, because the divorce has depleted emotional and material resources. Like young adult children, such parents may also worry about the future of the middle-generation woman, who faces her own aging with uncertain support.

Among divorced women, roughly one-third never remarry. Overall, remarriage is becoming a disproportionately male experience in our society, especially after the age of forty. After the age of sixty-five, remarriage rates for men are about eight times as high as for women.[29] This is in part due to dramatically imbalanced sex ratios; in part it reflects cultural norms regarding age differentials between spouses. Furthermore, research on remarriage following divorce in the early phase of adulthood has found that financial and educational resources operate quite differently in shaping remarriage probabilities among men and women. The more resources the woman has available (measured in education and income), the less likely she is to remarry.[30] For men, the trend is reversed. This suggests that the populations of those men and women who have divorced but not remarried are going to be quite different. Among women who divorced in the 1970s and 1980s, a number are resourceful individuals who already will have lived decades of life on their own as they face their early old age at the turn of the century.

Divorce and remarriage create more disruption in men's family networks than in women's. In a study of midlife divorce, my colleague and I found that many of the men expressed concern about the viability of family bonds. About a third felt that relationships with their children had suffered as a result of the break-up. More than half of the men reported that the parents were worried about losing touch with their grandchildren. The corresponding figure for women was under 10 percent. The men repeatedly expressed a sense of "not having a family anymore." What some seemed to be struggling with was the loss of their kin-keeper, the wife.

As we noted earlier, recent studies suggest that divorce may lead to an intensification of bonds to grandparents on the "custodial side," but to a weakening of ties to the "non-custodial" grandparents. Based on findings from the midlife divorce study, it seems reasonable to conclude that custody is not the critical factor. Rather, contact between grandparents and grandchildren is typically mediated through the middle generation, even after the children are grown. Because the mother often serves as a kin keeper for her husband's kin, divorce disrupts such mediation on the paternal side. The lack of contact between many divorced fathers and their children further aggravates this problem. Thus, a growing number of paternal grandparents face the loss of active grandparenthood as a ripple effect of their children's divorce.

A growing number of grandparents will also face the phenomenon of having step-grandchildren, although no figures are available on how common this experience is in our society. Much recent discussion has focused on how divorce and family reconstitution create complex kin relations for today's children. It has been argued, for example, that a growing number of children have more than two sets of grandparents. What we often forget is that marital disruption and remarriage have been part of childhood experiences throughout history; the only notable change is that the disruption now commonly is caused by divorce rather than death.[31]

Nevertheless, there are some ways in which divorce creates complexities in kin relations that are not encountered when death is the cause of marital endings. Recent estimates state the probability of children under sixteen experiencing the divorce of their parents at over one-third. Researchers provide some dramatic findings on the consequences of parental divorce for children's life course. A large number of children lose virtually all contact with one parent, typically the father. Furthermore, among children who experience remarriage following divorce, nearly 40 percent will experience divorce number two.[32] A growing number of children, parents, and grandparents will have the experience of expending a great deal of effort on making step-relationships work, only to find them eventually dissolve. At the present time, such ex-relationships have no legal protection. Recent trends in divorce and remarriage give rise to a number of complex questions. How will children of divorce, remarriage, and redivorce approach the formation and maintenance of attachments during their own adult years? What patterns of support will exist between aging parents and children in families where the mother was divorced and turned to her children for help in earlier adulthood? What will be the relationships between aging fathers and children with whom they had only sporadic contact for many years, and for whom they did not pay regular support? Will the mother-daughter axis become even more important as the mainstay of family organization and cohesion in the twenty-first century?

FAMILY WORLDS AND LIFE EXPERIENCES: A WIDENING GAP BETWEEN MEN AND WOMEN?

Many of the changes explored in this essay pertain more closely to life paths and family patterns among women than to those among men. Reduced mortality and greater longevity have been far more pronounced for women, and altered fertility patterns have reshaped women's adulthood more than men's. In addition, the more distinct demarcation between generations is more evident in female than in male lines, and the clearer sequencing of parenthood and grandparenthood is more typical of women's life course than of men's. The most durable intergenerational bond is that between mother and daughter, and more women than men experience life in multigenerational families.

Such contrasts in demographic trends, combined with recent cultural changes, may indeed have created new or sharper differences between the social worlds of men and women, both in the family realm and in society at large.

Increased Matrilineality?

As we have noted briefly, women are kin keepers, and the mother-daughter link is critical in the creation of family continuity and in the flow of intergenerational support. As Alice Rossi points out elsewhere in this volume, the historical shift from economic to emotional interdependence in the family, and the increasing role of non-family institutions in providing financial security for young and old, may have reduced core aspects of male family roles; however, they have further bolstered traditional female roles such as care giving and the provision of emotional support.

There are several reasons why families in the early twenty-first century are likely to have a stronger "female axis" than has recently been the case: the longer period of the joint survival of mothers and daughters; historical changes in their role patterns; trends in divorce and remarriage; and non-marital fertility.

The first part of the next century may witness generations of mothers and daughters who not only share the experiences of growing old, but whose adult lives have been more similar than was the case in the latter part of this century. Women born in the 1940s belong to "transitional cohorts" between strikingly different groups. It is not until the 1950 cohort that we see the emergence of "new women" who have high levels of education, smaller families, and fairly continuous work histories. These women will be young-old mothers of mid-adult daughters in the first decades of the twenty-first century.

If current trends in marital disruption persist, many mothers and daughters will spend a number of years when both are living without a spouse. It has previously been estimated that because of marital disruption, about 40 percent of children under sixteen can expect to spend some time with only one parent. In over 90 percent of the cases, that parent is the mother. Often, such projections did not consider the possibility of non-marital fertility. During the last few years, nearly 20 percent of all children born have had unmarried mothers. A current analysis that covers children born to married as well as to unmarried mothers provides some startling projections on the life experiences of children in the last two decades of this century.[33] The study estimates that by the time children born in 1980 turn seventeen, more than 80 percent of them will have spent some time living with only one parent. Recently, writers have voiced concern not only about how recent social change has affected fathers and male family lines, but also about how it has strained the quality of men's anchoring in community life.

Contrasts Between Men's and Women's Social Networks

Alice Rossi predicts that parenthood will be increasingly dissociated from marriage. She expresses concern that when a growing number of mothers are solo parents, men are missing out on significant mechanisms to tie them into communal activities. Most women in our society experience a time when their identity in the surrounding community is defined in terms of being someone's mother. To what extent they go through a later phase when they are defined as someone's daughter, we don't know. What we do know is that, throughout their lives, women find it easier to cross age and generation boundaries than men do. Research has found that men, starting in boyhood, regard age differences as more salient and tend to orient themselves to horizontal relationships with age peers.[34] In the adult years, women's social networks are larger and more diverse than those of men.[35] For example, women are much more likely to have confidant relationships which are vertical—that is, to span generational lines. Recent trends in fertility and marital disruption may further weaken men's involvement in vertical ties and lead to even greater contrasts between men's and women's networks.

Two demographers also discuss men's declining involvement with young children and express concern about it as a trend.[36] They point out that between 1960 and 1980, the average male life course showed a dramatic decline in number of years involved with children, and they suggest that this may have serious consequences for the psychological development of men, such as their ability to be nurturant and altruistic, or for the quality of their attention to values and life priorities. They also ask if men who do not have regular contact with children will be ready to support public spending on schools and social programs for the young.

All of this suggests that our society may currently be in a somewhat paradoxical situation. During recent decades, ideology has stressed equality between the sexes in their family roles. Yet, as we have seen, demographic and social changes have in many ways created very different family worlds for men and women. An increasing proportion of men have only precarious vertical ties, both up and down generational lines, while women's intergenerational ties are more varied, complex, and durable than ever before in human history.

Families are social arenas in which historical changes take on personal and shared meanings. They are also groups that meet critical human needs, and settings where biographies are written and rewritten as lives unfold, take on structure, and become interwoven. This chapter has reviewed some of the recent demographic and social changes that have transformed family life. Siblings, parents and children, grandparents and grandchildren, now look forward to decades of shared biographies. Altered patterns of mortality have not only created relationships of unprecedented duration, but have also made the timing of family deaths more predictable. As the number of children per family has decreased, differences in life experiences among siblings have become reduced, and a greater proportion of family relationships are conducted across generational lines rather than with generational peers. Trends in fertility and mortality have resulted in increasingly "top-heavy" families, and family care-giving has become more and more focused on very old members. Multigenerational families have become more common, which means that a wider spectrum of kinship roles and relationships are open to family members.

Finally, many of these recent changes have affected men and women quite differently, in some ways creating sharper contrasts between their family and social worlds.

ENDNOTES

Work on this paper was supported by a Research Career Development Award from the National Institute on Aging, grant no. 1 K 04 AG 00203.

[1]Ronald Blythe, *The View in Winter* (New York: Harcourt, Brace, Jovanovich, 1979).

[2]For further discussion, see Gunhild O. Hagestad and Bernice L. Neugarten, "Age and the Life Course," in Ethel Shanas and Robert H. Binstock, eds., *Handbook of Aging and the Social Sciences,* 2nd ed. (New York: Van Nostrand and Reinhold, 1985), pp. 35–61.

[3]This discussion is based on the work by Peter Uhlenberg, "Death and the Family," *Journal of Family History,* Fall 1980, pp. 313–20; and "Changing Configurations of the Life Course," in T. Hareven, ed., *Transitions: The Family and the Life Course in Historical Perspectives* (New York: Academic Press, 1978), pp. 65–97.

[4]Halliman H. Winsborough, "A Demographic Approach to the Life Cycle," in Kurt W. Back, ed., *Life Course: Integrative Theories and Exemplary Populations* (Boulder, CO: Westview Press, 1978), pp. 65–67..

[5]Tamara K. Hareven, "Family Time and Historical Time," *Daedalus,* Spring 1977, pp. 57–70.

[6]Arlene S. Skolnick, *The Intimate Environment,* 2nd ed. (Boston: Little, Brown, 1978); John Demos, *A Little Commonwealth: Family Life in Plymouth Colony* (New York: Oxford University Press, 1970).

[7]Uhlenberg, "Changing Configurations of the Life Course," op. cit.

[8]For a recent overview, see Candice Feiring and Michael Lewis, "Changing Characteristics of the U.S. Family," in M. Lewis, ed., *Beyond the Dyad* (New York: Plenum, 1984), pp. 59–89..

[9]Samuel H. Preston, "Children and the Elderly in the U.S.," *Scientific American,* Dec. 1984, pp. 44–49.

[10]Ursula Lehr and Wolfgang Schneider, "Fünf-Generationen-Familien: einige Daten über UrurgroBeltern in der Bundesrepublik Deutschland," *Zeitschrift für Gerontologie,* no. 5, 1983, pp. 200–204.

[11]Hagestad, "Continuity and Connectedness," in Vern L. Bengston and Joan F. Robertson, eds., *Grandparenthood* (Beverly Hills, CA, 1985: Sage Publications), pp. 31–48.

[12]John Modell, Frank F. Furstenberg, Jr., and Theodore Hershberg, "Social Change and Transitions to Adulthood in Historical Perspective," *Journal of Family,* Winter 1976, pp. 7–32.

[13]Matilda White Riley, "The Family in an Aging Society: A Matrix of Latent Relationships," *Journal of Family Issues,* Sept. 1983, pp. 439–54.

[14]Lillian E. Troll, Shiela J. Miller, and Robert C. Atchley, *Families in Later Life* (Belmont, CA: Wadsworth Publishing Co., 1979).

[15]Shanas and Marvin B. Sussman, eds., *Family, Bureaucracy, and the Elderly* (Durham, N.C.: Duke University Press, 1977).

[16]Kiyomi Morioka, *Family Life Cycle: Theory Research and Practice,* (Tokyo: Baifukan, 1973).

[17]Troll, et al., op. cit.

[18]Kari Waerness, "The Invisible Welfare State: Women's Work at Home," *Acta Sociologica,* supplement 1978, pp. 193–207.

[19]Elaine M. Brody, "Aged Parents and Aging Children," in P.K. Ragan, ed., *Aging Parents* (Los Angeles: University of Southern California Press, 1979), pp. 267–88.

[20]Eleanor Palo Stroller, "Parental Caregiving by Adult Children," *Journal of Marriage and the Family,* Nov. 1983, pp. 851–58.

[21]Betty Friedan, *The Second Stage* (New York: Summit Books, 1981).

[22] Brody, op. cit.

[23] James Morgan, "The Redistribution of Income by Families and Institutions in Emergency Help Patterns," in Greg Duncan and James Morgan, eds., *5000 American Families: Patterns of Economic Progress,* vol. 10 (Ann Arbor, MI: Institute for Social Research, 1983), pp. 1–59.

[24] Reuben Hill, Nelson Foote, et al., *Family Development in Three Generations* (Cambridge, MA: Schenkman, 1970).

[25] For a discussion of relevant work, see Barbara R. Tinsley and Ross D. Parke, "Grandparents as Support and Socialization Agents," in Lewis, ed., *Beyond the Dyad* (New York: Plenum, 1984).

[26] Hans von Hentig, "The Sociological Function of Grandmother," *Social Forces,* May 1946, p. 389.

[27] Furstenberg, Jame L. Peterson, et al., "The Life Course of Children of Divorce: Marital Disruption and Parental Contact," *American Sociological Review,* Oct. 1983, pp. 656–68.

[28] Noreen Goldman and Graham Lord, "Sex Differences in Life Cycle Measures of Widowhood," *Demography,* May 1983, pp. 177–95.

[29] Paul C. Glick, "Remarriage: Some Recent Changes and Variations," *Journal of Family Issues,* Dec. 1980, pp. 455–78.

[30] National Center for Health Statistics: advance report, final marriage statistics, 1980. *Monthly Vital Statistics Report,* vol. 32, no. 4, supp. PHHS pub. no. (PHS) 83-1120. Public Health Service, Hyattsville, MD, Aug. 1983.

[31] Graham B. Spanier and Paul C. Glick, "Paths to Remarriage," *Journal of Divorce,* Spring 1980, pp. 283–98.

[32] John Demos, "Old Age in Early New England," in Michael Gordon, ed., *The American Family in Social-Historical Perspective,* 2nd ed., (New York: St. Martin's Press, 1978).

[33] Furstenberg, et al., op. cit.

[34] Sandra L. Hofferth, "Updating Children's Life Course," *Journal of Marriage and the Family,* Feb. 1985, pp. 93–115.

[35] For a discussion of relevant work, see Hagestad and Neugarten, op. cit.

[36] Toni Antonnuci, "Personal Characteristics, Social Support, and Social Behavior," in Binstock and Shanas, eds., op. cit.

[37] David Eggebeen and Peter Uhlenberg, "Changes in the Organization of Men's Lives: 1960–1980," *Family Relations,* April 1985, pp. 251–57.

Harold A. Richman and Matthew W. Stagner

Children: Treasured Resource or Forgotten Minority?

I T HAS BEEN SAID THAT Americans hold a "conceit that no one has done as much or thought as much about children as we have in this century."[1] Yet the percentage of children in poverty today is one-and-a-half times the percentage of all people in poverty.[2] Our unemployment rate for youths ages sixteen to nineteen is nearly three times greater than the unemployment rate for adults over age twenty.[3] And while the adult suicide rate has declined, the suicide rate for children has risen dramatically over the last twenty-five years.[4]

It is indeed ironic that these should be the facts at the end of a century-and-a-half of changes designed to bring special status and protections to children—changes that began in the nineteenth century only as the mechanization of agriculture made it possible for farm children to begin to substitute school work for field work.[5] At the same time, rapid urbanization was altering the lives of city children, and the need for special protection for young people became increasingly apparent, a cause taken up by turn-of-the-century progressive reformers, aided by muckrakers' accounts of the plight of children in poverty. John Spargo's *The Bitter Cry of the Children* was one of a number of especially effective accounts that centered the nation's attention on the conditions of its children.

The demand for legislation to protect children began in earnest in the 1880s, but the early laws proved ineffective. Then, in 1899, Illinois created the nation's first special court for juveniles. Other states followed its lead, enacting legislation to limit child labor, establish compulsory school attendance, and promote child and maternal health.[6] These were the first effective laws to differentiate the world of children from that of adults. The White House Conferences on Children, first held in 1909 and repeated every decade thereafter, became a measure of the nation's increasing concern for the welfare of children, and public policies throughout the twentieth century have sought continually to define and extend further protections and benefits to them. How, then, have we arrived at the troubling conditions described by the figures that begin this essay?

THE PARADOX

Despite the importance of the social, economic, and political events that transformed the lives of children, two very different factors have come to account for the contemporary evolution of childhood as a period of special concern and investment: the gradual decrease in mortality rates—especially child mortality rates—and the increase in adult life expectancy. These demographic changes have altered American attitudes towards children in two ways.

First, the increased likelihood that individual children will live to adulthood makes it easier for parents to become emotionally invested in individual children and to plan for their future. One of the most lucid accounts of the effects of decreasing child mortality is found in Phillipe Aries's *Centuries of Childhood*. Aries argued that the indifference that prevailed toward children in earlier eras was a direct consequence of demography, as "people could not allow themselves to become too attached to something that was regarded as a probable loss."[7] Historically, emotional and financial investment in children began in earnest only after mortality rates for children fell.[8] By the early twentieth century, the rapid improvement in child mortality rates was accelerating the transformation of how Americans viewed children.[9] It is now a general expectation that an American child will live to become an adult,[10] but as late as 1900, more than one out of ten American children died before the age of twenty.

The second way in which we have altered our attitude towards children has to do with the steady increase in the number of years Americans expect to live after reaching adulthood, a development that makes it increasingly appropriate to view childhood as a time of preparation for adult life.[11] A century ago, Americans may have been fortunate to live to age fifty, while today's adults can reasonably expect to live beyond age seventy. One way we have reacted as individuals to this increased life expectancy is to determine that the preparation for adulthood—through education and segregation from the adult sphere of work—should encompass more of our early years.

It is paradoxical, then, that the same demographic forces that have contributed to a special social status for children have created an aging society in which that status may be threatened. As these demographic processes continue into the twenty-first century, public and private concern for children may begin to decrease for the first time since the early nineteenth century. The number of people who survive to old age will grow, the birth rate will probably continue to decline, and children will come to represent an ever-decreasing proportion of American society. Since 1960, when children under age eighteen made up over one third (35.7 percent) of the total U.S. population, the percentage of children in America has fallen dramatically. By 1980, their proportion of the population had dropped to just over a quarter (27.9 percent), and by 2030 it may drop to just over a fifth (21.6 percent).[12] At the same time, the fastest-growing segment of society will be older people, who as a group may require increasing amounts of private and public attention and resources, especially as the number of older people over age eighty-five expands rapidly.

THE CONSEQUENCES

The aging society poses two possible consequences for America's children. They may become a treasured resource, nurtured all the more for their scarcity and importance to the nation's future. Or they may come to be regarded, amid the increasing clamor for resources and attention by other dependent groups, as only another needy minority.

If we are to speculate responsibly on the consequences that an aging society might impose on America's children, we must recognize that children are unique among other dependents in our society. Most of the economic and emotional resources we direct towards children are provided by or transferred through the family. At the same time, society as a whole has a strong stake in the development of its future generations, and government has assumed ultimate responsibility for those children who are not adequately cared for by families. It is not possible, then, to consider either private or public policy investments alone as a barometer of our concern for children in an aging society. We must look at both separately and in concert.

The Optimistic View: Children as a Treasured Resource

The first possible consequence we have noted—the greater nurturance of children as they become a scarcer resource—suggests that in an aging society Americans will recognize the increasing need for young people who are healthy, well-motivated, and properly educated. Although they will be fewer in number, they will be relied on for labor, military defense, and the economic support of at least some portion of the aging population. The increase in life expectancy across all age groups, and the "bulge" in population created by the postwar baby boom, have created a situation in which Americans entering their productive years in the next few decades will be responsible for providing support to a greater number of older people than in the past—even though the *total* burden of dependency will be roughly the same as in previous generations. As table 1 shows, the *total* "dependency ratio"—that is, the ratio of those under age eighteen and over age sixty-five to those between ages eighteen and sixty-five—may differ little in 2030 from that of 1960. But the support of those who are over age sixty-five will be an increasing burden on those of working age. Unless unforeseeable changes are made in the Social Security system, most Americans over age sixty-five will be at least partially dependent on younger workers.

It may also be argued that, to grow and prosper, our society will increasingly need to explore new ideas and press forward with technological development. From this perspective, the young will experience growing pressures to provide the inspiration and innovation that will be required to retain America's economic and social strength. All these factors may create public pressure for increasing the nurturance and resources devoted to the children who will become the workers, providers, innovators, and defenders of our aging society.

Children in an aging society may also benefit from the decreasing competition for "children's items." This Malthusian argument assumes the existence of an approximately fixed amount of resources earmarked for children, and suggests that the decreasing numbers of children will result in the availability of more resources for each child.

TABLE 1. Number of Dependents per 100 Persons Age 18 to 65 in the U.S.

Year	Youth Dependency Ratio	Elderly Dependency Ratio	Total Dependency Ratio
1960	64.9	16.8	81.6
1980	46.0	18.6	64.6
2000	40.7	21.1	61.8
2030	37.8	37.0	74.8

SOURCE: U.S. Census Bureau, *Projections of the Population of the United States, By Age, Sex, and Race: 1983–2080*, Table D.

At first glance, such an argument seems improbable, yet for some "children's items"—educational resources, for example—it may hold true to some degree. The sheer number of children in the baby-boom generation overwhelmed the educational system; many were crowded into badly overextended facilities while authorities rushed to build new schools. The generation that followed now faces less competition for educational resources.

The very fact that American families will be composed of fewer children may imply that families will care more about children and provide more for them. Gary Becker refers to this issue as the trade-off between the "quantity" and the "quality" of children.[13] And as the costs of providing basic necessities for a child escalate, it can be expected that families will choose to have still fewer children, and to invest more in each child. (Empirical evidence suggests that smaller families spend more on each child.)[14] Becker also proposes that the increasing economic investment in each child shows that parents and children may be emotionally closer than they have ever been.[15]

The Pessimistic View: Children as a Forgotten Minority

On the other hand, the decreasing numbers of children in an aging society could *decrease* resources devoted to children. As they become a smaller part of each family and a smaller percentage of society as a whole, their claims may become overshadowed by those of other dependent groups, and their interests overlooked or ignored.

Families may well hope to increase the "quality" of their children by having fewer of them, but it is extremely difficult to document how much of a family's economic resources actually are directed toward its children. Neither the "public" goods that are contained within the household—such as heat and electricity—nor the "private" goods that are often shared—such as a bar of soap—can be easily assigned as exclusive expenditures for either adults or children.[16] Little research has been directed toward intrafamily transfers to children, but recent examinations suggest that such expenditures vary according to the location of the household, as well as the adults' ages, income, and education and the children's ages and gender. As household income increases, for example, children receive relatively less of the increase than do adults. On the other hand, a rise in the education level of a household's head raises expenditures on children.[17] The changes that we might expect an aging society to affect in the economic investment in children, then, are difficult to separate from the other changes that take place in American families.

Nevertheless, it may be that if the survival of older family members presents a greater financial responsibility for middle-age providers in a family, it will become difficult for those providers to spend as much as they now do on children. In 1980, the average forty-year-old couple had nearly identical numbers of living parents and children: 2.59 parents and 2.72 children. If the 1980 rates of fertility and mortality persist, a forty-year-old couple in 2020 can expect to have 2.88 living parents and 1.78 living children.[18] Faced with increasing pressures to assist older family members, families will find it difficult to avoid the transfer of at least some resources away from children.

What can we expect to happen to *public* investment in, and commitment to, children as American society ages? The effects of an aging society on public support for children can be documented more clearly than private support for children. Just as investment by the family varies according to the number of children in the family, investment by society may vary as the number of children in society changes. The percentage of children in the American population has decreased fairly consistently throughout the twentieth century. This decrease has been exaggerated by the brief rise in the percentage of children during the baby boom and by the rapid decrease that followed as that generation moved into adulthood.

The decrease in the percentage of children may have profound consequences for their public support. A society that requires young workers to help support an aging population may find itself demanding earlier entry into the labor market, forcing the shortening of childhood for some Americans. As other groups compete for resources, public expenditures for children may be cut back, and the tendency to consider children as special dependents who deserve protection from adult pressures may be reversed. In short, as society ages, it may become easier to ignore the special needs of children.

This prospect is particularly significant because it would mean a reversal in government's acceptance, since the nineteenth century, of its increasing responsibility for children. The growing focus on children has been most apparent in the accelerated expenditures for education, but government at all levels has strengthened its role in children's family life and economic well-being. Not only has it expanded its powers to remove a child from his home; it has also expanded its commitment to providing some level of economic support for poor families with children. While many public investments in children are made through the intervening mechanism of the family, public expenditures have represented an integral part of society's investment in children and symbolized a commitment to them.

THE EARLY EVIDENCE

We have presented both an optimistic and a pessimistic speculation about the consequences an aging society presents for America's children. The actual situation will most likely fall somewhere between these two extremes, but which trend can we reasonably expect to be stronger? Enough evidence now exists to make it possible for us to examine the record of the early stages of the aging society, and to determine how children have fared to this point. Two trends of the past twenty years suggest that there is good reason for concern.

First, Americans have not been particularly committed to supporting children as a group with growing needs. As the number of women in the work force expands, the necessity for daycare has increased greatly, but no national daycare program has been implemented. Even though there is virtually unanimous agreement that children belong only in special and separate facilities, the population of children in adult prisons has grown since the early 1970s.[19] And public support for education may be slipping as America ages: the 1983 Gallup poll of public attitudes toward the public schools found that for those respondents under age fifty, 45 percent supported an increase in taxes for public education, while 46 percent opposed it. At age fifty and above, only 28 percent supported increasing taxes for education, while 62 percent opposed it.[20] Surveys of voters in Massachusetts, following the passage of Proposition 2½—which cut property taxes—found that older people in households without children were less likely than other respondents to favor higher expenditures for education, and were more likely to favor decreases in education expenditures rather than decreases in other locally provided services.[21]

Perhaps more important than the declining concern for the needs of *all* children is that our basic economic support for *needy* children, never generous in the first place, is declining even further. We have observed that the economic resources devoted to children cannot easily be compared to those of other dependent groups, first because children have a special economic relationship within the family, and second because the changing proportions of children and older people within society at large suggests that aggregate public resources devoted to these groups cannot be compared over time. We would expect that groups increasing in proportionate size would require proportionately larger resources. Therefore, the best way to compare the economic well-being of children with that of other dependent groups is to use the post-transfer poverty rate. This is one measure of well-being that includes both public and private resources and is calculated on a per capita rather than an aggregate basis.

Table 2 shows that since 1969, children have been increasingly likely to live in poverty, while older Americans have improved their

TABLE 2. Poverty Rate by Age Group in U.S., 1959–1983

	1959	1969	1975	1983
Percentage in Poverty (Under Age 18)	26.9	14.1	16.8	22.2
Percentage in Poverty (Age 65 or Over)	35.2	25.3	15.3	14.1
Percentage in Poverty (All Ages)	22.4	12.2	12.3	15.2

SOURCE: Social Security Bulletin, Annual Statistical Supplement, 1983, p. 66, and U.S. Census Bureau, Current Population Reports Series P-60, no. 147, *Characteristics of the Population Below the Poverty Level: 1983*, p. 40.

economic well-being dramatically. Looking at the poverty figures in a slightly different manner, we can note that in 1970 the incidence of poverty among children under age fourteen was 37 percent less than the incidence of poverty among older people; by 1982 the incidence of poverty among children was 56 percent greater than among older people.[22] The reasons for this difference can be understood by looking at the manner in which we provide public resources for these two dependent groups.

The changing relationship between the poverty rate for children and the poverty rate for older people can be traced to three characteristics of the America public welfare system. First, older Americans have been granted the benefits of comprehensive economic and medical assistance programs—Social Security Retirement and Medicare, programs available to nearly all older people regardless of their economic standing. Children—or families with children—have no such programs to facilitate their support. Second, the means-tested economic assistance program for older people—Supplemental Security Income (SSI)—is indexed to inflation, and is available regardless of the potential recipient's living arrangements. In contrast, Aid to Families with Dependent Children (AFDC), our major economic support program for the young, is not indexed for inflation, and covers only children of single parents—and in less than half the states, children with two parents where the breadwinner is unemployed and meets certain other eligibility criteria. Third, programs for older Americans are national programs that avoid the dramatic state-by-state variations that characterize AFDC.

When we compare the benefit levels for each of these programs with the change in real value of benefit levels for each over the past two decades, much of the divergence between the poverty rates of children and older people becomes understandable. Table 3 shows the amount and percent of grant increases in each program between 1965 and 1981. Table 4 (page 172) compares the figures in a different way, measuring the benefit level of each program against the government poverty level. Note in particular the rapid decrease in AFDC benefits as percent of poverty level in Northern industrial states such as New York and Illinois. On the question of relative adequacy, the differences across states and the differences in how well the programs compensated for inflation speak for themselves.

The findings for the three programs displayed in tables 3 and 4 are not strictly comparable. In fact, as we indicate above, Social Security, SSI, and AFDC are very different on a number of dimensions. Tables 3 and 4 should not be read as a deliberate triumph of older people as a group against the interests of children; instead, the tables are intended to depict the effects of our historically different types and terms of assistance for children and older people.

Clearly, government economic support for older people has been improving, compared with support for children and their families during the early stages of the aging society. We can expect this trend to continue as the percentage of older people increases and as interest in their plight becomes a greater issue for the middle-aged. This is particularly alarming because children's need for public support will be increasing into the twenty-first century. First, a higher percentage of children will be living in single-parent families. The proportion of children not living with two parents (and primarily living with their mothers) will increase to over one-quarter of all children by 1990.[23] Second, a higher percentage of children will be members of minority groups. In 1950, 11.8 percent of all children under age nineteen were

TABLE 3. Amount and Percent Grant Increase 1965–1981 (in 1983 dollars)

	1965	1975	1981	% Change 1965–1981
AFDC and Food Stamps, Combined Monthly Benefit for Family of One Adult and Three Children with No Income[1]				
California	$674	$618	$628	−6.8%
Colorado	497	529	454	−8.6
Illinois	756	684	487	−35.6
Mississippi	185	249	268	+45.0
New York	769	760	558	−27.4
Texas	210	358	288	+37.0
U.S. Average	467	405	309	−33.9
SSI and Food Stamps, Combined Monthly Payment per Aged Person[2]				
U.S. Average	$219	$212	$198	−9.6%
Social Security, Monthly Payment per Retired Worker				
U.S. Average	$282	$394	$440	+56.4%

SOURCE: U.S. Department on Commerce, Bureau of the Census, *Statistical Abstract of the United States, 1982–1983*, p. 342; and 1966, p. 305.
[1] The states shown were chosen to present both a geographical balance and a range of benefit levels.
[2] Over half the SSI recipients in the nation also receive Social Security (Bureau of the Census, 1982–83, p. 340).

TABLE 4. Relationship Between Government Assistance Level and Government Defined Poverty Level, 1965–1981 (Government Benefit Level as Percent of Poverty Level: Poverty Level = 100%)

	1965	1975	1981
AFDC and Food Stamps, Family Benefit for One Adult and Three Children with No Income[1]			
California	79.4%	72.8%	74.1%
Colorado	58.6	62.3	53.5
Illinois	89.1	80.6	57.2
Mississippi	21.8	29.4	31.6
New York	90.6	89.6	65.8
Texas	24.8	42.3	33.9
SSI and Food Stamps, Monthly Payment per Aged Person[2]			
U.S. Average	56.1%	54.1%	50.7%
Social Security, Monthly Payment per Retired Worker			
U.S. Average	70.8%	99.2%	110.8%

SOURCE: U.S. Department on Commerce, Bureau of the Census, *Statistical Abstract of the United States*, 1982–1983, p. 342; and 1966, p. 305; and U.S. Department of Health and Human Services, *Social Security Bulletin, Annual Statistical Supplement*, 1983, p. 102.

[1] The states shown were chosen to present both a geographical balance and a range of benefit levels.

[2] Over half of the SSI recipients in the nation also receive Social Security (Bureau of the Census, 1982–83, p. 340).

black.[24] By 1980, the percentage of black children grew to 14.6 percent;[25] by 2030 that percentage may exceed 19 percent.[26] The percentage of children who are members of any minority group—including Hispanics, Asians, and others—will be even greater. By 2030, according to Census Bureau projections, nearly one-quarter of all children born in America will belong to a minority group.[27]

Both the increasing percentage of minority children and the increasing percentage of children who live in single-parent families suggest that, without significant changes, an increasing percentage of children will live in poverty. The incidence of poverty in female-headed families currently is more than five times greater than that in two-parent families.[28] The growth in the number of female-headed families has already added to the great expansion in the welfare caseload over the past two decades.[29] Based on the changing ratio of female-headed families to two-parent families alone, demographers expect that the number of children under age six living in poverty will increase twenty-seven percent during the 1980s.

Black children are much more likely to live in poverty than are white children. In Illinois, for example, the poverty rate in 1980 for black children was 38 percent, compared with a poverty rate for white children of only 7 percent. While some of this difference was due to the greater proportion of black children living in female-headed families, the poverty rate for black children in two-parent families was over three times that of white children in two-parent families.[30]

The trends towards increasing percentages of poor children who are in female-headed and minority families suggest that in the coming years children will require increasing public economic support—in addition to the support they now require for academic and vocational education, protection from harm, preventive health care, and assistance to the chronically ill and emotionally disturbed. This expanded need will come at a time when the aging of American society, the declining numbers of children, and the changing composition of the child population will all converge, potentially diverting the public's attention from their plight.

THE RESPONSE

In response to this real and projected decrease in attention to the needs of children in general, and to the needs of poor children and those with special problems in particular, several strategies might be considered for improving support and services for children and their families. Perhaps the most obvious strategy is to strengthen organized advocacy efforts on behalf of children. At the national level, the Children's Defense Fund has proven a durable and effective force, especially on behalf of the interests of poor and minority children. Yet it cannot do the job alone, especially because the most important target of present and future advocacy on behalf of children is not necessarily federal policy. Much of the primary public responsibility and activity now resides at the state and local levels, and while several effective state and local children's advocacy groups do exist, their numbers and strength are small for the tasks they confront, and they must cope with the inherent political weakness of a voteless constituency. One way to counteract that weakness is to build advocacy coalitions with stronger groups who also depend on continued public support. Here, older people are potential allies, both because they represent greater potential political strength, and because they already have organizational capacities for advocacy.

Whether the strategy of greater advocacy is enacted on behalf of children alone or in concert with advocacy for older people or others, it presents a major difficulty. Increased advocacy on behalf of one or even two interest groups inevitably pits one group against another in competition for available resources, a plight that can result in the erosion and fragmentation of community responsibility to all dependents. This kind of depletion can take its toll both on the resources that are available for the welfare of all dependents, as well as on the strength and cohesion of the community as it seeks to meet its responsibilities. Perhaps the fragmentation is best illustrated by the tendency within the children's field, as in many other areas, towards single-issue, rather than comprehensive, advocacy. The cry is for daycare *or* seatbelts for children *or* special education *or* aid for handicapped children *or* child-abuse prevention and treatment. When one attempts to turn the "ors" into "ands," enthusiasm diminishes, for the intensity that characterizes single-issue advocacy becomes diffused when the message is broadened to the need to invest in *all* children for the strength of our future. The immediate appeal that attracts constituents and media attention loses its glamor, and the impulse to action becomes dampened.

Rather than—or perhaps in addition to—increasing categorical advocacy, a different organizing principle might be developed, one that does not rest on competition in the public arena among dependent populations, but focuses rather on *common helping functions.* The process of assisting dependent populations should be one that helps the individual and his or her family, while at the same time building and strengthening the community rather than dividing it. Instead of organizing support for dependents in terms of their age, family structure, or economic group, organizing according to the kind of help they need can achieve both these goals.

Focusing on the common interest may present a more generally compelling case for community attention than insisting on the specialness and priority of each dependent group. The key to developing such a new organizing principle lies in the recognition among dependent groups that the conditions of their dependency need not create competition, but can create a shared interest and a claim in the community for certain common forms of support and assistance.

The usual manner of serving the common interest of two or more dependent groups is for each to "work for each other." In this manner, often called "double social utility," one dependent group supports another, usually either for pay or for some other form of recognition, thus achieving a gain for themselves as well as providing help for others: one example is for older people to serve in some helping capacity in day-care centers.

Double social utility is often a successful and mutually beneficial strategy, but another principle for aiding dependents rests on an even broader and more fundamental commonality of interest. As certain common helping functions become accepted as appropriate community responses to the needs of a variety of dependent populations, it might be desirable to organize services according to these functions, rather than by separate dependent populations such as children or older people.

For example, many temporarily or permanently homebound or disabled people of all ages can, with varying degrees of assistance, achieve some measure of independence and remain outside an institution. The organizing principle for services provided can be the type of service itself—be it assisting with chores, providing medical surveillance, doing social or educational visiting, or providing meals to assist both the dependent individual and his or her employed parent or primary caretaker. It is not only difficult, but isolating and wasteful, to organize, finance, maintain, and staff a separate care facility for each type of dependent individual and family situation. Here the focus is not on a categorical characterization by age, disease entity, or family structure, but on the need and the service to meet it.

Respite care and sheltered-work opportunities are other special community care functions that have the potential of transcending the competing demands of dependent groups. Organized by the community for all its dependent individuals and their families, respite care would allow the community to marshal and employ its limited resources on behalf of *all* its affected citizens. Sheltered-work opportunities are a dignified and constructive way for young people out of school, long-term unemployed, handicapped and physically disabled youths and adults, chronically mentally ill, and older people to spend as much productive time as their individual limitations allow. While it could not sustain separate operations for each dependent group, a community might well be able to manage a commonly available sheltered work program.

Moving from a categorically based service system to one that is functionally based would not be easy. The shift would require major changes in attitudes, institutional structures, and helping roles. But if the process of getting there might be wrenching, the probable result would justify it: more effective services for dependent groups, and strengthened communities.

Another possible course, and one that might approach the same results in a less potentially threatening, more functional manner, involves extending to children the two major strategies that have fostered the improved condition of older people over the last two decades. The first strategy is the direct provision of support to the dependent individual. Medicare and Social Security are primary examples of how this strategy now operates on behalf of older people. Both programs are virtually non-exclusionary and provide benefits directly to the individual, regardless of family structure. Even though there is uncontested agreement that medical care and cash subsistence are the bare essentials necessary for every child's development, we have no analogous provisions for all children. If our rationale for providing medical care and cash assistance to older people is that they deserve compensation for their contribution to our society, why it is not equally logical—and perhaps more compelling, given the increasing scarcity of children—to prepare the young for their contribution by providing the same necessities?

We have documented the dramatic differences in the financial support available to older people as compared with that available for children. There are strong historical reasons for the disparities, but they need not hold sway forever. Yet unless we find a new approach to our society's financial support function for children, the disparities will likely worsen. Applying the logic we have derived from our national experience with older people might provide the basis for rethinking our family income assistance dilemma, and for easing the alarming trend in child poverty. We are alone among Western industrial nations in not providing a support mechanism—such as a children's allowance—that is as non-exclusionary and non-stigmatizing as our provision for older people.

The second strategy that we might adapt from our programs for older people is to provide helping services to the dependent individual by empowering that individual's family to manage the situation. When special services are needed, this approach can both strengthen the family and provide for the needs of the dependent individual in the least intrusive, and often the least expensive, manner. As the demand for assistance policies and programs for the "frail elderly" and for older people in need of long-term care continues to grow, this strategy is assuming increasing importance. We are now beginning to recognize the need for a major effort to provide home help, chore services, health visitors, respite care, congregate or home-delivered meals, and other special supports for older people who are facing institutionalization because they cannot totally care for themselves, or because their families cannot carry the full burden. Why not extend this logic to children's needs? The current reality is that where we have needy families with troubled, sick, or handicapped children, we generally expect the families to manage on their own, or we go to the other extreme and assume total care for the child in an institution or foster home. Is it not as sensible, and as important, to strengthen families' abilities to cope with their children as well as their elders?

We have presented a sketch of how, as the population ages, the resources and attention that we now devote to creating and maintaining a special status for children in our society may be in a state of jeopardy. This endangered status comes at a time when children, although they comprise a smaller proportion of the total population, may present a greater claim on public resources because of their changing economic status and the changing composition of their families. Increased advocacy on behalf of children can help, but it can also have negative side effects in the community. Two alternative responses may be more beneficial for children. First, supports and services organized by function, rather than by presently defined target populations, may elicit fuller benefits than if children are competing as a separate entity for divided resources and fragmented attention. This approach can also engender a positive sense of community identity and obligation, fostered by a common concern and commitment for all dependent people in the community, rather than only for the temporarily favored or powerful. Second, why not strengthen our children for the responsibilities they will face in the future by applying the strategies that have improved the lot of older people over the last two decades? The burden our children will have to carry for us may be heavy. With fewer of them to manage it, we cannot afford a large margin of error in being certain that each child is fully prepared.

ENDNOTES

The authors wish to acknowledge the research assistance of Elizabeth Ruby.

[1]Bernard Wishy, *The Child and the Republic* (Philadelphia: University of Pennsylvania Press, 1968), p. viii.

[2]U.S. Dept. of Health and Human Services, *Social Security Bulletin, Annual Statistical Supplement 1983*, p. 40.

[3]U.S. Dept. of Labor, Bureau of Labor Statistics, *Monthly Labor Review*, March 1985, p. 62.

[4]National Center for Health Statistics, *Vital Statistics of the United States*, 1960 and 1983.

[5]Gary S. Becker, *A Treatise on the Family* (Cambridge: Harvard University Press, 1981), p. 111.

[6]Ray Ginger, *Altgeld's America: 1890–1905* (Chicago: Quadrangle Books, 1965), pp. 221–27.

[7]Phillipe Aries, *Centuries of Childhood*, trans. Robert Baldick (New York: Vintage Books, 1962), p. 38.

[8]These rates remained fairly constant from the thirteenth to the seventeenth centuries in Western Europe. In the late seventeenth century, only seventy to

eighty out of every hundred French children survived their first year, and only fifty out of a hundred survived to adulthood.

[9]Eighty out of a hundred American children born in the late eighteenth century survived to the age of five years. Sixty-seven out of a hundred lived to the age of twenty. See the essay by Jerome Avorn in this volume, for a discussion of how child mortality rates were lowered.

[10]National Center for Health Statistics, *Vital Statistics of the United States*, vol. 2, 1978.

[11]For example, in 1900 only three-quarters of all white females reaching age forty could expect to live to age sixty, and only one-third reaching age sixty could expect to live to age eighty. By 1978, nine-tenths reaching age forty could expect to live to age sixty, and nearly two-thirds reaching age sixty could expect to live to age eighty.

[12]U.S. Census Bureau, *Projections of the Population of the United States, By Age, Sex, and Race, 1983 to 2080*, series P-25, no. 952, May 1984, table E.

[13]Becker, op. cit., pp. 109–112.

[14]Robert T. Michael and Edward P. Lazaer, "Family Resources Available to Children," Economics Research Center/NORC, discussion paper 84–6, May 1984, p. 41.

[15]Becker, op. cit., p. 224.

[16]Michael and Lazaer, op. cit., p. 31.

[17]Ibid, pp. 39–43.

[18]Samuel H. Preston, "Children and the Elderly: Divergent Paths for America's Dependents," presidential address to the Population Association of America, May 4, 1984, Minneapolis, pp. 21–23.

[19]Harvery D. Lowell, et al., "Sentenced Prisoners Under 18 Years of Age in Adult Correctional Facilities: A National Survey" (Washington, DC: The National Center on Institutions and Alternatives, 1980), p. 50.

[20]Preston, op. cit., p. 25.

[21]Helen F. Ladd and Julie Boatright Wilson, "Education and Tax Limitations: Evidence from Massachusetts' Proposition 2½," discussion paper D82-2 in the series "Urban Planning Policy Analysis and Administration," Harvard University John F. Kennedy School of Government, Feb. 1984.

[22]Preston, op. cit., p. 5.

[23]U.S. House of Representatives, Select Committee on Children, Youth, and Families, *Demographic and Social Trends: Implications for Federal Support of Dependent Care Services for Children and the Elderly*, April 1984, p. 5.

[24]U.S. Census Bureau, *Statistical Abstract of the United States, 1955*, p. 37.

[25]U.S. Census Bureau, *Statistical Abstract of the United States, 1981*, p. 26.

[26]U.S. Census Bureau, *Projections of the Population of the United States by Age, Sex, and Race, 1983–2080*, Series P-25, no. 952, May 1984.

[27]Ibid, p. 10.

[28]Select Committee on Children, Youth, and Families, op. cit., p. 7.

[29]Heather L. Ross and Isabel V. Sawhill, *Time of Transition: The Growth of Female-Headed Families* (Washington, DC: The Urban Institute, 1975), p. 101.

[30]Mark Testa, Edward Lawlor, and Harold A. Richman, *The State of the Child, 1985* (Chicago: Chapin Hall Center for Children at the University of Chicago, forthcoming).

Rose C. Gibson

Outlook for the Black Family

WHAT IS IN STORE FOR the black family of the future? Blacks in every age group today are confronted with their own set of critical social problems, problems that, if not attended to effectively, will have serious consequences for the black family both in the near future and well beyond.

This chapter will concern itself with these specific social problems and their impact on black children, teenagers, the middle-aged, and elderly, as well as with the implications they pose for our society as a whole. Identifying the more critical social problems by summarizing census data and the findings of my own research—based on *The National Survey of Black Americans* (NSBA)[1] and on other major national studies—will give us a useful starting point.

There are several reasons why the problems confronting various age groups of black Americans may be difficult to resolve. First, the absolute number of blacks is smaller—and will always be smaller—than that of whites, and smaller groups can have more difficulty making their voices heard.[2] (This must be balanced against the fact that small groups without power or wealth can wield influence through the use of special voting patterns, lobbies, and coalitions with other groups; or by posing an imminent public threat, as blacks did during the civil disturbances of the 1960s and 1970s, and as victims of Acquired Immune Deficiency Syndrome—AIDS—do today.) Second, advocacy movements on behalf of particular age, income, occupation, or gender groups have usually focused on the needs of the majority within the group, even when the needs of its minority are vastly different.[3] Third, we have customarily focused legislative and societal attention on only a single group or issue at a time.[4] Finally, the relation between the absolute size and social position of a group seems to determine its importance as a "special group."[5]

These characteristic ways of focusing societal attention—coupled with the disproportionate growth of the elderly white population, which is better positioned socially—could have profound and deleterious effects on the black family of tomorrow.[6]

THE CHANGING DEMOGRAPHY OF BLACK AMERICANS

The first obstacle confronting the black family in the aging society lies in the absolute numbers of blacks compared with that of whites. The number of blacks age sixty-five and over has been increasing faster than the number of whites of those ages, but elderly blacks comprise—and always will comprise—a smaller group in absolute numbers than comparable whites. This black-white comparison of absolute numbers holds true in all age groups. Based on sheer numbers, this means that, age for age, whites may fare better when pitted against blacks for benefits, services, and programs as our society ages.

If we look at the two groups in our population most in need of help, children and the elderly, we find that the young outnumber the old in the black population, while the reverse is true for whites; the number of white elderly (age sixty-five and over) is larger than that of white children under five years of age, and of white teenagers from fifteen to nineteen years of age.

According to Jacob Siegel and Maria Davidson's 1984 monograph for the Census Bureau, this difference in proportions at younger and older ages stems from the higher fertility of black women, as well as from blacks' higher mortality at midlife. That the number of white children is decreasing while the number of white elderly is increasing means that there will continue to be a greater ratio of elderly to children among whites. This will not be the case among blacks. Although the number of black elderly is increasing, the number of black children is slowly decreasing, and there will continue to be a greater ratio of children to elderly among blacks for some time to come. Theoretically, then, the burden of support for the elderly of both races could fall disproportionately on the shoulders of today's black youth as they age. But as the black underclass has a higher rate of reproduction than the black middle class (as John Reid points out in his 1982 report), a majority of black youth will be born poor and without the personal resources as adults to be the mainstays of growing numbers of dependent elderly in an aging society.

The ratio of dependent blacks (under fifteen years of age and over sixty-four) to working-age blacks (ages sixteen to sixty-four) will be greater than will be the case for whites, and this will serve to heighten the black burden of dependency. The situation will be exacerbated if labor-force participation of middle-aged blacks continues to decline.

Individuals age seventy-five and older constitute a section of the black population that is growing disproportionately. (There is, in fact, a racial mortality crossover effect at about that age, a subject to which we shall return.) The most rapidly growing group of the black elderly are women who are eighty and over, and it is they who have the longest average remaining lifetime.

Certainly, the demographies of blacks and whites are changing, but, as we have noted, the small absolute numbers of blacks in every age group may hinder them from gaining societal focus on their particular social problems—that is, unless we begin to recognize those problems in a larger context: as an urgent task our society can ignore only at its peril. The problems of black children become especially important when we realize that, by virtue of their group size relative to white children, it is they who have the greater potential for bearing responsibility for the dependent in an aging society.

BLACK CHILDREN AT RISK IN AN AGING SOCIETY

Infants and Children

The major social problems confronting black children today are poverty, inadequate health care, and poor quality of education—three conditions that are closely related. Nearly 50 percent of black children live in poverty, which means that the black child has a fifty-fifty chance of growing up underprivileged, under-educated, and unemployed. It is these very black children who, as adults, will be expected to assume proportionately more responsibility for supporting the dependent black and white elderly than their white counterparts. For this reason alone, today's black children should be of particular concern to majority group members. Otherwise, society's indifference, or its simple lack of attentiveness, could produce black family heads who are poor in money, in education, and in health—conditions that could seriously undermine not only the economic stability of the black family of the future, but also their ability to support those of us who will look to them for assistance.

The percentage of poor black children is even higher in households headed by a woman. What is more, large segments of the low-income black population are not even being reached by most of the major government income-transfer programs for the poor and jobless. According to a report by Robert Hill in 1981, among black households with incomes under $6,000, only 51 percent received food stamps; 39 percent were covered by Medicaid; 33 percent lived in public housing; 25 percent received rent subsidies; 25 percent received free school lunches; and only 22 percent received Supplemental Security Income (SSI). Another reason for the continuing poverty of black children is the roll-back since 1979 of such major anti-poverty programs as Aid to Families with Dependent Children (AFDC) and food stamps.

Marian Wright Edelman of the Children's Defense Fund notes that, when compared with white children, black children are more likely to be in poor health, twice as likely to have no regular source of health care, more likely to be seriously ill when they finally see a doctor, five times as likely to have to rely on hospital emergency rooms or outpatient clinics, and twice as likely to be born to mothers who have had no prenatal care. Thirteen percent of all black children are born with low birth weights, a factor that is associated with poor prenatal care and makes them more vulnerable as a group to mortality, prematurity, and mental retardation.

In spite of these disturbing conditions, shrinking federal funding and restrictive eligibility requirements have limited the effectiveness of federal health-care programs. For example, 16 percent of black children are not covered by either Medicaid or private insurance. The Early Periodic Screening, Diagnosis, and Treatment program (EPSDT), which makes preventive care available to low-income children, renders ineligible those children who fail to qualify for Medicaid. This means that about five million poor children living in two-parent families do not meet the requirements for EPSDT. The Child Health Assurance Plan repeatedly failed to pass Congress until 1984, when a mini-version that reflected budget cuts and further reductions was passed. And the Special Supplemental Food Program for Women, Infants, and Children (WIC), a program that provides baby formula, diet supplements, and checkups for poor pregnant and nursing women and small children, is underfunded and has a steadily growing waiting list.

The curtailment of programs that are of special benefit to the health of black infants and children is a moral matter. A case in point is the WIC program, which has demonstrably reduced some of the negative effects of low birth weight. The moral issue is whether we have the right to eliminate health-care strategies that are known to have positive effects, and thus to determine which groups of children will have access to "the good life" and which will not.

Black children also receive poorer-quality educations than do white children. Evelyn Moore of the National Black Child Development Institute reports that black children are more than twice as likely to have their educations delayed by two or more years; three times as likely to be assigned to classes for the "educable mentally retarded"; twice as likely to be suspended, expelled, or given corporal punishment; twice as likely to drop out of school; twice as likely to be behind grade level; and more likely to score below the mean on national standardized tests, but only half as likely to be labeled gifted. In 1981, John Ogbu of the University of California at Berkeley suggested that inferior education for black children is a function of several subtle mechanisms: negative teacher attitudes and low expectations (teachers believe that blacks are less intelligent than whites); biased testing and classification; biased tracking or ability grouping; biased textbooks and inferior curricula; inadequate academic and career guidance; biased channeling into special education classes; the employment of less qualified teachers in black schools; and cutbacks in federal aid to education and to those programs—such as Headstart—that were successful in preparing black children for better academic performance.

The danger is that the curtailment of major anti-poverty, health-care, and education programs that especially benefited black children might be accelerated by the increasing needs and demands of the rapidly growing group of whites age sixty-five and over for similar types of programs. Samuel Preston of the University of Pennsylvania points out that child-welfare programs (such as AFDC) have already been rolled back, while programs benefitting the elderly (such as Social Security) have been maintained or expanded. He suggests that this is happening because entitlements are negotiated from demographic strength, and the elderly are simply more numerous than children—and their numbers are increasing. Furthermore, he states that the white elderly do not vote on behalf of children's welfare, and that they most assuredly do not vote for "other children's" (i.e., minority children's) welfare.

The effect of this erosion of child-welfare programs and increasing competition from other groups is that black children may not develop the resources of affluence, health, and education to live as independent adults, and must be prepared to bear greater burdens than their white counterparts in supporting the dependent. It is somewhat ironic, then, that the anti-poverty insulation, the health care, and the quality of education that black children receive is inferior, and that black children of today, a group with great potential for contributing to an aging society, are themselves in jeopardy partly *because* of an aging society.

Teenagers

Teenage pregnancies and out-of-wedlock births are especially disturbing problems among black teenage women. The rate of black teenage (age fifteen through seventeen) child-bearing in 1979 was more than three times the white rate: 77 per 1,000, versus 25 per 1,000. As John Reid reports, the proportion of births out-of-wedlock has increased from 90 percent to 93 percent for black women age fifteen through seventeen and from 36 to 42 percent for a comparable group of white women. In spite of this situation, few inroads have been made into the problem of black teenage pregnancy. If these trends continue, however, increasing numbers of young black women will be raising children without fathers in the home. Niara Sudarkasa presents evidence that black families headed by women can be highly functional, and the statement here must not be misconstrued to mean that black families headed by women are, by definition, dysfunctional.[7] The issue is economic. Black families headed by women with no male present are making up larger and larger segments of the black poor than are black husband-wife families. According to Reynolds Farley of the University of Michigan, over one-half of black female-headed families lived below the poverty level in 1982, in contrast to only 19 percent of black husband-wife families.

Programs and services that provide continuing education, job training, and child care for these teenage unwed mothers could help lift them out of poverty. But as they are now constituted, child-care programs tend to benefit higher-income women more than those with lower incomes. Evelyn Moore suggests that child care for poor black mothers is in fact a kind of "Catch-22" situation, in which rigid income cut-off levels for eligibility act as disincentives to full-time work, so that many black families must remain poor if they are to obtain quality child care. (It is interesting to note that child care became a national concern only when white mothers began to join the labor force in numbers.) In an aging society, where larger and larger numbers of elderly whites will demand continuing education, training for labor-force reentry, and their own day-care facilities, the needs of poor black unwed mothers may well go unmet.

Teenage black men have their own set of problems, including vulnerability to homicide, incarceration, and constantly high rates of unemployment. A black male youth is five times as likely as a white male youth to be a victim of homicide (frequently as a result of police intervention), and twice as likely to be detained in a juvenile or adult correctional facility. A black youth is three times as likely as a white youth to be unemployed. A black student who graduates from high school has a greater chance of being unemployed than a white student who dropped out of elementary school. A black college graduate is as likely to be unemployed as a white high-school dropout. James McGhee of the National Urban League has stated that the current estimate of 50 percent unemployment for black youths is probably an underestimation: 70 percent is more likely. This might mean that an overwhelming majority of today's black teenage men *will never work in any sustained or beneficial way in their lifetimes*. If that is an accurate assessment, they will arrive at adulthood and old age with even fewer skills and poorer work experiences than their parents and grandparents, for whom unemployment rates in youth were not nearly so high.

The increasing loss of black men through death and incarceration in youth and as a result of the failure to find employment may portend the virtual disappearance of the black male from the black family and, as Charles Willie of Harvard University suggests, further dissolution of the black family in the future.[8]

Homicide, incarceration, and unemployment, inextricably bound, dictate a hand-in-glove approach to preventive counseling and vocational training programs. Yet black youth are underrepresented in counseling programs and overrepresented in training courses that are geared toward low-wage, low–upward-mobility, and low-demand jobs (less than 15 percent of electronics students are black, for example, as against 65 percent of textile-production students). David Swinton of the Clark College Policy Center suggests that the solution to the unemployment problem of young black males lies less with job training than with the creation of suitable jobs. Yet the needs of burgeoning numbers of older white workers—for counseling services, for the creation of new types of jobs and for new training programs to facilitate them—may deter the possibility of creating those new jobs and job-training programs that focus specifically on the needs of disadvantaged black youth.

When viewed as a single phenomenon, the plights of the masses of black infants, children, and teenagers today might mean that the black family of the twenty-first century will be more economically disadvantaged than was its counterpart in the preceding century—a disturbing possibility indeed.[9]

BLACKS AT MIDLIFE: ANOTHER GROUP AT RISK

Middle-aged blacks (age forty-five to sixty-four) represent another segment of the black family that is at risk in an aging society. The critical social problems of the masses of middle-aged blacks today are divorce, separation, difficulties in psychological adjustment, low morale as workers, and declining physical abilities accompanied by decreases in labor-force participation. These fairly new social trends are creating the "unretired-retired," a new type of black retiree. If these work and retirement problems are characteristic of a life stage of blacks, the black middle-aged worker will be at an increasingly greater risk as the pool of older white workers grows in an aging society. Work and retirement may need reconceptualizing both for the benefit of these early retirees and for the economic welfare of their families.

Divorce and Separation

Divorce and separation are on the rise in black America. By midlife, only 55 percent of blacks are married and living with a spouse, in contrast to 79 percent of whites—figures that are due in part, of course, to the greater mortality of blacks than whites at earlier ages. The rise in the divorce ratio has been more dramatic for black than for white women (from 104 versus 56 in 1970, to 265 versus 128 in 1982). Findings from a study I completed in 1983 using the NSBA to compare the mental health of middle-aged and elderly blacks, suggest that divorced and separated black women are also among the least well-off of blacks at midlife on several measures of stress, distress, and morale. One of the reasons for these psychological states may be economic. Paul Glick, former senior demographer with the Census Bureau, pointed out that in 1979 only 29 percent of black women who had sole custody of young children were awarded child support payments (as compared with 59 percent for their counterparts in all other races); fewer black women than women of other races who were awarded child support payments actually received them (5/8 versus 3/4); and very few divorced black women were awarded alimony. Disrupted marriage thus takes a disproportionate economic and psychological toll on black American women at midlife.

Mental Health Status

Middle age may be the most tumultuous time of life for blacks, partly because the tasks of middle age are particularly difficult for blacks today.[10] Current thought assumes that good feelings accrue about oneself as one accomplishes the major tasks of midlife, some of which are assessing one's accomplishments, pinpointing one's position in society relative to others, and feeling mastery for the first time over one's own life and social environment. Blacks may fare less well than whites in these self-appraisals. Measuring one's accomplishments might be particularly difficult when racial discrimination in the marketplace has put a lid on the achievements of those blacks who are now at middle age. These may be the single group of blacks today for whom accomplishments fall shortest of aspirations. Younger middle-class blacks may be better able to bridge the gap between aspirations and accomplishments because of their greater opportunities, and elderly blacks may have a smaller gap because their aspirations have already been lowered by the time they reach old age. To aspire and not to reach, a quality that is thus more characteristic of middle-aged blacks than others, may be particularly stressful.

With respect to assessing one's position in society, while whites at midlife are at the pinnacle of their careers and incomes, today's midlife blacks are in straitened circumstances. They are keenly aware of their lower socioeconomic positions relative to younger (age thirty to forty-four) middle-class blacks—those beneficiaries of the social changes of the 1970s—and relative to middle-aged whites as well. For middle-aged whites, the reverse is true; they are higher in socioeconomic position than either younger whites or their black age-mates. Middle-aged blacks, then, find themselves in the least advantaged position, whether they compare themselves to middle-aged whites or young black adults.

The mental-health status of blacks at midlife is poorer than that of blacks at late life. My 1983 mental-health study, noted earlier, revealed this to be true by several measures of stress, distress, and morale. The black middle-aged who were the most likely to be stressed and distressed were women, members of the underclass, the divorced, and the separated. With respect to stress, distress, and morale, midlife black women appear to be at higher psychological risk than midlife black men.

The black underclass is also at serious risk in midlife. As income and education decrease, stress and distress increase. The most disadvantaged in that regard were those with incomes of less than $5,000 a year and those with less than an eleventh-grade education. The divorced and separated were the most likely of the marital groups to be seriously stressed and distressed.

Although the black underclass is more likely to be stressed and distressed, the black middle-class is more likely to have low morale. At particular risk in regard to morale—life dissatisfaction and unhappiness—were women who could be considered well off: those with incomes over $20,000, those who are college graduates, those in professional occupations, and those living in the suburbs. We might speculate that their low morale is due to the fact that they have set high goals for themselves and are experiencing wide gaps between these goals and their accomplishments. They may also be measuring themselves against the younger black women, age thirty to forty-four, who made the quantum leaps in education, occupation, and income in the decade between 1970 and 1980.

Family counseling services and programs carefully designed to address the different problems and mental health needs of both the black underclass and more affluent blacks will be needed in the coming decades. But at the same time increasing numbers of the white elderly will also need family counseling services, as will the growing numbers of white families that consist of several generations living together.

Competition for mental-health resources and mental-health dollars during the next decades may not only involve the white elderly versus teenaged blacks versus middle-aged blacks, but might also pit groups within the black middle-aged community against each other. This sort of competition could be minimized if counseling services were designed to address the problems of blacks comprehensively—across the life cycle and as family units.

Reconceptualizing Work and Retirement

Nearly 40 percent of non-working blacks age fifty-five and over can be categorized as the "unretired-retired," individuals who appear and behave as if they were retired, but do not call themselves such. My 1985 study of the retirement definitions of older blacks identified this group as the neediest of the black middle-aged. Because they do not meet the traditional retirement criteria—of chronological age, a clear line between work and non-work, income from retirement sources, and their own realization that they are retired—this very needy group finds itself screened out of major retirement research and deprived of the retirement-benefit planning and policy that stem from that research.

Who are these "unretired-retired"? They are older black workers, many in early midlife, who are making a gradual exodus out of the labor force mainly for reasons of physical disability. Among the middle-aged, disability in most categories increased more for blacks than for whites over the past twelve years, while over the past twenty-six years, decreases in labor-force participation were more dramatic for black men and increases in the labor force more dramatic for white women. The disturbing possibility is that, beginning at about age fifty-five—barring radical social intervention such as equalizing employment opportunities and creating jobs that would accommodate their declining physical abilities—a large group of older blacks will never work again in any systematic way; their work lives will effectively be over. To assure that they receive some type of benefits, "retirement" age may need to be moved back for older blacks—and eventually for other groups as well.[11]

One of the most interesting findings of the study James Jackson and I conducted was that, for many blacks, the retirement years are often the happiest and most secure of their lives. This finding is in direct contrast to the results of several empirical studies of work and retirement that indicate that the elderly would benefit from remaining in the work force, and would in fact prefer to do so rather than to retire at the traditional cut-off point of age sixty-five. In his study of the retirement of black and white men, for example, Herbert Parnes found that the morale of white retirees was lower than that of older white workers even after controlling for income, age, and health. The NSBA data, in contrast, reveal the reverse is true for older blacks: retirees have higher morale than workers. There are at least two possible reasons for this. First, the combination of declining physical abilities of older blacks, coupled with their restriction to strenuous and distasteful jobs at the bottom of the job hierarchy that do not accommodate their infirmities, makes work as it is now structured more punishing. Second, many blacks in retirement can look forward for the first time in their lives to the reliability of a monthly check coming in from Social Security plus SSI benefits. For a majority of older blacks it is not work, but retirement, that promotes adjustment.

If current trends in disability and early labor-force withdrawal continue, there is a distinct possibility that by the middle of the twenty-first century blacks will "cease" working and begin "retirement" *before* midlife. This will pose problems on the policy level: should we call this group "retired," although they do not meet the traditional criteria, so we can provide them with some type of benefits when their work lives are over? The problem intensifies when we realize that growing numbers of longer-lived white retirees will also need income supplements. We need to investigate new ways of supporting burgeoning numbers of black and white non-workers.

It is also possible that the lines between work and non-work will become even more blurred as older blacks work more sporadically as a result of competition with growing numbers of older whites for the scarce jobs that accommodate the declining physical capacities of older workers. Because disability pay is a mainstay of these middle-aged blacks who are leaving the labor force, the disability role may replace the retirement role. The result would be an increase in importance of disability-pay legislation over Social Security legislation for the economic welfare of blacks—especially when the proposed age of eligibility changes, as is now planned under Social Security. At this time, there will be an even longer wait between the end of work lives and the beginning of benefits, and growing numbers of black males simply will not live long enough to collect their benefits. Given the shorter life spans of blacks, this raises an even more fundamental issue—are age-based policies in general inappropriate for the masses of blacks in an aging society?

All of these work and retirement factors mean that, because the black family may be top-heavy with non-working dependents, its welfare may be seriously threatened as we approach the twenty-first century. Middle age, then, may be likened to a proving ground, a battle from which only the victorious—those who are physically and psychologically fit—emerge and get to play out old age. For blacks who survive these crises, old age may actually be a less stressful time than midlife. It should not be surprising, therefore, that blacks age seventy-five and over are regarded as psychological as well as physical survivors.

THE BLACK ELDERLY IN AN AGING SOCIETY

Attempts to solve the major problems of today's black elderly may encounter roadblocks in the form of the needs of increasing numbers of their white counterparts, who are living longer but in poorer health. If inadequate health care and insufficient economic support for the black elderly continue, the burden of caring for them may fall squarely on the shoulders of younger blacks, the masses of whom may be ill-equipped, as we have already pointed out, to bear the responsibility. A balancing factor, however, might be the notable psychological assets of these very old blacks.

The racial mortality crossover might be a case in point. The crossover refers to the fact that, up to about age seventy-five, whites can expect to live longer than blacks, but after that age, blacks can expect to live longer than whites. There are several speculations as to why this is so. First, blacks at advanced ages may be a more biologically select group—those who survived inadequate medical care earlier in life. It is also possible that aging is retarded in some ways among blacks at advanced ages—a possibility that might be attributed to race differences in aging at the cellular level. A third possibility is that blacks are especially insulated in some way at more advanced ages against the leading killer diseases—heart disease, cancer, stroke, and generalized arterioschlerosis. It is also possible that social factors might account for differences in the mortality of older blacks and whites.

Certain psychological factors may also serve to decrease the vulnerability of older blacks to disease and thus to mortality. These might include more positive attitudes toward life, effective ways of handling stress, and the use of special help-seeking patterns in times of great need. A good deal of recent research, including that of Stanislav Kasl and Lisa Berkman in 1981, suggests that each of these sets of social and psychological factors does indeed buffer the onset of certain diseases. In short, some particular insights might be gained into the racial mortality crossover by examining the biomedical, social, and psychological data of elderly blacks.

Even though these black survivors lack the attributes of financial security, adequate education, and marital company (more black than white elderly live without spouses), they seem to sustain themselves psychologically as they age. Certainly, in terms of one gross measure of adustment—suicide—older blacks fare well. In my analysis of data from the National Center for Health Statistics, I found that suicide rates among the elderly, ranking from lowest to highest, are ordered as follows: black females, black males, white females, and white males. Older black women are the most likely to be poor and the least likely to end their own lives; older white men are the least likely to suffer poverty and the most apt to die by their own hands. There is also an apparent inverse correlation between suicide and prayer: elderly black women are most likely to use prayer as a coping resource, while elderly white men are least inclined toward prayer. Black men and white women fall between these extremes. I suspect that it is the communal as well as the intrinsic aspects of prayer that are helpful to older blacks: "getting together to get things done." And as Emile Durkheim has suggested, greater bonding to social groups increases social integration and thus psychological well-being.

A recurring theme in several of my research studies is that not all aspects of old age have negative connotations for blacks. Elderly whites have somewhat higher morale than elderly blacks in most of the major national studies, but if we consider the great disparities between the races in functional health, income, education, and marital harmony, the gap in morale is not commensurate with the gap in resources. Is something putting a floor under the morale of elderly blacks? Is it merely a matter of long practice, of long experience in meeting adversity? Or have they found particular resources and strategies that sustain them? My 1982 analysis of national data collected in 1957 and again in 1976[12] suggests that some of the effective mechanisms of blacks may lie, not only in the role religion plays in their lives, but in their use of special patterns of help-seeking as they adapt to old age. In terms of using informal support networks in times of distress, older black Americans drew from a more varied pool of informal helpers than did their white counterparts, both in middle and late life, and were more versatile in interchanging these helpers one for another as they approached old age. Whites, in contrast, were more likely to limit help-seeking to their spouses in middle life, and when their spouses were no longer available for this support, to confine their attempts to replace it by calling only on single family members as they approached old age.

In spite of their economic and physical handicaps, the black elderly—the psychological survivors—may turn out to be part of the salvation of the black family of the future. The unusual strengths of very old black women (who are perhaps, not so coincidentally, experiencing the most rapid growth of all 80+groups, considered by sex and race) are well known. Elderly black women have been a wellspring of support and nurturance over time. The rapid growth of this group, coupled with the growing tendency of black families to be without men, may mean that a modal black family of the future (there could be other modes as well) will be composed of several generations of women. Publicly funded programs and services could encourage these roles of older black women as surrogate parents in families without fathers present. This would not be an unfamiliar role, for historically many have taken responsibility for raising the children of others—their own grandchildren, children of other family members and friends, and children of their white employers.

In summary, the renowned strengths of the black family will be put to a severe test as our society ages, and as larger and more powerful groups compete for limited resources. No age group of black Americans will be insulated against this effect: black infants, children, teenagers, the middle-aged, and the elderly each has particular economic, social, physical and/or psychological vulnerabilities—

problems that if not attended to may have profound and deleterious effects on the welfare and structure of the black family, and, in turn, on our society as a whole. Yet, there are enormous strengths within the black family's own ranks, and while the concerns are grave, the hopes are also great as we approach the twenty-first century.

It goes without saying, of course, that policies and programs that ameliorate the poverty of, improve the health care of, and create equal opportunities for black Americans of all ages will help the most to solve the problems of the black family in an aging society. The absence of sound knowledge about the effects of an aging society on the welfare of blacks in the future makes it premature to recommend specific policy or program changes that might buffer these effects. Systematic diagnosis and examination is needed; without them, policies and programs are bound to fall short and go awry. What is required is a programmatic approach that will allow researchers and policymakers from diverse disciplines and areas of interest to work together to identify and offer solutions to the problems.

Those who are vitally interested in the future of the black family can only urge that such studies will be undertaken that will result in helpful policies. Without intensive study and informed intervention, the problems of the black family can only worsen in the aging society.

ENDNOTES

[1] The *National Survey of Black Americans* is the first national probability sample of the adult black population that is truly representative of blacks in the continental United States. See James S. Jackson, *National Survey of Black Americans* (Ann Arbor, MI: Institute for Social Research, University of Michigan, 1979).

[2] Samuel Preston suggests that the power of special-interest groups to influence public decisions is a function of the size of the group, the wealth of the group, and the degree to which that size and wealth can be mobilized for concerted action. See Samuel Preston, "Children and the Elderly: Divergent Paths for America's Dependents," presidential address to the Population Association of America, Minneapolis, MN, May 1984.

[3] The Displaced Homemaker's Program is a case in point. The program was designed to address the work and training needs of midlife women, but it failed to address the particular problems of black women at midlife because it was targeted to housewives who had never worked. Black women have historically been workers.

[4] John Naisbitt, monitoring social change by using content analysis of newspapers over the years, documents the fact that our closed social system handles only a limited number of concerns at a time. He cites examples of issues of racism being

replaced by issues of sexism, and sexism by ageism. Congress acted at the crest of each movement. See John Naisbitt, *Megatrends* (New York: Warner Books, 1982), pp. xxiv-xxvii.

[5]Preston, op. cit., commenting on the problems of the elderly, suggests that higher-positioned, larger groups tend to elicit focus on their problems. This means that blacks of all ages, being less numerous and lower-positioned socially, might have difficulty gaining attention as a "problem group" (barring the group's potential as a public threat).

[6]This is not to say that the black family is dysfunctional, for its strengths are well known. See, for example, Robert B. Hill, *The Strengths of Black Families* (New York: Emerson Hall, 1972).

[7]See Niara Sudarkasa, in Rose C. Gibson, ed., *Blacks in an Aging Society: Proceedings of the Carnegie Corporation Conference,* held at Ann Arbor, MI, Oct. 16, 1984.

[8]There is serious debate among scholars of the black family as to whether "dissolution" should be used in describing conditions in black families. While there is agreement that the black family is not a pathological form of the American family, but rather takes on a variety of functional forms that might be different from the "norm," there is disagreement as to whether "dissolution" can take on strictly economic meaning. Willie attaches an economic meaning based on the fact that certain types of black families—families headed by women—are overrepresented among the black poor. See C. Willie in Rose C. Gibson, ed., op. cit.

[9]The civil rights movement, although it worked to secure voting and other civil rights, did not fully address the economic conditions of blacks in America. It is the opinion of some that middle-class blacks benefitted more than other blacks, and that poverty among the masses remains unattenuated, creating a small black elite and a massive black underclass. See, for example, William J. Wilson, *The Declining Significance of Race* (Chicago: University of Chicago Press, 1978).

[10]For a discussion of several tasks at midlife, see Bernice Neugarten, "The Awareness of Middle Age," in Bernice Neugarten, ed., *Middle Age and Aging* (Chicago: University of Chicago Press, 1968).

[11]This phenomenon of an increasing group of subjectively unretired blacks could be an omen for other groups of older Americans. Certainly this seems possible if we take as precedent the occurrences of negative social phenomena that appeared first in the black community and were then manifested in white America: two good examples of this are drug abuse and the high incidence of out-of-wedlock births. If we perceive these as a pattern, then we might speculate that the observed changes in work and retirement patterns among blacks are a kind of forewarning to the society at large.

[12]Data collected originally by Gerald Gurin, Joseph Veroff, and Sheila Feld in *Americans View Their Mental Health* (Ann Arbor, MI: Institute for Social Research, University of Michigan, 1957, 1976).

Harry R. Moody

Education as a Lifelong Process

AMERICA'S EMERGENCE AS AN aging society has profound implications for the role education plays over the course of life. As Philippe Aries has shown, education has a strategic role in society, for its structure serves to shape our image of the life cycle as a whole.[1] A century ago, a "modernized" life-cycle emerged which expressed a view of the life course that linked education to the mass industrial economy and drew rigid boundaries between the stages of life.[2] In this modernized life-cycle, education, work, and leisure were assigned sequentially to the life stages of youth, adulthood, and old age.

Today the advent of an aging society has begun to challenge this pattern. Education is no longer tied exclusively to youth, and we have begun to see declining numbers of young people among those age groups that traditionally have been served by colleges. Higher education has already responded to this demographic change with modest steps toward non-traditional learning, but there have been far fewer changes in educational philosophy, financing, or curriculum. Business and industry have promoted their own view of education in terms of "human-capital formation," but programs to retrain workers for the post-industrial economy have rarely included older workers.

These modest and halting steps are a weak response indeed to what must be seen as *the* decisive demographic revolution of the twentieth century: the aging of societies throughout the industrialized world. Loosening the boundaries between life stages and making them more flexible seems desirable, but fails to address the real question: how can the dramatic rise in life expectancy become the basis for new social productivity—for a genuine abundance of life? What role can learning play in preparing individuals *at every stage of life* for a society where most people can expect to live to old age? These challenges will demand a change in the relation between education and life stages.

THE EDUCATION OF CHILDREN IN AN AGING SOCIETY

Support for Public Education

For over a century, public policy has supported universal mass education for children and young people. That public support is now threatening to decline, in part because of our society's shrinking proportion of children and its growing proportion of elderly. Today, only 20 percent of American voters have school-age children, and opinion surveys show that older people are far less likely than other groups to support school-tax increases.[3] In the past, public support in this country for the education of children and young people depended on a variety of sources, and was an expression of the democratic ideal of common citizenship that united all generations. Public support for education was based on a willingness on the part of parents to make sacrifices in order that one's children may have a better life, and obligations to the next generation were tied to an ideology of social progress and upward mobility.

In recent times, this older ideal of citizenship has faded, leaving the desire for economic growth the chief rationale for public support of education. Today, even this economic rationale has been weakening, since education no longer guarantees a good job. While schools and colleges once had a monopoly on education, because they granted credentials that had value in the job market, the comparative advantage of credentials has fallen today, while competition for good jobs has heightened. Growing numbers of people are described as "overeducated" or "underemployed." Under these conditions, it becomes more difficult to justify educational expenditures on the old grounds. As a result, claims for support of public education are based increasingly on labor-market forecasts and on economic planning— on the need for a skilled labor force to attract high-technology industry, for example. But public support also depends on whether voters perceive that schools are doing a good job, and evidence of our public schools' effectiveness has weakened that support.

School Reform

It was the wide public recognition of these trends, along with a new environment of international economic competition, that were largely responsible for the clamor for "school reform" that arose in the early 1980s. But the challenge of school reform, which is open to several quite divergent solutions, has been posed for the public in very narrow terms. The strategy that has received the most public discussion is the one that would thoroughly upgrade public education, particularly on the secondary level. In some areas of the country—Texas for example—leaders from high-technology industries have been prominent advocates for such school reform, but, for reasons suggested earlier, financing public education when fewer families have children in the schools is a continuing problem.

If the general strategy of school reform does not bear fruit in producing a skilled, flexible labor force, then business may opt for a second strategy: targeting private "human-capital" investment in job training for highly specific occupational skills. This strategy has an advantage for corporate planners, since the control of education goals would then remain firmly in the hands of business. The business community could also find allies in the higher education sector; already, over half the colleges in the United States operate joint training ventures with private industry, and the trend is growing.[4]

It is comforting to imagine that this kind of human-capital investment approach might offer "second-chance" opportunities to groups that have so far been unsuccessful within the formal educational system. But if resources are invested according to the needs of the business community, we are more likely to see a further erosion of constituencies for the "open access" forms of education that have been vital for the disadvantaged. In one year, for example, the California community-college system experienced a 25 percent drop in enrollment after it had imposed a tuition charge. The issue ultimately confronts us with a choice between public or private control over decisions affecting human-capital investment—what we call education.

With an aging population, public education at all levels is likely to remain on the defensive. Schools will be further tempted to justify their effectiveness on narrow economic grounds. But government will continue to be faced with other competing demands, such as the rising health-care costs of the elderly. When struggles are waged through conventional interest-group politics, we risk the danger that young and old might be polarized. One alternative would be to convince all age groups that they have a common stake in educating the next generation.

A case that illustrates this point can be found in Brookline, Massachusetts, a community of 55,000 people with a very high proportion of the population—20 percent—over age sixty five.[5] At the same time, 25 percent of the school-age population is composed of minority children, chiefly black and Asian. In Massachusetts, as in California, a major property-tax limitation measure was approved. But in Brookline, despite its high proportion of predominantly white senior citizens, the community voted overwhelmingly *against* the property-tax limitation at the same time the measure was winning elsewhere in the state. One reason for the voting pattern lay in the strong support for schools by Brookline senior citizens, support that was cultivated as a result of years of community effort.

Three elements were key to the Brookline success: public information, school-based services for older people, and the active recruitment of senior citizens as school volunteers. The public schools were used as sites for serving hot lunches to senior citizens and for other services such as health screening and recreation. Adult education programs were moved to community locations, while unused school buses were made available to senior citizens for shopping during the day and for transportation to cultural events in the schools at night. Older people were recruited as volunteers for tutoring, for teaching English as a second language, and for the sharing of life experiences. When the drive came to limit school expenses, the senior-citizen vote in Brookline was substantially against the state-wide trend.

Is it possible to generalize or to replicate the Brookline experience in other communities in America? There are some signs that this is already happening. In many localities, closed school buildings have been turned into community centers. The National Organization of School Volunteers showed striking success in recruiting the elderly as volunteers in cities across the United States. These are promising efforts, for they incorporate the elderly as a new constituency and as contributors to the learning process. But volunteerism also has its limits. The predominantly white elderly of Brookline are unlikely to travel to Roxbury ghetto schools, for example. Schemes for voluntary action must be balanced by changes in public policy.

Our current public policies continue to reinforce the century-old "modernized" life course, with its linear separation of education, work, and leisure. Social Security, which depends on younger workers, is part of a federal taxing system, while school and property taxes are assessed by local government. These taxation policies end up pitting age groups against each other, raising the specter of elderly homeowners repeatedly voting down school-bond issues—as happened over a period of years in the Sun City, Arizona, retirement community.

We are faced not simply with the task of convincing older people to volunteer in the schools, but with reminding people of all ages that each generation has taken on an obligation to preserve a free society for the next generation. Younger adults without children, as well as grandparents with no children currently in school, need to understand this obligation in far broader terms than they now perceive it. Like military service, public education has provided a basis of common citizenship, of ties to community that reach beyond any single generation. In the present political climate, the policy dilemma may come down to two quite different versions of conservative ideology, one that emphasizes self-interest in the marketplace model (that is, human-capital formation), and the other based on some version of obligation to a common good that transcends any single generation.

Children and young people will have to be educated in ways that strengthen, rather than erode, these intergenerational ties. Promoting more positive attitudes towards all stage of life, including old age, would be one way to begin. This is a task that must extend from elementary education right on through the most advanced professional schooling—for example, to the education of physicians, who often display either a lack of interest or an openly negative attitude toward the chronic diseases of geriatric practice, despite the fact that in most fields of medicine geriatric patients already constitute more than a third of the patient load, a figure that will surely increase. It is promising that some positive models for gerontological education in the professions are beginning to emerge.

RETRAINING MIDDLE-AGED AND OLDER WORKERS

The Aging Work Force

With population aging, the relations between work, retirement, and retraining are likely to change. In the past few decades, while the average age of retirement has been falling, recent federal legislation has been moving in the opposite direction, raising the Social Security age to sixty-seven and the mandatory retirement age to seventy, for example. By the year 2000, half the work force will consist of people age thirty-five to fifty-five. With fewer young people seeking employment, we may be unable to forgo the productivity of older workers. These trends make it imperative to rethink the role of worker retraining from the perspective of the entire life span.

The prevailing pattern has been for employers to provide job training, either directly at the work site or by means of tuition reimbursement plans. Yet far fewer employees than might be expected have taken advantage of retraining opportunities. Experience suggests that simply offering educational programs or financial assistance is insufficient; individuals must also be convinced that it is both worthwhile and feasible to take advantage of the available opportunities. In the past, many companies believed that it was cheaper to hire and train younger people than to retrain older workers, and a widespread bias has remained in favor of providing training resources to relatively young employees.

A Life-Span Approach to Retraining

Proposals for retraining middle-aged or older workers must take into account the serious problem of social *expectations* about what is appropriate in later life. We have noted that people were generally locked into a "linear life plan"—a sequence that consisted of education, work, and leisure, in that order. An optimal model for the future would integrate life planning over the entire life course. This would create workers who are not only well prepared, but who are highly motivated to participate in training and retraining.

The Role of Colleges and Universities

Like industry, institutions of higher education have generally accepted a youth-oriented, age-decremental model of human resource development. While industry remains preoccupied with very specific job skills, colleges could certainly adopt a more comprehensive model of life-span development, and provide education accordingly. Given such a model, it might be possible for people beyond age fifty to become re-educated, to learn a whole new career. Instead of thinking of themselves as on a downward slope toward retirement, they could think about beginning a new phase of life.

John McLeish, in *The Ulyssean Adult*, has documented a range of examples of creativity, continued learning, and second careers in later life. In a few cases, educational institutions have responded to this possibility with innovative measures, such as the successful program at the Harvard Graduate School of Education, which offers mid-career retraining that permits engineers—average age fifty—to become high-school science and math teachers.

The key problem with this optimistic picture of second careers in later life is motivation. What prompts people to take the risk? One answer is that certain life changes—divorce, or plant closings in smokestack industries—often impel people to give up old patterns and take the chances necessary to begin new occupations in mid-life.

In 1976, for example, the Vocational Education Act turned federal attention for the first time to the educational needs of middle-aged displaced homemakers.[6] ("Displaced homemaker" refers to a person who, through divorce, separation, or the death or disability of a spouse, finds herself needing to move back into the job market at age forty or more.) This national effort at retraining has demonstrated the feasibility of public initiatives to build on the capacities of age and experience.

The successful programs have provided practical skills training in such areas as personal financial management or job-search techniques. They have also been helping older women to translate their knowledge from life experience in homemaking or volunteer work into paid employment. Local chapters of the Older Women's League, often in collaboration with community colleges, now offer training programs on financial and retirement planning, housing, health needs, and family life, as well as skills acquired in leadership development and advocacy training.

HUMAN-CAPITAL INVESTMENT IN LIFE-SPAN PERSPECTIVE

If we are to insure economic productivity and growth in a competitive international economy, technological innovation is a necessity. At the same time, there are serious doubts whether high-technology skills will provide the kind of career flexibility that we have been advocating over a longer life span; in many ways, it may actually contribute to de-skilling and even trivializing jobs. New technology can also cause older workers to lose the advantages of age and experience, increasing their fears of being replaced by automation.

The public policy response to this situation has been inadequate and even misdirected. Under the old Trade Adjustment Act, for example, initiatives have largely failed, and little retraining of older workers has even been attempted. Further, the federal tax code prohibits those engaged in retraining for a new occupation from claiming an educational deduction, while it permits deductions for those who improve their skills within their current occupations. Even the recent Job Training Partnership Act represents a meager response to the structural transformation of the American economy. Federal leadership will achieve little indeed unless it provides serious incentives in the form of training subsidies, tax credits, new adult retraining services, and other such programs. Prevailing policy fails even to address these questions.

Financing Retraining for Older Workers

Some recent proposals approach the task of financing worker retraining in novel ways. Under one, which calls for so-called Individual Training Accounts financed by joint contributions from workers and companies, a worker could draw upon an account if he found himself displaced from a job. Still more ambitious plans would offer general educational entitlements, based, for example, on Social Security, to be set aside for use at any period of the life course. Such policies would weaken the grip of the linear life plan, and might promote greater occupational mobility for middle-aged and older workers.

One liability of these plans is that they would appeal primarily to upper-income workers; people with more modest incomes, who could not benefit from tax incentives, are less likely to participate.

There is also the fact that, for those older workers who have built up significant equity in home ownership but now face high mortgage rates if they try to move, relocation assistance is as vital as retraining. Current policy in effect subsidizes immobility and inflexibility in an aging labor force—a major problem in a post-industrial economy, where mobility and flexibility are essential for growth.

Public Policy for Life-Span Development

Because of the historical geographic mobility of the American labor force, our private firms and local governments have under-invested in education and training compared with other industrialized countries. Under-investment was traditionally tolerated because companies could recruit younger workers who had acquired the necessary skill levels through public education. Here is an instance of the limitation of the human-capital investment perspective as applied to worker retraining: it is unrealistic to expect either private firms or local governments to make investments if they cannot expect to recoup benefits. In a period of "hypermobility" of international capital, it is easier for industries simply to abandon a local area when their human resource costs become excessive.[7]

The effect of our current national policy is to offer incentives for economic dependency in retirement through pension and Social Security transfers. In contrast, our local and private policy bears the entire burden of offering incentives for human-capital investment. The result is that individuals and private firms alike end up supporting publicly subsidized dependency while avoiding risky human-capital investments in retraining older workers. The aging society, then, confronts a contradiction: increased longevity means an abundance of life in the later years with a potential for continued social productivity, yet the political economy channels older people away from productive roles in the workplace.

Work, Aging, and Post-Industrial Society

Many observers express deep pessimism about future job growth in advanced industrialized economies. On the one hand, new technology is needed to insure healthy productivity, while, on the other, an aging work force is threatened by skill obsolescence or by the vanishing of jobs altogether. We can anticipate that many older people will resist innovation and be reluctant to take risks, while employers will continue to maintain inelastic salary levels and job rationing by age and seniority.

As we move away from the concept of the linear life plan, we also move away from security and predictability. One response to an unpredictable world has been a version of *protectionism:* for example, guarantees of lifetime job-security. Western European societies, with their aging populations, have already begun to experience the long-range cost of the protectionist strategy, a defensive response that often results in an inflexible labor force, and the setting of the old against the young. A better response would be to promote skills of adaptation and development over the entire life course. Instead of regarding older workers as unproductive burdens, we would invest in their retraining as a way of developing their abilities to contribute in many different settings.

LIFELONG LEARNING IN THE AGING SOCIETY

Adult Learners and Non-Traditional Education

The coming of an aging society is likely to accelerate the trend toward "non-traditional" higher education. American higher education has already demonstrated impressive flexibility in its ability to reach out to adult learners. The main thrust of the innovation to date has been to remove the most obvious barriers to adult learners[8]—by providing evening programs, weekend colleges, and initiating outreach efforts to bring education to sites beyond the limited time and place of the traditional campus. But these separate programs never quite achieve parity with the standard educational offerings; they always remain examples of "learning at the back door."[9] The academic mind persists in making status distinctions between regular education and continuing education, between credit and non-credit offerings, distinctions that are reinforced by educational policy and financing patterns.

Other issues may be far more important for older learners than simply promoting access. For one, the pedagogical traditions of the university are not always compatible with the active learning interests and the individual learning styles of adults. With the process of aging, people become more, not less diverse, a condition that gives rise to conflict between the expectations of experienced adults and the curriculum of most post-secondary institutions.

We must take care not to be deceived by the conventional assumptions of assessing educational needs. Patricia Cross has reminded us that the results of surveys of perceived educational demands are always related to a respondent's prior experience with education;[10] people really have no sense of what their need for education might be until they actually experience a concrete alternative program and are able to measure the difference. The successful experience of the Open University in Great Britain has demonstrated this point. Educational innovation for an aging society will demand not merely *access* to predetermined programs and materials, but *redesign* of those offerings to meet the needs of learners who bring with them the special strengths of age and experience.

Education for Older Adults

There is abundant evidence that people can continue to learn at any age. As successive generations of older people continue to show rising levels in the years of schooling they complete, we can expect interest in lifelong learning to grow in the future.[11] Today, comparatively few older people are enrolled in formal education, and the degree of their participation is correlated to their prior educational attainment, a pattern that holds true at all ages. But the participation rates of older adults are rising. The 1974 Harris Survey recorded only 2 percent engaged in adult education, while the 1981 Survey identified 5 percent.

Older learners tend not to be interested in credentials or degrees; tests, grades, and competition hold little attraction for them. The fields they pursue range widely, from the arts or methods of coping with social change, to programs that teach information about hobbies, physical health needs, and personal growth. They tend to prefer the kind of participative learning that allows them to be involved and active, as opposed to courses presented in the typical lecture format. The most effective programs have been those that respond directly to the special interests of older learners.

One example of a successful program is "Elderhostel," which was founded in 1975 as a summer residential college program for people over sixty. It offers non-credit courses in the liberal arts and sciences. Elderhostel's growth has been extraordinary. It began with two hundred participants, and by 1985 nearly 100,000 were enrolled at eight hundred campuses around the United States. Elderhostel is now both a year-round option and an overseas activity. One of its key features is its residential format, and the fact that it offers an opportunity for travel. The residential program provides a degree of intimacy and socialization that is an important part of the program as a whole. Elderhostel entails no homework, no papers, and no grades; participants enroll simply for the joy of learning. Its participants enjoy a new retirement lifestyle that reinforces feelings of self-worth and personal growth.

In many ways Elderhostel resembles the American Chattauqua Movement, now revived in the era of the aging society. The trend it demonstrates is worldwide in nature, as is evident in the spread of the "Universities of the Third Age" in France, Spain, Scandinavia, and, more recently, Japan. The phenomenon suggests further possibilities for the future of higher education in an aging society. College faculty members are increasingly troubled today about declining skills, poor motivation, and an almost single-minded focus on career-orientation on the part of their younger students. At many American campuses, professors compete to teach in Elderhostel, because older students, with their rich life experience, have proved themselves ideal audiences for liberal education.

While the socioeconomic status of Elderhostelers tends to be above average, we should not assume that liberal education can appeal only to the upper-middle-classes. Other program models exist as well:

The Senior Center Humanities Program, sponsored by the National Council on Aging, brings humanities learning to senior citizens in local neighborhood settings. It is funded by the National Endowment for the Humanities and relies on local discussion groups conducted by voluntary leaders at senior centers, nursing homes, nutrition sites, and other community locations. Groups focus on such subjects as "The Remembered Past: 1914 to 1945," and "Exploring Local History."

The program combines high-quality texts with a sensitivity and awareness about adapting materials to local interest. Carefully prepared anthologies serve as a basis for discussions and include selections from literature, philosophy, autobiography, folklore, and the arts. While using materials that are nationally produced and distributed, the Humanities Program has demonstrated its appeal to widely diverse groups of elderly people. The educational and socioeconomic profile of its 75,000 participants is virtually identical with a profile of the U.S. population over age sixty-five.

One of the greatest challenges America faces in the transition to an aging society is how to increase the availability and the quality of services in a period when government funding is tighter than ever. The answer may be found in educational programs that help older people learn skills for self-sufficiency to cope with the problems of aging. A last example suggests the potential of late-life education for encouraging productive roles for older people outside the market-place:

The *Senior Health and Peer Counseling Center* of Santa Monica, California combines older-adult education with organized self-help groups. Classes and workshops are focused on blood-pressure control, nutrition, stress management, exercise, and health education. Health screening and referral services, linked to nearby hospitals, are also available. The Santa Monica Center is nationally known for recruiting and training peer counselors, elderly people who work with other older people in emotional distress.

The Santa Monica Program illustrates the potential of older people to learn new skills when the motivation and the opportunity are present. Institutions, professionals, volunteers, and self-help groups all collaborate in a comprehensive approach. What the experience suggests is that more institutional and professional support could encourage other programs that build on the capacity for self-help and self-change in later life. Any list of the concerns of the elderly today would have to include health care, nutrition, crime prevention, and long-term care. These are areas where government at all levels has tried to respond, but typically the response has been only to provide more services for people in immediate need, with never enough money to provide services for all who actually need them. In health care, for example, we spend billions of dollars on treatment, but virtually nothing on preventing illness or on teaching older people how to care for themselves.

An alternative strategy would be to invest in educating older people to do more for themselves. Education for older people is sometimes viewed as a "frill," a view that seems short-sighted indeed, especially at a time when the "self-help ethos," as Frank Riessman has called it, is growing rapidly as mutual self-help groups have proliferated;[12] by some estimates, they now involve over 15 million Americans. Mutual-aid groups are especially appropriate for certain concerns of old age—widowhood, vulnerability to crime, and coping with chronic illnesses such as arthritis, hypertension, and diabetes, for example. Their experiential learning style offers an approach to education that is tied to concrete motivation for change. Instead of a "hard path" of constantly expanding services for a dependent population, we would opt for a "soft path," where education through self-help builds coping skills along with self-esteem.

The hard path is not only expensive; it also reinforces the "learned helplessness" of old people in the face of bureaucracy and professional interventions. By contrast, the soft path provides new skills and knowledge to make older people productive in ways that are not measured by the marketplace. Perhaps the most exciting potential of self-help lies in its possibilities for encouraging older people and professionals alike to transform their images of what "dependency" or "productivity" in old age might mean, a critical step in re-fashioning social policy for an aging society.[13]

SCENARIOS FOR THE FUTURE

Beyond the Linear Life Plan

Willard Wirtz, among others, has argued against the linear life plan, with its rigid separation of learning, work, and leisure.[14] Indeed, survey data suggest that most Americans would prefer alternative work schedules: not merely schedules that make working time more flexible, but those that radically break up the three "boxes" of life. In one survey, 80 percent of respondents favored some version of a "cyclic" life plan—that is, one that offered reduced schooling during youth, more flexible retirement, and greater options for education and leisure throughout the life course.[15]

Individual preferences aside, there are convincing policy-based arguments for favoring a more flexible life course: as a way to reduce the rising cost of student-aid dependency; as a device to avert financial threats to Social Security; and as an incentive to engage people in productive work during more years of life. Why, then, has employment been progressively compressed into the middle period of life? The real answer, it appears, is that our economy is not structured to create enough jobs for youth and for those elderly who want to work. It is pressures to achieve higher levels of productivity which require the intensive use of skilled human resources during the middle period of life. The linear life plan, far from being based on the mere "human convention" that Wirtz decried, is sustained by the most deeply rooted drives of the advanced industrial economies—the impetus towards maximizing profits and promoting efficiency.

While it is true, therefore, that flexible work schedules have come to be adopted at the margin, it is worth noting that total hours in the work week have not fallen since World War II, even though the years of completed schooling have risen, and the average age of retirement has dropped. These long-term trends suggest that there may be limits to just how far the linear life plan can be modified. If this conclusion is true, then it follows that much more attention should be devoted to education for *non*-monetized forms of productivity for older people. Retraining for paid employment will remain an important option, but clearly it should not become the exclusive criterion for policy.

The Information Economy

The structure of the century-old "modernized" life course is now being reshaped by new economic forces as America becomes a post-industrial information economy. In turn, education will be broken down into new categories corresponding to a new economic imperative for the production and distribution of knowledge:

• the formal educational system, which is the largest sector of the human services and provides the principal occupation for most people during the first quarter of their lives;

• a parallel but "invisible" instructional system sponsored by business and industry, now operating on a scale that exceeds the total expenditures for formal higher education;

• the still more informal and widely dispersed learning systems that we identify with publishing, mass media, culture, entertainment, and the communications industry.

Each of these segments of the information economy promotes learning over the life course, but each does so in very different ways and with different policies and purposes. Roughly speaking, each of these subsectors of the knowledge industry can be correlated with the "modernized" life cycle, that is, with the life stages of youth, midlife, and old age. Thus, the formal education system, with the near-monopoly it wields over the uses of time during the first quarter of life, has concentrated on youth. Business and industry have concentrated on the second quarter of life, but have largely ignored middle-aged and older workers.

Finally, we have the informal learning system that occupies an increasing part of most people's lives. Older people are linked to the information economy chiefly through the mass media. The elderly watch television more than any other age group, and for many old people TV provides the major leisure activity of their lives. The advent of an information economy, then, has not fundamentally altered the "modernized" life cycle, with its segmentation of education, work, and leisure. Apart from the informal learning system, major institutions have neglected to provide—or even to conceive of providing—learning for people in the third quarter of life or beyond.

Those analysts who have seen the outlines of a "learning society" in the new post-industrial economy are surely correct; the role of knowledge workers, the primacy of human-capital formation, and the spread of an information economy are all trends likely to favor lifelong learning. But this version of lifelong learning may not mean that greater resources are available for the formal educational system. On the contrary, it is industrial training and the informal learning system that may become the primary educational channels, drawing funding away from the formal system. This could mean a loss in our capacity for long-range thinking about human resources, a loss that would be particularly damaging in an aging society.

The Need for a Long-Range Perspective

The formal educational system—our schools and colleges—still represents the central vehicle that we have for developing human resources in our society. For a period of nearly two decades, on average, we turn over our children and young people to institutions charged with developing those capacities that will sustain them throughout their lives.

Here the contrast with corporate education and training is striking. With rare exceptions—such as IBM or Xerox—American business enterprises do *not* approach employee training with a long-range view to nurturing skills and abilities. Short-range thinking prevails. In an aging society, we will begin to pay the price for this limited view of human development, in the same way that American business is now recognizing the limits of short-range thinking tied only to the current year's balance sheet.

It would be less damaging if this kind of short-sighted, present-oriented thinking were characteristic of business and industry alone. Unfortunately, higher education has been guilty of it too, both in the "marketing" orientation of continuing-education offerings, and in the very narrow career-education programs that have displaced liberal education in many colleges and universities. Early specialization to gain an advantage in today's market leaves students ill-equipped to develop deeper and more widely ranging capacities as they grow older.

Yet the extended life span, combined with the obsolescence of so much knowledge, means that the time frame will have to be stretched still further. If a fifty-year-old worker still has twenty years of work life and perhaps a full thirty or thirty-five years of life expectancy ahead, then short-run thinking no longer makes sense.

Life-Span Development or Market Imperatives?

There is no longer any question about the ability of older adults to learn or to benefit from education, but there is an astonishing lag between what is now known about development over the life span and what our major social institutions prescribe for the different stages of life. Our traditional images tell us that youth, not age, is the time for learning, and the new boom in non-traditional learning has not really challenged that traditional image. Instead, we have expanded our image of youth into middle adulthood, and the advent of continuing education has introduced market imperatives while driving out human development goals at every turn.

The effect of market imperatives has been to extend the dominance of credentialism over the entire life course. This is not human development so much as it is defensive education in a competitive job market. In a period of rapid social and technological change, this middle-class style of lifelong learning becomes increasingly necessary for those who wish to get ahead or to appear well-informed; it is a style of adult education that may allow little room for older learners, for it regards them as superfluous to the tasks within the economic system. Unlike education for the young, education for the older adult is not perceived as a necessity for the maintenance of society. From this credential-obsessed perspective, old people may pursue education, but it is strictly a private pursuit for leisure-time activity, with no larger meaning or purpose. Here we see a view of old age as a phase of life that is separated from past and future generations, and finally cut off from any shared future.[16] It is the persistence of this view that feeds our secret despair about the last stage of life.[17]

The most gloomy scenario would perceive the aging society as an *age-polarized* society, with older and younger generations pitted against one another by opposing interests. Diminishing numbers of children would mean that support for public education would decline, while late-life education would remain a private affair among the elite. In this scenario, both higher education and business move increasingly towards a human-capital model of learning under the control of private decision-makers. While an enlarged information economy would provide unending entertainment to distract the very young and the very old, short-term interest would be determined solely by marketing considerations.

An alternative scenario would envision the aging society as a society where education at last becomes a lifelong enterprise, an opportunity for both young and old. The "three boxes of life" would give way to an ideal of continuing human development that extends over the entire life course. This ideal implies a vast expansion of retraining for middle-aged and older workers, just as it calls for a redesign of educational curricula to take account of the rich experience of older learners.

The greatest difference between these two scenarios lies not so much in their differing economic forecasts as in a fundamental question of values. Is the new abundance of life now produced by gains in longevity to be regarded as a problem or an opportunity? Are younger and older generations simply "interest-groups," or are all generations bound in obligations toward a common good? The experimentalism and vitality of American education at all levels has always been based on a shared public vision of individual opportunity working towards the common good. That history gives some reason to hope that the aging society will rediscover opportunities for learning in each of the stages of life.

ENDNOTES

The author is grateful for support from the Andrew Norman Institute for Advanced Study at the Andrus Gerontology Center, University of Southern California, as well as the Mina Shaughnessy Fellowship Program of the Fund for the Improvement of Post-Secondary Education during the period this article was written.

[1]Philippe Aries, *Centuries of Childhood* (New York: Alfred A. Knopf, 1962).

[2]Gerald Gruman, "The Modernization of the Life Cycle," in D. Van Tassell, K. Woodward, and S. Spicker, eds., *Aging & the Elderly: Humanistic Perspectives in Gerontology* (Atlantic Highlands, NJ: Humanities Press, 1978).

[3]See Samuel H. Preston, "Children and the Elderly in the U.S.," *Scientific American,* Dec. 1984, pp. 44–49.

[4]Nell P. Eurich, *Corporate Classrooms: The Learning Business,* (Princeton, N.J.: Carnegie Foundation for the Advancement of Teaching, 1985).

[5]I am indebted to Dr. Robert Sperber, former Superintendent of Schools of Brookline, Massachusets, for background information provided at the Carnegie Project Conference on Education and the Aging Society.

[6]I am indebted to Cindy Marano for background information on the Displaced Homemaker Programs.

[7]Michael Harrington, *The New American Poverty* (New York: Holt, Rinehart, & Winston, 1984). Barry Bluestone and Bennett Harrison, *The Deindustrialization of America: Plant Closings, Community Abandonment and the Dismantling of Basic Industry* (New York: Basic Books, 1983).

[8]I am indebted to Russell Edgerton, president of the American Association for Higher Education, for background information provided at the Conference on Education and the Aging Society.

[9]Charles A. Wedemeyer, *Learning at the Back Door: Reflections on Non-Traditional Learning in the Lifespan* (Madison, WI: University of Wisconsin Press, 1981).

[10]K. Patricia Cross, *Adults as Learners: Increasing Participation and Facilitating Learning* (San Francisco: Jossey-Bass, 1984).

[11]The best overall treatment of education in later life is David Peterson, *Facilitating Education for Older Learners* (San Francisco: Jossey-Bass, 1983).

[12]Alan Gartner and Frank Riessman, *The Self-Help Revolution* (New York: Human Sciences Press, 1984).

[13]Peter Townsend, "The Structured Dependency of the Elderly: A Creation of Social Policy in the 20th Century," *Ageing and Society,* March 1981, pp. 5–28; Alan Walker, "The Social Production of Old Age," *Ageing and Society,* Nov. 1983, pp. 87–95.

[14]Willard Wirtz, *The Boundless Resource* (Washington, DC: New Republic Book Co., 1975).

[15]Survey by Fred Best, cited by Robert Hamrin in his *Managing Growth in the 1980s* (New York: Praeger, 1980), p. 282.

[16]See the chapter on "Old Age" in Christopher Lasch, *The Culture of Narcissism* (New York: W.W. Norton, 1977).

[17]On ego-integrity versus despair in old age, cf. Erik Erikson, *Insight and Responsibility* (New York: Norton, 1964) and Erikson, *The Life Cycle Completed: A Review* (New York: Norton, 1982).

Fernando Torres-Gil

Hispanics: A Special Challenge

I N AN AGING AMERICA, cultural pluralism represents a social force that will help define the future character of our country. Multiculturalism reflects our growing numbers of ethnic and minority populations, particularly the national minority groups: blacks, Asians and Pacific Islanders, Hispanics, and Native Americans—groups whose members are much younger than the population as a whole. Together they will make up a large percentage of the U.S. population, and in many regions of the country will become the new majority. How we choose to respond to this situation will say much about us as a nation. Will blacks continue to be an underclass: impoverished, disillusioned, and increasingly rebellious? Will Hispanics and Asians become separatist nations within the U.S, maintaining their cultural identities and aligning themselves exclusively with their countries of origin? Or will the current dominant population—the primarily white, English-speaking descendants of eighteenth- and nineteenth-century Anglo-Saxon and European immigrants welcome them into the ever-changing American mosaic?

This essay will approach the aging of our population and the implications for cultural pluralism by examining one dimension: Hispanics in an aging society.* Not only are Hispanics becoming the

---

*Even the question of what to call Hispanics is fraught with controversies and frustration. "Hispanics," as a term, was not created by Puerto Ricans, Cubans, or Mexican-Americans for self-identity, but is rather a convenient sociological and demographic term that functions as an umbrella to describe those three groups, as well as Central and Latin Americans, in the United States. The U.S. Bureau of the Census used the term "Spanish-origin or descendant" in the 1980 Census as a "self-identifier" for those who designated themselves as being Mexican, Mexican-American, Chicano, Puerto Rican, Cuban, or other Spanish/Hispanic. For the purposes of this

largest minority in the country, but they are remarkably diverse, composed of Puerto Ricans, Cubans, Mexican-Americans, and Central and Latin Americans. Their presence also forces us to acknowledge a reality that we have too long ignored: the Western hemisphere is composed primarily of Spanish-speaking persons with a Latino heritage. As the populations of the countries of the Caribbean, Brazil, and Spanish-speaking America continue to grow at tremendous rates, and continue to provide the United States with large numbers of young immigrants, Canada and the United States are diminishing in terms of their numerical importance.

With the growth of young Spanish-speaking populations in the United States, the aging of the U.S population will bring problems, challenges, and opportunities. If we are to respond dispassionately and constructively, we must be prepared to understand these trends as they develop. The U.S is not the only country facing these circumstances. Other parts of the world—Canada, Israel, China, and the Soviet Union—are also experiencing rapidly aging populations that contain increasing numbers of linguistically and culturally diverse groups. But as the world's leading industrial, technological and economic power, we have, through default, become the mirror of the future that faces the rest of the world. How we respond to these challenges will be noted carefully, and taken either as models to emulate or mistakes to avoid.

HISPANICS IN AN AGING AMERICA

Assessing the impact of an aging society on the Hispanic population and posing its problems, challenges, and implications for policy and cultural change is not a narrow exercise. Although many of the issues involved are equally relevant to other minority groups in this country, the differences between Hispanics and blacks, Asians and Pacific Islanders, Native Americans, and white ethnic groups—Poles, Germans, Irish, Italians, Jews—are such as to merit their study as a group distinct from other minority and ethnic populations.

The 1980 census indicates that 14.6 million Hispanics live in the mainland United States and about 3.5 million in Puerto Rico. They

paper, however, Hispanic will be used in lieu of "Spanish-origin" unless reference is made to a specific Hispanic subgroup.

constitute at least 6.4 percent of the U.S population. Between 1970 and 1980, the Hispanic population, as counted by the census, grew 61 percent, compared with a 9 percent increase for non-Hispanics—a surge that makes Hispanics the fastest-growing population group in the country. Mexican-Americans, or Chicanos, constitute 60 percent of this population, followed by Puerto Ricans (14 percent), Cuban Americans (6 percent), and Central and South Americans and others of Spanish origin (20 percent).[1]

People of Spanish origin have given the United States some unique statistical characteristics. We are now the fifth largest Spanish-speaking country in the world, after Mexico, Spain, Argentina, and Colombia. If Puerto Rico is included, the United States would be placed even ahead of Colombia. Spanish is the fourth most frequently spoken language in the world, after Chinese, English, and Russian.[2] After Mexico City, Los Angeles has the second-largest concentration of residents of Mexican descent in the Western Hemisphere.[3]

Important subgroup variations exist within the U.S Hispanic population. Generally, Puerto Ricans have higher unemployment rates, lower family and per-capita incomes, and lower median school years completed than Mexican-Americans or Cubans. Cubans have generally completed the highest median school years, and account for the highest individual and family incomes and the lowest unemployment rate of the three subgroups. Mexican-Americans usually fall between the other groups. Median age among Hispanics differs greatly from other groups. Persons of Spanish origin presently have a median age of twenty-three years, which is lower than that of whites (thirty-one), Asians (twenty-nine), and blacks (twenty-five). Among Hispanics, Cubans tend to be older (thirty-eight), followed by Mexican-Americans (twenty-two) and Puerto Ricans (twenty-two).[4]

ISSUES

The aging of society will affect education, health care, and jobs; economic, political, and governmental systems; and our attitudes about the aging process itself. For Hispanics in American society, this phenomenon raises particular social, political, and economic implications. As relatively recent immigrants to the United States, Hispanics' assimilation will differ substantially from that of previous immigrant groups such as Jews, Italians, Germans, and Irish.[5] The United

States is embarking on a new technological and re-industrialization course, reducing the number of those blue-collar jobs that have required little education but afforded middle-class income and status to earlier immigrant groups. The Hispanic population is also larger than any group other than blacks, so their numbers alone will make them highly visible. Unlike previous groups, their cultural reinforcement is literally next door; Mexico, Puerto Rico, and Cuba are only a short flight, boat trip, car ride—or, for some, a short walk—away. This proximity, coupled with mass communication systems, may mean that Hispanics will be able to retain their cultural identity longer than previous immigrant groups.

The most profound aspect of this matter is the growth of a young Hispanic population precisely when the United States itself is aging. No other American immigrant group has had to evolve, assimilate, and attempt to achieve full participation in American social, economic, educational, and political life while the country was being increasingly affected and redirected by its aging population. How might these parallel trends of the Latinization and the aging of the U.S population affect our future? What issues do they raise, and where does their intersection occur?

To illustrate the consequences that an aging society poses for Hispanics, it is helpful to compare their situation with that of two other cohorts: today's elderly, and those who will begin to turn sixty-five by the year 2010—the "baby-boomers." Both groups have disparate historical profiles that provide clues to the issues and tensions that may arise as they, along with the Hispanics, mature in an aging society. Today's elderly, the products of the Great Depression and World War II, are both conservative and liberal: they value individualism, self-reliance, and strong family ties, but the Depression has also made them adherents of a strong federal role in the provision of public benefits and services. Even while they approve of the "bootstrap" theory—that everyone should pull themselves up by their own efforts without relying on government—they also support Social Security, Medicare, and the Older Americans Act, public benefits that have protected many of them from abject poverty.

It is no surprise that a majority of the elderly voted for President Reagan in 1980 and 1984 while opposing his administration's efforts to cut back programs for the aged.

The baby-boom group represents the "golden generation": those who are enjoying the benefits of their parents' military and economic victories.[6] They take for granted that social stability and public benefits (e.g., student financial assistance, subsidized mortgage interest rates, environmental protections, a volunteer military) will continue. They expect to be better off economically than their parents, and they have an overriding concern for job security, upward mobility, job advancement, and the "good life."[7] The youth culture of the 1960s and 1970s was promulgated by baby-boomers, and it is they who will redefine a "middle age" and an "aging" culture. Yet this group may be forced to compete directly with a young Hispanic population for scarce resources and may become a "generation of risk," wondering whether they will face reduced public benefits such as pensions and health care.[8] If the "law of numbers" thesis is accurate,[9] where the large post–World War II generation finds life difficult because of large numbers competing for jobs and upward mobility (and conversely, the small generation born in the 1930s finds the labor market favorable because of their scarce numbers), then this cohort may have additional reason to compete with young minority populations. What clues do these tensions and uncertainties offer for assessing the impact of an aging society on Hispanics? The answers are related to political power and competition, to resource allocation and financial security.

Political Power and Competition

Much has been written about the growing sophistication and political clout of Hispanics. Since the 1950s, they have shown dramatic gains in registration and voting, and the number of Hispanic elected officials has increased nationwide. In several states—California, New York, Texas, Illinois, and Florida—they are considered the "swing vote" in close state-wide elections. Yet the Hispanic vote has yet to live up to its potential, and despite the increases in registration and voting rates, Hispanics as a group are still a "sleeping giant."

Registration and voting rates remain low. In the 1982 elections, only 35 percent of the Hispanic population was registered to vote, compared with 59 percent of blacks and 64 percent of whites. Low Hispanic registration and voting rates are due to the large proportion who are not citizens (32 percent) and to the relative youthfulness of the population.[10]

Older persons face an entirely different situation. They have political power, at least in terms of the percentage of their numbers who are registered and vote. In 1982, 65 percent of persons 65 to 74 years of age and 65 percent of persons 55 to 64 years old voted, compared with 60 percent of persons aged 45 to 54, and 52 percent of persons aged 35 to 44.[11] Some analysts argue that the elderly are not a voting bloc, and that any claims to the effect that they wield inordinate power solely because of their collective numbers is a political bluff.[12] In part, this is accurate. Older persons are a diverse group whose members differ by gender, income, race, background, and class. They do not always have common concerns.[13] However, on selective issues such as public benefits, where they are directly affected as older persons, the elderly do tend to vote as a bloc and are an important political force.[14]

Hispanics are at a distinct disadvantage when they are forced to confront the potential political power of older persons. Not only are the absolute numbers of eligible Hispanic voters fewer, and their registration and voting rates much lower, but the percentage of Hispanic elderly who vote is very small. This is further aggravated by the large percentage of undocumented Hispanics and by the general youthfulness of their population. Hispanics cannot expect to win when issues become posed as a choice between a Hispanic priority and an elderly priority—a situation that is bound to arise in such policy areas as education, health, Social Security, and retirement programs. And given the demography of Hispanics, they will not display a competitive stance until well into the early twenty-first century, when the large section of young Hispanic voters matures and reaches the peak voting ages of forty to sixty.

What about the baby-boomers? What role do they play as a political force, and how does this affect Hispanics? The baby-boomers were raised during the affluent decades of the 1950s and 1960s, and can afford to be liberal on social issues: pro-environment, pro–gun-control legislation, and pro–liberalization of drug abuse laws; and conservative toward government and large organizations: anti-establishment, anti–big government, anti–big institutions, and anti–big labor.[15] When Hispanics expect government to intervene on social and public policies, they may find the baby-boomers are not an ally. It may well be too early to assess the potential clout of baby-boomers, for individuals born between 1946 and 1961 (the commonly accepted age period for the baby boom) are still not at their peak voting rates. Their real impact on the political system is yet to come, and as that time nears, it will become increasingly important to assess their attitudes, values, and political behavior to determine to what extent they will work for or against Hispanic interests.

Resource Allocation

The unequal political power among young Hispanics and aging whites affects other political and policy issues, particularly the allocation of resources in a constrained economy.

Perhaps the single most important priority for Hispanics is education. American immigrants have often seized upon education as "a way out." The development of public education in the 1800s was a milestone for American social policy, because it guaranteed every child an opportunity, if not a guarantee, that he or she would be educated. Along with this has been the public's belief that support of public education should be a top priority, regardless of the tax dollars involved. Unfortunately, public education has been declining since the 1960s—in quality, availability, and public support.

This trend has directly affected recent immigrants (e.g., Hispanics, Vietnamese, Haitians) who were to have followed the same path as Italians, Germans, Jews, Japanese, and other immigrant groups. It is ironic that just when the second generation of Mexican-Americans and Puerto Ricans are beginning to attach a priority to their children obtaining an education, Hispanics find schools overcrowded, plagued by crime, dependent on out-dated instructional materials, and staffed by non-minority teachers who are near retirement and are tired of the hassles of teaching in inner-city schools.

Yet the young Hispanic population greatly needs renewed support for public education. Hispanics are the least educated minority in the United States. For every hundred children entering school, fourteen whites fail to obtain a high school diploma, compared with thirty-three blacks and forty Hispanics.[16] Forty-five percent of Mexican-American and Puerto Rican students who entered high school never finished, compared with 17 percent of Anglo-American students.[17] The implications of this are serious. Hispanics are receiving inferior education, and are not completing high school or entering professional or graduate schools in proportion with their growing population. An underclass of ill-prepared, uneducated persons may be developing that will last for generations. Compounding this lack of educational preparation is the change in skills now required for full participation in a technological, computerized, and communication society—skills not being acquired by most Hispanic children, and without which in the future even blue-collar jobs will be unattainable. This underclass will present scant comfort for the relatively few Hispanics who have "made it," for these few will increasingly be perceived as an elite whose members are part of the system that is unaccessible to most young Hispanics. This elite will become the subject of the same bitterness and distrust currently directed to others.

Education presents one of the most critical areas of discrepancy between the priorities of today's elderly, the baby-boomers, and Hispanics. In an aging society, more resources will go towards adult education, midlife career training, pre-retirement planning, second and third careers for homemakers re-entering the work force, and retirees. If education is a barometer of occupation, income, and class mobility, Hispanics will, as they garner political power, come into direct conflict with a population that is reluctant to tax itself for public education, and uses its political power to support tuition tax credits, educational vouchers, and federal aid to private and parochial schools. Many of this group will send their children to private schools (as will many Hispanic middle-class families) rather than sending them to inferior public schools.

Employment is a second critical area that will be affected by an aging society. Unemployment in 1983 ranged from 12.3 percent to 13.3 percent for Hispanics, while it hovered between 9.5 percent and 8.8 percent for the overall U.S population.[18] Lack of education is a major cause of employment problems, particularly for Mexican-Americans and Puerto Ricans. But discrimination and lack of proficiency in English are two additional major problems facing Hispanic workers in the labor market. The percentage of Hispanics in managerial and professional occupations was lower than for the total population, although Cubans had higher percentages than Puerto Ricans and Mexicans.[19]

The relative disadvantages Hispanics face in the labor force contrast with the increasing importance they have gained there. In an aging society, fewer young whites will be available to replace those who are aging. As the baby-boom generation ages, insufficient numbers of non-minorities will be available to fill labor-force and military manpower needs, and young minority populations, particularly those representing the two largest minority groups (blacks and Hispanics), may become the mainstay of the labor force and the military—particularly in elite units such as marines and paratroopers. It is these young minority populations that will become vital to the support of the aged population—a population that is primarily white.

This trend creates a set of tensions for a young Hispanic population facing greater demands for its labor. Will the general population be willing to support improvements in public education and re-training programs? Given that the public educational system that now serves minorities has yet to incorporate high technology, computers, cybernetics, and communications, are Hispanics and blacks being prepared for technologically obsolete skills? Or will major initiatives be undertaken to revamp public education and to provide it with the resources to train minorities for the new industries?

Financial Security

Hispanics are twice as likely to be poor as the general population. In 1982 they made up 12.5 percent of America's poor, although they constituted only 6.4 percent of the U.S population. Poverty varies across subgroups: Puerto Ricans live in the "rust-bowl"—the central cities of the Northeast and Midwest, where unemployment and poverty are exacerbated by plant closings and other economic problems—while Cubans are concentrated in Florida—a "sunbelt" state with a growing economy—and Mexican-Americans are found in the Southwestern states of the Sunbelt which have growing economies.

In an aging society, the continued existence of these rates of poverty will raise serious issues about employment, labor-force participation, and education. The more salient issue, however, given their present circumstances, is the extent to which Hispanics and other minority groups will be at greater risk when they age. How likely is it that in an aging society, policy decisions will be made that affect the economic circumstances of Hispanic aging?

It is around Social Security and the protection of retirement and pension plans that major policy conflicts will emerge as Hispanics mature in an aging society. In 1983, for example, the U.S Congress instituted major structural changes to preserve the fiscal integrity of the Social Security system. It avoided benefit reductions for current recipients, but for future beneficiaries it raised the eligibility age for receipt of full benefits to sixty-seven for those individuals who will reach age sixty-two after 2022. This type of public-policy action raises the prospect that future generations of older minorities may not have access to benefits now enjoyed by the elderly, particularly those groups with lower life expectancies, or without full citizenship.

Health policy is another possible area of tension. Health care delivery is developing into a two-tier system: one level for those with private health insurance, Medicare, or the means to pay for expensive medical treatment; and another for those forced to rely on Medicaid, public charity, or to do without health care altogether. The services provided at this second level are fewer and of lower quality; this situation is exacerbated by cutbacks in Medicaid, by the expansion of a for-profit medical-industrial system that caters to middle- and upper-income consumers, and by state and local government unwillingness or inability to provide health care to the poor.[20]

Hispanics and baby-boomers are facing reductions or elimination of those features that benefit today's elders. But baby-boomers are caught in the middle: they are too young to benefit from current retirement policies, but old enough to become alarmed. They will increasingly come to see the raising of eligibility years, the reduction in costs-of-living indexes, the taxation of pension benefits, and the reduction of retirement income as working against their interests. They may respond to these actions in one of two ways: by supporting legislation that ensures that pensions and Social Security will continue to be generous to all age groups and tax themselves accordingly; or by supporting legislation that benefits only their own age group and still taxes the public—as the elderly did in 1983. They may use their political leverage to raise taxes on a labor force that is increasingly black and Hispanic—a group that will be politically disadvantaged for another decade or two.

Hispanics, on the other hand, have not yet made financial security in old age a political priority. Their political leadership is more concerned with such short-term priorities as education, employment, and cultural issues (bilingual programs, for example). Yet critical decisions will be made in the 1980s that will affect the pension, retirement, and Social Security systems for the year 2010 and beyond. It may be too late to wait for the Hispanic youth to reach their full voting potential in the year 2015 to influence those decisions. By then, they may react to perceived inequities and create more conflict—not just with the elderly of today, who will be dying, but with the baby-boomers caught up in their own retirement activities.

Early signs of this conflict can be gleaned from data on pension coverage. In 1980, Hispanic civilian workers had the lowest rates of pension-plan coverage (35 percent), compared with whites (45.5 percent) and blacks (40.9 percent).[21] Among workers participating in private pension plans, Hispanic workers are less likely to have vested rights benefits than their white counterparts. The difference is particularly large among older participants—those getting ready to retire. Among all ages, 35 percent of Hispanics were vested, compared with 49 percent of whites and 41 percent of blacks. In the forty-five and older range, 44 percent of Hispanics were vested, compared with 66 percent of whites and 58 percent of blacks.[22]

CONSEQUENCES

An examination of the areas of political power, resource allocation, and financial security highlights the issues and conflicts Hispanics will face in an aging society. Our current dramatic shift in social policies towards the aged and aging, and away from youthful populations, portends those tensions. Since the 1960s, we have given increasing priorities to creating, expanding, and maintaining public benefits and programs for older persons. Yet public outlays for children have been reduced since the 1970s. The costs of public entitlement programs, specifically Medicare and Social Security, are becoming so great that in a period of a restrained economy, they overshadow other equally important public policy choices such as public education. Samuel Preston found that since the 1970s, the total federal outlay on child-oriented programs (AFDC, Head Start, food stamps, child health, child nutrition, and aid to education) was about 36 billion dollars for 1984, about a sixth of the total spending for the elderly.[23]

An increasingly large proportion of American children are from minority groups: 24 percent of those younger than fifteen are black or Hispanic, compared with only 11 percent of the population that is sixty-five or older.[24] That raises the critical issue of race in determining public priorities. Some may argue that as children become fewer they will be more highly prized; with fewer children, it is argued, more resources and attention can be devoted to them. On the other hand, if those children are minorities, will they, in fact, receive greater attention? Will we invest more public funds in inner-city black and Hispanic schools? Race and racism may be mitigating factors; minority children have always been a minority, yet they continue to have the highest rates of unemployment, the lowest rates of education, and greater incidences of crime. In an aging society, the color and ethnicity of children may continue to work to their disadvantage. Where government has to choose between Medicare and public education, it may choose the former. Where a state has to choose between contributions to civil service retirement systems and retraining for minorities, it may choose the former. Where Hispanic advocacy groups have to compete against senior-citizen lobbies in city councils, the latter is likely to come out ahead.

As the intersection of aging and cultural pluralism draws near, then, we are faced with tensions related to age, race, and ethnicity. David Hayes-Bautista and his colleagues refer to this tension as the emergence of a population that is stratified by age and race.[25] Using California as a case study, they identified three social forces—deaths, births, and migrations—that affect the size and composition of a population. They found that the Latino population is much younger, has a higher fertility rate, and grows as a result of constant immigration from areas such as Mexico. The white population, on the other hand, is aging, increasing in longevity, and not replacing itself by births. California is therefore likely to become highly stratified by age and race within the next thirty to fifty years, and the burden of support of the large elderly population may fall onto the shoulders of a smaller working-age population—a population that will be predominantly black and Hispanic, and one that may well ask why it should sacrifice to support the elderly.

The issue of long-term care provides an interesting illustration of the reality facing Hispanics in an aging society. After families, the major source of long-term care is nursing homes. Yet the residents of nursing homes, particularly of proprietary homes, are overwhelmingly Caucasian females, the owners and administrators are largely white males, and the non-professional staff—the orderlies, janitors, nurses' aides—are frequently minorities: blacks, Hispanics, and undocumenteds. This is so, in part, because there are fewer Hispanic elderly in the general population, and they are more likely to be cared for in their homes.[26] But the larger issue in the occupational segmentation of the nursing-home industry is an underlying attitude of racism. The industry is only too willing to hire workers who accept very low wages and who are not likely to join unions (undocumenteds), but it will not hire or train minorities as administrators or provide them with opportunities to become owners and investors. Nor does it make extensive efforts to increase minorities in its patient pool, for Caucasian patients may be uncomfortable with a mix of minority residents, and because minority elderly will require linguistic and cultural services.

The purpose of raising these disparities is not to add fuel to fires—that is, not to fabricate a polarization between aging whites and young Hispanics. Robert Binstock warns of using the aged as scapegoats when we focus on how well-off the elderly are in comparison with other groups. Scapegoating the elderly diverts attention from a host of deficiencies in political leadership and public policy, at a time when the problems of society should be viewed in a "non-ageist political context."[27] But in order to move toward a non-ageist approach in examining the position of Hispanics in an aging society, it is necessary to assess and acknowledge the conflicts that may arise between distinct groups, and to do so while there is still time to develop constructive solutions. The perception that a problem exists is often more important than the reality. The media and various Hispanic organizations are already raising these perceived disparities, and it is important to acknowledge and address them.

Immigration and nativism are other factors to contend with. The economic dislocation of the 1970s and 1980s has resurrected a fear of immigrants and migrants, particularly those from Southeast Asia and the Pacific Islands, the Caribbean, and Latin America. Nativism—the fear of "non-American" immigrants—is not new. It was raised in the 1860s when Irish immigration hit its peak after the potato famines of the 1840s, in 1880 when the railroads reached the West Coast and the Chinese workers employed to build them were no longer needed, and in 1900 when the United States received its largest number of immigrants from Eastern and Southern Europe.[28] The 1980s is witnessing the peak arrival of Latin Americans—immigrants who are arriving at a time when America is undergoing major economic and political changes and is in no mood to tolerate, let alone be generous towards, those who are not already citizens.

The population arriving from Latin America and the Caribbean is young and eager to come to the United States. For example, the age pyramids of Mexico and the United States are reversed, with the very young comprising a large portion of Mexico's population, just as the old comprise a large portion of the United States'.[29] The high birth rate in Mexico creates tremendous pressures on an economy that cannot provide the jobs, education, or housing that its population desperately needs. Many of the same trends are occurring throughout the Caribbean and Latin America. Puerto Rico, Cuba, Central America, Mexico, and Latin America are relatively young populations with high birth rates.[30] Each in turn is faced with economic, political, and social transitions that are causing many of its young to come to the United States. As the United States becomes more Latinized, much of its population growth will be accounted for by Hispanic immigrants, constantly reinforcing and replenishing those generations who are beginning to assimilate. It seems certain that immigration and nativism will continue to provide important sources of conflict or opportunity well into the next century.

Alongside the Latinization of the United States and the constant immigration of Latinos are the accompanying pressures and dilemmas over cultural maintenance. Unlike previous groups, Hispanics— particularly Mexicans, Puerto Ricans, and Cubans—appear to be unlikely candidates for either full assimilation or full acculturation, at least in our lifetime. Many individuals have assimilated, but the bulk continue to retain their language (Spanish), their customs, their in-group solidarity and interests, and for some, their involvement with their countries of origin. We have noted that much of this cultural maintenance can be attributed to the ease of travel and communication, as well as the proximity of these three regions. But it is also due to the sizable numbers of Hispanics, and to their growing political influence. It is this political influence that is making itself felt in policies that promote bilingualism and biculturalism, practices that will also lead to policy conflicts. The development of bilingual programs as a matter of national policy, the use of Spanish on bilingual ballots, the pressure in some states to make Spanish an official language, and the pervasiveness of Spanish names and symbols in food, dress, and towns reflect the influence of Hispanic culture and language. And as Spanish language and culture grow with the size of the Hispanic population, further tensions will be added to those that already face young Hispanics in an elderly population composed primarily of Anglo-European background.

These issues are essential to our understanding the difference between Hispanics and other minority and ethnic groups in the United States. Blacks cannot easily promote an African language or African culture; nor can Asians or Pacific Islanders use their presence to promote public policies to reflect their special cultural characteristics, for they are too few in number. But Hispanic numbers guarantee that demands for cultural identity will play a role in their political and policy priorities.

POLICY

Having identified the potential conflicts posed by maturing Hispanics in an aging society, we need to explore the range of constructive and compassionate solutions. Proposing specific responses is difficult, given the exploratory nature of this essay and the many questions that have yet to be explored by other writers and researchers. Nonetheless, it is possible to take advantage of a window of opportunity that exists in the 1980s, and to suggest policy directions that may prepare us for a multigenerational and multicultural society.

First, our society's elderly must assume some leadership on issues that benefit the non-aged. Today's elderly have paid their dues to their country and their society: they have lived through the Great Depression, World War II, the Korean War, and the prosperity of the 1950s, 1960s, and 1970s. They have earned their share of public benefits and programs, and that cannot be denied them. But the aged of today have a responsibility to future generations as well: to their children and grandchildren, and to the children and grandchildren of America's newest immigrants. That responsibility requires them to support those policy directions that may not benefit them directly in the short term, but will benefit the future elderly in the long term. Do we put more resources into Supplemental Security Income, disability insurance, and other programs that primarily serve the young and the elderly poor? Do we tax Social Security benefits? Charging the elderly to take part in these decisions does not burden them with the sole responsibility for ensuring that society responds to younger minority groups, for the larger responsibility lies with the entire society—its social, economic, and governmental institutions. But the elderly *will* be required to broaden the extent of their current participation in these issues if our nation's response is to be constructive.

We have described some of the improvements that will be necessary if Hispanics are to be vital partners in an aging society—improvements in their health, education, employment, and income circumstances. But there are other directions and policies that go beyond these areas, that arise not only from their unique cultural, political, and economic status in the United States, but also from the state of U.S relationships with Latin America and the Caribbean.

Redefining Ethnicity

In the United States, ethnicity is often couched in terms of those who are considered "Americans" and those who are considered members of minority groups, a distinction that creates the illusion that minority groups are somehow "un-American" if they retain their language, culture, and heritage. It fails to recognize that today's American culture is an amalgamation of the cultural characteristics of those groups who arrived in the nineteenth century and the early "Anglo-Saxons" who colonized the Eastern seaboard. Just as the immigrants of the eighteenth and nineteenth centuries created today's American culture, so the immigrant groups of the twentieth century—Hispanics, Asians, and Pacific Islanders—will contribute their influence and redefine American culture in the twenty-first century. During that transition, an aging society will need to grapple with the cultural homogeneity of an elderly population and the cultural diversity of its younger minority populations, who will not be a significant portion of the elderly population until after 2015.

The growth of young immigrant populations in the United States at a time when the society is aging can be viewed as either a problem or a set of opportunities. If we perceive it as an asset, then ethnicity, multiple languages, and links with these groups' countries of origins will imbue the United States with a dynamic flavor, as well as provide it with a young, industrious work force. If we perceive it as a problem, then nativism and ignorance about cultural pluralism will dictate policies that treat these minority groups as second-class citizens, and pit the dominant American culture now reflected in the elderly population against the young immigrant cultures from Latin

America, the Caribbean, and the Pacific Basin, polarizing them and pitting them against each other.

Bilingualism-Biculturalism

The need to redefine the American character is reflected in the current debates about whether to adopt Spanish as an official language, and whether to require bilingual ballots, documents, and education. The specter of French Quebec is raised as a dire example of what could befall the United States if we allow Spanish to become official policy in areas with high concentrations of Hispanics. Will it promote separatism? Will certain regions (e.g., South Florida, Los Angeles, South Texas, New York) identify more with Cuba, Mexico, and Puerto Rico and demand separate status? But using French Quebec as a warning ignores the uniqueness of the Canadian experience: French culture and language were promoted there, not to *encourage* separatism, but to *keep* French Quebec in the Canadian union—a solution that appears to be working.[31]

Unfortunately, bilingualism has become a political issue that polarizes instead of unifying. Some argue that bilingualism is a civil and political right, while others assert that only English can be the official language. Each side argues a strong case, and the debate is unresolvable for now. What is certain is that the discussion is divisive, and must not be allowed to serve as the standard by which cultural pluralism and the status of Hispanics in an aging society is judged. Far more serious subjects—e.g., education, public services—demand our immediate attention, and both sides in the current debate are at fault for polarizing and ignoring the real issues bilingualism raises.

Multilingual abilities of Americans are an asset, as they are in Europe, and teaching Spanish in public and private schools helps not only immigrants, but all those who speak only English. Yet, bilingual advocates are at fault for confusing or ignoring a vital priority: English-language proficiency. Hispanic children and immigrants must master English, and while bilingual educational programs are needed in schools, they must focus only on English-language proficiency rather than on cultural maintenance. The latter is a private matter that is best attended to in the home and the communities.

Political Participation

The intersection of multiculturalism and aging will most likely occur first in the political realm. As Hispanics grow in numbers, and age, their political influence will increase. The full weight of this will not be felt until 2010, when the upwardly mobile Hispanics of the 1970s and 1980s will reach their peak voting ages. That will lead either to political conflict, or to alliances with those who are devoted to promoting policies that benefit Hispanics, the elderly, and society. Discrimination, racism, gerrymandering, and other measures that create obstacles and postpone full political participation of Hispanics will only create an animosity that can lead to selfishness and vindictiveness among Hispanics when they acquire their political influence.

As Hispanics grow in numbers and political influence, there may well develop a "Hispanic lobby" capable of affecting an aging society. America in this century has had a tradition of ethnic lobbies in foreign policy.[32] The Greek lobby influenced American foreign policy in the conflict between Greece and Turkey, and the Jewish lobby influences U.S relationships with Israel and the Middle East. Will there be a lobby representing Hispanic groups that attempts to influence American foreign policy with Latin America? Whether a Hispanic lobby develops that compares in sufficient political and economic influence with the Jewish lobby remains to be seen. But if it does—and there is evidence that it will—it could introduce a new tension, between priorities at home (e.g., health, pensions) and priorities for the larger Hispanic community—the economic and political conditions in Latin America (e.g., political repression, economic development, immigration).

Latin America

Conditions in Latin America and U.S policy in the region will be increasingly important issues for Hispanics in an aging society. Mexico's economy, the United States' relationship with Cuba, and the status of Puerto Rico are immediate concerns for Mexican-Americans, Puerto Ricans, and Cubans.[33] But the social and military turmoil in Central America, drug problems throughout South America, political instability in the Caribbean, and poverty, repression, and economic instability in Latin America are also of great concern to the United States, and will especially affect Hispanics.

One immediate issue confronting us is immigration. This is both an internal issue for the United States—large numbers of undocumented persons arrive each year and play an important role in the U.S economy—and a foreign policy issue to the extent that it depletes resources in Mexico, Central America, and other nations.[34] Immigration to the United States increases the presence of Hispanics, reinforces their cultural heritage, and keeps their median age low. Those who immigrate are generally the youngest, poorest segments of Latin America, although large numbers of older, affluent Latin Americans also arrive whenever their political or economic position is threatened in their countries. Immigration also serves as deliberate foreign policy strategy for other nations: it is, for example, Mexico's safety valve, for without it Mexico would face far more severe pressures for internal reform. It also acts as a brain drain, drawing from Argentina, Brazil, and other countries their brightest and most ambitious individuals. The United States benefits from immigration, but it also creates further tensions, adding to the youthful nature of the Hispanic population and, over time, increasing its political presence, strengthening its influence, and affecting its public-policy priorities. It should therefore not be surprising that immigration may also exacerbate any already existing tensions or discrepancies between Hispanics and an aging society.

THE RESPONSIBILITY OF HISPANICS IN AN AGING SOCIETY

It is not enough to assign responsibilities to society in general, and to the aged and the baby-boomers in particular, if we are to avoid the real and potential conflicts that await us in our aging society. Hispanics share equal accountability to ensure that a multigenerational and culturally pluralistic society can count on compromises, sacrifices, and joint ventures by all its constituents. As their numbers increase and they become the majority in certain regions of the United States, Hispanics cannot afford to consider only their own specific priorities (e.g., immigration, Latin America, bilingualism); they have a larger responsibility to the entire society and its priorities: economic prosperity, internal cohesion, and political stability. Just as American society must recognize their unique experience, Hispanics must understand the historical development of the United States, the dichotomous immigration (from Europe and the Third World) that creates a schizophrenic response to the new immigrants, and other issues that create fear and concern in the American public. Hispanics in the U.S cannot afford to be perceived as a special interest group, wanting and not giving.

Hispanic political and economic elites have been guilty of becoming interest groups with a narrow set of agendas that do not take into account the broader needs of our society. Demands for bilingual education, affirmative action, and a focus on immigration, without an accompanying awareness of how they affect other public and social policies, cannot help but elicit animosity and resentment, both from the public at large and from other ethnic and minority groups. In short, Hispanics have as much to learn about the changes affecting an aging America as the society has to learn about Hispanics. There is self-interest at stake; despite the continuing influx of young Latin American immigrants, Hispanics will not always be a young population. They are aging too; already, 5 percent of their number is over sixty-five.[35] In fact, Hispanics are aging at a faster rate than whites; a greater percentage become sixty years old every year than in the white population.[36] These figures should serve to emphasize the stake Hispanics have in ensuring that *all* elderly are treated fairly.

Hispanics have a responsibility to participate in the redefinition of the American mosaic and to assure the American public that they are not pursuing separate policies. In order to avoid polarization and intergroup conflicts in their struggle for resources, they must also devote themselves to including other ethnic and minority groups. Hispanic intellectuals and policymakers must also beware of romantic ideologies from Latin America. There is bias and self-centeredness on the part of some Mexican and Latin American intellectuals who automatically and simplistically blame their ills—many self-induced—on the United States. We cannot always assume that Latin American criticisms of the United States are accurate or fair, and our own difficulties with U.S domestic policies cannot overshadow or color U.S foreign policy concerns.

Finally, the separate subgroups that comprise the Hispanic population in the United States must make it a priority to minimize conflicts among themselves. It is confusing and self-defeating for

Cubans, Mexican-Americans, and other Hispanic subgroups to have competing public agendas. On the major public policy issues of education, income, and jobs, they are all equally affected and should develop common agendas. On those issues where there are separate concerns—relations with Cuba, Puerto Rico's political status, and the plight of undocumenteds, for example—Hispanics must be aware of the line that divides working together from pursuing specific interests, and of how to responsibly negotiate it with a minimum of conflict.

The United States is at an exciting but unpredictable crossroad, aware of the changes before it yet uncertain about what directions to take. It has always had the capacity to respond to social, political, and demographic changes, but not without much soul-searching, tension, and confusion. Response to the Latinization of an aging society will not be easy, and will be replete with conflicts, uncertainty, and frustration. But if the public at large can understand the demographic changes that will be affecting the United States in the twenty-first century, and if the options for responding to those changes are developed and clarified, it would not be unrealistic to assume that the right decisions will be made. The simultaneous aging of the population and the increasing presence of Hispanics provides an opportunity to redefine the American character for the next century without altering its basic political and social structures. But the process will require renewed commitment of those public policies that allow Hispanics to feel part of this country and that prepare the entire society for an older population. It will also require greater understanding by the United States, its government, and its people about Latin America—its history, its concerns, and its hopes. The Western hemisphere is already a Spanish-speaking continent, and despite its mercurial relationship with the United States, Latin America continues to look to this country for guidance and leadership. How we respond to the needs of Hispanics in an aging society will say much about how we respond to Latin America and the coming crisis in the aging of its population, as well as how we are prepared to respond to the needs of our society as a whole.

ENDNOTES

[1]U.S. Dept. of Commerce, Bureau of the Census, "Conditions of Hispanics in America Today" (Washington, D.C.: U.S. Government Printing Office, 1984), p. 4.

[2]The rankings are based on estimates of world populations with data obtained from the 1984 World Population Data Sheet. See Mary Kent and Carl Haub, "1984 World Population Data Sheet" (Washington, D.C.: Population Reference Bureau, Inc, 1984). The Spanish-speaking population of the world is approximately 281 million, which includes the Spanish-speaking portion of Latin America (about 235 million), Spain (38 million), and Hispanics from the United States and Puerto Rico (18 million). This compares with the Republic of China (over one billion persons); the English-speaking countries of India (746 million), the United Kingdom (56 million), and the U.S. and Canada (261 million), which have a combined population of 1063 million persons; and the Soviet Union, with a population of 274 million.

[3]Emily McKay, "Hispanic Statistical Summary: A Compendium of Data on Hispanic Americans" (Washington, D.C.: National Council of La Raza, 1981).

[4]U.S. Dept. of Commerce, "Conditions of Hispanics in America Today," op. cit., p. 6.

[5]Immigration in the course of U.S. history has fluctuated dramatically. In the early 1800s, immigration figures were less than 50,000 immigrants a year and hit a peak in 1900 with 900,000 per year. That level dropped to its lowest point in the Great Depression but has climbed steadily, so that by 1980 legal immigration totaled 500,000 per year with an additional 125,000 to 250,000 undocumented immigrants per year. In addition to the changing number of immigrants, their composition has shifted. Between 1820 and 1899, 90 percent came from Europe and 1 percent came from Latin America. Between 1900 and 1949, European immigration dropped to 78 percent and Latin American immigration increased to 7 percent. Since 1950, Latin Americans and Asians account for 75 percent of legal immigration, with Latin Americans making up 36 percent of total legal immigration and Europeans comprising 31 percent. The "ports of entry" reflect this shift. In the nineteenth century, the East Coast urban centers served as the primary settlement for immigrants, while today the West Coast, primarily Southern California, is the "new Ellis Island" for Latin Americans and Asians. See "Southern California: A Region in Transition," (Los Angeles: Southern California Association of Governments, 1984).

[6]Jerry Hagstrom, "Baby-Boom Generation," *National Journal*, April 28, 1984, pp. 804–810.

[7]In the 1980s, the younger members of that cohort became euphemistically known as "Yuppies"—young, upwardly mobile professionals. The term implied a level of selfishness and materialism that contrasted with the idealism that characterized some elements of the older cohort of baby-boomers, the Vietnam generation. Just as the idealism of the 1960s was not entirely altruistic—there was a large amount of selfishness and anarchy—so the self-centeredness of the Yuppies does not apply to many young persons. Within the baby-boom generation and among the Yuppies are considerable numbers of Hispanic baby-boomers who benefited from the "golden period"—that time between 1967 and 1975 when civil rights pressures provided affirmative-action policies, student assistance, and public receptivity towards benefits to disadvantaged minorities. Those Hispanics who

benefited from that period are the idealistic elite who will provide leadership for the Hispanic population during the 1980s and 1990s.

[8]Robert Butler, "A Generation at Risk," Hogg Foundation for Mental Health (Austin, Texas: University of Texas, 1984), p. 3.

[9]Richard Easterlin, *Birth and Fortune: The Impact of Numbers on Personal Welfare* (New York: Basic Books, 1980).

[10]U.S. Dept. of Commerce, Bureau of the Census, "America in Transition: An Aging Society," *Current Population Reports,* series P-23, no. 128 (Washington, D.C.: U.S. Government Printing Office, 1983), p. X.

[11]U.S. Senate Special Committee on Aging, *Aging America: Trends and Projections* (Washington, D.C.: U.S. Senate Special Committee on Aging, 1984).

[12]Binstock, "Interest Group Liberalism and the Politics of Aging," *The Gerontologist,* Autumn 1972, pp. 265–80.

[13]See Fernando Torres-Gil, "The Politics of Aging and Health Care Policy," paper presented to the conference on Health Policy Issues in the 80s, School of Medicine, University of California, San Diego, 1984.

[14]Neal Pierce and Peter Choharis, "Gray Power," *National Journal,* Sept. 11, 1984, pp. 1559–62.

[15]See Hagstrom, "Baby-Boom Generation," *National Journal,* April 28, 1984, pp. 804–10.

[16]McKay, "Hispanic Statistics Summary: A Compendium of Data on Hispanic Americans," (Washington, D.C.: National Council of La Raza, 1981), p. 3.

[17]Hispanic Policy Development Project, *"Make Something Happen": Hispanics and Urban High School Reform,* vol. 1 (New York: The Hispanic Policy Development Project, 1984), p. 10.

[18]McKay, "Demographic Summary of Hispanic Americans" (Washington, D.C.: National Council of La Raza, 1983), p. 2.

[19]Dennis Roth, "Hispanics in the U.S. Labor Force: A Brief Examination," (Washington, D.C.: Congressional Research Service, Library of Congress, 1984).

[20]Medicare and Medicaid reflect the schism of public support for federal programs. Medicaid is perceived as a welfare program targeted to the poor, blind, and disabled, including many very poor older persons. Medicare, on the other hand, is open to all older persons and is therefore considered worthy of public support; Harris polls have consistently demonstrated the public's opposition to cuts in Medicare. That schism in public perception of what will be supported by their tax dollar has important implications for proposals that would "means test"— target—Medicare and Social Security benefits to the "truly needy" and the poor. Although means testing makes inherent operational sense, it may result in loss of public support if these become "welfare" programs.

[21]Fred Romero, "The Hispanic Population in the United States: Increasing Numbers and Increasing Poverty," unpublished report, 1984, p. 16.

[22]U.S. Dept. of Health and Human Services, "Private Pension Coverage and Vesting by Race and Hispanic Descent, 1979," by Gayle Thompson Rogers, Social Security Administration, (Washington, D.C.: U.S. Government Printing Office, 1982).

[23]Samuel H. Preston, "Children and the Elderly in the U.S.," *Scientific American,* Dec. 1984, pp. 44–49.

[24]Ibid, p. 48.

[25]Hayes-Bautista, Werner Shinek, and Jorge Chapa, "Young Latinos in an Aging American Society," *Social Policy,* Summer 1984, pp. 49–52.

[26]Torres-Gil and Eve Fielder, "Long Term Care Strategie for the Hispanic Population," paper presented at the annual meeting of the American Public Health Association, 1983.

[27]Binstock, "The Aged as a Scapegoat," *The Gerontologist,* Feb. 1983, pp. 136–43.

[28]See Thomas Sowell, *Ethnic America* (New York: Basic Books, 1981).

[29]Dudley Kirk, "Recent Demographic Trends and Present Population Prospects for Mexico," *Food Research Institute Studies,* vol. xix, no. 1, 1983, pp. 93–111.

[30]The median ages in 1985 for Latin America and the Caribbean were 20.5 years and 22.1 years, respectively. The estimated median age for Cuba in 1985 was 25.8 years, and the median age for Puerto Rico was 25.5 years, making those two areas older than Mexico (median age of 18.2 years) and Latin America. The major sending countries of Central America are particularly young, with a median age in 1985 of 17.5 years for El Salvador, 18.3 years for Guatemala, and 16.1 years for Nicaragua. (Data obtained courtesy of the Sloan Foundation.)

[31]Milton Esman, "The Politics of Official Bilingualism in Canada," *Political Science Quarterly,* Summer 1982, pp. 233–54.

[32]See Charles Mathias, Jr., "Ethnic Groups and Foreign Policy," *Foreign Affairs,* Summer 1981, pp. 975–98.

[33]Between now and 2010, several scenarios may occur that would place considerable pressures on American society. If Mexico collapses internally as the result of political, military, or social upheaval, the United States may intervene—in which case, another major conflict will engulf this country, and new waves of Mexican immigration will enter the United States. If the U.S. and Cuba open diplomatic relations and allow free movement, vast numbers of Cubans will immigrate to the United States. If Puerto Rico becomes a state, there will be a major increase in Hispanic political power (two new senators and seven additional congressmen) and new demands to make Spanish an official linguistic and cultural policy.

[34]Kirk, op. cit.

[35]Torres-Gil and Mona Negm, "Policy Issues Concerning the Hispanic Elderly," *Aging Magazine,* March–April 1980, pp. 2–3.

[36]U.S. Dept. of Health and Human Services, Administration on Aging, "Characteristics of the Hispanic Elderly," *Statistical Reports on Older Americans* (Washington, D.C.: U.S. Government Printing Office, 1981).

Edward A. Wynne

Will the Young Support the Old?

A MERICA IS MOVING TOWARDS an era in which declining proportions of working-age adults will be expected to provide goods, health care, and other services to increasing numbers of elderly who are seventy-five, eighty-five years old, and older. Many factors might moderate the responsibilities this change will produce for the working generation. Shifting popular values may raise the typical retirement age, or growing numbers of immigrants may help to reduce the median age of our population. Still, whether and however the increased responsibilities are moderated, it is certain that the burdens on the working population will rise, and the major question is: how much? This vexing prospect leads to another, less apparent issue: will the working-age population accept such an increased burden?

The brute fact is that the working-age population—those, let us say, who are between the ages of twenty and sixty-five—is always the largest voting group in the country. Even if elderly voters should realize the greatest possible increase in their proportions, they will still account for less than 25 percent of the voter pool. Certainly, mobilized groups of elderly voters have had considerable effects recently on decisions that affect programs for the aged. But if the economic costs generated by these programs continue to increase, one cannot assume that such disproportionate political influence will persist, and there may well come a point of rebellion. The majority may then decide to vote against those legislators who favor increased tax burdens to support programs for the aged.

In the long run, government benefits can be available to the elderly only if the majority of Americans choose to make them available. For a number of years, the comparatively moderate tax burdens generated by systems such as Social Security masked this issue. The benefits provided were portrayed as "earned" by the elderly by way of the insurance-like premiums they had paid when they were younger. But it is increasingly being recognized that the old-age security and health system is actually a tax on the working generation to help those who are currently elderly: there is no real trust fund or pool of accrued premiums. Given this situation, how can the elderly—or those who will become elderly—enforce the increasing obligations the young presumably owe them?

It is true that some legislation now exists that articulates the theme of "filial obligation." It establishes principles that permit elderly persons (or the state, acting in their behalf) to sue in order to compel younger relatives to provide them with certain economic support. Even though this legislation contains important principles of responsibility, it can settle only a minute proportion of the economic problems that may arise as our elderly population increases. As the chapter in this volume by Gunhild Hagestad emphasizes, the potential variety of intergeneration support situations that may arise—such as grandparents being asked to support great-grandparents—is so great that much of the support must come from society as a whole. It is possible for an elderly person to successfully sue a younger relative for support under a specific law. But even if elderly persons collectively and successfully sued the federal government to compel the imposing of taxes to increase benefits or health-care levels, how could the verdict be enforced if the majority of voters oppose such taxes?

In sum, the economic security of our present and future elderly Americans rests partly on the goodwill and sense of obligation of the working majority then in command, and partly on the economic efficacy of that majority—since, if workers are highly productive, there are more goods and services available for all to share.

The non-working elderly survive largely on the economic surplus produced by the working population. Strictly speaking, the working population needs only produce enough goods and services to keep itself alive. If that could be accomplished during an average twenty-five hour work week, the working population might well find it desirable to adopt a twenty-five hour work week, and to spend the rest of their time on holiday. Or, workers might choose to keep our current work week, but to perform at a more relaxed pace. Attractive as these approaches might appear to the working population, they drastically lower the level of benefits potentially available to the elderly. Thus, the elderly have a great interest in being succeeded, not by generations of hedonists, but by efficient workaholics.

RIGHTS VERSUS RECIPROCITY

The conceptual issues that are highlighted by the increase in the proportion of the elderly are not particularly novel.[1] All societies have different classes of dependents. The first class is children and young persons, and any continuing society must provide for this group, for these young dependents cannot survive and grow without help from both their immediate families and the larger community. Next, almost all adults suffer from periods of illness and disability during their lives, and they need indeterminate amounts of support. Finally, all societies, except those living on the threshold of starvation, provide forms of help for the economically unproductive aged. Sometimes, to guard against future periods of dependency, adults are urged to save. But even with savings, the vagaries of life are such that systems of human interdependency are inevitable. In general, these systems operate under the principles of reciprocity: "I'll help you during this overload situation, and you'll do the same for me later."

This reliance on reciprocity can be contrasted with the notion of "rights," a concept that is often popular in our era. Rights are inherent, and need not be earned. We have rights simply by reason of being members of a society; even a vicious convicted murderer has some rights. In contrast, reciprocity means that a benefit has been earned by previous conduct, or that the acceptance of a benefit makes the beneficiary duty-bound to repay it at some future date. Reciprocity thus stresses the concept of "deservingness," or obligation.

The differences between rights and reciprocity have important practical effects. Ideally, when we exercise rights, we do so at little or no cost—making it understandable why we prefer to have many rights. Reciprocal benefits, on the other hand, have strings attached: we must either show that they have been earned, perhaps by arduous efforts, or we must accept possibly burdensome future obligations. The English philosopher Jeremy Bentham nicely articulated the tension between rights and duties in some remarks occasioned by the popular strivings for broader rights in the early nineteenth century:

The things that people stand most in need of being reminded are, one would think, their duties; for their rights, whatever they may be, they are apt to attend to themselves . . . The great enemies of the public peace are the selfish and dissocial passions . . . . What has been the object, the perpetual and palpable object, of this declaration of pretended rights. To add as much force as possible to those passions, already too strong, to burst the cords that hold them in; to say to the selfish passions—There, everywhere is your prey! To the angry passion, There, everywhere is your enemy![2]

Bentham's warning makes clear why we may be reluctant to encourage the broadening of "rights," as opposed to the ease we may feel when reciprocal benefits are proposed. Yet the obligations that prevail in reciprocity systems are often not explicit, but implicit. *Explicit* reciprocity is akin to a formal, legal contract, which parties might enforce with legal action. *Implicit* obligations are generated when individuals accept gifts, or favors. Exactly what obligations are created is sometimes a subtle question, which is why the concept of "duty" is complex. Essentially, it is the standards of the group in which the donation occurs that define the substance of the implicit obligations. Those standards often informally generate established patterns of reciprocity. The (sometimes) very diffuseness of the standards provides a valuable flexibility: if you help your neighbor jump-start his car, you may later be entitled to borrow his electric drill. Or if you risk your life to save a stranger you are, in some way, "owed" something. It is neither practical nor desirable for such "debts" to be precisely defined. The essential norms persist because— and if—successive generations are socialized to apply them, and expect, in turn, that the same standards will be applied to them.

Given this, let us assume that successive generations of retired elderly Americans expect to receive help, largely by way of government benefits, from contributions by working generations. They claim they deserve this help because of the earlier help they gave the young and elderly by paying taxes and providing other forms of support and security; in other words, they claim that they are reciprocally entitled to help. Some of the people formerly helped by these now-elderly were, themselves, members of an older generation, and thus, most of them are dead. These deceased persons cannot repay their now-aged benefactors, and so the entire burden of helping the elderly falls on the middle generation, which has received only part of its own generational benefits; ostensibly, its benefits for being aged still lie ahead.

We might propose that the middle generation will always choose to assist the elderly, in the interest of earning its "entitlement" to assistance when it ages. But even such self-interested generosity must meet the criterion for reciprocity. It will not be prudent for the middle generation to choose to help the elderly unless its generosity engenders a future collectable debt. We all know of situations where persons have given generously and still have not received reciprocal recognition. And so, in the end, while giving is a key element of establishing entitlement to generosity, debts or duties are not established unless the giving occurs in an environment in which people recognize that accepting gifts generates powerful obligations. This raises the question of whether our young are being taught to honor and respect the elderly for the sacrifices they have made on their behalf; whether they are being imbued with a sense of duty; and whether they are developing an understanding of the importance of economic productivity and diligence.

PRINCIPLES OF RECIPROCITY

As we have seen, reciprocity can be either explicit or implicit. It can reside in families or other small groups, or it can operate between large social classes—between one generation and another, for example. We might also refer to the "debt" we owe our war veterans, and we can characterize the two contrasting situations of the "debt" family members owe one another and our society's "debt" to veterans as separate examples of "simple" and "complex" reciprocity. We also can compare "immediate" reciprocity, where the exchange occurs over a short period of time, with what I call "remote" reciprocity, where you give to me, and then I "owe" you something, but I make the repayment—on your behalf—to another party.

Let me combine these three principles—explicit/implicit, simple/complex, and immediate/remote—into a more elaborate example. When American troops landed in France during World War I, General Pershing announced, on a public occasion, "Lafayette, we are here!" This signified that Americans, in the twentieth century, were paying the "debt" owed to France generated by the conduct of

Lafayette (and the French monarchy) during the eighteenth century. Pershing was recognizing a debt of *honor*—the ultimate cement of many reciprocal relations. The event was an example of an implicit, complex, remote reciprocal relationship.

Some of the debts elderly Americans believe they are owed are part of implicit, simple, direct reciprocal relationships. Thus, grandparents may help their married adult children with child care, or give them funds, and they may concurrently receive visits or obtain help around the home from these adult children. But many of the important debts that affect elderly Americans are part of implicit, complex, remote, reciprocal relationships. These include benefits such as Social Security, many forms of health care, public housing reserved for the elderly, and the like. These debts are implicit because they are not evinced by legal documents, cannot be sued for, and cannot be defined with any great precision. They are complex because they exist between large groups: the class of elderly persons and the class of working adults. They are remote because many of the working adults being asked to make reciprocal sacrifices to help the elderly never received any benefits—perhaps even indirectly—from the people who are now seeking help; and some of the benefits are provided to the elderly in recognition of their help to former generations now dead. In effect, B helped A and C, then A died, and C helped B and D, and B died, and D now helps C and E. But there is always the temptation for someone or some group to break the chain—to benefit without reciprocity by being only a taker.

IS OUR HONOR SACRED?

There is a natural tendency for subgroups to take more than they give. If it is carried too far, the whole benefit system will dissolve. Still, each tempted (or even "sinning") subgroup hopes that other subgroups will stay loyal. Thus, no claim of exemption from obligation is ever based on raw selfishness. The plea is usually made that special circumstances should excuse one group or another from payment; however, the assumption is that everybody else, of course, should pay in full, and that the basic obligation is valid. And there are inevitably good cases that can be made for some exceptions, leaving us with the puzzle of how things can be managed so that growing pressures for special exemptions do not tear the reciprocity system to pieces.

The chain of reciprocity is maintained by the socialization system, and it depends on how effectively we imbue children and young people with the sense of obligation to repay debts. The spirit of that obligation extends far beyond simply paying one's bill, or saying "thank you," and the system must also transmit an appreciation of implicit, complex, remote, subtle obligations. Thus, suppose we reflect on Pershing's words about Lafayette with pride (in our country's national display of responsibility). If we do so, we are disclosing that we have learned some sense of honor. We "believe" that we should be proud to honor publicly implicit, remote, complex obligations—or that we should be ashamed if we act dishonorably. But there is nothing innate in that sense of pride or shame. I assume, for example, that some readers regard remarks such as Pershing's as the product of macho romanticism, or as pretentious demagoguery.

Brecht's *Threepenny Opera,* for example, is replete with caustic sarcasm about notions of obligation and honor, and such scorn makes a great deal of psychological sense. We are often strongly attracted to the notion that people generally are dishonorable and ignore their obligations. Even if untrue, this belief provides its proponents with an excuse for choosing to avoid their own commitments. And since most of us are, at some times, more debtors than creditors, the theme of ignorance of debt can be very appealing: there are many attractions to the concept of declaring bankruptcy.

Given the logical appeal of selfishness—or the disavowal of debts—it is striking to realize that generalized patterns of implicit reciprocity are common in societies. In war, people often serve in the armed services because of their sense of obligation. In "return," we feel obligated to provide various patterns of benefits to veterans, and to honor their "sacrifices" by producing symbols like the Vietnam Memorial in Washington, D.C. Recently, we formally recognized Martin Luther King Day, to honor the martyred civil rights leader. Abraham Lincoln, in his eloquent Gettysburg Address, memorialized the debt we owed to the "honored dead" of Gettysburg, "who *gave* their lives that this nation might live." But the theme of reciprocal exchange is not original to American society. It has pervaded the public and private life of all important, persisting societies.

Thus, Thucydides, in his history of the Peloponnesian War, described the great Funeral Oration by the Athenian leader Pericles. The text may not quote the oration precisely, but it is surely a statement of what a contemporary Athenian—Thucydides—expected an important public leader to say, and it thereby articulates the norms of Athenian society in that era. The speech was delivered at a memorial ceremony for the Athenians who had fought and died in the war. It portrayed Athens as a city-state worth fighting and dying for, and itemized its special virtues. It concluded with a description of the character of the deceased:

> . . . the Athens I have celebrated is only what the heroism of these and their like have made her, men whose fame, unlike that of most Hellenes, will be found only commensurate with their desserts. And if a test is wanted, it is to be found in their closing scene, and this not only in the cases in which it set the final seal upon their merit, but also in those in which it gave the first intimation of their having any. For there is justice in the claim that steadfastness in his country's battles should serve as a cloak to cover a man's other imperfections; since the good action is blotted out by the bad, and his merit as a citizen more than outweigh his demerits as an individual. But none of these allowed either wealth, with its promise of future enjoyment to unnerve his spirit, or poverty with its hope of a day of freedom and riches to tempt him to shrink from danger . . . . Choosing to die resisting, rather than to live submitting, they fled only from dishonor, but met danger face to face, and after one brief moment, while at the summit of their fortune, escaped, not from their fear, but from their glory. So died these men as became Athenians.
>
> You, their survivors, must determine to have as unaltering resolution in the field . . . you must feed your eyes upon the beauty of Athens from day to day, 'til love of her fills your hearts; and then, when all her greatness shall break upon you, you must effect that it was by courage, sense of duty, and a keen feeling of honor in action that men were enabled to win all this, and that no personal failure in an enterprise could make them consent to deprive their country of their valor, but they laid it at her feet as the most glorious contribution they could offer.[3]

DEFINING OUR OBLIGATIONS

Pericles's speech is replete with reciprocal themes: what it was that citizens had received from Athens which now placed them at an obligation; how the dead soldiers now being honored had met their obligations; how service as a brave soldier wiped out personal deficiencies; the obligation to honor those who have served; the honoring of the deceased in an eloquent speech by a prominent person before a large, respectful audience; the suggestion that the sacrifices of the dead obligate the living to similar sacrifices; and the recognition, by the audience, that their own potential future sacrifices were of a glorious nature, and might be similarly memorialized. This speech is a prominent and microcosmic example of how ceremonies are employed to socialize citizens to reciprocity—and to maintain their disposition to it once it has been created. Ceremonies are only one tool toward these ends; the example demonstrates the many virtues and problems that underlie the total process of maintaining reciprocity.

Vital socialization systems can obviously stimulate citizens to high levels of dedication. Our own pragmatic age may tend to belittle notions like loyalty, honor, or moral obligation, but the simple truth is that far greater sacrifices may be (and have been) made on behalf of such principles than we can ever hope to stimulate through simple appeals to coarse self-interest. Furthermore, the generalized nature of such "noble" concepts provides the concepts themselves with a certain utilitarian flexibility. Where loyalty begins and ends is sometimes debatable, and thus the application of such principles is usually surrounded with discussion, analysis, and emotional appeals. Indeed, Pericles's oration was, in part, an apologia for the war: an argument as to where true "loyalty" should lie. Such debates generate high degrees of public involvement in the "decision-making" process. For the war to proceed, loyalty to principle had to be pervasively reinforced. And that reinforcement was part of the function of the "glorious" Athenian statuary, of the elaborate aesthetic and gymnastic training provided for the Athenian young, of the great eloquence of Pericles's oration, and of the many similarly attractive characteristics of Athenian society. These forms and processes enhanced the sense of obligation of Athenian citizens, regularly reminding them that they owed a great deal to their society, and that these debts were to repaid. And the payment of these debts was enforced not so much by lawsuits, as by powerful social norms.

It is not incongruous to recognize here that, at this point in history, Americans are intrigued by the considerable success of Japanese industrial and commercial corporations. One of the unique elements of these organizations is the special attention they devote to employee loyalty among workers at all levels. The Japanese undoubtedly assume that this kind of loyalty provides a base for constructive, flexible, and economically beneficial reciprocal relationships, and the available evidence suggests that their assumption is correct.

Developing and maintaining a pro-reciprocity environment is expensive. Precious time, goods, and imagination must be applied to communicate appropriate values to citizens. Time must be taken away from productive work to conduct ceremonies such as the Funeral Oration, at which the whole community would come together and listen. Works of art—statues, pyramids, churches and palaces, triumphal arches, medals, poems, murals, plays, operas, special garments—must be provided to communicate symbolically the central importance of reciprocity as well as its principles: what has been given; on what terms; what is owed; and how it can be paid. Talented persons must be involved in the creation and presentation of these works, and these persons must be trained and supported. Citizens' time must be expended in absorbing the basic iconographic material that suffuses the environment: in memorizing the *Odyssey,* or the *Bible,* or the *Baltimore Catechism,* or in learning the elements of the Passover feast, where traditional Jews are informed and reminded of their peoples' "debt" to Jehovah by the very text and activities of the ceremony.

The preceding catalogue reminds us that the theme of reciprocity is a central element in many great works of art. In Shakespeare, for example, we can recognize questions such as: what did Hamlet "owe" his dead father; what did Romeo and Juliet "owe" their parents and one another; and what did Romeo "owe" Mercutio, who died on his behalf. On another scale, many of Shakespeare's historical plays portray, to the English people, how their society was built—and what they owe to their predecessors. We might contrast Shakespeare to Brecht. To Shakespeare, reciprocity is the norm: the question is, what are the confines of the debt. To Brecht, the idea of a strong, persisting obligation is essentially an aberration.

THE GREAT TRANSFORMATION

In *The Great Transformation,*[4] the economist Karl Polanyi presented an insightful contrast between life in traditional societies and life in many contemporary environments. Polanyi's analysis focused on economic exchanges—where goods or services were bought and sold—in traditional and modern societies. (Support from the young to the aged is an instance of such a transaction.) He observed that in traditional societies, the elements of these exchanges were surrounded with ceremonial aspects: prayers, ritualized gestures, the recitation of special rubrics, or the parallel exchange of symbolic gifts. All exchanges were pervaded with elements of "honor." Polanyi proposed that these traditional forms served a multiplicity of social needs, that the raw exchange of goods or services was coupled with forms that reaffirmed the larger context of the exchange. In effect, the "gods" participated in, and blessed, the exchange.

The "transformation" Polanyi described occurred when the larger context of the transaction was lost, and the process evolved into the typical, modern, single-purpose, raw economic exchange: "I give you money, and you give me what I buy, and our relationship then is at an end." It was as if one had substituted prostitution for sex with love; this might seem to have simplified a highly complex process, and to have fostered more, more diverse, and less stressful copulation. Yet a dimension that most readers would think critical is lost.

In the specific context of general economic exchanges, the benefits of this shift from complex to simple transactions are evident. Exchanges could now take place between relative strangers, and without complex interactions. The transformation also facilitated the spread of networks of exchange. But it also drained much of the emotional juice from many transactions, and meant that breaches in the execution of modern transactions would be matters to be decided by courts: the essense of obligation is no longer left to priests, auguries, or public debate. In effect, this bureaucratization of exchanges simplified the process of enforcement, and also accelerated the diffusion of economic exchanges.

To recapitulate, the transformation Polanyi identified was "great" because it dramatically altered the nature of human exchanges, or transactions. While exchanges had once taken place within limited groups, been pervaded with symbolic and poetic elements, generated obligations of a relatively diffuse nature, and been enforced through an appeal to popular and symbolic values, many now occur within large groups, have a relatively explicit nature, and depend for their ultimate enforcement on specialized, formal bodies of courts of law.

It is evident that the great transformation was related to a variety of other changes in Western society—among them the Reformation, the Industrial Revolution, and urbanization. It is also evident that one cannot propose revitalizing the nature and the spirit of complex reciprocity simply by turning back the clock. Nevertheless, despite the vast medley of changes, the great transformation has not been complete. Our contemporary society still contains a great variety of reciprocal relationships in which implicit obligations are important, and are not defined or enforced in terms of formal contracts. And sometimes these relationships are accompanied by ceremonial aspects, such as engagement rings and marriage ceremonies, or inauguration ceremonies that include the recitation of oaths. Indeed, the issue of whether and how Vietnam veterans should be memorialized in Washington D.C. presents a classic example of a traditional debate about the obligations of reciprocity in our society. For even modern societies reflect a continuing need to maintain important patterns of implicit reciprocity. Human life is simply too complex to be managed largely in contractual terms.

CARING FOR THE AGED IN A "TRANSFORMED" SOCIETY

American society likes to consider interpersonal and intergroup obligations in precise, contractual terms. They are acts of explicit reciprocity. This is the significance of the concept of Social Security as *insurance.* "Insurance" is a relatively modern social invention which assumes that each person who pays premiums will get back, *on the average,* the same amount he or she paid in. The virtue of insurance is that each insured person is protected against extraordinary mischance, and the forms of protection provided by actual insurance are quite precise, and calculated by actuarial formulas. The terminology of insurance was deliberately applied in the design of our Social Security system. One reason the federal government employed this (misleading) terminology was to assure beneficiaries that they would not be burdened with the obscure (that is, complex) responsibilities generated by traditional reciprocity systems. Furthermore, the operation of the system provides no ceremonial elements. Payments are deducted in an almost invisible manner, and they are rendered to beneficiaries with even greater secrecy; no one knows who, in the neighborhood, is receiving Social Security payments, or under what conditions; nor do we know how much individual workers are paying to support their elderly contemporaries. The whole process seems to be a private matter between each individual taxpayer and beneficiary, and the government—nice and clean.

The trouble is that the logical formal framework is a fiction. For the foreseeable future, each middle generation will pay higher dependency costs (for both maintenance and health) than have been paid by their predecessors. It is even possible that the total dependency costs (for both young and elderly) of the middle generations will be greater than those for their predecessors, since the costs of maintaining the elderly may be disproportionately higher than for maintaining the young. The tensions generated by this development may stimulate individuals, or groups, to try to withdraw in various ways from the intergenerational compact that underlies the system, by drawing more earnings from the untaxed off-the-books economy; by fighting to maintain lower levels of benefits, with the assumption that one's own group will be more securely protected by various private old-age security systems; or by seeking other forms of exemption from the system of taxation for benefits. Some of these measures may be illegal, while others may involve only the conventional politics of special-interest groups.

Yet the rising costs of care for the elderly is only partly an economic issue. We are now one of the richest societies in history. We can surely afford to provide more funds for the elderly—if we just "choose" to give up something. But whether we make that choice depends more on our philosophic values than on our economic productivity. Of course it is easy to suggest that requests for help be framed in terms such as honor or loyalty, but the real problem arises in attempting to win acquiescence to the requests. Putting it simply, if such requests are directed to people whose ideals have been largely derived from the themes expressed in the work of such writers as Bertolt Brecht, Joseph Heller, or Kurt Vonnegut, one might be pessimistic about the responses. Regardless of the stated aims of these authors, the fact is that they portray worlds pervaded with venality, cynicism, and selfishness. No reader who takes such portrayals seriously will be encouraged to enter into complex, reciprocal relationships. The efficacy of appeals to honor or obligations toward social institutions, and other aspects of implicit, complex reciprocity, rests largely on the listener's prior socialization. Effective socialization to these norms is a long and costly process, and indeed, the costs are one of the reasons for the great transformation: it seems cheaper to keep reciprocal relations on explicit, legalistic terms. Unfortunately, such terms do not enable individuals—or societies—to deal with diffuse, unexpected contingencies. Formal, legalistic relations encourage people to pursue ignoble exemptions, and the thrust toward legalism and private rights actually frustrates flexible responses to large, dynamic problems. The moral is that, if we want to provide more secure assurance for the future elderly, we must invest more resources into appropriately socializing our contemporary young.

The resources required cannot be purely monetary. Historically, our education system has been the formal unit that is primarily responsible for this kind of socialization. And our society—by a variety of measures—has been expending more per pupil in education (up through college) in the recent past than ever before in our history. The issue is, what are we using our money to buy? It is notorious that children can receive high levels of "help," and still grow into hedonistic, selfish, litigious adults. Spending additional education dollars simply to buy more of the same is unlikely to be of much help in solving the problem we are exploring. We need *different* education services. Part of these broadened services would include the use of new materials in the formal curriculum—in literature, social science, and history as well as in the readings presented to elementary school students. The materials would stress such themes as loyalty, students' "debts" to previous generations, the benefits that previous generations have won for the students by their sacrifices, and the centrality of character and honor in social life. Readers will recognize that there is a vast body of existing—but not necessarily contemporary—materials that can serve these ends.

Another part of these broadened education services will consist of employing different activities to engage students during their non-curriculum school hours, for schools instruct not only by presenting formal materials, but by the other ways in which they organize students' time, as well as by the role models teachers put before students. For example, consider the text of the Pledge of Allegiance: "I pledge allegiance to the flag of the United States of America, one nation, under God, indivisible . . . ." What are the implications (about obligations) of having students recite such a pledge three thousand times during their school years under the leadership of teachers who treat the activity as one that is at least as serious as driver education? What are the implications of mandatory community service activities for all public school pupils—to symbolize their obligation to begin to pay back the debts they are incurring? Or what about transforming periodic school holidays—Veterans Day, Presidents' Day—into *school days,* instead of relegating them to be time

for TV, or hanging out? On such occasions, students could participate instead in artful, appropriate, and significant ceremonies, which
could help form them into generational units that owe gratitude, and
thus, a "debt," to those who preceded them. And suppose a variety
of older adults—not teachers—were invited to the school to enlist
students in well-designed activities that would engage them and
heighten their respect for these seniors. The activities would also
demonstrate the willingness of the elderly to continue to meet their
own reciprocal communal obligations. (Indeed, the idea of nearly
absolute retirement, into nearly "pure" leisure, is very much a
modern phenomenon. Very few people in earlier societies, or
throughout American history, ever attained such a status. This
modern development undoubtedly complicates the transmission of
the concept of reciprocity, since a number of our retired elderly
appear to the young as solely passive takers.)

As I have already emphasized, such activities, if well-managed, will
require some economic and institutional costs. But we are trying to
buy love and loyalty, and they are expensive goods. I should also
mention, speaking from my own experience in in-school research,
that the activities proposed are not entirely unique in contemporary
American public schools. A wide diversity of practices now exists,[5]
and readers may be surprised to know that some public and private
schools in our era still work hard to communicate relatively pro-
reciprocity values to their students.

The real problem is not the economic costs of the proposed
socialization process. Indeed, it is not even a matter of whether
modern young people can be made to believe in loyalty or honor. The
values of young people are malleable, and new generations of
students appear continuously. The problem is that "we"—or many
adult Americans—may not want to change our message to the young,
and that strong adult resistance can veto, or seriously undermine,
efforts to socialize the young to practice reciprocity. Once that
happens, it can be argued that activities to promote reciprocity simply
don't work. The issue, then, is the matter of adult *will*.

In this regard, we must consider the possible sources of adult
resistance to the measures we are proposing. They are multifold:

(1) Adults may resist because the proposed changes may compel
them to work harder, or to change their present habits. Educators

will have to change the style and broaden the content of much of their work. Textbook publishers will have to revise what they produce and sell. College professors, who advise educators, will have to adopt new perspectives on the kind of advice they provide. Some educators may find their status threatened because their current advice will be obsolete. But the matter will extend far beyond adults who are paid for working with the young. All older adults must become more deeply involved in engaging in and demonstrating reciprocity princi-ples to the young. Parents must organize their home lives so that their children have frequent occasions to enjoy significant and deferential contacts with grandparents and elderly adults. And elderly adults must become more available to the young—instead of removing themselves permanently to Florida or Arizona, for example.

(2) Adults will resist because many influential people in our society earn their livings defending and enlarging the rights of individuals and groups: defense lawyers, social workers, and diffuse categories of activists who may feel that teaching obligation contradicts their own principles. Others are members of groups whose members have obtained valuable benefits by their successful assertion of rights—as opposed to showing they have *earned* something by a deliberate sacrifice. All of these persons are implicitly threatened by the prop-osition that benefits must be earned, or that apparently unearned benefits generate serious future obligations. The kind of transforma-tion we are proposing may inhibit the willingness of many people to claim certain apparent benefits; alternately, grantors of benefits may be strengthened in their resistance to demands for them.

(3) Many adult Americans resent being dependent (or having others dependent on them).[6] But the admission of dependency is a vital element of the function of reciprocity. If a truly dependent person refuses to admit his status, then he will refuse to express gratitude. (One way that we try and escape the "weight" of depen-dency is to stress the concept of rights.) But objectively, elderly people will be increasingly dependent, and their unwillingness to admit that status will surely aggravate the challenges that lie before us. It is difficult to persuade people to sacrifice for others; it is even more difficult when the person helped refuses to solicit help, or even to say "thank you." We must recognize that the special pressures that are now building will entitle the working generation, which must make

extra sacrifices, to various forms of deference—just as they, too, should provide deference to their elders.

(4) Artists and other creative people play an important role in the reciprocity process. They provide many of the clues and reinforcers that stimulate a sense of public obligation. Even where that stimulation is by non-artists—by a politician such as Lincoln, articulating the Gettysburg Address—societies that stress reciprocity must generally strive for elevated forms of expression. The problem might be described as a deficiency in patronage. In most eras when great art was produced, the artist was responding to commissions or other bounded requests from purchasers and patrons. Unfortunately, in our era artists are all too often left with open-ended commissions or with competitions that are poorly defined. We might perform a service for our artists and our whole society by expanding the horizons of our art patronage systems. If it is important to communicate perspectives of reciprocity throughout the society, we must urge, stimulate, and commission artists to communicate such values through songs, operas, statues, plaques, and paintings.

(5) The concepts of obligation, loyalty, and reverence for tradition and for the elderly are relatively alien to American values. We are a comparatively new nation, founded through a conspicuous and deliberate break with the past. We succeeded in settling a continent partly by disregarding old techniques of development and exploitation, and by inventing new policies and principles. We have followed the policy of giving significant weight to the unrefined wishes and aspirations of the young, and our high evaluation of "equality" has encouraged many citizens to envy others who have succeeded in having earned unusual benefits or status.

All of these forces suggest that we may be reluctant to celebrate values that provide elderly persons with unique prestige, or that "burden" younger generations with strong obligations, or bind them to collective loyalties. There are two replies to this contention. The first is brief. We are facing a historically novel situation—the extraordinary enlargement of our elderly population. As an adaptable society, we must use original measures to confront novel situations. And if loyalty and obligation are the themes that will generate the necessary social cement, then so be it. On with the adaptation!

WHY OBLIGATIONS ARE GOOD THINGS

The new responsibilities symbolized by our rising obligations to the elderly are not solely bleak, or limiting. During the nineteenth century, many observers bemoaned the limited role of significant art in American life. As Tocqueville put it, "Nothing conceivable is so petty, so insipid, so crowded with paltry interests, in one word, so anti-poetic, as the life of a man in the United States."[7] In our era, these criticisms have become muted. Contemporary American art is regarded as a model and a style-setter throughout the world. It is not so much that American art and life have become more "poetic," but that contemporary art and life in the whole industrial world have simply moved closer to American modes. Let us assume we want to elevate the quality of art and life in our society—as an aesthetic goal. If we do, then we should assign art a more important task than simply filling our free time, or expressing only the artist's lonely vision. One such task would be to increase our awareness and reverence for the social bonds on which reciprocity is founded. This "assignment" will not automatically generate great art, but it will at least meet one important condition for fostering important art: many people are interested and affected by the message underlying the work.

If we award deference to the elderly, this deference implies that the achievements of the past (and of past generations) are also entitled to respect, a proposition that assumes a relative social stability. Americans admittedly have mixed feelings about such propositions, for they seem to denigrate the importance of change, or the probability or necessity of continuing social improvement. But the comparative virtues and drawbacks of the past, present, and future are essentially ideological issues, and they are not subject to evidentiary analysis. Obviously, one can recite ways in which the present is "better" than the past, but one can also recite the obverse of that position. For instance, the available data indicates that the rates of youth self-and-other-destruction (rates of death by homicide and suicide), levels of out-of-wedlock births, and arrests for crimes have increased by hundreds of percents over the past fifteen to twenty-five years,[8] and that youth drug use in America is still higher than in any other industrial nation. How does one compare these distressing patterns with the prolongation of adult life, with the extraordinary increases in leisure time, or with the general expansion of years spent in formal education? The reply is that comparisons like these depend on philosophic and personal imponderables, but the admission means that the question of how much weight we should devote to "tradition" versus "progress" is an open one. If this is so, the clear need to heighten our respect for the elderly constitutes evidence that may affect the process of the weighting. Indeed, it is even possible that the general increase in our social stability that would be caused by our demonstrating greater respect for the past might provide us with a number of precious social benefits.

Most readers will recognize that some of my contentions fly against popularly regarded values, but it is also true that America is confronted with an historical anomaly. A diverse series of developments seems to be moving on a collision course. Either we will accept increased obligations toward the elderly, or levels of assistance will decline. Some assumptions will have to yield: the preceeding analysis and its contentions offer a case for one pattern of yielding. Analysts who prefer different scenarios are obligated to identify what other, but also unpleasant, pill they prescribe for us.

ENDNOTES

[1] For a broad discussion of the themes of group and individual reciprocity, see Edward A. Wynne, *Social Security: A Reciprocity System Under Stress* (Denver, CO: Westview Press, 1980).

[2] Jeremy Bentham, quoted in A.V. Dicey, *Law and Public Opinion* (New York: Macmillan, 1905), p. 171.

[3] *The Complete Writings of Thucydides* (New York: Modern Library, 1951), pp. 103ff.

[4] Karl Polanyi, *The Great Transformation* (New York: Farr and Rinehard, 1944).

[5] For evidence of the diversity among schools, including adherence to "traditional" values, see Edward A. Wynne, *Looking at Schools* (Lexington, MA: Heath/Lexington, 1980).

[6] For one work critical of the American fear of dependence, see Takeno Doi, *The Anatomy of Dependence* (New York: Kodansha International, 1973).

[7] Alexis de Tocqueville, *Democracy in America* (New York: Harper & Row, 1966), pp. 453–54.

[8] For one summary of data about youth disorder, see Edward A. Wynne, "Trends in Youth Character Development," *Communio,* Fall 1983, pp. 256–81.

James E. Birren

The Process of Aging: Growing Up
and Growing Old

I N THE ANCIENT EPIC OF Gilgamesh, the hero, Gilgamesh,
wants to obtain immortality. He is told to search for a thorny
plant at the bottom of the sea and that eating it will impart
immortality. Unfortunately, after struggling to secure the plant,
Gilgamesh refreshes himself by bathing, and a serpent comes along
and eats it. According to the legend, it was this plant that gave snakes
the capacity for renewing their skins and, presumably, long life as
well. The clay tablets containing the epic poem appear to date back
to about 650 B.C.; the legend itself dates back as far as 3000 B.C.
Throughout history, similar legends have documented our continuing desire to understand the aging process and to prolong life.

What makes aging such a magnetic subject for myth-building is the
complexity of the changes it brings. Aging is at once a biological,
psychological, and social process. Today, as we continue to improve
the conditions of life, many of us are haunted by a new question: is
our biological heritage, which results from thousands of years of
evolution and appears to fix the upper limit of our life, within our
grasp to manipulate?

AGING AS A CONCERN

Growing older is a biological, social, and psychological process that
begins at conception and ends with death. In earlier centuries,
because it was common for so many people to die at early ages from
infectious diseases, one of life's most poignant ingredients was the

lack of an opportunity to grow old. Many societies believed that the length of life was limited by obscure powers that lay beyond human understanding.

Although the scientific era of thought about aging essentially began in the last century, it still faces the legacy of deeply entrenched early beliefs. Many of us still entertain convictions about the healing powers of spas, while others revel in legends that a faraway people are particularly long-lived, or that we were once very long-lived ourselves but have lost the secret. The quest for rejuvenescent drugs still pervades contemporary society and, in fact, constitutes a significant economic activity. In short, the subject of aging is probably encrusted with more odd beliefs than any other aspect of human existence.

In this century, old people are no longer rare. Given the fact of increased life expectancy and decreased fertility, the proportion of the aged in the population is relatively high, and the extent to which aging has come to absorb media attention is not surprising. John Naisbitt points out that in the 1960s almost all the press stories devoted to rights issues were focused on issues of race. By mid-1975, half of this space was devoted to racism and the other half to sexism. But by the late 1970s, two-thirds of the rights space was given to ageism, reflecting the growing interest in our increasingly aged population.[1]

In this chapter, we will provide a unified view of the contributions of the various sciences to our present understanding of the processes of aging. Biologists have approached the subject by seeking to understand it as a physical process—how the body grows up, is susceptible to disease, grows old, and dies. Psychologists have explored our abilities and capacities, the way we process information, and how we extract meaning and derive contentment from our new longevity. Social scientists have looked at the roles and various statuses of older persons, working to determine the social processes of change that transform a young adult into an old person and how that old person is integrated into—or left out of—our society.

Our task here is something like putting together a giant jigsaw puzzle. The biological, psychological, and social pieces, after all, should be fitted together in a way that makes sense of one's personal experience.

LEARNING ABOUT AGING: AN OVERVIEW

It is only since the early part of the last century that science has had the tools to study aging. The early scientific discoveries of the sixteenth and seventeenth centuries were made in fields like astronomy and physics, and the step from observing stars and planets to observing and recording data on human beings was not an easy one to take, or an obvious one. Organized religion was a powerful influence during these centuries, and the Church was not enthusiastic about extending scientific studies to man, a special creation of God. In its eyes, examining the soul's earthly vehicle—the body—was an idea bordering on sacrilege.

In the early part of the nineteenth century, the Belgian Adolphe Quetelet began to study, measure, and document the characteristics of human development and aging—our physiology, behavior, and society—in a manner that formed the basis for creating a science of mankind. A genius interested in every aspect of human experience, Quetelet published his data in 1835 in a book entitled *On the Nature of Man, and the Development of His Faculties.*

Quetelet's interest had been piqued by some earlier studies in France, which had demonstrated that secluded monks and nuns lived longer than the general population. The Church objected to these inquiries too: the length of one's life was a matter to be decided by God. Quetelet nevertheless began to accumulate his own data.

Quetelet's contribution to the development of contemporary science is enormous. First, he broke with tradition by affirming that humankind was a suitable subject for objective study. Second, he originated the method of collecting data from a large number of people, analyzing it, and developing both a statistical average and a measure of the range of individual differences. He created the term "the average man" to express the traits revealed by his calculations. And finally, he arranged all of his data so that he was able to detect changes in abilities and experiences according to age groups.

Francis Galton, Charles Darwin's cousin, corresponded with Quetelet and began to develop similar research in England. Galton, who was later to become well known for his work in eugenics, was a geographer, anthropologist, and psychologist who devised statistical methods to describe the data he gathered. By 1877, Galton had devised seventeen separate tests and administered them to thousands of men and women of various ages. His findings demonstrated that the average characteristics of his subjects were associated with their ages. Three of his observations, later rediscovered, were that (1) there is a tendency towards loss of hearing of high tones with age, particularly for men; (2) there is slowness in movement in older men and women; and (3) the capacity of the lungs (vital capacity, as physiologists call it) decreases with age. Out of this research came the concept of interactions and the knowledge that there are constellations of factors that operate in the process of aging.[2]

On his death, Galton left his fortune to University College, London, to endow a professorship in biostatistics. The first holder of the professorship, Karl Pearson, developed a new method of separating chance effects from causal effects, permitting statistics to become a powerful tool of the late nineteenth and twentieth centuries. Today, the combination of statistical methods and the computer enables us to look in greater detail at the factors that influence how long the average person lives.

If we want to study why some people live a long time, we must compare groups of people of known backgrounds who are exposed to different environmental conditions. In the past, the folklore that surrounded the aging process could not be separated from the facts. Now this sorting can be accomplished.

The development of statistics alone, however, did not trigger a flood of research on aging. As a field, the study of aging is still very young, for we have learned most of what we now know about the aging process only since about 1945. The early years of the twentieth century saw biological scientists preoccupied with a number of more immediate problems, in particular with the effort to fight those infectious diseases—tuberculosis, influenza, pneumonia, typhoid, diphtheria, and smallpox—that were responsible for the largest numbers of deaths.

In the 1920s, one of the early students of public health in America, Raymond Pearl, pointed out that people who have long-lived grandparents tend to live longer than the average person. While this was a correct interpretation of the data, it led to an over-generalized point of view that "living long is a matter of having the right grandparents." While heredity does play a role in how long we live and what diseases we are susceptible to, it is also clear how powerfully life circumstances can modify the lengths of our lives. Were heredity the only important factor, the dramatic increases in life expectancy that have occurred in this century could never have come about.

The average length of life in the United States in 1900 was about forty-seven years. By 1980, the figure was seventy-two, an increase greater than that that took place from pre-Roman days to 1900. The primary factors that have determined these recent changes in longevity have been the improvements in the environment and the control of infectious diseases. In 1959, when Hardin Jones summarized the many factors that were then known to influence life span, he estimated that having a mother and father who lived for ninety or more years gives an individual seven years advantage over the general population. Yet we now know that smoking two packs of cigarettes a day subtracts twelve years from life expectancy, regardless of parental longevity—an example that makes it obvious just how powerful environmental influences can be.

The increase of about thirty-five years in life expectancy in this century is so large that we have almost become a different species. Retirement used to be rare, because most people died during their work lives. At least one parent had usually died before the last child left home. Orphans were common and old people were scarce. Now the opposite is true.

This huge and unprecedented increase in life expectancy brings with it both unease and optimism. We are poorly prepared for the change and are still surrounded by the old legends and mystiques, by embellished traditions and outmoded social conventions. On the other hand, we remain optimistic about science's ability to extend our life span still further in the near future. The change is being accompanied not only by faddism in life-promoting practices, but by great uncertainty in public policies as we struggle to understand an aging society. No society of the past has had to cope with these issues.

THEORIES OF AGING: WHY DO WE GROW OLD?

Why living things grow old and, in so doing, become more likely to die is a universal question, and most people are no longer willing to accept an answer based on antiquated superstitions. Many early pioneers in medicine conducted autopsies that provided descriptions of old tissues and vital organs. They observed that hardened arteries, softened bones, and shrunken organs are characteristics of old age.

As a result, the common opinion arose that old age was *caused* by these manifestations of pathology. In actuality, the dramatically altered appearance may not be a *cause,* but rather an *effect* of growing old (or possibly even an adaptive change that was desirable for the survival of the organism).

According to Lewellys Barker, pathological aging is the premature breakdown of an organ system as a result of disease or trauma, while physiological or normal aging involves a gradual involution of the body as a whole, a process in which cells and organs slowly atrophy. Barker observed that "the conscientious clinician makes it a point . . . to secure . . . careful macroscopic and microscopic examinations of the organs and tissues of persons dying at different ages as these afford a knowledge of the gross anatomy and finer histology of the body in disease and also reveal the more characteristic changes that the human body undergoes in successive periods of life." He adds that after long experience the physician can form ". . . a general and composite picture of the average conditions that exist in human beings at different ages of life and thus arrive at fairly valid conclusions regarding the processes that are characteristic of ageing."[3]

Barker's views are similar to those of many distinguished students of the anatomical changes that occur in the body with age. Yet, one cannot tell from these descriptions whether the observed pathology is primary, in the sense that it leads to the other observed changes and eventually to death, or whether it is secondary and without effect on the process that leads to such changes. As a result, throughout the history of research almost every tissue has at some time been suspected of serving as *the* primary pacemaker of aging. This is because there is nothing in the descriptive process itself, no matter how detailed and painstaking, that enables us to point to the primary phenomena from which others may follow. These valuable data, in short, do not solve the problem of separating cause from effect.

A similar error in logic was made by Benjamin Franklin, who devoted serious thought to the riddles of aging. One of his regrets was that he had been born too early to see the dramatic advances he believed lay ahead for science. Franklin was especially impressed with the fact that bodies grow cold with dying. It was but a further step for him to suggest that, once dead, a body might be revived. He believed, as did other educated persons of his time, that life might be suspended for a period and later brought back by applying heat or electric shock. This error in logic resembles the thinking of the early physicians: by associating a feature of the organism with age or with death, a causal relationship was assumed, resulting in the belief that by supplying the missing feature—in this case, heat—the body could be revived. The success of future research on aging will depend on the researcher's ability to separate cause and effect in the many changes that accompany growing old.

Hardening of the Arteries

Changes in the arteries with age have been noted for centuries, and some researchers still believe them to be causal in the aging process. The reasoning here seems credible in that, if arteries become clogged as one ages, circulation will ultimately fail to supply vital organs with oxygen and nutrients. In the beginning of this century, William Osler, a leading internist, pointed out the close relationship between aging and the state of the blood vessels. The mental incapacity, or senility, that occurs in some older people was thought to be primarily caused by the hardening of the arteries in the brain. Others have continued to draw similar conclusions, although the popularity of this theory has waned in the face of evidence that only some older people show hardened (sclerotic) major blood vessels.

Changes in the blood vessels are currently viewed as a condition that is avoidable, not one that is intrinsically linked with advancing age. This view is supported by the facts that human populations display wide variations in the occurrence of these changes, and that they usually do not appear in other species of animals except under unusual experimental conditions. In his 1942 review of research on cardiovascular aging, Alfred Cohn tried to determine whether the arteries and the heart age. He concluded: ". . . the evidence depends for its credibility on a combination of common sense and statistical inference, aided perhaps by the use of examples not particularly obvious."[4] Here, the elements of statistical inference and the use of exceptional examples are added to the common sense that earlier clinicians used to answer the question: Why do we age?

Digestive Putrefaction

One of the more novel early theories of aging was that of Elie Metchnikoff, the Russian biologist, whose views attracted consider-able attention at the turn of this century. He and his followers theorized that noxious bacteria flourish in the digestive tract and produce putrefactive products, or toxins, that are lethal to the organism. Metchnikoff and his followers encouraged people to eat yogurt to combat the increasing toxicity of the digestive tract. Today, yogurt is even more widely consumed than in Metchnikoff's time, but of course its current appeal is as a nutritious and low-calorie dietary item.

Later research determined that gastrointestinal flora may, indeed, be useful. For example, if laboratory rats are given antibiotics that kill the bacteria in their digestive tracts, the animals become vitamin-deficient because they depend upon the bacteria for synthesizing vitamins that the species lost the ability to synthesize in the course of evolution. Metchnikoff, in this case, had inverted the interpretation of the symbiotic relationship between the host and the bacteria. This illustrates the great difficulty in separating those features associated with age that are life-promoting from those that are deleterious. Even today, it is far from obvious how to interpret many commonplace facts.

Endocrine Functions and Aging

With the discovery of the individual endocrine glands—the thyroid, the pancreas, the gonads, the adrenals, and others—and of their great significance for our well-being, it seemed natural for researchers to focus on them in the search for the general pacemakers of aging. Recent research has shown how closely these glands are linked to each other, as well as how they interact in development and aging. Yet hormone levels, by themselves, apparently do not tell us much of biological significance. A 1982 review of the evidence emphasized that "measuring hormone levels alone, even during perturbation tests, may not characterize a defect."[5] It is now clear that early research on the role of endocrines in aging was an ill-fated effort that regarded aging as a lock-and-key problem—as if there were one critical organ whose diminished function resulted in the aging of the entire organism.

In no area was this error as clear as in some of the research devoted to sexual function. The observation that sexual activity in the human diminishes with age prompted investigators to focus on the male testes and the female ovaries. It was particularly popular in Europe between 1910 and 1920 to transplant ovaries and testes, both in animals and humans. But transplantation of an organ is a failed effort, if it is the endocrines that stimulate the organ from the brain that are deficient, or if the target tissues are unable to utilize properly the organ's output of endocrines. Today, we recognize that the testes and ovaries are not primary factors in aging. Castrated animals, in fact, live normal, or in some cases longer, lives than intact animals. Early in this century, when the castration of retarded boys was permissible in institutions for the mentally impaired, follow-up studies showed that the boys lived longer than their intact peers. These findings support the conclusion that changes in the sex organs can claim only a secondary role in the aging process. Sexual potency may diminish with age, but this is less a matter of primary change than it is a reflection, in many instances, of either the presence of disease or a reaction to certain medications.[6] Given appropriate levels and timing of stimulating endocrines reaching the ovaries and testes, both can continue to function almost indefinitely. Most likely, the early concern with the aging of sexual function was a result of the general mystique that still surrounds fertility and sexual behavior. While much research is properly directed toward the aging of the reproductive systems, the pacemaker of aging must now be regarded as residing elsewhere.

Immunity and Age

Influenza and pneumonia have often been looked upon as the friends of the very old, for in the past infectious diseases often served to end a life of pain and debilitation. As a result, little research was conducted on why resistance to infectious diseases declines in late life. Today there is growing recognition of the immune system's contribution as a source of general aging.

The debilitated older person may not only come to forget events, names, and familiar faces, but may also gradually lose the *biological* memory necessary to recognize and fight previously encountered viruses and "unfriendly" proteins. Two processes are involved: the first is the recognition of the noxious agent; the second is the capacity of the immune system to mobilize its resources to combat it. Recent discoveries have given rise to *immune theories* of aging. As these theories have developed, the availability of drugs capable of reducing the occurrence of infectious diseases has limited inquiries into how the body's defenses are mobilized. Instead, attention has been focused on the body's inability to distinguish friendly from unfriendly proteins: our own proteins can become antigens and our bodies may mistakenly attack these necessary substances. It is the mobilization of our immune system's defenses against our own vital proteins that gives rise to "auto-immune" disease.

Immune theories of aging are new on the scientific scene. Research suggests that while our response to outside, or exogenous, antigens may reduce as we age, as sometimes happens with hay-fever, our response to some internal or endogenous antigens may increase. What is appealing about linking the immune system to aging is that it, along with the endocrine and nervous systems, is one of the body's three great regulatory systems: the failures of all three can be transmitted or diffused broadly throughout the body. It should be kept in mind, however, that lower forms of life without specialized immune systems also show characteristics of aging. So we must wait for further evidence before we can commit our enthusiasm to the immune system.

Genetic Diseases and the Control of Aging

Ever since Raymond Pearl's work on familial tendencies to longevity, there has been considerable interest in the extent to which the potential for long life is inherited. Two components affect longevity. One is our inter-individual differences in characteristic length of life; the other is the tendency for our species to live long. There is no doubt that different families have different potentials for longevity; in fact, siblings of the same parents may also vary. Franz Kallman and Lissy Jarvik found that identical twins tend to have greater similarities in lifespan and cause of death than fraternal twins or non-twin siblings.[7]

We now know that many chronic diseases of later life are also heritable; Alzheimer's disease, for example, may involve familial predisposition. Nevertheless, the question of why particular persons are susceptible to a given disease in late life is not the same as why living things age and have a greater probability of dying with advancing age. And the question of why people live longer than dogs or mice is separate from why a person with long-lived grandparents has an advantage in life expectancy. Science tends to seek the most general answer; we should look to evolution for clues about our species and, within the species, for clues about individual differences.

The Brain and Longevity

In the course of evolution, there was apparently a survival advantage in having a large brain. Generally, the larger the brain of species, the longer its life expectancy. This fact has significant implications: animals that survive longer have more effective regulatory control over their bodies. Not only does the human brain give us the advantage of providing rapid and precise control over our bodily processes—such as metabolism, temperature, and blood pressure—but it also enables us to adapt to novel environments through learning and memory. The human species is probably the only one that has influenced its own evolution to a considerable extent, thanks to our capacity to learn. And we humans may influence it still more dramatically by exercising genetic manipulation in the near future.

While early theories of aging emphasized individual vital organs, the theoretical emphasis of contemporary research has shifted gradually to the role of the central nervous system as a critical force in aging. Compared to the two other major biological systems—the immune system and the endocrine system—the nervous system is clearly the most critical in disseminating influences to remote tissues and cells. The ratio of a species' brain weight to body weight is more closely linked to that species' longevity than either brain weight or body weight alone. This suggests that the fineness of control over the functions of the organism has been an evolutionary advantage in human aging.

By evolving a brain with a great capacity to learn, store, and retrieve information, the human animal has developed three ways of regulating its development and aging. In addition to the genome—the mass of genetic information—it is the programming of the individual through learning and the passing of this information to others that gives rise to culture, the accumulated products of individual learning. If DNA is the biological basis of the species, then culture is the DNA of society, the basis for many influences that bear on the way we grow old—such as our diets, the amount of exercise we get, and the drugs we use.

Mankind's great capacity for learning, storage, and retrieval is apparently a function of the neurons of the brain. Three other types of cells in the brain, called glial cells, function to support the neurons. While they are vital to the maintenance of the brain, glial cells are not regarded as the basis of the modifications in behavior that occur as a result of experience. The neurons are the cells most likely to serve as the archive for storing the engram, or the traces of the learned past that can influence future behavior.

The neurons are long-lived, an important feature that affects the process of aging. After early infancy, the neurons in the brain no longer continue to divide, and our original cells remain with us until we die. Most other types of cells can continue to divide over the course of life. Thus, the human nervous system is stable and consistent over time not only because of the genome, but also because of the accumulation of learning. It may be said that the immune system has a "memory" for substances it has met before, but only the nervous system can anticipate what it will do in the future—that is, engage in strategic planning.

The specialization of the human brain, while imparting a selective advantage for survival, may also dictate our fate in late life. As the nervous system goes, so goes the collection of unique experiences that make up our individual identities. The death of an individual is most clearly marked by brain death. Legally, once the brain ceases to function, the cells of many otherwise living organs and tissues may be taken for transplanting. The "I," or ego, dies with the brain.

In lower animals, such as the flatworm, the nervous system can regenerate. If we cut a flatworm in half, the tail half without a nervous system will regenerate a new one. Think of the implications of this for the retention of learning. If the flatworm depended on *retaining* what it learned in order to avoid noxious or toxic conditions, then the tail portion would not long survive. During the long process of evolution, the human species has become committed to a long-lived nervous system whose cells do not divide. This confers one type of survival advantage in terms of longevity and adaptation, but with it comes a disadvantage: we go the way of our nervous system.

Experiments with mice have been successful in transplanting neurons that have a neurosecretory function. Embryonic cells can be transplanted into a mature host, in which they perform their normal function. It may be asked whether such experiments do not contradict the notion of the fixed neuron. It is possible that the transplanted neurons function in a nonspecific way in the brain; they synthesize and secrete needed endocrines but need not have a role in a complex information network. Future possibilities for success in replacing brain cells and other cells through transplantation would seem to be greatest where the cells play the least differentiated role, are primarily regulated by the genome programming, and do not participate in the organization of functions that result from learning.

Very little of the genetic material in a cell is used to program the cell's differentiation and mature functioning. This is true for neurons as well, and the potential for adaptations to future conditions may lie in this large reservoir of unused genetic material. What turns DNA on and off in cells during stages of development is still a mystery. In the study of late-life diseases such as Alzheimer's, puzzling questions arise as to why, if the illness is genetic, the genes do not express themselves until late in life. By learning more about the expression and repression of genes, biomedical research may show us how to repress genes that predispose us to Alzheimer's and other diseases.

Some genes that have late-life expression in disease may have served a desirable function in earlier life. The term *pleiotropism* refers to this multiple function, which bears on the important point that normal development and aging require the proper timing of genetic expression.

Aging as a Counterpart of Development

It may be both intriguing and useful to think of aging as a counterpart of development. The way we age may be a translation of the way we grow up, biologically, psychologically, and socially. (The term "counterpart" is not used here to imply that aging is a mirror image of development, but to refer to aging as development's complement.) Freud viewed very early learning as the basis for the adult personality. From this perspective, adult personality and psychopathology form a close counterpart of development, with less significance attributed to the events of mid- or late-life and greater significance attached to the effects of early experience. From my perspective, however, aging should be viewed as more loosely linked. Menopause, for instance, is not merely a regression of function back along the lines of early development; it is not merely the inverse of puberty.

Biological Counterpart

One of the dominant views of aging during the 1950s held that aging resulted from random biological damage that accumulated to a lethal level. The idea was derived from the era's experience with radiation, which taught that the cumulative effects of radiation on organisms resulted in damage and, eventually, death. The crucial element in this model is that the damage was not deterministic or planned but was, rather, the consequence of random insults—to the DNA, for example. Biologists in the 1950s defined development as an organized process, and aging as the disorganization of organisms permitted by evolution after the optimum time of reproduction. The idea was that in late life characteristics of the organism are beyond the reach of selective pressures. But given the evidence sketched earlier in this chapter for genetic factors in longevity, there must be some programming for longevity beyond simple wear and tear. Longevity could derive from a given metabolic capacity—like a fixed number of heartbeats that can be used up quickly or slowly, or a fixed capacity to repair damages to genetic material. Yet if we reverse the logic, observing that there is some evidence that longevity is heritable, then the question becomes one of accounting for its origin in selective pressures during the course of evolution.

The counterpart theory stresses the specialization that is involved in development and how it may affect longevity. Maynard Smith speculated, for example, that humans might pay for their ability for rapid mobilization in early life with a tendency to late-life hypertension. I pointed out some years ago that in preliterate societies, long-lived elders imparted a selective advantage to their families and tribes by providing memories from earlier experiences with famines, droughts, and the management of plants and animals.[8] In this way wisdom may have become linked to a long life and the combination became heritable.

If the characteristics of late life were not heritable, they would be increasingly random. Traits that favored survival and reproduction at puberty would be selected in a gradiant around the age of reproductive maturity—and would evolve into a gathering of random assassins waiting to assault us in the later years. If true, this picture would suggest that there is no organization to the processes that make us more likely to die with age. The very old would be victims of many genetically unrelated diseases, all relatively independent in their expression.

Thus far we have drawn a picture of aging at the biological level which is organized partly on a genetic basis and partly as a process of random degradation. This means that as we control environmental stresses, we can expect to improve the likelihood of survival in old age. Japan is an example of this, having progressed dramatically in the period following World War II so that its population today has the highest life expectancy in the world.

Behavioral Counterpart

Every human being is a unique combination of the parental genes. To this genetic uniqueness is added a lifetime of unique personal experiences. It is not surprising, therefore, that behavior in the later years is highly individualized. In some people, this produces a complex pattern of temperamental, intellectual, and motivational dispositions that we call wisdom.[9] In others, unfortunately, it leads to problems of poor mental health. Perhaps it is true, as Ernest Hemingway said, that "life breaks us all, but many are stronger in the broken places."

Some events are so overwhelming that they leave indelible marks on the individual involved. For example, in a major review of the literature on the effect of war, including captivity in prisoner-of-war and concentration camps and participation in resistance units, Arve Lonnom suggests that these stressful situations carry residual effects, and that premature aging may appear *after* the event.[10] In such persons, many factors combine to bring on the early appearance of diseases usually associated with the later years. For some, the psychological damage is sufficient to derail them for the remainder of their lives. "There are, however, many who did not suffer actual injury but who nevertheless have been incapable of switching from wartime to peacetime life. They lost touch and did not manage the readjustment to a normal civil life."[11]

Social Counterpart

It is perhaps in the province of social science where the counterpart theory is most useful. The cultural patterns that socialize individuals into their roles clearly contribute to the conditions of later life. In our productivity-minded society, for example, the emphasis on work brings with it attitudes that are negative for older adults. Evidence indicates that young adults view the life circumstances of older adults more negatively than do older adults themselves. Hence, the young regard aging as moving *from*, rather than *toward*, an ideal state. It has often been suggested that America is youth-oriented, a society in which ageism is deeply rooted. Yet Congress has recently raised the age limit on employment, and it is quite possible that, in the near future, all age limits on employment will be removed. For the present, we should remember that our own image of old age is transmitted to the young.

Modification of the Length of Life

What are our prospects for extending our lives significantly? One of the consistent findings about the human life span is that little length has ever been added to the later years. Life expectancy is inversely related to age: the younger the age at the time of prediction, the more years are added to life expectancy. In 1900, life expectancy at birth was 47.3 years, in contrast to 73.2 in 1977, a gain of about 26 years. In 1900, however, further life expectancy at age sixty-five was 11.9 years, compared to 16.3 years in 1977, or a gain of only about 4.5 years. Since 1900, the increase in life expectancy at age eighty is small—just over three years. These data include the effects of infant mortality and do not fairly represent changes in the later years. In 1900, for example, life expectancy at age ten was greater than at birth due to high infant and childhood mortality from infectious diseases. Life expectancy at age ten for males in 1900 was 50.6, in comparison with 71.7 in 1978, an increase of 21.1 years, which is still larger than the increase in life expectancy at age sixty-five. Despite many improvements in the standard of living, then, life expectancy has not changed much for the very old, though it has changed significantly for the young. As a guide for the future, this suggests that gains in life expectancy will be easiest for a society to attain in the middle years, when, perhaps, the effects of the environment and stress are most apparent.

Evidence for the effects of stress can be seen in the fact that, in the 1960s, the death rates rose somewhat for mature men, many of whom were World War II veterans in the process of fitting back into competitive civilian life.

One of the more puzzling facts about life expectancy in the United States is that once the non-white population survives past the age of sixty-five, its life expectancy is greater than that of the white population. However, fewer non-whites survive to late life in the first place. Still, if we hold that life expectancy reflects the health of a population, then the young and middle-aged have become notably healthier in the twentieth century. Do we then reverse this reasoning for non-whites at age sixty-five and hold that life expectancy reflects something else? The logical conclusion is that the non-white population has been exposed to selective pressures that result in better health in the later years.

THE FUTURE OF AGING

Japan's example of having become, in only two decades, the country with the highest life expectancy should make us cautious about predicting what aging will be like in the future. But if the United States continues to show reductions in heart disease, it too will have a remarkably increased older population. If the life expectancy in the United States matches that of Japan by the year 2000, U.S. women will have a life expectancy at birth of about eighty years, and men of about seventy-seven.

Historically, predictions about the size of the older population have tended to be too low. G. Stanley Hall, in his 1922 book on senescence, quoted Pearl as concluding that the United States population would reach an upper limit of 197,274,000 by the year 2100.[12] His estimate was already exceeded by the time of the 1970 census. One recent projection shows a population of 274,000,000 by 2010, with 12.7 percent over age sixty-five.

The percentage of people over sixty-five is influenced by the fertility rate, which fluctuates on the basis of the attitudes of persons at child-bearing age. The number of older persons is more easily estimated, for those who will become old are already alive at the time of estimation. If present employment trends continue, not many people will be working in the labor force after age sixty-five. Hall quotes sources which indicate that in 1880, 73.8 percent of males over sixty-five were employed; by 1900 the percentage had fallen to 68.4 percent, and this trend has continued. If life expectancy is notably increased, then there will be still larger numbers of persons over sixty-five seeking significant roles in society.

The prospects for additions to life expectancy are probably greater in the middle years, when changes in health habits such as diet, smoking, and the use of alcohol and drugs can contribute positively to health. The fruits of genetic engineering also offer prospects for adding to life expectancy although they are far from application.

Neal Cutler has written that "demographic analysis predicts that tomorrow's older persons will be, perhaps, in a better position to deal with ... problems on the basis of both individual and collective action."[13] The growth of organizations for retired persons also suggests a new context for older adults. The American Association of Retired Persons had about 20 million members at the end of 1985, and its magazine attracted the third largest readership of all magazines published in the United States. Here a dramatic social change is demonstrated, which G.S. Hall forecast in 1922 when he wrote:

The time is ripe for some kind of senescent league of national dimensions . . . with committees on finance, on the literature of senescence, including its psychology, physiology, hygience, etc. . . . and an organ or journal of its own that should be the medium of correspondence, keeping its members informed to date upon all matters of interest or profit to them, perhaps keeping tab on instances of extreme longevity or unusual conservations of energy, with possibly a junior department eventually for youngsters of fifty.

Given our current and anticipated increase in the number of older people, research on aging should continue to grow considerably in the immediate future. It is currently being discovered that such research is greatly facilitated by a unified view of all the psychological, biological, and social influences. Future aging research is expected to reflect still further this need for an interdisciplinary understanding.

This brief review has established the fact that there are different principles of aging depending on the complexity of the biological organization of the species being studied. The purpose of the developing organism is always to establish the capacity for self-regulation. In the case of the human, this means not only regulating its biological systems, but its social and behavioral systems as well. Aging is a highly complex phenomenon that should perhaps be viewed not as a single circumstance, but as a wide array of processes. This nudges us toward an ecological view of aging, in which our length of life is influenced by extrinsic environmental factors of a physical and social nature; by intrinsic factors related to our species and to our unique individual heredity; and by how and what we learn in a particular culture.

Just as we recognize the complexity of aging, so we must expect that the contribution of various factors to the average length of life will shift again with time. There may be some unpredictable positive developments that will lengthen our lives, but civilization also brings lurking dangers of toxic environments and destructive lifestyles. How we will age in the future is in our own hands.

ENDNOTES

[1] John Naisbitt, *Megatrends: Ten New Directions for Transforming Our Lives* (New York, Warner Books, 1982), p. 5.

[2] Y. Koga and G. Morant, "On the Degree of Association Between Reaction Times in the Case of Different Senses," *Biometrica*, vol. 15, 1923, pp. 346–72.

[3] Lewellys Barker, "Ageing from the Point of View of the Clinician," in Edmund Cowdry, ed., *Problems of Ageing* (Baltimore: Williams & Wilkins, 1942), pp. 832–54.

[4] Alfred E. Cohn, "Cardiovascular System and Blood," in Cowdry, ed., op. cit., p. 135.

[5] Stanley Korenman, *Endocrine Aspects of Aging* (New York: Elsevier, 1982), p. 4.

[6] Ronald S. Swerdloff and David Heber, "Effects of Aging on Male Reproductive Function," in Korenman, ed., op. cit., pp. 119–35.

[7] Franz Kallmann and Lissy Jarvik, "Individual Differences in Constitution and Genetic Background," in James E. Birren, ed., *Handbook of Aging and the Individual* (Chicago: University of Chicago Press, 1959), pp. 216–63.

[8] James E. Birren, *The Psychology of Aging* (Englewood Cliffs, N.J.: Prentice Hall, 1964).

[9] Vivian Clayton and Birren, "The Development of Wisdom Across the Life Span: A Reexamination of an Ancient Topic," *Life Span Development and Behavior*, vol. 3, 1980, pp. 103–35.

[10] Arve Lonnum, *Delayed Disease and Ill-Health* (Oslo: Norwegian Association of Disabled Veterans, 1969).

[11] Ibid, p. 18.

[12] G. Stanley Hall, *Senescence: The Last Half of Life* (New York: Appleton, 1922).

[13] Neal Cutler, "Age and Political Behavior," in Diana Woodruff and Birren, eds., *Aging: Scientific Perspectives and Social Issues*, 2nd ed. (Monterey, Ca.: Brooks/Cole, 1983), p. 49.

[14] Hall, op. cit., p. 194.

Jerome L. Avorn

Medicine: The Life and Death
of Oliver Shay

O NE COMMON MISCONCEPTION about the aging of society throughout the industrialized world is that the great changes the population is undergoing are almost entirely attributable to improved medical care, particularly of the high-technology sort. The truth is that while it clearly plays some role in the increasing survival of the very old multiply impaired elderly, medical care per se has until recently played a rather modest part in generating the population changes we are currently experiencing. The foundation (as well as the first several stories) of this changing population pyramid was built of far more unassuming stuff, earlier in this century. The alarmingly straightforward observation that under-lies this concept is that one cannot live to become sixty-five if one has not lived to become ten. By far the most important reason for the brief life-expectancy of the early twentieth century was the era's extraordinarily high rates of infant mortality and death prior to early middle age. While conventional wisdom holds that the dread diseases of the turn of the century—influenza, tuberculosis, pneumonia, diphtheria—have been put in their place through the miracles of modern medicine, a number of authors have clearly documented that the striking reduction in mortality from these killers took place in large part before any biomedical intervention was available to forestall or cure them.[1] The discovery of bacteria, the practice of immunization, and the arrival of antibiotics all occurred well after major strides had been made in reducing the impact of these diseases on society.

What, then, caused the precipitous drop in mortality from these infectious diseases, a factor that plays such a large role in the demographic transitions we are considering? The best evidence indicates that it is *social* interventions, rather than biomedical ones, that deserve the credit: the availability of adequate nutrition, of clean water free of sewage, of sufficient housing to prevent crowding and exposure to the elements, and the institution of rudimentary sanitation practices. Likewise, while the drop in the birth rate has been another important cause of the relative ascendancy of the old in the population, it, too, was well entrenched before the introduction of the birth-control pill, although this medical intervention has probably made the fertility rate drop somewhat more steeply than it otherwise might have been.

A more modern example of the impressive power of "low-tech" changes to reduce morbidity and mortality can be found in the area of the most serious and most frequent medical problem in the United States: cardiovascular disease. Beginning in 1968, a striking and unexpected drop was noticed in mortality resulting from the diseases of the heart.[2] The best current evidence indicates that this drop is continuing, and is likely to do so well into the next century.[3] In a recent analysis of this phenomenon, Lee Goldman and E.F. Cook analyzed the relative contribution of such "lifestyle" changes as diet, smoking, and exercise, compared to such medical interventions as coronary care units and medications, in causing this change.[4] Their conclusion was similar to that of other researchers: most of the reduction in mortality (and, it is likely, in morbidity as well) should be credited to changes in our behavior and our health habits, rather than to curative medical interventions.[5] Had this remarkable reduction in death and disability been the result of a new medical procedure or therapy, it would have been greeted with accolades and headlines—and, if a new wonder-drug were responsible for the change, a doubling of the net worth of the company that produced it. But since the intervention takes as humble a form as avoiding cigarettes and eating fish instead of beef, this "life-saving discovery" has been the subject of somewhat less public attention and policy action.

Nevertheless, as we underline the importance of non-biomedical factors in preventing disease and making old age itself possible, it is important not to lose sight of the legitimate role of curative medicine, which is becoming increasingly significant (though perhaps never as significant as those of us who practice it would like to believe). The fifty-year mark is a convenient, if somewhat arbitrary, marker to delimit the point at which medical technology begins to have its greatest effect—both in the life of the individual and in the course of the present century. Most of the modern medical interventions familiar to us today became widely available only after the mid-point of this century: antibiotics (in widespread use only after World War II), cardiac pacemakers (in the 1960s), hemodialysis (in the late 1960s), coronary artery surgery (in the 1970s), to name a few.

With the exception of the birth-control pill, each of the medical-technology interventions developed since the 1950s has its most widespread impact on people who are past their fifties—the further past their fifties, the greater the impact. If the public health and environmental advances of the first half of this century made it possible to create a cohort of people who survived into middle age—and who could then go on to become old—then it is the biomedical discoveries of the second half of this century that are making it possible for these same people to live into advanced old age in a way that has never before been possible in human history.

It is in this area that the aging of individuals has its greatest impact on the aging of society. It is paradoxical that at the same time that we are supporting—some would say creating—the largest group of chronically ill elderly the world has ever known, we are witnessing a trend in the opposite direction. This phenomenon has been named "youth creep," and represents the other side of aging in the late twentieth century: large numbers of people coming into their sixties and seventies healthier than their grandparents were at the same age. These seemingly different phenomena are in fact both offshoots of the same process. It is as if the health of older Americans has been ratcheted up a notch or two in recent decades. While on the one hand, this results in an improvement in health for the non-ill elderly, on the other hand, this ratcheting up will cause many chronically ill people, who otherwise would have died, to remain one notch below death. "The rising tide lifts all ships equally," including those that might otherwise be resting at the bottom of the harbor. (One side effect of this is that, in the aging society, fully 40 percent of the Medicaid budget for the poor of all ages is consumed by the elderly, an unsettling statistic that will be considered later in this chapter.)

The emerging awareness about aging that is spreading through all age groups, combined with an increase—some would say a glut—in the number of physicians, may well result in physicians devoting greater attention in office practice to preventive care, something that has until now been disdained by much of the medical profession. Forestalling the onset of disability rather than effecting a cure may increasingly come to define the goal of health care for everyone past the age of thirty-five. As awareness of the specter of geriatric malfunction spreads among ever-lower age groups, attention will focus on what can be done in midlife to ward off the ravages of senescence. In this sense, there may be a strong connection between society's growing awareness of its own aging and the escalating interest among people of all ages in fitness, nutrition, and various other means of protecting one's earthly container.

There is certainly good reason to believe that for some geriatric infirmities preventive behavior throughout life can make an important difference: smoking and diets that are high in saturated fat as causes of heart disease and various forms of cancer are probably the most convincing examples. Yet we still lack good evidence of any preventive actions that will fend off other ravages of old age, such as the terrible chronic illnesses of Alzheimer's disease or diabetes. Nonetheless, as we continue our evolution from a society preoccupied with youth to one that is preoccupied with age, we can expect greater public attention to be devoted to those voices of preventive medicine that were so often ignored in the past.

From the point of view of sociology or psychology or demographics, the emergence of the vigorous "young-old" is of considerable significance. But from the perspective of the health-care system, the young-old—despite their growing numbers—have considerably less impact on society than the sicker old-old. It has frequently been noted that the fastest growing segment of the U.S. population comprises those who are in this category. While those over seventy-five currently represent about 4 percent of the population, by the year 2040 this group is expected to comprise 11 percent of the population, reflecting a quadrupling of their numbers from 3.6 million to 13.8 million.[6] As Karen Davis shows in this volume, this group is of the greatest interest to us from both economic and medical perspectives, since the 75-and-up cohort consumes the greatest amount of medical care per capita. It is people of this age group that most heavily employ the pacemakers, the replacement organs, and the intensive life-support systems, and whose lives are most deeply affected by them.

A clinical vignette may help to illustrate some of the primary biological, economic, and ethical issues involved in applying the medical technologies of the mid-1980s to a patient in his mid-eighties. Let us then consider the story of the fictitious Oliver Shay.

Oliver Shay was born into a lower-middle-class household at the turn of the century. The periods just before and after the birth of little Oliver were marked by a series of crucial but lackluster non-events. His mother came to her pregnancy well-fed and protected from the elements by a sturdy row-house. During gestation she had adequate access to nutritious, if uninspired meals. After weaning, baby Ollie drank water uncontaminated by human wastes, ate copiously, and shared a room with only two other children. He did not begin work until he was sixteen. These are not exactly the makings of a Theodore Dreiser novel or even a television mini-series—but, repeated by millions of other children during the early twentieth century, Ollie's experiences did provide the makings of a demographic transformation.

After a relatively uneventful adult life working on an assembly line, in 1965 Oliver Shay stopped working at age sixty-five, in keeping with his company's mandatory retirement policy, and began to collect Social Security. Fortunately for Mr. Shay, this was also the period during which the Medicare program came into existence, and he was soon covered by it for most, if not all, of his acute medical needs. In the winter of 1967, Mr. Shay came down with a severe case of bacterial pneumonia, and was admitted to a hospital in a state of respiratory failure. Before World War II, this illness might well have caused his death, but with the widespread availability of antibiotics and new sophistication in the management of respiratory failure, Mr. Shay was just a "routine case," managed successfully by an intern in the intensive-care unit, and discharged in good health less than two weeks after admission.

Two years passed, and Mr. Shay began to notice pressing left-sided chest pain when he exerted himself, a condition that worsened steadily over time. Cardiac catheterization revealed that he had a near-total narrowing of one of the main coronary arteries, which, if allowed to progress, would likely result in death within a few years. Mr. Shay was scheduled for an elective coronary artery bypass operation, which he underwent successfully at age seventy-three. Six years after the operation, Mr. Shay began to notice increasing pain in his left hip when he walked or climbed stairs. X-rays revealed advanced degenerative arthritis, and he underwent an elective total replacement of his hip joint. Within eight months of the operation, he was dancing at his granddaughter's wedding, and proclaimed, "I feel like a new man!"

On the day of his seventy-ninth birthday, Mr. Shay visited his children (themselves now in their late fifties) in a neighboring suburb. When he failed to return from an upstairs bathroom, a grandson found him sprawled on the floor in his own vomit and feces, mumbling incoherently. He was rushed to the nearest hospital, where computerized tomography of his head revealed that he had suffered a cerebrovascular accident (stroke), leaving him severely paralyzed on his right side, unable to swallow, feed himself, or walk. Two days later, a nurse found him lying in bed immobile, unresponsive, and pallid. He had no pulse and was not breathing. A cardiac-arrest emergency was announced over the hospital paging system, and within minutes, closed-chest cardiac massage was implemented by the resuscitation team, a tube was placed in his windpipe to facilitate breathing, and he was attached to a respirator. Electric defibrillation and a variety of intravenous medications followed, and within thirty minutes Mr. Shay once again had a normal heartbeat and blood pressure. The respirator was detached after he was moved to the intensive-care unit, and within five days he was transferred out of intensive care. Within two more weeks, impeccable nursing care and aggressive rehabilitation efforts restored Mr. Shay to a point at which he could be discharged from the hospital to a skilled-care nursing home.

After living in the nursing home for two years with essentially no improvement in his paralysis and speech disorder, Mr. Shay was noted to have episodes of falling, at least two of which resulted in broken bones and admission to the orthopedic service of his local hospital. Work-up by an internist during the second admission revealed that Mr. Shay's pulse was very slow and irregular, with occasional periods of no detectable heart beat at all for up to five seconds. A cardiologist suggested that degeneration of the heart's conduction system was responsible for Mr. Shay's repeated falls, and a permanent cardiac pacemaker was implanted. At age eighty-four, family members began to notice that Mr. Shay no longer seemed to be as "with it" as he had been, and he seemed even less able to care for himself in the nursing-home setting than he had been previously. Several months later, he became irascible and combative, but was still alert. A neurologist advised the family that the likely diagnosis was Alzheimer's disease, and that no specific treatment was possible. His mental status continued a slow downward course, but he remained able to converse in garbled speech with those around him and continued to take pleasure in certain activities, such as eating. At age eighty-eight, blood tests revealed a major electrolyte imbalance, and a diagnosis was made of chronic renal failure. The family requested that he be put on hemodialysis (an artificial kidney machine) for the remainder of his life. This was done, and his course remained relatively stable for the next three years, until he developed severe abdominal pain at age ninety-one; he was sent to the emergency room of the nearest hospital where a rupturing aortic aneurysm was diagnosed, and he was rushed into surgery. After five hours in the operating room, he was transferred in very critical condition to the surgical intensive unit where he remained for ten days with a variety of complications, and then died.

The composite story of Mr. Shay is not at all atypical of the medical life-history of many geriatric patients. At numerous points, beginning with his pneumonia at age sixty-seven, he experienced acute medical problems that, just a few decades earlier, would often have proved fatal. Instead, he was rescued by one medical technology after another: antibiotics cured his pneumonia, resuscitation literally reversed his dying, a pacemaker kept his heart pumping, and an artificial kidney freed his body of impurities, much as a real one would do. Nevertheless, it was his chronic disabilities—his stroke and his senile dementia—against which the armamentarium of modern medicine had relatively little to offer. He was kept alive in his state of ever-decreasing functional capacity until the occurrence of his terminal catastrophe, which was itself prolonged for nearly two weeks, at exorbitant cost.

Mr. Shay's case can illustrate many things, but for our current purposes, I would like to focus on the matter of "the compression of morbidity."[7] This appealing but probably specious concept holds that since the human life span is finite, and because we are developing various acute and chronic diseases later in life than our counterparts in previous generations, we are entering a period in human history in which people will live active, vigorous lives until advanced old age, and then experience most of their illnesses during a relatively brief period immediately before death.[8]

Unfortunately for all of us, this seductive scenario flies in the face of available demographic information, clinical observation, measures of health status over time, and common sense.[9] Whatever the theoretical upper limit of the human life span, it is demonstrably the case that the *average life expectancy* of people in industrialized countries is indeed increasing each year. As the vignette of Mr. Shay illustrates, the successes of modern medical care have assured us of an increase, rather than a decrease, in the number of people who survive previously fatal illnesses—but often only to be afflicted by disabling chronic conditions for years. While the "compression of morbidity" theory would paint the reassuring picture of less and less burden of disability on our aged population in the decades to come, the best evidence we have suggests quite the opposite view, and one that is far more sobering: that it is precisely the cohort of very old individuals that is increasing the fastest and living the longest. It is unlikely that breakthroughs in medical research in the coming years will enable us to cure or prevent Alzheimer's disease, arthritis, stroke, diabetes, or all the other chronic afflictions of old age. Barring such an unforeseen set of discoveries, the demand on the health-care system and related social supports by this burgeoning group will indeed be awesome. Burdened by multiple chronic illnesses, the elderly themselves will pay an increasingly high price for their longevity in terms of the disability they will have to bear. And yet the toll will not only be on the old. Such "geriatric" issues affect all age groups in the aging society—for it is the middle-aged offspring and their children whose lives are often limited in the attempt to provide long-term care for the elderly.

How are health-care professionals affected by this changing complexion of the patient population, in which those over age sixty-five occupy more than 40 percent of hospital beds on any given day, and take up a considerably larger percent of general medical services? The evidence is not encouraging. Several studies have compared the attitudes of medical students toward the old or chronically ill at the start and at the end of their training. In general, a worrisome deterioration is seen to occur in their disposition toward elderly patients and in their desire to care for them.[10] For many, the processes of bedside medical education and the socialization that is part of medical training seem to bring with them a transformation from idealism to cynicism or, at best, apathy.

Much of this transformation can be related to the mismatch of conventional medical paradigms with the changing epidemiology of illness. In 1910, Abraham Flexner prepared a report on medical education in the United States and Canada for the Carnegie Foundation for the Advancement of Teaching. His landmark work helped to lift medical education from a collection of scattered programs of very uneven quality to a level at which it became concentrated in a much smaller number of university-affiliated institutions that were deeply committed to the scientific basis of diagnosis and therapy.[11] This empirical tradition developed in parallel with the new life-sciences that were emerging in the early part of this century. Of all of them, it was perhaps bacteriology that most helped to define the conceptual models that have formed the cognitive backbone of medical training up to the present. A good example of this is the treatment of pneumococcal pneumonia: it is as if medicine became "imprinted" with the concept that disease is brought on by a single cause, is characterized by reliably typical clinical manifestations, and can eventually be completely cured by administering a specific "magic bullet"—in this case, penicillin—leaving the patient as fit and functional as before the acute illness.

This paradigm of illness and cure—certainly one of the high points of our struggle against disease—has set the mold for virtually all medical education up to now. Yet we practitioners have become victims of our own success. We have become so good at curing acute diseases like pneumococcal pneumonia that the patients who suffer from them now require relatively less and less of our attention. In many instances, they may be treated as outpatients, and may never even occupy a hospital bed. Increasingly, those who are left in the beds are the people whom we don't know how to cure—the Oliver Shays with degenerative chronic illnesses who do not—cannot—leap out of bed after forty-eight hours of antibiotic treatment, utter a hearty "Thanks, Doc!" and return to active, vigorous lives.

Despite these changes, the models used to train us—and which we still use to train others—continue to feature the orientation that there is a correct single diagnosis and a correct "magic bullet" to fix a given illness. Given the conceptual mismatch between what medical students are taught and the burden of illness they later confront, it is not surprising how many of them feel frustrated and even appalled by the realities of geriatric practice.

It is interesting to note that other groups of health professionals have fared better in this regard. Nurses, for example, have been taught for generations that their primary responsibility is to care for patients, not to cure them. Helping patients cope with their diseases, learn about them, and adapt—these have been the classical roles of the mother-figure nurse, while the father-figure physician worried about diagnosis, intervention, and cure. It is only recently that we physicians are coming to understand how much we can learn from our nurse colleagues on this issue of care vs. cure.

The consequences of the aging of society are diverse, and they touch on every aspect of human life. It is in the realm of biology, however, that this process will confront its most fundamental and most difficult challenges. A sense of genuine emergency now permeates most informed discussion about the nature of health and medical care for the coming decades. As the number of Oliver Shays and heroic high-tech interventions at our command increases, will we have the economic wherewithal to continue to provide everyone with all that is available? Given that it is the old who will continue to require the most from our medical-care system, will we begin to see a battle between the generations for health-care resources? When Mr. Shay's grandchildren are in their senescence sometime in the next century, will they face resource limitations in their care that are unthinkable today? What moral, clinical, political, and economic principles will guide us through that uncharted territory?

One course of action stands out from all the rest as being the simplest to implement and the one that would produce the most predictable consequences: continuation of present policies. Not much speculation is required to document that maintaining our current approaches to health care, with their reliance on curative medicine, institution-based long-term care, and fee-for-service reimbursement underwritten by government expenditures, will lead to such a progressive escalation in the costs of medical care that the funds in the Medicare Trust Fund will surely be depleted before the end of this century.[12] (Although halting steps are currently being taken to replace fee-for-service with reimbursement with prospective payment, skepticism abounds concerning the capacity of such an approach to maintain control over escalating health-care costs.) There is a slim chance that the public and its representatives would tolerate the increased costs of health-care expenditures that would be reflected in an additional 5 to 7 percent of the gross national product being devoted to medical expenses, but this is not very likely. Far more plausible is the likelihood that other means will be found to impose a brake on escalating costs of health care for the elderly in order to free up funds for other worthy purposes—including health care for the non-elderly. Some of these can be summarized briefly, as follows:

Rationing. As is currently the practice in Great Britain in the case of expensive health-care interventions such as hemodialysis,[13] the United States might develop policies that discourage the use of certain costly technologies for elderly patients, or that withhold public funding for these interventions. This issue will become acute in the immediate future, as technologies such as artificial organs and widespread transplantation programs guarantee an enormous excess of demand over supply in this area, whether supply is expressed in terms of dollars or available tissue parts. The ethical, legal, and human problems this approach would create are not hard to imagine.

Prevention. Our experience in the last two decades with the treatment of hypertension and with the unexpected drop in cardiovascular mortality has made clear that, despite our fascination with the high-tech dramatic "saves" of which curative medicine is capable, relatively inexpensive, unglamorous activities—whether medical or behavioral—have enormous power to prevent devastating illness and death. Nonetheless, such interventions consistently fail to capture the imagination of policymakers, and have only recently begun to be of much interest to individuals. Strong commercial interests, on the other hand, have had considerable success in opposing large-scale attempts to reduce the consumption of commodities of particular interest to them, such as tobacco or saturated-fat products. Despite this, there is encouraging evidence that even in the absence of concerted governmental action on this front, individuals in every age group of our graying population are manifesting greater interest in preserving their own health through diverse means, of widely varying effectiveness. Far more must be learned about the efficacy of various purported ways of preventing illness, as well as about how best to motivate people to adopt and maintain health-promoting behaviors. While it would be utopian to suggest, as some do, that the widespread adoption of preventive practices by Americans will spare us the brunt of chronic disability in late life, the evidence is accumulating impressively that such changes can make important differences in the need for medical care and the occurrence of disability.[14]

Research breakthroughs. It is quite possible that specific diseases of the elderly might well be vanquished in dramatic and unexpected ways by discoveries in basic biomedical research, as was the case with that oft-cited example, polio. As Lewis Thomas and others have pointed out, biomedical research is ultimately the most efficient way for society to deal with the burden of illness, since half-way solutions (wards full of iron lungs, in the case of polio) are inevitably more expensive and far less satisfactory from a medical point of view.[15] Recent advances in the understanding of the neurochemical basis of Alzheimer's disease may, in a decade or two, lead to the next major breakthrough in medicine's assault on diseases that afflict the elderly. Promising research leads, analogous to those that resulted in the use of L-dopa to treat Parkinson's disease, are beginning to develop in the area of neurotransmitter therapy.

As important as such research is and will become, however, it is crucial that we set into policy perspective its possible impact on morbidity and mortality. The major diseases of the elderly from an epidemiologic point of view (and therefore those most relevant to health-care delivery questions) are not, in general, specific lesions in a particular organ, as has been the case with many previous breakthroughs in the history of therapeutics. This paradigm has been described in an insightful, if obscure, way by Michel Foucault.[16] Instead—and the distinction is one that repeatedly eludes many planners and clinicians—the "name of the game" in the medical care of the elderly is the predominance of overlapping multi-system diseases that are degenerative in nature. While great expectations— and funding—are due research into these problems, it would be inappropriate to base public policy on an assumption that the coming years will provide breakthroughs analogous to the polio vaccine for such problems as arthritis, arteriosclerosis, incontinence, depression, or various forms of central nervous system degeneration. It has been documented for several millenia now that human beings are, in fact, mortal and that one must die of some terminal event.[17] And it is in the management of those last years, which we shall touch on now, that some of the most important challenges will be faced.

Re-thinking therapy and death. One traditional view of the role of medicine holds that the physician should at all times struggle against disease and death in much the way that a lawyer struggles to win acquittal for his client, regardless of the merits of the case.[18] In the past, when the tools of medicine were more limited in their power, nature tended to take its course in any case, and in the first half of this century the notion of using medical technology to keep people alive beyond the duration of any recognizably human existence was simply not an issue; we were unable to do so even if we wanted to. With the growth of curative technology, however, the practice of medicine became imbued with an ideology of "automatic therapy," aimed at restoring physiological normality to patients in virtually all circumstances. This ideology is currently prevailing with near-frantic intensity, particularly in tertiary-care medical centers. Its practice has been bolstered by a series of unfortunate legal proceedings, which have contributed to the discomfort that many physicians feel in withholding any form of therapy from a patient, even when it is not clear that it is in the interest of that patient to have life prolonged.[19]

Only recently has an opposing view been voiced with any degree of clarity or consistency. Grounded in either humanitarian or economic perspectives, the case is increasingly being made that, in view of our new power to keep patients alive well beyond what was once considered the point of death, we must begin to face up to the question of when additional medical care is *not* in the best interest of the patient. More attention is being devoted to the concept of the "living will," or, more satisfactorily, durable power of attorney as a means of authorizing the cessation of care when it is no longer meeting the stated goals or desires of the patient. Considerable confusion persists on the part of both physicians and family members over how to put this approach into practice, but consensus is slowly growing that in many instances no good is served by prolonging the dying of a particular individual by days or weeks of intensive, often uncomfortable, and generally expensive therapies.[20] Abuses of this concept are certain to become commonplace in future years, but it is equally certain that the medical profession and society as a whole will learn to live with this new kind of control over our fates. If we fail to address this very difficult issue squarely, the result will be our keeping every desperately ill person technically "alive" well beyond the limits he or she would have established, and at an increasingly unaffordable cost in both dollar and human terms. As the practice of mindlessly extending life is widely becoming regarded as unacceptable, we must develop a more thorough understanding of the issues being raised, and we must do so before we edge perilously close to policies that might be economically plausible but ethically unacceptable.[21] It is the old of today who are the subjects of these concepts and decisions, but it is all of us—including the non-old of today—who will be their subjects in the not-too-distant future. It has often been noted that the aged comprise the one minority group that nearly all of us will enter. A slightly altered version of that well-known statement of Pogo's might well serve as the motto of the aging society: "We have met the elderly—and they are us."

ENDNOTES

[1] Rene Dubos, *The Mirage of Health* (New York: Anchor Books, 1959); Thomas McKeown, *The Role of Medicine* (London: Nuffield Provincial Hospitals Trust, 1976); Edward H. Kass, "Infectious Disease and Social Change," *Journal of Infectious Diseases* (1971): 110–14.

[2] Ralph S. Paffenbarger, *Proceedings of the Conference on the Decline in Coronary Heart Disease Mortality* (Washington, D.C.: NIH Publication no. 79-1610, 1979).

[3] Dorothy P. Rice and Jacob J. Feldman, "Living Longer in the United States: Demographic Changes and Health Needs of the Elderly," *Milbank Memorial Fund Quarterly/Health and Society* (1983) 61: 362–396.

[4] Lee Goldman and E.F. Cook, "The Decline in Ischemic Heart Disease Mortality Rates: An Analysis of the Comparative Effects of Medical Interventions and Changes in Lifestyle," *Annals of Internal Medicine* (1984) 101: 825–836.

[5] Julius B. Richmond, et al., *Healthy People: The Surgeon General's Report on Health Promotion and Disease Prevention* (Washington, D.C.: U.S. Government Printing Office, DHEW (PHS) Publication no. 79-55071, 1979); W.J. Walker, "Changing U.S. Life Style and Declining Vascular Mortality: A Retrospective," editorial in the *New England Journal of Medicine* (1983) 308: 649–651.

[6] See Rice and Feldman, op. cit., and the essay by Siegel and Taeuber in this volume on demographic changes.

[7] James F. Fries, "The Compression of Morbidity," *Milbank Memorial Fund Quarterly/Health and Society*, Summer 1983, pp. 397–419.

[8]James F. Fries, "Aging, Natural Death, and the Compression of Morbidity," *New England Journal of Medicine* (1980) 303: 130–135.

[9]Kenneth C. Manton, "Changing Concepts of Morbidity and Mortality in the Elderly Population," *Milbank Memorial Fund Quarterly/Health and Society* (1982) 60: 183–244; Edward L. Schneider and Jacob A. Brody, "Aging, Natural Death, and the Compression of Morbidity: Another View," *New England Journal of Medicine* (1983) 309: 854–856; A. Colvez and M. Blanchet, "Disability Trends in the U.S. Population," *American Journal of Public Health* (1981) 71: 464–471.

[10]Janet Gale and B. Livesley, "Attitudes Towards Geriatrics," *Age and Ageing* (1974) 3: 49–53; Donald L. Spence, et al., "Medical Student Attitudes Toward the Geriatric Patient," *Journal of the American Geriatrics Society* (1968) 16: 976–983; "Geriatrics Is Medicine," editorial in *Lancet* (1974): 663.

[11]Abraham Flexner, *Medical Education in the United States and Canada* (New York: The Carnegie Foundation for the Advancement of Teaching, 1910).

[12]John Iglehart, "Medicare's Uncertain Future," *New England Journal of Medicine* (1982) 306: 1308–1312.

[13]Henry J. Aaron and William B. Schwartz, *The Painful Prescription* (Washington, D.C.: The Brookings Institution, 1984).

[14]Barry M. Stults, "Preventive Health Care for the Elderly," *The Western Journal of Medicine* (1984) 141: 832–845.

[15]Lewis Thomas, "On the Science and Technology of Medicine," *Daedalus* (1976) 106: 35–46.

[16]Michel Foucault, *The Birth of the Clinic: An Archaeology of Medical Perception* (New York: Random House, 1973).

[17]John W. Rowe and Richard W. Besdine, *Health and Disease in Old Age* (Boston: Little, Brown, 1982), *passim*.

[18]Franklin H. Epstein, "The Role of the Physician in the Prolongation of Life," in *Controversies in Internal Medicine*, vol. II, ed. by Franz Inglefinger, et al. (New York: W.B. Saunders, 1973).

[19]Allen E. Buchanan, "Medical Paternalism or Legal Imperialism: Not the Only Alternatives," *American Journal of Law and Medicine* (1979) 5: 111; Alexander M. Capron, "The Development of Law on Human Death," *Annals of the New York Academy of Sciences* (1978) 45: 55; New Jersey Supreme Court, "In the Matter of Claire C. Conroy." Docket No. A-108. January 17, 1985.

[20]President's Commission for the Study of Ethical Problems in Medicine and Biomedical and Behavioral Research, *Deciding to Forego Life-Sustaining Treatment* (Washington, D.C.: U.S. Government Printing Office, 1983).

[21]Jerry Avorn, "Benefit and Cost Analysis in Geriatric Care: Turning Age Discrimination into Health Policy," *New England Journal of Medicine* (1984) 310: 1294–1301.

Karen Davis

Paying the Health-Care Bills
of an Aging Population

T HE AGING OF THE POPULATION in the United States has
particularly important implications for the nation's health
sector. It will increase the frequency of chronic illness, disability, and frailty in our society, and raise the demand for health and
long-term care services. The proportion of the GNP devoted to health
care has increased from 5 percent in 1960 to almost 11 percent in
1983—and seems certain to climb even further.

While the aging of society is characteristic of most industrialized
nations, the unique features of the U.S. health system raise important
concerns. First, we have no explicit mechanism for controlling the
level of resources devoted to health care. Most health services are
provided privately, and are financed by a mix of public programs,
private insurance plans, and direct patient payments. Patients are
largely free to choose the physicians or providers of health services
they prefer; the financial consequences of these decisions are masked
by insurance coverage. The government, either alone or in combination with other payers, does not establish budgets for health services,
and, except in a few states, there is no regulation to govern rates
charged by hospitals. Physicians may charge patients whatever they
choose and are virtually unchallenged in their decisions about the
health services patients need and receive. As a result, in the United
States there is neither effective market control nor governmental
regulation of health expenditures. As the population ages, we shall
either have to develop mechanisms for limiting the public resources

devoted to the health sector or be prepared to accept an ever-increasing diversion of economic resources for that purpose.

Unlike other industrialized nations, the United States publicly finances the health care of its elderly, but the health care for the remainder of the population is financed for the most part by private health insurance. As the population ages, government budget outlays for health care will increase disproportionately. The resulting budgetary pressures will add to those generated by increased outlays for Social Security pensions for the elderly, by reduced tax revenues from a relatively smaller working population, and by public resistance to higher taxes. The separate public financing of health services for the elderly also tends to focus policy options solely on health care—rather than fostering a policy that considers the health system as a whole.

Resolving the conflict between the expanding health needs of an aging society and the pressures to constrain budgetary and economic resources devoted to health care will not be easy. One relatively painless strategy would be to reduce the health-service requirements of the population by investing in preventive health measures and in biomedical research to prevent or to cure those diseases that now demand such heavy health expenditures. Unfortunately, we know very little about how successful such a strategy would be.

Another approach—but one that would encounter political difficulties—would be to introduce more effective controls for health expenditures. These could take the form of market-oriented strategies that either ration services directly on the basis of one's ability to pay, or that give physicians and other health-care providers incentives to ration services on the basis of medical need. Or the controls could require that government act to limit payments to hospitals, physicians, and other health-service providers, or to challenge physicians' decisions regarding patient care (for example, by screening out those services shown to be ineffective in improving health outcomes or the quality of life).

Still another, not mutually exclusive approach, would be to share the burden of health-care expenditures for an aging population more equitably among all members of society. In the U.S., the financial burden of health-care expenditures now falls most heavily on certain segments of the population—the uninsured or inadequately insured (mostly poor and near-poor non-aged, unemployed, or workers in low-wage jobs), the chronically ill and the terminally ill, those in nursing homes, and—because of gaps in public coverage—the near-poor aged. If the financing of health services were reformed, the burden of health-care expenses could be distributed according to one's ability to pay.

The foregoing choices are complicated. It may be useful, in expanding public understanding of these various approaches, to describe the current and future projected course of health expenditures in the U.S. in the context of prospective population; to examine inequities in the current health financing system; and, finally, to analyze options for altering the future course of the health-care system in the U.S. and for resolving the conflict between the expanding health needs of an aging population and a climate of constrained resources.

HEALTH EXPENDITURES AND THE AGING OF THE POPULATION

In 1984, the U.S. spent $387 billion on health, or about 11 percent of the gross national product. About one-third of all personal health-care expenditures went to care for aged persons, a proportion that reflects their greater needs and their greater use of health services. The average expenditure for personal health services for persons age sixty-five and over was $3140 in 1981, compared with $828 for those under age sixty-five.[1]

Much of the difference in expenditures is attributable to the fact that the aged make greater use of hospital and nursing-home care than their younger counterparts. The average annual per-capita hospital expenditures of the aged were $1381 in 1981, compared with $392 for the non-aged. Nursing-home expenditures average $732 per aged person, compared with only $30 for the non-aged. Differences also exist in expenditures for ambulatory care services. Physician expenditures per aged person were $589 in 1981, compared with $189 for the non-aged.[2]

Sources of Financing

The government picks up a substantial share of the health expenses of the elderly—primarily through the Medicare program, which finances acute health services for the elderly and disabled, and through

FIGURE 1. Per Capita Health Care Expenditures by Age, 1981

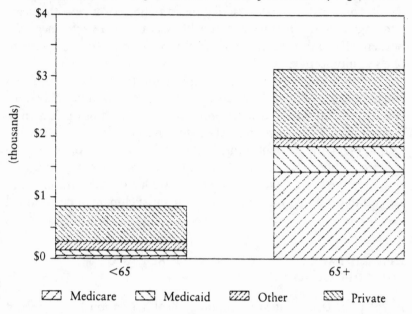

Medicaid, which finances acute and long-term care services for the poor, including the aged poor. As shown in figure 1, in 1981 Medicare paid 45.3 percent, or $1422, of the per-capita bill for the elderly. Other sources of funding included Medicaid (13.7 percent, or $430 of the per-capita bill), other public programs (4.9 percent, or $154), and private payments, including private health insurance and out-of-pocket expenses (36.1 percent, or $1130).

By contrast, for those under age sixty-five, only 29 percent of health expenses were paid by public programs. Private health insurance plans and patient out-of-pocket expenses accounted for 71 percent. Despite the greater percentage contribution of public programs for the care of the aged, on a per-capita basis the elderly pay more for private health care than do the non-elderly ($1130 for the aged and $588 for the non-aged in 1981). This reflects the much greater total health expenses of the aged.

The Financial Burden of Health Costs

As we have noted, the financial burden of health-care costs is very unevenly distributed. Among the non-aged, those without private health insurance or coverage under Medicaid can face quite significant financial burdens if they become ill and require health care. As shown in figure 2, the proportion of income spent on health care declines as income rises. Those with incomes below $3000 paid 10.2 percent of their income in health care in 1977 as contrasted with 1.7 percent of income for those with incomes above $15,000.

The financial burden of out-of-pocket expenses also falls particularly heavily on certain groups of elderly. Some elderly people enjoy good health and rarely use health-care services. Others are seriously disabled and require extensive treatment. Medicare and Medicaid assist many of those with serious health problems, but even with these programs, many elderly, especially the near-poor, can suffer financial hardship from health-care bills.

Because of the differences among them, health expenditures for the elderly as a group are very skewed. In 1981, 79 percent had annual

FIGURE 2. Average Out-of-Pocket Personal Health Expense for Persons with a Medical Expense, by Income, 1977*

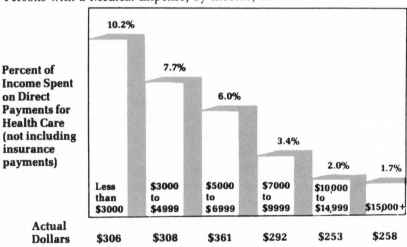

Percent of Income Spent on Direct Payments for Health Care (not including insurance payments)	10.2%	7.7%	6.0%	3.4%	2.0%	1.7%
	Less than $3000	$3000 to $4999	$5000 to $6999	$7000 to $9999	$10,000 to $14,999	$15,000+
Actual Dollars	$306	$308	$361	$292	$253	$258

SOURCE: Unpublished data from the 1978 National Health Interview Survey, National Center for Health Statistics, Department of Health and Human Services.
*Income is factored at categorical midpoint.

Medicare reimbursements of less than $1000, including 38 percent who received no Medicare payments. At the other extreme are those who require extensive care and treatment; 7.5 percent of the elderly accounted for two-thirds of all Medicare payments, with an average payment of over $11,000 in 1981.

For the most part, the elderly are not a prosperous group. Half of all families with an elderly member have incomes below twice the poverty level. (In 1981, the poverty level for an aged individual was $4359; twice the poverty level was $8718.) By contrast, 30 percent of persons in families without an aged member have family incomes below twice the poverty level. In 1981, 15.3 percent of the aged had incomes below the poverty level, compared with 14 percent of all persons. For single, white, aged women, 28 percent had incomes below the poverty level, while 64 percent of single, black, aged women had incomes below the poverty level.

Medicare and Medicaid are extremely important to the elderly in meeting their health-care bills. In 1981, these programs together spent $49 billion on health care for the elderly. Almost 40 percent of Medicaid expenditures go for the care of 3.5 million elderly people. But despite these programs, many elderly people already face serious financial burdens in meeting their health-care expenses. In 1980, 6 percent of the elderly had out-of-pocket health-care expenses (not counting health insurance premiums) exceeding $1000, and 16 percent paid more than $500 directly for health-care bills. These private payments by the elderly reflect gaps in Medicare coverage. Medicare has substantial cost-sharing requirements for covered benefits, and many health services are excluded. The elderly are required to pay a deductible for the first day of hospital care ($400 in 1985), one-fourth of that amount for each day of care between the sixtieth and ninetieth days of hospital care in a given episode of illness, and half of that amount for each day of care in a ninetieth-day lifetime reserve. Once these days of hospital care have been exhausted, the elderly must pay all of their hospital expenses.

The elderly incur especially heavy costs for physician services. Medicare covers only half of their physician expenditures. The elderly pay the first $75 of physician bills during the year, 20 percent of Medicare-allowed physician fees above the deductible amount, and the excess of all charges physicians make above the Medicare allowable fee. These charges can quickly become an enormous burden. Older people also incur heavy financial burdens from services that are not covered by Medicare. Most nursing-home care is not covered, nor does Medicare cover prescription drugs (except when a patient is hospitalized), dental care, hearing aids, eyeglasses, and many other health services that are essential to daily living.

The Congressional Budget Office estimates that out-of-pocket expenses for Medicare cost-sharing were \$505 per enrollee in 1984; the Supplementary Medical Insurance premium (the physician services part of Medicare), cost-sharing, and the deductible account for 80 percent of the cost. In addition, it is estimated that the average beneficiary paid an additional \$550 in 1984 for non-institutional care not covered by Medicare, most notably for prescription drugs and dental care. If nursing-home care were included, it would add another \$650 per person, for a total out-of-pocket cost to the elderly of \$1705.[3]

Out-of-pocket medical expenses are a particular burden for those elderly who do not have supplementary coverage to Medicare—either from Medicaid or private health insurance—and for those with serious health problems. Data from the National Medical Care Expenditure Survey for 1977 indicate that households containing elderly (excluding those elderly who live in nursing homes) who are covered only by Medicare spend 11 percent of their household incomes out-of-pocket on health-care expenses, compared with only 5 percent for those covered by both Medicare and Medicaid, and 8 percent for those with both Medicare and private health insurance.[4] Part of the reason that the lower-income elderly suffer such a heavy financial burden is their inability to afford supplementary private health insurance to fill in the gaps left by Medicare. Overall, 66 percent of the elderly have private health insurance in addition to Medicare. However, this varies widely by income. Of those poor or near-poor elderly, 47 percent have private insurance, compared with 78 percent of the high-income elderly.[5]

Even those who carry supplementary coverage can suffer quite burdensome medical expenses if they are seriously ill. For elderly of all incomes with health-care bills exceeding \$2500 in 1977, those who were covered by Medicare alone spent 37 percent of their incomes on health care; those who were covered by both Medicare and Medicaid spent 9 percent of their incomes on health care; and those with Medicare and private insurance spent 18 percent of their

incomes on health care. For the poor and near-poor elderly households with total health-care bills exceeding $2500 in 1977, those with
Medicare alone spent 53 percent of their incomes out-of-pocket on
health-care expenses, those with Medicare and Medicaid spent 10
percent of their incomes, and those with both Medicare and private
health insurance spent 30 percent of their incomes on out-of-pocket
expenses. These figures are based on those living at home; the
financial burden of nursing-home care for those elderly not eligible
for Medicaid can pose even greater hardships.[6]

Catastrophic medical expenses can occur even for those elderly
who purchase private health insurance to supplement Medicare. Few
"Medi-Gap" policies pick up physician charges in excess of
Medicare's allowable fees. In addition, these supplementary policies
can be extremely expensive, and they return few benefits in exchange
for high premiums.

Future Trends in Health and Population Aging

Future demographic and economic trends will strain the ability of
public programs to maintain the current level of assistance, and will
further magnify the gaps. Even with the uncertainties of technological
change, biomedical research, and health-related behavior of the
population in future years, it seems safe to predict that the gap
between expanding health-care needs and limited economic resources
will widen.

Major demographic shifts seem certain. In 1980, 26 million
people, or 11 percent of the population, were age 65 and over.[7] As
the post–World War II baby-boom generation reaches retirement,
the aged population is expected to grow to 59 million, or 19 percent
of the population, in 2030. The traditional age pyramid will become
increasingly rectangular over time as the baby-boom population ages.
Given current estimates of mortality trends, we can expect major
increases in the numbers of older women. The female population age
eighty-five and over will triple between 1980 and 2030.[8] Over
three-quarters of these women will be single or widowed, and there
is strong evidence that people living alone or without a spouse are at
greater risk of needing long-term care assistance. This is one way in
which the changing demographic composition of the population has
important implications for the health sector.

The dramatic growth in the size of the elderly population, of course, is testimony to the remarkable progress that has been made—and seems likely to continue to occur—in extending life expectancy. In 1960, a woman reaching age sixty-five could expect to live until age eighty-one. In 1980, she could expect to live until age eighty-three, and by the year 2000 she will be able to expect to live to age eighty-six. Life expectancy for men upon reaching age sixty-five has increased from seventy-eight years in 1960 to seventy-nine years in 1980 and is expected to increase to eighty-one in 2000.[9]

Reductions in mortality from heart disease and stroke have been especially noteworthy in recent years. On the other hand, death rates from cancer are increasing in the elderly population, and there is considerable controversy about whether the average age-adjusted health status of the elderly will improve or decline. What is clear is that as the number of old people increases, so will the number of people with chronic illness or limited functional ability. The aging of the population means that more people will need assistance to function at home. Those who need help to get around within their own homes, for example, will increase from 1.9 million to 2.7 million between 1980 and 2000. The number of elderly who are limited by chronic conditions will increase.[10]

In light of the serious health problems many aged persons face, it is not surprising that they make heavy use of a range of health-care services. As the elderly population grows, major increases can be expected in the use of hospitals and other health-care services by the aged, if past patterns continue. Total hospital patient days of persons age sixty-five and over would increase from 105 million in 1980 to 273 million in 2000—almost tripling the use of hospital care by the aged in a twenty-year period. This would increase elderly patients' share of hospital patient days from 38 percent in 1980 to 58 percent in 2000. The number of aged in nursing homes will also rise, from 1.2 million in 1980 to an estimated 1.8 million in 2000, if current age-specific rates of institutionalization continue.[11]

These projections, based on historical experience, are not immutable. We can devote greater efforts to caring for the aged at home or on an ambulatory basis, rather than relying so heavily on in-patient hospital and nursing-home care. Technological advances to prevent or to better control chronic illness may also markedly reduce our reliance on high-cost institutional care. But if no steps are taken, serious strains could be generated on the health-care system.

With the growth in the number of older people, total health expenditures on the aged are expected to increase from about $50 billion in 1978 to almost $200 billion in 2000, in constant 1980 dollars.[12] A large portion of the increased health expenditures for the elderly will be borne by federal, state, and local governments. Publicly financed expenditures for the aged will increase from approximately $29 billion in 1978 to $114 billion in 2000 (in constant 1980 dollars). Current tax revenues will not be adequate to meet these increased expenditures. The Medicare trustees estimate, for example, that the hospital insurance trust fund of the Medicare program will be depleted by the late 1990s. More rapid increases in the elderly population between 2010 and 2030 should further strain this payroll-tax–financed program. All of this should make it clear that extended life expectancy and improved health of the elderly will bring with it a cost—a cost that is clearly affordable to a growing and prosperous society, but one that challenges us to develop innovative approaches to providing quality health care more economically than we do now.

THE POTENTIAL FOR COST CONTAINMENT

If we create new systems of payment that offer incentives to hospitals and other health-care providers to restrain costs, these future trends could be substantially modified. The most significant step in this regard has been the enactment, under the Medicare program in 1983, of a prospective payment system for hospitals. Since then, hospitals have received a fixed amount per patient, based, in part, on the diagnosis of the patient. The new payment system—sometimes referred to as the Diagnosis Related Group (DRG) prospective payment system—is being phased in over a three-year period, and permits allowable rates to vary in accordance with wage differences across geographical areas. Special allowances are provided for teaching hospitals and for those exceptional cases where little experience has left no predictable basis on which to set a rate.

The principal savings in the system comes from limiting the increases that might otherwise occur over time in the average payment rate. The initial legislation held rises to the rate of increase in the prices of goods and services purchased by hospitals (the hospital market-basket price index) plus one percentage point. It specified that this level of stringency was to be maintained until 1985, at which point the Secretary of Health and Human Services would be permitted to set the annual rate of increase, which was still frozen as this volume went to press. The limitation has an enormous impact on total Medicare expenditures. For example, if the rate of increase were set at the hospital market-basket price index plus 3.5 percentage points between 1985 and 1995, Medicare hospital expenditures would be about $150 billion higher than if the rate is held to the hospital market-basket index plus 1 percent.[13]

The DRG system should radically alter the incentives that often determine hospital decisions. For the first time, a hospital that keeps patients unnecessarily long, that orders unnecessary tests, or that provides care less efficiently than possible will be penalized. Under the previous cost-based reimbursement system, hospitals were paid more the more they did and the higher their costs turned out to be.

At present, the new system applies only to those hospital services received by Medicare enrollees, and it is likely that it will need to be modified over time. In the short term, it offers hospitals an incentive to avoid genuine cost restraint by charging privately insured patients higher rates. If hospitals are paid less for the care of Medicare patients than for non-elderly patients, and if Medicare payment rates increase at a much slower rate than hospitals can collect from other patients, the disparity in payments between Medicare and non-Medicare patients could become quite marked in time. This could conceivably lead hospitals either to refuse Medicare patients or to provide them with a substandard level of care. One way to avoid this would be to extend the current system of prospective payment to privately insured patients as well; this would provide hospitals with a greater incentive to contain overall costs and would eliminate some of the potential for discrimination against Medicare enrollees.

Another difficulty with the new prospective payment system is that it does not eliminate—in fact, it exacerbates—the incentives for hospitals to increase the number of people they admit for treatment. The DRG system could encourage hospitals to admit patients for procedures that have formerly been undertaken on an outpatient basis. In addition, while the system provides incentives for hospitals to discharge patients earlier, it also encourages them to re-admit patients for the same or a different condition. One long-range solution for avoiding some of these undesirable incentives would be to develop capitation (per-capita) systems of payment that would reward hospitals and other providers for reducing hospitalization. However, such systems have their own limitations, the most serious one being that, as yet, we have no methods for adjusting the rates to take into account the actual health risk of the population covered.

Another disadvantage of the DRG system is that it does not take into account the severity of the patient's illness within the context of a given diagnostic category. Because hospitals are paid the same rate for the relatively more difficult cases as they are for the simpler cases within a given category, they may have an incentive to refuse admission to patients with more complicated cases, or to transfer them to other settings. Hospitals with a high proportion of more complicated cases would find their payment rates inadequate to cover costs, while other hospitals would receive bonuses.

The new prospective payment system is to be phased in over three years, and the substantial variations in hospital costs across different geographic regions mean that hospitals in particular areas of the country could suffer serious financial hardship when uniform national rates are imposed at the end of that time. Facilities in the northeast and in the north central regions of the country could be faced with serious problems, while those in the south and the west could generate considerable profits.[14]

All these limitations make it clear that the DRG system requires considerable modification, and that its effectiveness in containing overall increases in hospital costs remains to be determined. Because adjustments will have to be made over time, its full fiscal impact is difficult to predict. And although the cost restraints it will impose should solve a portion of the fiscal problems now projected for Medicare, they will not be sufficient to prevent inevitable future deficits.

Attention is now being shifted to reforming methods of paying physicians under the Medicare program. Part of the Budget Deficit Reduction Act of 1984 imposed a fifteen-month freeze on increases in physician fees for all patients. Enforcing this provision is difficult, but it signals the intention of Congress to develop stable and effective methods to curtail rising physician expenditures in the Medicare program. Congress has called for a major report on physician payment, including an analysis of how it might be contained under a DRG type of system. Other options that have been advanced include imposing fee schedules based on the time and skill required to perform procedures, clustering services together so that all-inclusive fees can be set for related procedures, creating capitation systems of payment, and programs that include physicians as partners in financial risk-sharing. These proposals, which suggest possible ways to curb rising physician expenditures in the Medicare program, promise to be a major source of debate in coming years. Clearly, any fundamental reform of Medicare must address physician cost-containment incentives as well as those for hospitals.

Reforming the current payment incentives for hospitals and physicians offers the most promising possibility for slowing future increases in health expenditures for the elderly. However, other approaches may also be used to direct resources to high-priority areas and to limit those expenditures that contribute little or nothing to improved health. Professional review organizations have been established to set guidelines on the appropriate use of services—for example, to determine surgical rates by type of procedure for given geographic areas. If costly new technology is assessed with more care, it might be adopted far more cautiously than it is today. Protocols that determine the kinds of patients who might appropriately benefit from expensive interventions, or the types of conditions that justify them, may become more common in the future. Greater emphasis on prevention, healthier diets, life-long patterns of physical activity, and biomedical research breakthroughs on the major diseases that kill or disable the elderly may also affect future expenditures.

Despite the real potential for cost savings that some of these measures offer, it seems inevitable that an increasing share of gross national product will be devoted to health care in the future. As a result, some of the most difficult policy decisions will involve determining who shall bear the financial burden for rising health expenditures on the elderly: the old themselves, the relatively well-to-do, whether young or old, or the working population, as part of an implicit social insurance contract to assure protection for themselves in their old age.

REFORMING MEDICARE

The growing inadequacy of protection afforded by Medicare, coupled with the very real fiscal problems that the program will face in the twenty-first century, call for imaginative and far-reaching reform of our current approaches to financing health care for the elderly. Reforming the financing of acute and long-term care services for older Americans should address several problems that are inherent in the current system. These include the financial burdens the elderly now incur because of serious gaps in coverage and limitations on benefits; the projected deficit in the Medicare Hospital Insurance Trust Fund; the general problem of rapidly increasing expenditures for both hospital and physician services for the elderly; and the particularly fragmented and inadequate coverage of long-term care.

If Medicare is to be reformed to remedy these problems, those reforms should be designed in a fiscally responsible manner. This involves rethinking the entire structure of the program, including current eligibility provisions, benefits, financing sources, methods of payment to providers, administration, and the need for innovative features to improve the delivery of services. One approach would be to improve Medicare coverage, but to finance the expansion with greater premium contributions from the elderly on an income-related basis. The basic strategy would be to merge Part A of Medicare, which covers primarily hospital services, with Part B, which covers primarily physicians' services. This would result in a single plan with a ceiling on out-of-pocket expenses. The strategy would also seek to improve coverage for prescription drugs, and to add a new long-term care plan. These benefit improvements would be financed by an income-related premium. A separate Medicaid program for Medicare beneficiaries would provide wrap-around protection for low-income elderly.

Coverage

This new Medicare program would cover all persons age sixty-five and over (not just those covered by Social Security) and disabled persons who qualify under current eligibility provisions. The new Medicaid wrap-around coverage would be extended to all poor elderly, with a spend-down provision for the near-poor.

Benefits

Part A and Part B Medicare benefits would continue in the new Medicare plan, but the limits on covered hospital days would be removed. Deductible and co-insurance provisions for hospital and physician services would be continued. However, a new ceiling on out-of-pocket expenses of the elderly would be incorporated and indexed over time with the growth in program expenditures. Expenses that count toward this maximum ceiling include all out-of-pocket expenditures for hospital, physician, and other Medicare benefits, plus prescription-drug costs.

The long-term care plan under Medicare would cover nursing-home care (in qualified, skilled nursing facilities and intermediate care facilities), home health services (in addition to the more limited home health benefits available in the acute-care Medicare plan), and day-hospital services. These services would be subject to a co-insurance charge, and to a maximum ceiling on out-of-pocket costs. Beneficiaries could enroll in the plan beginning at age sixty, but benefits would not begin until one has been enrolled for at least five years. Everyone would be required to enroll by age seventy. The plan would be supplemented with a direct grant program to public and non-profit community organizations to provide home-help services such as chore assistance and personal-care services to the functionally impaired.

The Medicaid wrap-around plan would pay the cost-sharing required under the acute- and long-term care part of Medicare for all elderly with incomes below the federal poverty level. A spend-down provision would assist those elderly who otherwise would have their incomes reduced to below poverty after out-of-pocket expenses.

Financing

Part A and Part B Medicare trust funds would be merged into a single trust fund. The current Part A payroll tax would be retained as a source of revenue to the new trust fund, continued at its current legislated rate. The general revenues currently projected to support Part B of Medicare would be added to the fund. The current Part B premium would be replaced with an income-related premium, which would be administered through the personal income-tax system. The definition of income would be broadened, to be consistent with provisions in the Social Security program for taxing social security benefits of higher-income elderly. The new premium would be capped at the actuarial value of Medicare, or at some fraction of the actuarial value, and a minimum annual premium would assure that all elderly make some contribution. Additional revenues for the Medicare trust fund would be raised by increasing the current tax on cigarettes. These funds would be earmarked for Medicare, and added to the trust fund.

Long-term care coverage would be available with the payment of an income-related premium. The premium would be increased for those who postpone enrollment. As noted earlier, everyone would be required to enroll by age seventy, and benefits could not be initiated until one was covered for at least five years under the plan. Federal general revenues would be used to meet any long-term care expenditures not covered by the premium. Categorical federal grant funds would be used to establish home-help service programs through public or non-profit community organizations.

Provider Payment

Improved benefits and expanded financing of acute and long-term care services would be coupled with stringent cost-containment measures. The current prospective payment system for hospitals under Medicare would be retained and strengthened. A residual "all-payer" hospital prospective payment system that covers privately insured patients as well as Medicare and Medicaid beneficiaries would be adopted for those states that do not voluntarily adopt such systems. A prospective physician payment system would be established, and physicians would be required to accept Medicare prospective payment rates for all services they render to hospital patients. A prospective payment system for nursing homes would also be established, taking into account the level of complexity involved in the care of patients with different functional impairments. Health maintenance organizations would be encouraged to accept payment on a capitation basis. The plan would institute demonstrations to test capitation payment for nursing-home patients, covering both acute- and long-term care, as a basis for evolving a longer-term prospective payment system based on capitation.

System Reform

The plan would encourage appropriate care patterns by assessing patients' conditions, and by making entitlement to long-term care benefits contingent upon necessity, as determined by qualified physicians. It would establish profiles of practice patterns for all benefits, and it would institute utilization review for all claims that fall outside accepted practice pattern norms. It would emphasize that institutional care is to be avoided, where possible, both in hospitals and nursing homes. Pre-admission assessment would be required for admission to nursing homes.

Day-hospital services would be covered under the voluntary long-term care plan as an alternative to institutional care. Respite care would be provided so that family members supporting a functionally impaired elderly person at home could have periodic breaks. The plan would offer grants to public or non-profit organizations in exchange for home-help assistance—such as chore services and personal care services—to enable more functionally impaired elderly to remain in their homes. These home-help services would also be based upon one's level of dependency, and upon the need for such assistance. Volunteer workers in home-help agencies could earn credits to be applied toward their own voluntary long-term care premiums.

COMPREHENSIVE HEALTH REFORM FOR ALL

A major policy strategy for the present would be for us to prepare now for the aging of the population by undertaking comprehensive reform of the entire system of financing and delivering health services in the United States—not just those that serve the elderly. Universal coverage for health care could be provided through a phased-in national health plan, a measure that could involve the fundamental restructuring of our current entitlement programs. Medicare and Medicaid could be merged into a single program, and coverage would be extended to all those who fall outside private health insurance plans.

A phased-in plan could begin by expanding coverage, starting with those who are most in need—those with incomes below 55 percent of the federal poverty level, for example—and gradually increasing the eligibility level to 100 percent of the federal poverty level. Similarly, the plan would improve coverage for all workers and their families by requiring employers to cover them in a basic insurance plan that includes a ceiling on the costs that any family could be compelled to contribute. This ceiling could initially be set at a relatively high level, and then gradually be reduced to assure adequate coverage. Similar ceilings would also be a part of the public plan, so that the elderly and the disabled would be protected from undue financial hardship. Buy-in provisions would permit anyone who falls outside private employer group plans to purchase coverage at a subsidized rate, depending upon income.

This fundamental reform of the coverage and financing of health-care services could be coupled with comparably far-reaching reform of the provision of health-care services. Payment for hospitals, physicians, and other health-care providers could be established on a prospective basis to encourage efficiency in the provision of care, with stringent limits set on rates of increase in expenditures over time. The scheme would encourage organized systems of care delivery, such as health maintenance organizations, which charge on a per-capita rather than a fee-for-service basis. Standards built into the benefit package would promote prevention and primary care.

This option undoubtedly would be costly. It would involve a substantial restructuring of public programs, require the review and monitoring of employer health insurance plans, and entail major shifts in current methods of paying physicians and other health-care providers. At the same time, it would guarantee adequate access to health care for all, remove the threat and the actuality of financial ruin from health-care bills that now confront so many Americans, and provide a vehicle for instituting the major cost controls and incentives in the health-care system that are missing from the current patchwork of private and public coverage. This kind of transformation could also be a lever for shifting away from a continued reliance on costly high-technology acute care, and moving toward the increasing use of preventive and primary care. Finally, it would provide a more rational framework for making choices about the allocation of resources to the health sector as our society ages.

THE ROAD AHEAD

The United States is ill-served by the absence of a conscious policy to shape the course of the health sector over time. As the population ages, an increasing proportion of economic resources will be diverted to the health sector, but with no assurance that those resources will be used effectively, or even that they will be distributed to those who need them most. Whether we accomplish it by establishing market forces, by empowering more governmental intervention, or by a combination of approaches, we must make far greater efforts to ensure that we deliver health services efficiently, and that we eliminate the use of those services that are medically unnecessary. Even if we succeed in our efforts to assure that the health services provided yield real benefits, we can still anticipate that more health resources will be required to care for an aging population.

Another important task is to assure that the financial burden of meeting these expenses is equitably distributed, rather than concentrated—as it is now—on a small segment of the population that falls through the cracks of adequate health insurance coverage. We need major reform of health financing mechanisms, both to assure access to health care for those who need it and to reduce the financial hardship that illness or injury can bring.

We also need far greater public debate on the options for meeting these objectives if we are to generate a consensus on a national health policy. Rather than postponing action until the U.S. is faced with a major growth in its elderly population—when the conflict between generations could become intense—it is urgent that this effort begin now.

ENDNOTES

[1] U.S. House of Representatives, Committee on Ways and Means, *Background Information on Programs under the Jurisdiction of the Committee on Ways and Means,* Feb. 1983.

[2] Ibid.

[3] Congressional Budget Office, *Changing the Structure of Medicare Benefits: Issues and Options* (Washington, D.C.: U.S. Government Printing Office, March 1983).

[4] Karen Davis, "Catastrophic Coverage Under Medicare," testimony before the Joint Economic Committee, U.S. Congress, March 29, 1984.

[5]Gail Wilensky and Marl Berk, "Medicare and the Elderly Poor," testimony before the Special Committee on Aging, Hearings on the Future of Medicare, Washington, D.C., April 13, 1983.

[6]Davis, op. cit.

[7]Dorothy Rice and Jacob Feldman, "Living Longer in the United States: Demographic Changes and Health Needs of the Elderly," *Milbank Memorial Fund Quarterly/Health and Society,* Spring 1983.

[8]Davis, "Health Implications of Aging in America," in Office of Technology Assessment, *Impact of Technology on Aging in America,* 1983.

[9]Ibid.

[10]Ibid.

[11]Ibid.

[12]Ibid.

[13]Paul Ginsburg and Marilyn Moon, "An Introduction to the Medicare Financing Problem," *Milbank Memorial Fund Quarterly/Health and Society,* Spring 1984.

[14]Judith R. Lave, "Hospital Payment under Medicare," proceedings of the Conference on the Future of Medicare, Subcommittee on Health of the Committee on Ways and Means, U.S. House of Representatives, (Washington, D.C.: U.S. Government Printing Office, Feb. 1, 1984), pp. 87–100.

Daniel Callahan

Health Care in the Aging Society:
A Moral Dilemma

T HE GREATEST SOCIAL BENEFIT now enjoyed by the American elderly comes from a social security system that provides a minimal level of welfare and heavily subsidized health care. What those who designed the health portion of the system did not reckon with, however, was that its high and ever-escalating costs could in the long run threaten its viability. Federal expenditures for Medicare, for example, have been projected to rise from $74 billion in 1985 to $120 billion in 1989, a 60 percent increase in only four years. The threat that escalating figures of that kind portend—an eventual need to scale down benefits—seems a cruel blow to the gains so recently achieved. It is a direct thrust at a basic dream of an aging society: that old age and good health are biologically compatible and financially affordable. It may turn out to be no less unsettling morally, forcing choices that could well corrode values and principles that are centrally important and deeply cherished.

From one perspective, health care for the elderly presents an array of issues that are difficult but not unfamiliar. Among them are cost-effectiveness, the allocation of resources, methods of insurance, and the establishment of priorities for basic research and the delivery of care. Similar issues can be raised about the care to be given to any age group. Yet no sooner do we begin grappling with problems of the aged in those familiar terms than we discover some deeper and far more disturbing problems. Experience is teaching us that medicine can keep some elderly people alive far longer than is of any benefit to them—but also that a "premature death" is a flexible social and medical concept, one subject to constant change. Experience has also taught us that money invested in research on this or that costly and disabling disease will usually have a health payoff—but also that the cumulative effect of all those payoffs is a higher, not lower, medical bill, and perhaps an insupportable one.

Is the costly situation I describe limited to the care of the aged? Similarities can surely be noted in the case, say, of caring for severely handicapped newborns, or for other groups of patients where the interventions are exotic, the costs high, and the results problematic. Yet the difficulties of caring for the elderly display three unique features. The first is the increasingly endemic nature of their illnesses, which are less curable than they are controllable. In exchange for extending the life span for the elderly, we pay the price of a growth in chronic illness. The second feature follows from the first: the sheer number and proportion of the elderly as a pool of ill or impaired people. The third is the increasing necessity to make painful moral choices in the care of the dying elderly as a class, particularly among that growing number who end their days incompetent, incontinent, and grossly incapacitated, more dead than alive.

These problems would no doubt have been difficult even if the birth rate had remained high and the relative proportion of young and old had remained stable. But the skewing effect of an aging society is that the economic imbalances caused by the provision of health care for the elderly potentially threaten the welfare of younger generations and of society as a whole. If high and ever-escalating health-care costs are inherent in an aging developed society—and there is no evidence whatever to suggest otherwise—then the stage is set for a profound confrontation. We will have to face severe moral questions about the desirability of never-ending medical innovation, about the value we place upon preserving and improving the health of the elderly, and about the comparative rights of different generations to the necessary resources of life.

There is a sense of poignancy and paradox in these developments. We seem at once to fear the ministrations of medicine in our old age and to fear being deprived of them. As individuals who will inevitably age, sicken, and die, many of us have become terrorized at the thought of ending our lives in the oppressive company of a relentless and implacable high-technology medicine, cunningly lying in wait for us with its tubes, respirators, and invasive surgeries. We are no less terrorized by the fear of Alzheimer's disease that will take our mind long before some other malady takes our body. If that is the way we have come to feel as individuals, we nonetheless continue to be enthralled by the endless medical struggle against death, the ever-present hints of a cure for dread diseases, and the drama of lives saved by devices hardly dreamed of even a decade ago.

Of course we recognize in the back of our minds that a cure for cancer increases our chance of dying from stroke or heart disease, just as a cure for all of these enhances the likelihood of living out our days with dementia. But that ironic way of assessing medical triumphs is no more popular now than it was in those enthusiastic years during the 1950s and 1960s when the various "wars" against cancer and other diseases were initiated. Those wars continue, fought as always with the tubes, drugs, and machines so desperately dreaded as our possible personal fates. We thus spend an enormous and increasing amount of money to propel ourselves inexorably toward that which we most fear—hoping, of course, that in our own case the technology will be just enough to save us but too little to oppress us. Achieving just the right balance has proved to be an elusive goal.

These ironies may provide some clues about what should be sought and what avoided in providing health care in an aging society, and thus about how we might responsibly frame the moral problems such a task poses. The problems present themselves at three stages. These days, the first stage is typically displayed in legislatures and administrative agencies. There is a great deal of tinkering with the present entitlement system, but without any overt suggestion that its underlying values should be challenged. The question at this stage is: given our present social values, what options are available to control costs and thereby to preclude or forestall a significant reduction in adequate health care to the elderly? At the second stage, we begin to move out of the realm of existing values and commitments and ask a more probing set of questions: just what are, or what ought to be, the moral foundations of health-care programs and benefits for the elderly? How many and what kinds of economic burdens ought our society reasonably be prepared to bear for their sake? Are the moral premises that animated the establishment of Medicare still acceptable? The third stage raises a still more difficult set of issues, those that bear on the way in which we ought to understand aging and its place in human life. Should we interpret aging as a natural and inescapable biological process, to be accepted with grace and dignity—or as one more disease and corporeal derangement, to be fought with all the power that science and money can bring to bear?

I will consider each of these stages, exploring how we are being socially and economically forced to fall back from one to the other. My use of the metaphor "to fall back" is deliberately chosen. In my imagination, I see the three stages as a set of moral fortifications, with the first stage as the outer ring and the third as the final redoubt. Will the present crisis in the cost of health care for the elderly be solvable at the first stage? Or will that line of defense fail, forcing us back to the second stage, or to the third?

STAGE I: SOCIAL VALUES AND ECONOMIC REALITIES

The most obvious feature of the present system of providing health care for the elderly is that, if present values remain unchanged, we will face constantly rising costs in the decades ahead. The growing number and proportion of the elderly, the never-ending introduction of new medical technologies, and a set of well-entrenched social and medical values that encourage high costs leave little room for any other expectation. Socially, the most relevant current value is the strong belief that society has an obligation to provide health care for the elderly. The Medicare program is now only two decades old, but even the most dedicated opponents of government programs speak circumspectly about the possibility that it might be a good idea eventually to dismantle it. The notion of a societal obligation toward the elderly is paralleled by a widespread belief in a personal entitlement to health care when old.

Taken by itself, so powerful a social value would seem to guarantee a heavy economic cost, given the accompanying demographic impetus in the number and the proportion of the aged. But two other values serve as powerful reinforcers: the almost unwavering devotion to preserve life at any cost as a central social and medical goal, and the relentless drive of medical science to cure disease. For all the accusations about needlessly burdensome and expensive medical treatment of the elderly, particularly those elderly who are dying, there is still a strong presumption in favor of aggressive treatment. Most of us, including the elderly, are not now ready, much less eager, to die; and physicians are still trained to aggressively combat death.

In cases of doubt, life is still preferred to death, treatment to non-treatment, vigorous intervention to passive relinquishment.

It has become all too easy to scoff at, or to deplore, the conviction that life should always be preserved without regard to individual circumstance. Almost everyone knows or has heard of instances of horrible abuse, where unwilling or hopelessly moribund people are energetically treated regardless of the misery it will entail. But it is by no means easy to disentangle those excesses from the complicated web of impulses that drives the conquest of disease. The outraged cry to stop inflicting excessive technological wizardry on desperately ill elderly individuals is not accompanied by a demand to stop seeking cures for the illnesses and disease that affect them as a group. Much medical progress has historically been built, so to speak, on the backs of the dying—the testing of one more drastic remedy, one more radical innovation, when otherwise all would have been lost. If, at the moment, one tends to hear more about patients overtreated by technology, it is still just as easy to collect stories of apparently hopeless cases snatched, as the tabloids like to put it, from the jaws of death, and happily so. Not all of those stories in the *National Enquirer* are false.

It is hardly an accident, then, that health-care costs for the elderly continue to rise, even though alternatives are actively being pursued, efforts that can be characterized by the popular slogan "trim the fat." The most visible and significant of the cost-containment strategies seek to establish prospective payment plans, the most salient of which is the DRG (diagnostic-related groups) system as applied to Medicare hospital reimbursements, a plan that is likely in the future to be applied to other types of hospital insurance and to physician fees as well. By paying hospitals a set fee for carrying out a specific medical or surgical procedure, its main purpose is to provide hospitals with an incentive to control costs. If they can carry out the treatment at a cost less than the reimbursement fee, they can keep the difference; if greater, they must bear the additional costs themselves.

From my perspective, that is a system that operates within the framework of the stage 1 social and medical values noted earlier. It assumes that costs can be contained without disturbing the present level of entitlements, without threatening the life or health of the elderly in any way, and without hindering the progress of technological change. Yet the new DRG system provides many possibilities for bringing about precisely those unpleasant outcomes. It is a strategy that introduces, in principle, an alien utilitarian economic motive as a competitor to a traditional ethical commitment, a commitment that holds that patient welfare takes primacy over every other consideration. The evidence so far has not borne out those worries to any significant degree, but the system is too new to pass any definitive judgments. What is most striking is that it is assumed in any case that the DRG system, even if successful in its own terms, will not make any important difference in reducing the major cause of the growing cost of care for the elderly—their rising numbers.

While there are many other current schemes aimed at reducing government health expenditures on the elderly, three of those being considered deserve special note: a shift upwards in age eligibility standards, a reduction in costs for the terminally ill (a majority of whom are the aged), and a move from an age-based to a need-based Medicare program. The first is attractively simple. Raise the age of initial Medicare eligibility to sixty-eight or seventy or even seventy-two—today's equivalent in mortality expectation of what age sixty-five was when the Social Security system was introduced in 1935. That plan would require in principle no change in the prevailing social and medical values, though its political feasibility is uncertain.

The second possibility is morally more problematic: working to find ways of reducing the disproportionately high costs of care that maintain us in the last year of life. Victor Fuchs notes that the United States "spends about 1 percent of the gross national product on health care for the elderly who are in their last year of life," and adds that "one of the biggest challenges facing policymakers for the rest of this century will be how to strike an appropriate balance between care for the dying and health services for the rest of the population."[1] Yet that task will prove almost intractable unless there is a radical change in medicine's moral presumption that the benefit of doubt should be given to the preservation of life. Within the context of that value, moreover, the available evidence makes it difficult to prove that money is being squandered on the elderly dying, or that savings of any significant magnitude will be possible.[2]

The most feasible for cost-containment effort would be to shift from an age- to a need-based Medicare system. That tactic could also pose the sharpest threat to the social values that have undergirded guaranteed health care for the elderly. The most obvious wedge for introducing a need-based system is the otherwise appealing fact that the elderly are no longer an economically needy group. In 1959, when 35.2 percent of the elderly were below the poverty line, so were 22.4 percent of the entire population. By 1981, when 15.3 percent of the elderly were poor, the same was true of 14.0 percent of the entire population. When poverty increased among the general population during the recession of the early 1980s, the rate of poverty among the elderly remained relatively stable. Today, poverty among those over sixty-five may have declined below the level that prevails in the general population.

Since a basic reason for the 1965 introduction of Medicare was the then-low economic status of the elderly, a significant change in that status patently undercuts its rationale. Some leading gerontologists also now believe that an age-based program stigmatizes the elderly, and public opinion surveys show strong support for a need-based program. Those are surely signs of a receptivity to change in the moral and political basis of Medicare.[3] One argument against a move away from the age-based system is that it would subvert what was initially understood to be the real long-term goal of the Medicare program: to provide the basis for a national health insurance policy. An additional argument against a shift in that direction is the fact that Medicaid—organized from the outset in 1965 as a need-based program—has failed to provide consistently decent care for the poor.

Nonetheless, Douglas Nelson appears correct in arguing that "the aging movement in America now encompasses and identifies with a range of programs and policies that individually rest on fundamentally incompatible and inconsistent definitions of what it means to be old and on contradictory conceptions of where old people fit into the larger society."[4] If one of those definitions is that the aged are as a class financially impoverished, and if in fact that is not the case, then we must move on to an altered perception of the issue's morality: the present form and amount of health assistance provided the aged may be not only expensive, but discriminatory as well.[5] That possibility cannot be assessed, however, without a closer look at the ethical foundations of social policy toward the elderly.

STAGE II: ETHICAL FOUNDATIONS AND SOCIAL POLICY

A remarkable feature of policies on aging in the United States is that they rest on ethical foundations that are as vague and unanalyzed as they are popularly appealing. There is a general conviction that the state rather than families should bear the main responsibility for the costs of social security and health care, that we somehow owe it to the elderly to make their last years tolerable, and that the aged have as great a claim on resources as any other age group. Yet unlike traditional societies, we devote no special respect to the aged as a repository of wisdom or a special object of veneration. The claims made in their behalf seem to have been more pragmatic in their motivation than reverential—the aged exist, they have made some useful contributions, and it would be unseemly and impractical to have them spend their last days in needless pain and poverty.

The high cost of health care is now forcing a closer examination of those loose ethical and practical premises. Just how much do we owe the elderly, and why? What is our relative obligation to the elderly in the face of health-care claims by other age groups? If care is to be provided to the elderly, what legitimate claims can be made upon their family members in comparison with what claims should be made upon the state? And if the elderly themselves have sufficient financial means, should it not be they who have to bear the costs of their own care rather than their families or the state?[6]

These are large questions, and they cannot be fully examined here. But we can touch on them by briefly tracing the shift that has taken place in the locus of ethical responsibility over the centuries. Traditional societies, though not without considerable conflict or controversy, assumed that it was children and other family members who were to bear responsibility for the care of the weak or destitute elderly. As Edward A. Wynne has argued, reciprocity was the primary basis for traditional obligations toward the elderly.[7] Given the relatively short life span, the elderly's contributions of knowledge and wisdom, and a strong extended family network to share the care, the burden was not necessarily an excessively heavy one. In England, the Elizabethan Poor Laws of 1601 tried to enshrine that moral tradition in statutory form, making care of aged parents a legal obligation of their children. That spirit survived more or less intact in the New World: some twenty-six states still have laws on their books that can require family financial support of aged parents (and the Reagan administration in 1982 declared that the states would not be acting in a way inconsistent with Medicaid legislation if they required children to provide financial help to needy parents).

Such statutes have an obvious flavor of anachronism today, and they have not in fact been much employed or enforced. The coming of the Social Security system in the mid-1930s, and the advent of Medicare in the mid-1960s, were far better signs of a major change in values, shifting the locus of financial responsibility from family to state. None of this quite amounted to a situation in which the elderly explicitly insisted on a "right" to Social Security or health care on the basis of their age alone; little such language was then current. But it did amount to an implicit entitlement claim based on a mutual advantage to the young and the old. The young could look forward to the shaping of their own lives unencumbered by burdensome financial obligations to their parents. The elderly could achieve a long-sought goal, that of "not being dependent upon my children," a refrain my own mother constantly sounded while I was growing up. I would add an important qualification here. It was the sense of family *financial* obligation that was altered, not the sense of family obligation in general. For even if neither the old nor the young tend any longer to much believe in the notion of financial obligation, there still appears to be a robust sense of the obligation to provide time and affection when needed.[8]

Nevertheless, even the development of a new and different moral stance toward filial obligations would turn out to be only part of the larger ethical problem. At the time Medicare was introduced, its financial burden was still manageable; but the past decade has seen a dramatic increase in costs. It is now possible to find otherwise sympathetic commentators pointing to the singularly large amount and proportion of money devoted to the elderly, and—perhaps not accidentally—to the relative decline in funds available for children.[9] Moreover, the failure of Medicaid to meet the health-care needs of the poor in an adequate or consistent way—while many affluent elderly are having their health needs met by Medicare—directs still more attention to an apparent injustice.

What is the proper—or at least the acceptable—proportion of public resources that should be devoted to the elderly, both in relationship to the health needs of other age groups and to other social requirements as a whole? I can offer no direct answer to that question, but some speculation might be useful.

A few aspects of the health-care needs of the elderly need underscoring in any attempt to devise a fair allocation. The elderly are the only age group about which it can generally be said that illness and decline are an inevitable part of their life. That generalization can be qualified by stipulating that it will be more true of the "old-old" than the "young-old," and by conceding that some proportion of the elderly may die before experiencing any significant illness or disability. Yet for the most part, the idea of "squaring the curve"—a healthy life followed by a quick illness and death—remains more an ideal than a foreseeable reality.[10] Moreover, as James Storey has noted, before anyone concludes that the question of age or need as the foundation for health-care support has decisively tilted toward need, it should be taken into account that by 2025, "those seventy-five and older will rise by 70 percent to 17 million. Elderly women will increase by 75 percent to 27 million. The number of aged blacks will rise by 40 percent in only twenty years to a level of 3 million. Thus, the problems associated with old age—low income, large health care costs, long-term care requirements, and isolation from community services—could increase."[11] In short, it could be premature indeed to pronounce an age-based policy no longer necessary and thus to jettison the age/need nexus as a moral foundation for policy at a time when society may still face serious future problems.

Quite apart from whether "need" is still serviceable as a moral foundation, are there additional possibilities, especially for the care of those who are otherwise financially able to care for themselves? In practice, a need-based foundation stresses only the present situation of the aged—what their present welfare requires rather than what they may have done in the past or will do in the future to merit assistance. By contrast, Edward Wynne's idea of a return to "reciprocity," or Douglas Nelson's suggestion of "veteranship" ("old age ... [as] the occasion for repayment by the larger community") provide the basis for a policy that would not have to make distinctions among the aged, as a need-based policy must do.[12] Yet it is by no means evident why mere survival, the living of a life through adulthood, in and of itself merits the bountiful social blessing of fully subsidized health care. Just as not all of the aged are financially needy, not all of them will have led lives worthy of automatic honor.

More critically, a moral foundation for policy centered on honor due the aged for their past lives and their contributions to the community offers little guidance about what a just allocation of health resources among and across the generations might be. If the elderly could claim their past services to society, younger adults could claim their present services, and children could claim those that they will contribute in the future. No one generation can easily show the superiority of its own claim; in a good society, one might suppose, all generations will be respected, and everything possible would be done to reduce competition among them for scarce resources.

The very interdependence of generations should militate against competition, which can hardly be socially productive in any case. Until recent decades, no one generation automatically required a disproportionate share of health resources. The conquest of infectious disease drastically changed that situation, reducing the healthcare needs of the young while helping to prolong the life span of the elderly. But with the accompanying persistence of chronic disease, the health needs of the elderly are now grossly disproportionate in comparison with their numbers; and that circumstance promises to get worse before it gets better.

What, then, of the honor owed the aged? Is their claim on that basis strong enough to dominate those of other age groups, as in fact seems to be happening—especially when it is abetted by the strong political power of the elderly as a group? I know of no argument that would support such a powerful moral claim. Still, if a social decision were made (openly or tacitly) to reduce the proportionate share of health care that they receive, it would require a distasteful strategy—not mere neglect, but positive discrimination. Could that be justified? The traditional medical answer is that age alone provides no basis for discrimination against the elderly; those who are ill should be treated, whether young or old. We ought, Dr. Mark Siegler has written, to "retain need-specific criteria for medical decisions with respect to elderly patients."[13] A failure to do so "would undermine the traditions of clinical medicine, which are based upon medical need and patient preferences."[14] James Childress makes a related point in a somewhat different way: ". . . The use of an age criterion in the provision of health care in our society at this time could itself have negative symbolic significance: abandonment and exclusion from communal care."[15]

Yet the actual consequence of a non-discriminatory policy results in nothing less than giving de facto preference to the elderly. Their needs are in the aggregate predictably greater, and the meeting of those needs more expensive, per capita, than is true of other age groups. Let us assume, as some have argued, that money spent on the elderly is money taken from the young. If, then, the actual effect of holding onto what can readily be conceded to be an admirable part of the traditional medical ethic is the deprivation of the young, some adjustment would seem in order. There is severe complication, however, in trying to determine how a better balance might be struck. Most health and welfare comparisons between the young and the old will reveal, not a deprivation of the lives of the young while the elderly are being saved, but a severe weakening or a paucity of assorted social and educational services that affect not the young's sheer physical survival, but their future social and intellectual well-being. Is there any moral calculus available for making comparisons of that kind? If so, I have not heard of it.

That example alone points to the weakness of a much-touted method for making allocation decisions of a moral kind: the use of cost-benefit techniques.[16] The difficulty is that, on the one hand, their use will ordinarily work against the elderly because of the diminishing long-term benefits that health-care expenditures will bring in their case. On the other hand, we have no good way of comparing the benefits, say, of the physical mobility that an expensive hip-and-joint replacement imparts to an older person (for about $50,000) with those of an improved secondary education for a teenager. Norman Daniels has been exploring the provocative idea of a moral theory of resource allocation based on age, an "attempt to assure individuals a fair chance of enjoyment of the normal opportunity range for each life stage."[17] The problem with this notion is, first, that there must be "an underlying commitment to equity in replacement ratios enjoyed by successive birth cohorts"[18]—that is, the old cannot be allowed to monopolize wealth and benefits in a way detrimental to the young— an understanding that could be difficult to achieve and enforce; and, second, that, given steady medical advances and changing expectations, it has become difficult to say what, even now, much less in the future, will constitute a "normal opportunity range" for the elderly. After all, were it not for the widespread desire to expand the "normal opportunity range" from its earlier boundaries, and for the success of medicine in responding to that desire, we would be facing no problems about health care in an aging society. At the heart of the moral problem lies the question of what should constitute our standard in determining, in the light of available and foreseeable resources, a reasonable "range." If that is the preliminary theoretical task, one that has barely been undertaken, then the devising of practical policies to encompass such theories would be a formidable assignment indeed, the work of decades and perhaps generations.

I am not painting a happy picture of the moral options available at this second stage to cope with the health-care costs of the elderly. That is hardly surprising if one stays within the traditional categories of medical ethics, which gives primacy to individual patient welfare and knows nothing of choosing among equally needy patients, and stays also within the heady domain of the technological hopes and expectations that have been the very stuff of biomedical advancement, where enough is never enough. We would not be facing the problem of health-care costs at all, or be confronting an aging society, had not that commitment to individual welfare and medical progress been so powerful and so potently complementary to our desire to create a different kind of old age than the one that previous human generations experienced. A full and genuine coping with the moral problems might require nothing less than a severe reduction in, or alteration of, that commitment; that in turn could require still broader changes in moral perspective of consequence to many other aspects of communal life as well.

The ethical thread that binds together the triad of health care, respect for life, and the welfare of the aged is not merely decorative. To what extent can it safely be tugged at or rewoven? The answer to that question is not yet clear. An ancient medical and moral tradition of the sanctity of life—which in practice has ordinarily taken the form of vigorous efforts to preserve and extend life—has now been complemented by a "quality of life" perspective. For all of its popularity, the meaning of that phrase is hardly self-evident, nor are all of its possible implications altogether reassuring. It has on occasion been seized on as a way of reacting against the sheer vitalism that has sometimes been read into the older tradition (although the notion that life had to be preserved at all costs appears historically inaccurate). More often, it has been employed out of a desperate sense that the power of medicine to prolong brutally a kind of life that is no more than a biological Potemkin village requires attention to the kind as well as to the fact of life.

The concept of "quality of life" appears to offer a way out of the moral wilderness of the insupportable personal, social, and economic costs of open-ended health care for the aged. Under its tutelage we might, for example, cease to provide expensive health care when a patient's quality of life no longer makes that beneficial, and under more extreme circumstances, even stop the provision of water and nutrition. We might also allocate health-care delivery resources to favor those age groups whose potentiality for an extended quality of life is greatest (self-evidently the young), and allocate research resources to concentrate on those diseases or other conditions that predominantly kill or cripple them. In short, could we not, by a rigorous adherence to a quality-of-life standard, and without any radical unraveling of our traditions, find a suitable *modus vivendi* between the moral claims of the elderly to decent health care and economic good sense? This would amount to spending only up to that point at which it stops doing any good and then cutting it off.

That strategy will not work, or at least the odds are extraordinarily high that it will not. Quite apart from the notorious difficulty of achieving a consensus on an acceptable individual quality of life, at least part of the notion of "quality" should encompass the inclusion of hope in the future. This hope would simply not be fully possible in a society that rigidly judged what health care people should be allowed according to the potentiality they possessed for maintaining their future health and well-being. In addition to its natural liabilities, the approach of old age would then come to carry with it the inevitability of social abandonment, with all potentiality eventually consumed and the future quality of life found wanting by a society. How could there be a decent quality of individual life in the absence of a socially reinforced belief that one is respected for who one is, regardless of age, and not simply for what one has the potentiality to become? So it is that "quality of life" as a standard for terminating health-care benefits can contain a powerful self-contradiction.

Even if that contradiction could be circumvented, what are the prospects that medicine will learn just when the optimal moment for terminating treatment on sick patients has arrived? There is only one conceivable way this could be learned: by stopping all medical research and innovation, freezing present modes of health-care delivery, and then accumulating a great deal of experience from the ensuing stasis. Such an experiment might succeed—in some other world, peopled by some other human beings. In our world, the very meaning of medicine includes a perpetual effort at improvement, obsessively persistent experimentation, and the constant fueling of hope that suffering can be reduced and death somehow pacified.

It is not, then, simply that "quality" can be an elusive concept to apply to a human life, or a dangerous one if not handled with great moral care, although both of these statements are true enough. The ability of medicine to combat ever more successfully conditions that lead to a poor quality of life, and steadily to improve the nature of even what was initially or earlier of poor quality, means that any standard must be to some extent context-dependent, subject to change. The standard of "quality of life" we have at hand, therefore, is at once necessary to invoke and at the same time extraordinarily flabby. It helps a little in cutting through the confusion of our moral duties toward the sick elderly, but it does not give us as much help as we need.

STAGE III: INTERGENERATIONAL OBLIGATIONS AND THE ACCEPTANCE OF DEATH

I believe that we have been driven back to the final redoubt, even if that has yet to be generally recognized. A satisfactory general solution to the rising costs of health care for the elderly is unlikely to be reached without a fundamental reassessment of those values—moral, social, and cultural—that created the problems in the first place. While token gestures will be possible, efforts to shift the burden of health care back to families or to the elderly themselves, or to find ways of radically reducing the costs of such care by imposing cost-containment techniques, will meet with only limited success. The magnitude of the impending costs far outstrips those possibilities.

No less important, those possibilities leave untouched the deeper values that animate the entire enterprise of providing health care for the aged. Something much more fundamental is thus required, and I commend three aspirations for an aging society. The first would be that society become willing to desist from pursuing those medical goals that combine the following three features: the beneficiaries are primarily the elderly, the costs are high, and the population-wide gains are marginally slight. The second proposal would be that the old shift their priorities from their own welfare to that of the young and of generations to come. The third would be that we enter a pervasive cultural agreement to alter our perception of death from its being an enemy to be held off at all costs, to its being, instead, a condition of life to be accepted, if not for our own sake, then at least for the sake of others.

Each of these three aspirations for an aging society raises an enormous set of difficulties, and of different kinds. The first would no doubt trip us up immediately, and not only because of our culture's deep commitment to conquering disease and forestalling death. It would also confront us with the problem of finding a way to distinguish between cures for diseases that predominantly benefit the elderly and those that benefit younger age groups. Locating any sharp line of demarcation would be rare, for what helps one age group almost always has benefits for other groups as well.

Still another profound puzzle would present itself. Costs of providing care for the elderly will remain high because of benefits that were gained from earlier research investments in the cure of diseases affecting younger age groups. Much of that research will not lead to perfect cures, but simply to the management of the diseases; as a result, it will generate a large class of people who are chronically ill and in continuing need of health-care resources. Their lives will be saved while they are still relatively young, but the cost of salvaging them will linger, often for the rest of their lives. Not only will their original cures cost money; so too will their ensuing chronic illnesses.[19] They will also manifest what might be called the "twice treated, once dead" phenomenon: that is, since the aged will die of some illness, the costs of that final illness must be added to the costs of those earlier illnesses from which they were successfully saved. Many elderly people now incur multiple diseases as they age, any one of which could have been fatal in earlier times. Now they are saved, often at great cost, from one disease, only to be guaranteed death from still another, at equally great cost.

The present popularity of emphasizing the high costs of terminal care for the elderly obscures far more important economic realities. How are we going to find a way to call a halt to, or radically slow down, the entire process of aggressive life-saving interventions for our population as a whole? For it is that *process* that generates a series of costly procedures, before what may be the most costly one of all, that of trying to save a life that cannot be saved. Since it is rarely known in advance which intervention is the final one, the ultimate source of the problem is really the *cost of the whole series of life-saving interventions over time.*[20] The most effective ways of saving money in the future, therefore, would be to refrain from investing research funds in methods of cure that are likely to produce only chronic illness and a relatively short life thereafter; to cease attempting to conquer those diseases that would not significantly increase average life expectancy or greatly improve the quality of life; and to find ways to determine which life-saving interventions should be denied on the grounds that they only set the stage for still another needed intervention, which might well be the final and futile one.

Let us assume that ways might be found to cope with these problems. Would it even be possible to reduce the general social pressure to wage war against those diseases that afflict the elderly, an effort that consumes large amounts of money? That would depend in part upon the willingness of the aged both to forgo the use of their political power for their own improved health care and to shift their political energies to the needs of the young; and upon the willingness of the young to forgo scientific investments in their future old age that will effect deprivations for the generations that will follow them. It would also depend on returning to (or devising a more contemporary version of) a traditional way of looking at life that emphasized two features: the primary collective responsibility of the old for the welfare of the young and the generations to come, and the acceptability of death after a reasonable length of life.[21]

As a society, perhaps we have just passed through a period that encouraged us to believe that those traditional values could be set aside, or even that they could be actively combatted. During the 1950s and 1960s, there seemed to be sufficient money to enact health and welfare programs that could benefit all age groups; there appeared no need to worry that the elderly might benefit at the expense of the young, or that a commitment to the young could not be sustained in full vigor. At the same time, the never-ending string of medical triumphs over illness and disease has encouraged a widespread belief that any insistence on setting limits to the aspirations of medicine expresses an outdated fatalism. Why not aspire to a greatly increased life span? Why not, indeed? Why not also aspire to a vision of old age that is not marked by severe illness, or decrepitude, or senility? Who was—or who is—to say that it is not possible?

Only a fool would any longer prophesy what science cannot do. As a matter of prudence, then, we should not make the mistake of thinking that medicine will sooner or later run up against some intrinsic barriers in its ability to improve health and to extend life, and use that possibility as the basis for evading the hard moral questions that now face us. We should instead assume that medical science will continue to offer improved prospects for the elderly, but that neither our society nor any other will be able to afford all the costs. For, to the extent that we accept those costs and try to meet them, we will be indirectly depriving younger generations of circumstances, goods, and wealth they need to realize their full potential.

The phenomenon of an aging society has resulted in nothing less than the destruction of a moral and biological balance that has historically been of great importance. This moral balance stemmed from the fact that, on the whole, the elderly did not live long enough for their legitimate needs to impinge upon, much less usurp, those of the young, as many believe they are doing today. The biological balance stemmed from the fact that most people lived only long enough to insure their ability to raise children; nature conveniently removed them by the time those children procreated their own children. A great shift has since taken place. Viewed from that earlier moral and biological perspective, the aged—defined as those who have lived well past the time needed to raise their children—have become a biologically surplus and financially burdensome group. Worse, in a technological society they have little wisdom to pass along; younger generations have to face unique conditions, about which the elderly can offer little based on their own quickly outdated experience (or so many of us—probably mistakenly—assume).

Yet is it not the story of science in general, and of medicine in particular, to free us from the bondage of those earlier moral and biological balances, to understand them not as a fortuitous combination of need and aspiration, but as a slavery to biological need and social necessity? Tutored by the vision of liberation from the limits of the body—a body that too early faded and died—and by the prospect of release from a social life dictated by the physical and environmental needs of younger generations, an aging society opens up an entirely new possibility: that of people who can live for many decades for themselves alone, shaping a life free of the demands of children (either because they are long since grown, or because, for an increasing number, they were never chosen in the first place). Under this dispensation, the aged are not at all a surplus group. The kind of healthy, self-directing, self-realizing lives they are now able to live becomes the medical, political, and social goal, the ultimate reward of a progressive and medically enlightened society. From the perspective of health-care costs, an aging society is only a *moral* problem if it is assumed that the most important point of a society is to assure the welfare and future of its young people and, through them, its own future as a society. Otherwise the high costs of health care for the elderly are simply the price to be paid for creating a society whose aim is no longer the welfare of the young, but the preservation of those now enabled to break from the biological and familial constraints of the past.

To what extent that viewpoint is widespread is not clear. But there can be no viable or morally tolerable future if such an aim is pursued, certainly not for the young—who may be deprived of much they need in order to support the elderly—or even for the elderly themselves, who will need a sympathetic younger generation willing and able to support them. The present generation of elderly have that kind of sympathy, and they are well supported. But should the young come to believe they are penalized by the aging society's commitment to the health needs and demands of the elderly, their sympathy could well evaporate. Why should the young harm their present prospects, and their own prospects as the next generation of the aged, to make heavy sacrifices for a generation of elderly people who have become able, through the blessings of affluence and medicine, to live for themselves only, and are content to do so?

One way or the other, I believe, we will be forced back to some form of the balance between the needs of the young and the old that was the mark of most human life in the past. That kind of balance cannot be transcended, even though it will doubtless take a different form now from what it did then. A limit will have to be placed on the length of individual lives that a society can sensibly be expected to maintain at public cost, and on investments in the kind of research and health-care delivery that will constantly raise expectations about such a life. This strikes me as the only possible way to limit one side of the balance, a side that will, in the absence of controls, encourage a never-ending escalation of demand on the part of the elderly to better health and longer life. It may fall to the young to impose those limits. Yet it would be better if they had the help of older generations, so that the sense of limits would emanate from within the ranks of the elderly as well; they would know that they must ascribe boundaries to their own aspirations. The new balance ought to be one that is worked out mutually between the generations. That is the only way I can see to avoid the inevitable nastiness, competitiveness, and mutual hostility that the present costs of health care in an aging society must otherwise carry with them.

ENDNOTES

[1] Victor R. Fuchs, " 'Though Much is Taken': Reflections on Aging, Health, and Medical Care," *Milbank Memorial Quarterly/Health and Society*, Spring 1984, pp. 164–65.

[2] Ronald Bayer, Daniel Callahan, et al., "The Care of the Terminally Ill: Morality and Economics," *New England Journal of Medicine*, Dec. 15, 1983, pp. 1490–94; Anne A. Scitovsky, " 'The High Cost of Dying': What Do the Data Show? *Milbank Memorial Quarterly/Health and Society*, Fall 1984, pp. 591–608.

[3] See, for instance, Bernice L. Neugarten, "Policy for the 1980s," in Bernice L. Neugarten, ed., *Age or Need: Policies for Older People* (Beverly Hills, CA.: Sage Publications, 1982), p. 27.

[4] Douglas W. Nelson, "Alternative Images of Old Age as the Bases for Policy," in Neugarten, op. cit., pp. 138–39.

[5] A powerful argument for this conclusion can be found in Samuel H. Preston's "Children and the Elderly: Divergent Paths for America's Dependents," in *Demography*, Nov. 1984, pp. 435–57.

[6] I have discussed this problem in "What Do Children Owe Elderly Parents?" *Hastings Center Report*, April 1985, pp. 32–37.

[7] See Edward A. Wynne's chapter in this volume.

[8] See, for instance, Ethel Shanas, "The Family Relations of Old People," *The National Forum*, Fall 1982, p. 10.

[9] Cf. Phillip Longman, "Taking America to the Cleaners," *Washington Monthly*, Nov. 1982, pp. 24–30; and Preston, op. cit.

[10] James F. Fries has been the most articulate proponent of such a possibility. See his "The Compression of Morbidity," *Milbank Memorial Quarterly/Health and Society*, Summer 1983, pp. 397–419. But this view has been effectively criticized by Paul H. Black and Elinor M. Levy, "Aging, Natural Death, and the Compression of Morbidity: Another View," *New England Journal of Medicine*, Oct. 6, 1981, pp. 854–56.

[11] James R. Storey, *Older Americans in the Reagan Era* (Washington, D.C.: Urban Institute Press, 1983), p. 3.

[12] Nelson, op. cit., p. 156.

[13]Mark Siegler, "Should Age Be a Criterion in Health Care?" *Hastings Center Report*, Oct. 1984, p. 27.

[14]Ibid.

[15]James F. Childress, "Ensuring Care, Respect, and Fairness for the Elderly," *Hastings Center Report*, Oct. 1984, p. 29.

[16]Cf. Jerry Avorn, "Benefit and Cost Analysis in Geriatric Care," *New England Journal of Medicine*, May 17, 1984, pp. 1294–1301.

[17]Norman Daniels, *Just Health Care* (New York: Cambridge University Press, 1985).

[18]Ibid., p. 177.

[19]See Lois M. Verbrugge, "Longer Life but Worsening Health? Trends in Health and Mortality in Middle-Aged and Older Persons," *Milbank Memorial Quarterly/Health and Society*, Summer 1984, pp. 475–517.

[20]Cf. Scitovsky, op. cit., pp. 605–606: "A consensus has gradually developed about the ethics of forgoing treatment for such patients for whom care is, in some real way, futile. But no such consensus exists for patients who, although very sick, might still be helped by various diagnostic or therapeutic procedures and whose days might be prolonged. Thus, if we ask whether the costs of care for this group are excessive, we face new ethical problems of major proportions."

[21]See Leon R. Kass, "The Case for Mortality," *American Scholar*, Spring, 1983, pp. 173–91; and Daniel Callahan, "On Defining a 'Natural Death,' " *Hastings Center Report*, June 1977, pp. 32–37.

Malcolm H. Morrison

Work and Retirement in an Older Society

*The remedy of social ills cannot be exclusively achieved
through repression of excesses but must at some time
envisage constructive measures for the improvement of the
worker's welfare.*

—Otto von Bismarck

*The most essential ingredient for implementing the
proposed changes [in policies and practices for the aging]
is the societal expectation that people will remain
productive, in the broad sense, throughout the third
quarter of life and will thus be accepted as full
contributing members of the community.*

—Alan Pifer

T HE MAJOR CHARACTERISTIC OF THE twentieth century
continues to be rapid economic and social change. In less than
one hundred years, revolutionary developments in health care
and labor-saving technology have transformed demographic patterns
in developed nations, leading to their characterization as "aging
societies." These societies typically share two particular qualities: a
low fertility rate and longer life expectancy resulting in large increases
in the proportion of "older" persons, and highly developed social
welfare systems that devote most of their resources to this population. These developments have been accompanied by the significant
reduction in work-force participation by "the aged," achieved
through the social pattern of retirement.

Many developed nations, and the U.S. in particular, have created increasingly sophisticated public- and private-sector retirement income programs to improve the economic status of the aged and simultaneously to reduce their employment in national economies. As a social institution, retirement enjoys wide support as a goal to be maintained through public and private policies. For an institution of very recent origin, it now appears to be gaining additional structural support from economic and social policies that both mandate and induce its acceptance by the large majority of older persons.

Despite this widespread social consensus about the value of retirement and its apparently benevolent consequences, serious economic and social questions have arisen about whether the institution of retirement can or even should continue in its present form in an aging society. The economic questions center around the ability and willingness of society to continue to support increasing numbers of older persons through public retirement-income and health-benefit programs that depend primarily on the taxation of the work force. (In the private sector, a corollary concern has been raised about the costs of private pension systems and private health-insurance programs for increased numbers of older people.) It has taken national legislation to forestall the insolvency of the Social Security retirement program and the Medicare program in the United States, and although the measures enacted or proposed appear to remedy fiscal problems for the time being, few informed observers believe that today's benefit levels can be maintained in the future without further program modifications that would involve additional taxation of workers and the retired themselves, and/or substantial reductions of benefits. Similar problems may develop with private pension plans and health benefit programs, particularly if benefits are legally required for the retired and cannot fluctuate with the changing financial capabilities of individual business firms.

At present, U.S. government expenditures for older persons (age sixty-five and over), who represent just 12 percent of the population, are nearly 30 percent of the annual federal budget. If present expenditure levels are maintained, by the year 2030 (when 20 percent or more of the U.S. population will be age sixty-five or over) these expenditures will represent about 60 percent of the annual budget. It is difficult to foresee a social policy that would allocate three-fifths of the annual budget for support of the older population. The Social

Security legislation of 1983 that increases taxes on earned income, taxes Social Security benefits, and raises the eligibility age for full benefits after the year 2000 may portend future policies designed to raise the revenue necessary to provide benefits for older persons. Thus, the "economic argument" for modifying retirement as an institution is based on the view that society will be unwilling or unable to allocate the very large expenditures required to maintain benefits for the future retired population, and that this will eventually lead to a change in retirement patterns.

Social policy commentators point out that retirement bears positive and negative consequences for the older population. On the one hand, retirement—if it is accompanied by financial sufficiency—provides a period of time in which regular paid employment is not necessary and personal desires can be maximized. On the other hand, it poses serious problems for those older persons whose lives and identities have been closely tied to work, family, and community roles that are diminished or unavailable during retirement. This is especially so when they confront the assumption that their further productivity—in the broad sense—will be neither required or expected. For these "older" persons, retirement becomes a penalty that deprives them of a continuing productive role in society.

Although it would be inaccurate to describe retirement as total leisure without productivity, its social definition certainly excludes economic productivity, emphasizes leisure, and implies that even non-economic productivity (voluntary work, etc.) is not necessarily expected. It is this definition that has led social scientists to label retirement a "roleless role," a paradox that also accounts for why retirement, despite its popularity, instills disappointment or feelings of unproductivity in so many older people.

The increasing availability of public and private resources has led to an early retirement trend in the U.S. and many other developed nations. Historically, return to employment after retirement has been a relatively rare event. Today, of 27 million persons age sixty-five or over in the U.S. only 3 to 4 million report employment during any year, and most who do so are 65 to 72 years old and work part-time. There is evidence that more of the recently retired (since 1980) work for several years after receiving Social Security benefits, but these decisions are based almost exclusively on personal motivations and desires, for few policy incentives encourage longer-term employment during the retirement years.

It is perhaps because of the social value of retirement that new questions are being raised as to its meaning and content. As more people spend long periods of time as "retired pensioners," as the average retirement period lengthens, and economic benefits for the retired increase, "retirement" takes on the characteristics of a separate life stage, and some have suggested that greater specification of retirement norms is needed. Given that many "older" people have few significant personal barriers to continuing their productive contributions to society, both economic and non-economic, it is reasonable to question whether limiting the overall productivity for as much as 20 percent of the U.S. population is a "good" social policy. In other words, an aging society may well require changes in expectations about the roles of older persons, changes that elicit their continued contribution to social, cultural, and economic life.

Whether these changes will occur through modification of the retirement institution remains an open question. But both economic and social imperatives are already developing which will, at the very least, either redefine retirement or structure a new life-cycle period as a flexible and multi-option life stage for older persons. Achieving enough flexibility for older persons to remain productive presents many barriers, among them the social attitudes, perceptions, and beliefs that stereotype and underestimate their capacities, skills, and potential. This view continues to be widely held by people of all ages in the United States—including the old—despite evidence that many older people remain productive. If older persons are to be encouraged to remain productive, the entrenched beliefs that assume decline, redundancy, and dependency on their part will have to change to reflect their actual capacities. The economic and social policies that define retirement would also need to be altered to reflect the new social conception of productive roles for older persons.

This perception of aging as an opportunity for broadly extending productivity in society contrasts sharply with the view of older people as an economic and social burden. A new concept of retirement, or the acknowledgment of a productive life stage between middle and older age, is not only today's vision, but tomorrow's social imperative. Attaining this goal is a key challenge of an aging society, for it is the one major alternative to relying excessively on very large economic transfers to an older population, a practice that would seem to lead inevitably to escalating intergenerational tension.

Meeting this challenge involves reaching a social consensus about mutual obligations that link generational interests, and finding new ways to demonstrate that consensus through modified values and institutions. While most would agree that an ongoing historical process creates and redefines shared societal myths and values,[1] we should also be aware that major social choices significantly influence the success of generational relationships. It is important, when we consider this ongoing historical dialectic, to focus on those generational obligations that involve the rights and responsibilities of older people as well as younger ones. In an aging society, some responsibilities may become newly reciprocal, involving older people in unfamiliar roles and relationships. Our increasing obligations in an aging society will require two-way relationships in which the old assume greater responsibility for themselves and the welfare of all members of society.

Given today's values and policies—that generally exclude older people from social, economic, and cultural participation in society—conditions that might encourage greater productive participation on the part of the elderly may appear nearly unattainable.[2] But we must consider that these policies all tend to require that a diminishing number of younger and middle-aged persons support a growing aging population, and that the young and middle-aged are now questioning the extent and the magnitude of their commitment to an older population that is increasingly affluent. In addition, today's society is composed of cohorts of persons whose life experiences and expectations differ significantly from former generations in terms of their desire to remain socially productive. Thus, as the society ages, the old themselves may be both more able and eager to remain active participants in social and economic life. (Productivity in this context should be broadly defined to include both remunerative employment as well as a variety of "volunteer" roles such as teaching, mentoring, providing care for the frail and sick, and community service—the kinds of activities from which the retired population has usually been excluded because of societal expectations.)

As we have noted, this view of an aging society challenges most contemporary analyses, which suggest that older people must accept a combination of familiar and new kinds of dependency. Yet both historical and contemporary analyses of work and retirement indicate the dynamic nature of the social values and institutions that affect the aged, and the ways in which work and retirement choices respond to myths, values, and institutional policies.[3] Both past and present may be guides to the future: the changing perceptions of the roles and responsibilities of the old in an aging society, and the values and expectations that underlie them, is being conditioned by both the historical American experience that has focused on the dependency of the old, and by contemporary circumstances that are producing their emergence as a major and growing group in society. For the challenges of an aging society to be met, our social values and norms will need to acknowledge and facilitate productive roles for older persons. Let us now examine this process more closely.

WORK AND RETIREMENT: THE AMERICAN EXPERIENCE

If retirement is perceived as a social institution, then it must reflect and incorporate social ideology and values, alternatives established by the culture, rewards or constraints that influence choices, and the organizations and mechanisms through which the institution functions in society.[4] As an institution, retirement is subject to modification by changing social values and the combination of demographic, economic, and political circumstances that affect the culture over time.[5] From this perspective, retirement is neither inevitable nor unchangeable; its existence and its goals respond to changing sociocultural circumstances. Adopting a dynamic view is important, for while the definition of retirement as a transition from work to non-work has remained stable (particularly since it became an expected part of the life course), its objectives have undergone significant changes.[6] Recent analyses have begun to consider it as one of the three major life stages—education, work, and now leisure— and have documented the expansion of the time devoted to the first and the third stages and the commensurate reduction of the time spent at work.[7] The changes in this continuum demonstrate the dynamic nature of social expectations and behavior and the variations these have undergone throughout our nation's history.

Labor-force participation by older persons remained substantial until well after 1900 primarily because of the continued growth of industry and the demand for labor. Retirement was uncommon, for the most part the result of unusual circumstances. But industrial development brought important changes that were the precursors of retirement as an expected life stage. Between 1850 and 1900, industrial unions emerged, and with them the development of an ideology that supported a government role in providing income security for wage earners in society. The first appearance of private pensions was another element that, although embryonic during the late nineteenth and early twentieth centuries, would become a major factor in engendering the later institutionalization of retirement.[8]

Industrial unions expended special energy on maintaining job security for senior workers in order to protect them from layoffs. Nevertheless, management's acceptance of a job-security system based on seniority was won at the cost of accepting the imposition of uniform mandatory-retirement rules for workers considered to have reached an age of diminished productivity. The linkage between seniority and mandatory-retirement rules was originally perceived primarily as a protection for senior (and older) workers. It became evident only later that the seniority/mandatory-retirement policy trade-off resulted in a serious limitation of their employment.

Another feature of industrialization was the widespread unemployment caused by cyclical business conditions, a new problem that caused further economic deprivation and dependency in old age. Europe's attempts to solve this problem in the late nineteenth century led to the development of a new social ideology that invested government with the responsibility for the working classes of society. It was Bismarck who most clearly articulated the new ideology, which challenged the Poor Law system and encouraged state protection for workers in the areas of employment, health, and old age. The state was to assume responsibility for difficulties that were not the fault of individuals, but which resulted from social circumstances beyond their control.[9] This led to a nationally legislated old-age pension system, and so began to legitimate retirement as a time when basic economic sufficiency could be maintained if work was not available or possible.

Finally, it was during this period that the military and judicial sectors of the U.S. government, along with a small number of private companies, initiated pension plans for their employees. (Most of these required compulsory retirement, and their eligibility and benefit provisions varied widely.) The concept of private pensions was by no means an established one in America at this time, and the few organizations that provided pensions, private or public, were considered unusual. As a result, neither the seniority system, the notion of state responsibility for income security of the aged, nor the few existing private pension plans had much effect on the general expectations that employees would continue working until stopped by ill health, debilitation, or death.

Many of the negative stereotypes about older workers developed during the rapid industrialization and labor-intensive employment expansion that took place in the United States from 1920 to 1940, long before retirement became institutionalized as an expected social pattern. As industrial organizations grew in size and complexity, the increase in bureaucracy was accompanied by the launching of "scientific management techniques" to improve production efficiency—practices that often required increases in the speed of work regardless of the consequences for employees. Management's concentration on speed was based on the theory that a worker's lifetime individual capacity was relatively fixed, and that it declined over time until it was exhausted. The intense speed required for industrial work was thought to increase stress, which, it was assumed, would result in an absolute decline of productive capacity with age. With an increasing immigrant labor supply, union demands for reduced weekly work hours, and the advent of automation, this "wear-and-tear" theory gained wide credence and was used to justify both the dismissal of older workers as well as the imposition of age limitations in hiring.

Although there was never much objective support for beliefs about the relationship between age and declining capacities, these views have persisted over time and have hardened with the addition of negative assumptions about skills obsolescence, reduced learning capacity, resistance to change, and slower decision-making with aging. Despite considerable scientific evidence that for most tasks age is not related to reduced performance and, moreover, that individual variations preclude any valid generalizations about age and performance, the belief that age results in declining productive capacities has proven extraordinarily difficult to modify.

The early years of the twentieth century did much to shape future employment and retirement policies, as the new concepts of mandatory retirement, private pensions, and state responsibility for economic security in old age paved the way for a subsequent national retirement policy. And the negative attitudes about the performance capacities of older persons would take their place as relatively permanent parts of employer belief systems, to be reflected in growing discrimination against older workers.[10]

Some interpreters have proposed different explanations for the development of retirement as a social institution, locating it in the context of industrial capitalism. They usually suggest that the concentration of capital and the centralization of business control changed the nature of production, transforming the use of labor and selection of the labor force. The new approach involved the emergence of the "managerial class," which was responsible for supervising the operations of business firms. These managers adopted the early principles of "scientific" management, and its assumption that capacity declined with age. As a result, according to these interpretations, the new managers supported the development of retirement policies that would permit them to exercise greater control over the composition and the movement of the labor force.[11] This explanation of the institutionalization of retirement gives little weight to the influence of labor unions, or to the role played by the government and private pension plans. Instead, it suggests that the retirement institution was primarily a response to the requirements of industrial capitalism, which demanded policies of "superannuation" based on the view that older workers were unable to maintain their productivity, and thus created production inefficiency.

Although the historical record is not altogether clear, it appears that the early development of retirement was very much influenced by industrialization, the union movement, serious problems in the economy, and negative views of the productive capacity of older persons. But, clearly the most important historical development in the *institutionalization* of retirement in the U.S. was the enactment of the Social Security program. Some interpretations suggest that the program developed as a response to the economic crisis of the Depression years, a period that evoked a social vision that contained major elements of a welfare state.[12] Others suggest that the program was primarily a political response to large-scale unemployment and the accompanying destitution of older persons, as well as a way of rationalizing mandatory retirement and age discrimination in employment.[13] In any case, it was part of a social ideology that supported major federal responsibility for managing the economy and for providing social welfare policies for the population as a whole.[14] Whatever disagreement may exist as to the reasons for the development of Social Security and its multiple goals, few people question its profound impact in establishing retirement as an expected life stage, and in providing incentives to encourage retirement. While Social Security's emergence was clearly a response to the growth and intensity of poverty among the old during the Depression, its subsequent role in removing workers from the labor force and "reducing" unemployment should not be minimized. Social Security's early impact on encouraging retirement was not great, but its influence grew dramatically as program eligibility and benefits were broadened.

The large demand for labor during World War II briefly suspended negative attitudes toward older workers. Thousands were employed with little difficulty, and there were few complaints about performance. Yet this experience only served to reinforce the view that the labor-force participation of older persons could be significantly controlled by federal employment and retirement policies: government could develop policies that would either encourage the hiring or retention of older workers or help channel them into retirement from the labor force. In the postwar years, government, labor unions, and private employers adopted the latter strategy as a vital element of their employment policies.

The postwar period saw two major developments that formed the basis of today's retirement patterns. First, the Social Security program was extended to cover nearly all wage earners and self-employed; the permissible retirement age was lowered to sixty-two; and a national disability income program was added to Social Security. Second, based on legal interpretations of the Taft-Hartley Act, private pension plans became a legitimate area for collective bargaining, which led to very substantial growth of pensions between 1950 and the present. The major consequence of these changes was the gradual development of a retirement norm in America.[15]

In the last twenty years, retirement has grown into a major social institution. Retirement at earlier ages has been endorsed by virtually all sectors of our society, including government, private employers, and unions. Numerous surveys indicate that retirement as a concept is strongly supported by all age groups in the society.[16] Benefits in the Social Security program were significantly liberalized during this period; private pension plans proliferated; a national health-insurance program for the aged and disabled (Medicare) was added to Social Security, and its coverage and benefits were gradually expanded; and a national program that protects most economically disadvantaged aged from destitution was enacted—the Supplementary Security Income Program.

National policy regarding retirement has therefore strongly supported early withdrawal from the labor force and encouraged the development of multiple sources of *retirement* income, presumably to sustain longer periods of leisure on the completion of "working life." But another variety of legislation may portend a broader view. In 1967, the Age Discrimination in Employment Act (ADEA) was passed to protect older workers (forty-five to sixty-four) from a variety of discriminatory employer practices, including age-based discrimination in hiring and firing, in providing employee benefits, and in determining promotions, training, and so forth. Later legislation extended this protection to all employees age forty to sixty-nine, and also banned mandatory retirement before age seventy. Although the increasing legal protection against age discrimination in employment has not led to significant increases of older workers in the labor force, the ADEA does demonstrate a change in perspective in national policy, recognizing that it may be legitimate and valuable for some older persons to continue productive employment. While the impact of the ADEA may thus be modest in terms of changes in labor-force participation by older workers, in its modification of views and policy related to retirement it may prove far more significant.

Quite recently (1983), public policy was revised so that the normal Social Security retirement age will gradually rise from sixty-five to sixty-seven after the turn of the century. Due to rising national budget deficits, attempts are also being made to limit cost-of-living adjustments in the program, and to shift costs for health benefits from the government to private insurers and individuals. But these efforts emanate from budgetary constraints, and are neither designed nor intended to modify retirement patterns. It can be argued, in fact, that public policies concerned with retirement lack coordination and consistency, offer little flexibility in their approaches, and fail to reflect changing values and behavior underlying the continuing dynamic of retirement as a social institution.

Over time, social values and expectations about older persons and their role in society have changed considerably in response to demographic, economic, political, and sociocultural circumstances. Early devaluation of older persons had little effect on work participation, but it was followed by the development of seniority employment systems and mandatory-retirement rules that soon became linked to beliefs about diminished work capacity with age, and about the inability of older persons to adapt to the pace of work required by automation. By this time, the older worker was clearly facing increasing discrimination in the work place. General economic problems and severe unemployment made reduction of the labor force both necessary and pervasive. Since older workers were ostensibly worn out, they clearly were the most appropriate group to be encouraged to leave the work force, and as a result, retirement became regarded as an *unwelcome transition* from employment to what was often a period of economic constraint, if not deprivation. Its rationale was based primarily on the goals of creating jobs for younger persons, reducing unemployment, and containing costs, with older workers the most convenient group at whose expense these objectives could be achieved.

Enhanced economic support programs for the retired shifted the focus of the problem of "aging," but did not alter the underlying belief pattern: the old "deserved" a reasonable level of economic support after a lifetime of labor on behalf of society, and since they were no longer capable of productive work, society had a moral obligation to provide for them in their declining years. This led to viewing retirement as an *earned right* to be secured as soon as economically feasible. Moreover, once retirement became commonplace, the old recognized and acquiesced to the view that they should be supported by the young and had no responsibility to continue to support themselves. It was in this way that the old became defined as a dependent group in society, a group whose members could not and should not work, and who needed economic and social assistance that the younger working population was obligated to provide.

The recent fuller acceptance of early retirement by the majority of "older" workers has given rise to a revised view of dependency, one that regards retirement not only as an earned right, but also as a *reward*—which implies there is no longer any need or obligation to remain productive in society. As people have retired earlier, the relationship between retirement and old age has diminished. But age is still used as a major rationale for the maintenance of retirement as an institution,[17] and despite the recognition that "retired" people are often healthy, alert, and capable, society has yet to create norms for their continued productivity both within and outside of the labor force.

Are today's social values congruent with the institution of retirement? Is the intergenerational compact that stresses the obligation of the young to maintain the old a permanent part of the retirement institution? Can a new set of values emerge that involve the goal of productive participation of older persons?

While a *transition* from employment to retirement is likely to remain a common practice in an aging society, the mechanisms by which it occurs, and the socially endorsed goals to be achieved, will change as new choices are made that reflect changing ideology, economic conditions, and political developments. The actual choices older persons make today do not always reflect the social ideology that regarded the old as dependent and non-productive. Many older workers are already continuing productive participation in society, demonstrating not only that they can still maintain their former roles, but that they can create new roles as well— roles that involve both direct participation in the economy and voluntary activities. This, combined with great improvement in the economic status of the old, is changing social views of aging as a period of loss, dependency, and debilitation. Older age is becoming more highly valued as a period during which a continuing contribution to society is possible.

Because of existing fiscal constraints and the growing recognition by the young that their support burden will increase dramatically in an aging society, there is considerable discussion today about reducing total economic obligations, shifting income support and health costs to private auspices and to older individuals, and requiring longer work lives. The intergenerational compact may be in the process of changing to become more reciprocal, at least for the growing number of older persons who are healthy and active. One implication of such a shift is that, despite the continuing prevalence of negative beliefs about the capabilities of older persons, other social needs considered to be more important—such as sharing the costs of economic support—may result in policies that permit and encourage productive participation by the old.

Today's early retirement pattern does not preclude productive roles later in life. On the contrary: the opportunity to "retire" relatively early from a long-term job creates a choice for mature persons about whether and how to continue productive social participation. Although many barriers still exist—particularly the lack of cultural norms and defined roles for post-retirement life—early "retirement" may actually stimulate *more* productive activity in older age.

Thus, while the costs of an aging population continue to dominate public policy activity, social values and expectations about the aging are changing in response to demographic, economic, and political developments. Although one cannot predict future values and expectations regarding older persons, it appears that productive activity is becoming a more prevalent goal and expectation. Fuller development of new values, norms, and roles for the aging awaits the influence of social patterns and new public and private policies that will emphasize optional approaches to later life involving work, education, and leisure.

AGING, HEALTH, AND WORK IN TWENTIETH-CENTURY AMERICA

In a society whose aging population has achieved improved education and better health, it might be expected that a substantial number of older persons would participate in the economy. But, it is also possible for the economic status of a society—its gross national product, consumer expenditure patterns, and income distribution—to make leisure a valued societal goal, reducing the incentive for older persons to be economically productive. This is especially the case if the society has sufficient productivity and resources to provide for the economic sustenance of a large leisure class of older persons. Contemporary experience in the United States has been closer to this second scenario than to the first. Yet, while the dividends of higher productivity have been used to provide economic support for an increasing retired population, the required investment to maintain this policy has grown exponentially. In 1950, total social insurance expenditures of $5 billion were 1.7 percent of the GNP, but by 1982, they amounted to $300 billion, nearly 10 percent of the GNP. (All social welfare spending by federal, state, and local governments was

8 percent of the GNP in 1950 and 19 percent in 1982; and the federal government paid respectively 45 percent and 62 percent of these costs.) Retirement income-support payments are 50 percent of all social insurance outlays, and the federal government (through Social Security) pays four-fifths of these costs.[18]

Growing public expenditures are the result, not the cause, of social choices related to retirement policy. These choices had their genesis during the early history of our society, when the proportion of older persons was small. The long-term consequence of these choices, while anticipated by some, could not have been completely or accurately predicted, and it was assumed that policies could be modified to reflect future circumstances and needs. One consequence of the emphasis on early and complete retirement is the growing economic support burden; another is the paradox of maintaining an essentially younger and middle-aged work force by encouraging the early labor-force withdrawal of mature persons long before they reach old age. While the labor force will age over the next several decades, and the proportion of the middle-aged will increase (as that of entry-level workers declines), this will have little effect on labor-force attachment of workers over age fifty-five, whose participation is predicted to decline even further in coming decades, and into the next century.

Although most concerned observers recognize the many changing characteristics of the labor force—the coming dominance by the middle-aged, the increasing participation by women, the changing occupational structure, the growth of dual- and single-earner house-holds, etc.—few have questioned the desirability of maintaining early retirement as a social goal. The potential intergenerational tension that may result from an increasing old-age dependency ratio, and the social and legal obligations of the young to support the old, are not major subjects of public debate. Yet some of the unintended consequences of the earlier social choices about retirement have been to increase the economic support burden for the remaining working population, to establish the norm of retirement, and to extend its application to an enlarged group of aging persons. In a society that is undergoing significant changes in the social definition of work, including work patterns, roles, and mobility, a retirement norm based on a flexible and sometimes ambiguous chronological defini-tion may be subject to significant modification because of changes in social values and goals. This change might consist of endorsing later retirement, "post-retirement" employment, and/or other productive activity with minimal economic reward but broad social benefits.

The development of upward flexibility in the retirement-age norm would require more structural pressure than the increasing economic support burden brought about by a much enlarged group of retirees and a smaller group of workers. For a society can, at a certain social and economic cost, maintain an inflexible retirement norm. That is, it is *not* inevitable that an aging society, with high proportions of older persons, will provide more opportunity for productive activity by its older members. It can be very difficult to modify retirement norms, as recent policies to reduce the costs of Social Security by restricting periodic cost-of-living increases and by taxing benefits attest. Other social developments are beginning to affect retirement behavior, however, and they may soon lead to a re-conceptualization of retirement as a social institution.

Probably the most important changes involve the health status and the educational attainment of the population, both of which have been improving significantly during the last fifty years. These are improvements that pose both short- and long-term consequences. For example, chronic diseases and the subsequent utilization of health services by older persons are increasing, as are limitations in activity and work disability with extended age; declining death rates for older cohorts have not led to improved health and reduction in work disability.[20] Personal health habits, however, have been changing dramatically, a factor that can reduce the prevalence of major health problems, including heart disease, cardiovascular disease, and cancer. In all probability, these changes will lead to: *(1)* an increase in the proportion of those persons who are able to maintain very good health almost until death; *(2)* a smaller but increasing proportion of persons with severe functional limitations; and *(3)* a decline in the proportion of persons with moderate degrees of impairment.[21] We also know that educational levels continue to increase, and that labor-intensive employment is declining in our society. Although the proportions are uncertain, we can be reasonably sure that many more older persons, especially those younger than age seventy-five, will be functionally capable in the future; thus, the *chronological* definition of "middle-aged" will be extended.

Today, middle-aged men and women generally anticipate early retirement, and many face uncertainty about what that extended period will be like. Whether they are in a situation of social anomie, however, is debatable, for many create new roles and activities. Nevertheless, good health, functional capacity, and continued or new activity for more of the middle-aged "retired" have not led to a re-definition of retirement, or to the modification of the retirement norm to include productive work activity. This is partly a result of the pressure to maintain employment for "younger" cohorts, and reflects one of the major historical objectives of the retirement institution. No simple prescription can resolve the issue of intergenerational equity when considering jobs, but our economic system has proven very flexible in terms of the expansion of employment, and this strongly implies that job availability is not a zero-sum situation. If financial and social policy disincentives to employment could be reduced, there is no a priori reason to believe that the economy would be unable to expand gradually to accommodate more "retired" persons, especially in part-time, self-employment, and service capacities. This is not to suggest that unlimited expansion is possible, but to point out that intergenerational job competition is not direct, and that job-for-job substitution of younger for older employees is not common.[22] For older workers, productive activity might better be viewed in a context of more flexible work patterns.[23]

Continuity and discontinuity characterize today's retirement patterns. Half of Social Security's beneficiaries abruptly leave the labor force, and the other half engage in some short-term labor-force participation after they retire. No one pattern predominates. However, *entry into retirement* is very predictable, and, in recent years, more than 60 percent of those eligible now accept early Social Security retirement benefits. However, the definitions of activity and the ways in which time is used during the retired years continue to change. More variations in retirement lifestyles can be anticipated, involving extended employment, return to work, later-life training and education, and combinations of leisure and employment.

The most prevalent alternative work options that have been implemented are:

Phased retirement. Generally designed to permit job retention by older employees, this arrangement provides reduced work schedules with partial retirement, a salary that usually is prorated, and benefits that are either continued or prorated. Partial pension payments are sometimes permitted, along with continuation of contributions for time worked; periods vary, but they sometimes extend from two to five years or more.

Annuitant pools. This alternative usually involves the employment of a company's own retirees for temporary full- or part-time assignments; it sometimes involves restructuring jobs to permit retirees to work permanently on a part-time basis. Full retirement benefits usually continue, and the employed are paid regular wages, which are monitored so as not to exceed the Social Security earnings-test limitations. Employees are usually approached before their retirement as to their interest in joining such pools, and some programs provide training in skills to be used when those who do join return to work.

Contract work. This option entails the employment of older persons as independent contractors on a fee-for-service basis. Employers are often in the fields of sales, technical consulting, and temporary personnel services that hire many older persons with different skills. It sometimes involves specialized training for older persons, which is subsequently used in future contract employment.

Retraining. This approach is most often used by businesses where recruitment of trained personnel is difficult and costly. It usually involves employees forty-five to sixty years old, who normally remain with the firm on a full-time basis after training.

Multiple flexible work arrangements and job redesign. When experienced employees have long-standing clients (financial, insurance, real estate) and the firm values older workers, this approach is sometimes implemented. Salary and benefits often do not affect the receipt of pensions. Adjustment of job responsibilities and time at work are easily accommodated, but full-time work remains a possibility. Although these programs are usually not offered specifically for older workers, it is older workers who use them most.

Part-time employment. A wide variety of organizations provide part-time employment on a permanent or semi-permanent basis for older persons. Most are "new hires" who receive basic wages and minor fringe benefits.

By making use of these options, older persons can develop second careers, participate in phased retirement programs, receive additional training and education, engage in part-time work (clearly the most popular alternative), and obtain flexible work schedules. Many retired people will continue to choose self-employment and small-business development and remain productive through these alternatives, while others may become engaged in a wide variety of voluntary productive activities.

In addition to the work options that are being provided for older "retired" persons today, it is also possible to foresee another approach for older employees who might remain in the work force instead of retiring early. This would require employers and workers to accept a different view of work life, including such policies as horizontal job mobility without increased pay, reduced responsibility and income, and gradual diminution of responsibility and reward. In a society that values and requires the productive participation of greater numbers of older persons, these types of human-resource policy adjustments may become increasingly necessary. But they will be feasible only if the social values that now emphasize progressively upward mobility and increasing reward can be modified to reflect a continuum of work life, encompassing upward, horizontal, and downward mobility.

These flexible work alternatives can bring about social and economic changes, which in turn may increase the likelihood of significant modification of retirement as a social institution.[24] Whether this modification will occur, and the extent of its impact, will be determined by the relationship between social and economic changes and changes that take place in public and private policy.

THE IMPACT OF PUBLIC AND PRIVATE POLICIES

We have noted that the institution of retirement in the U.S. developed as a side effect of policies designed to insure job security, to exchange "energetic" for "worn-out" employees, and to provide income security for "superannuated" employees. As society matured, retirement took on other functions based on different values—among them balancing the labor force and fulfilling the desire for leisure—and a variety of policies, laws, regulations, and procedures developed to maintain the institution. These were generally based on the assumption of a social consensus about the values contained in retirement norms, and little revision has occurred either in these values or in the retirement norms themselves. This has led to discussion of the "leisure society" and to predictions that even fewer persons will need to be productively employed in the future technological society.[25] Yet we still have no substantial understanding about the future implications of population aging, the shift to a service economy, technological production methods, communication expansion, and the changes in lifestyles they portend. The technological and service economy has produced far more new occupations and jobs than it has eliminated, for example, and displacement is of relatively limited significance in the overall economy.[26]

A less labor-intensive economy that places greater emphasis on services and communication, improved methods of production, and more flexible work patterns does not imply the exclusion of mature persons. On the contrary, such changes *increase* the possibilities for participation by older persons, and if negative attitudes about their productive capacities recede and positive self-images grow commensurately, then their increased social and economic participation in society becomes more likely. It is therefore not social, economic, demographic, or technological change that precludes or limits the productive participation of older persons, but the conflicting goals of public and private policies that have limited their ability to adjust to changing social conditions.

Viewed in terms of reducing the work force and providing income security, the goals of retirement policy certainly have been achieved in our society. Until recently, the additional cost for maintaining the retired population has been considered an acceptable trade-off for creating and maintaining jobs in the economy. The general principle has been that the costs of retiree support are "recovered" by enhancing employment for "younger" persons and by retirement income transfers that stimulate consumption. A major change to *increase* pension eligibility ages will likely conflict with employment policy and be inefficient in terms of forcing the retention of an older and more expensive work force. However, as income- and health-support costs have increased for the growing aging population, recommendations have been made for the development of more balanced or age-neutral employment and retirement policies. This could occur if the principle of retaining more older employees could be accepted.

It is possible, however, that a general norm for lengthened work life might prove unacceptable, either to individuals or major social institutions. When proposals have been made to mandate later retirement, they have been rejected by large portions of the population, including the currently employed. On the other hand, the growing preference for later-life employment that has been documented seems to be related both to educational and occupational status; this suggests that health, education, and occupational variables may define a group of older persons for whom a lengthened work life may be particularly suitable. This would not, of course, exclude others from participating in later-life work, and perhaps a growing proportion of the mature population might gradually want to work.

Some commentators are convinced that no extension of work life is possible without a clear demand for the productive services of older persons—i.e., without norms for productivity or a demand for labor, and with continued incentives for early retirement, the rationale for a new definition of retirement is unsupported. On the other hand, public policy has begun to recognize the limits of the support burden for the retired, and although private policies do not yet provide incentives for continued employment, exceptions to rigid retirement rules are increasing.[27]

While we are approaching the limits of resource allocation for the aging, a new value consensus about work and retirement has yet to emerge. But the characteristics of an aging society, including demographic, economic, technological, and health changes, can be expected to bring about new values regarding the productivity of the old. In this sense, an aging society characterized by renewal and change creates new values and norms that merge with and continue the historical development of social institutions. How will this process affect the future work-retirement continuum?

RECONCEPTUALIZING WORK AND RETIREMENT

An aging society requires the development of a new social value consensus about mutual obligations and social relationships among generations. Part of this consensus involves values and norms about the productive participation in society by older persons. We have seen that an aging society does not necessarily imply decline, but that it may well be characterized by change and innovation in many of its institutions and practices. Such changes may produce social and economic strains that require accommodation if the society is to function smoothly. This accommodation must be based in part on reducing intergenerational tension by creating an improved balance of obligations between young and old.

Before the pattern of intergenerational relationships can be changed, a value consensus must develop about certain issues, among them the need for productivity, the costs and benefits of dependency, social integration, and the allocation of resources. If the old are to remain productive, social values emphasizing the *need* for their contributions must be established. These values probably cannot develop solely in response to fiscal constraints; they must also derive from the character of an aging population in an aging society.

The idea that the old can and should remain productive is the most fundamental change in belief that will be required. Of course, social choices are made not only on the basis of needs and capabilities, but also on the basis of economic factors. In the recent past, it has been considered cost-effective to maintain large numbers of persons outside of the work force through income-transfer programs. Given the benefits thus imparted to the remaining work force, the resulting financial costs have been assumed to be acceptable. The cost-benefit calculus is clearly being challenged, however, as the full magnitude of the retiree support burden becomes evident. Yet there is considerable reluctance to shift the support-cost burden by delaying the timing of retirement for large numbers of older persons. Any shift in the cost-benefit trade-off would affect the productivity-need continuum as well, and would require different social values about the roles of the aging in society.

A new framework of public policy that takes as its goal greater productivity for the aging could significantly influence the development of such new social values. Resources would have to be allocated to encourage the continued integration of mature persons in society in both paying and non-paying productive roles, and policies that exclude the old would have to be modified, as would social expectations about productivity and age. Alterations in existing policies could lead to improved social integration and to a change in social values. More flexible Social Security eligibility requirements, for instance, and the use of a partial pension program could encourage more flexible work patterns, including delayed retirement and return to work after retirement. Such changes could also encourage similar flexibility in private pension arrangements.

It is unlikely that different intergenerational exchange relationships can develop in the absence of this kind of public policy modification. For while the example of more older persons in productive roles can inform policy, it does not establish a requirement for policy change. In a society with more older members, such a mandate depends heavily on the recognition of the need for new policies because of a changing balance of intergenerational relationships.

We have now reached the point where values based on obligations of the young toward the old are being reexamined in light of the new circumstances of the aged. The resilience of social institutions to adapt to these conditions is being tested, and if a new consensus about age and productivity is emerging, its outline is only dimly perceptible. But the conditions for this consensus are present, and each modification of a social institution towards greater flexibility with regard to the aged brings the consensus closer. It is by means of such small-scale reforms that social values will change and that a new concept of the productive potential of older people will emerge.

We have observed how employment and retirement policies have been used primarily to secure balance in the work force to achieve national economic objectives and to diminish intergenerational tension. The same goals are relevant in an aging society that will, however, place a higher social value on using the creativity, talent, and motivation of people *throughout their lives*. This broad social goal can be achieved by adopting the concept of a work-retirement continuum that involves lifelong education and training. Only then will the definition of *retirement* gradually change, will public and private policies be modified to bring about a society that offers innovative alternatives for work and retirement, and will there be major enhancement of the roles and responsibilities of older persons.

ENDNOTES

[1] See W. Andrew Achenbaum's essay in this volume.

[2] Lois F. Copperman and Frederick D. Keast, *Adjusting to An Aging Workforce* (New York: Van Nostrand Reinhold, 1983); Richard Barfield and James Morgan, *Early Retirement: the Decision and the Experience* (Ann Arbor: University of Michigan, 1969); James W. Walker and Harriet L. Lazer, *The End of Mandatory Retirement: Implications for Management* (New York: John Wiley and Sons, Inc., 1978).

[3] Achenbaum, *Old Age in a New Land: The American Experience Since 1979* (Baltimore: John Hopkins University Press, 1978); David Hackett Fisher, *Growing Old in America* (New York: Oxford University Press, 1978); William Graebner, *A History of Retirement: The Meaning and Function of an American Institution 1975–1978* (New Haven: Yale University Press, 1980).

[4] Robert C. Atchley, "Retirement: A Social Institution," *Annual Review of Sociology*, 1982, pp. 263–87; Wilma Donahue, Harold L. Orbach, and Otto Pollak, "Retirement: the Emerging Social Pattern," in Clark Tibbitts, ed., *Handbook of Social Gerontology* (Chicago: University of Chicago Press, 1960).

[5] William Buckley, *Sociology and Modern Systems Theory* (Englewood, New Jersey: Prentice Hall, 1967).

[6] Graebner, op. cit.

[7] Fred Best and Barry Stern, "Education, Work and Leisure: Must they Come in that Order?" *Monthly Labor Review*, July 1977; Fred Best, *Flexible Life Scheduling, Breaking the Education-Work-Retirement Lockstep* (New York: Praeger, 1980).

[8] Achenbaum, *Old Age in a New Land,* op. cit.

[9] Wilma Donahue, Harold L. Orbach, Otto Pollak, "Retirement: the Emerging Social Pattern," in *Handbook of Social Gerontology,* op. cit.

[10] Graebner, op. cit.

[11] John F. Myles, *Old Age in the Welfare State, The Political Economy of Public Pensions.* (New York: Little, Brown, and Co., 1984).

[12] J. Douglas Brown, *An American Philosophy of Social Security* (Princeton, N.J.: Princeton University Press, 1972); Eveline M. Burns, *The American Social Security System* (Boston: Houghton Mifflin Co., 1949).

[13] Graebner, op. cit.

[14] Fred Cottrell, "The Technological and Societal Basis of Aging," in *Handbook of Social Gerontology,* op. cit.; Henry J. Pratt, *The Gray Lobby* (Chicago: University of Chicago Press, 1976).

[15] Atchley, op. cit.

[16] Louis Harris and Associates, "Aging in the Eighties: America in Transition," paper for the National Council on the Aging, Inc., Washington, D.C.: 1981.

[17] Jennie Keith, *Old People As People, Social and Cultural Influences on Aging and Old Age* (Boston: Little Brown and Company, 1982).

[18] Ann Kallman Bixby, "Social Welfare Expenditures, 1981 and 1982," *Social Security Bulletin,* Dec. 1984 (Washington, D.C.: U.S. Department of Health and Human Services, Social Security Administration, 1984).

[19] Malcolm H. Morrison, "The Aging of the U.S. Population: Human Resource Implications," *Monthly Labor Review,* U.S. Dept. of Labor, May 1983; Howard N. Fullerton, Jr., and John Tschetter, "The 1995 Labor Force: A Second Look," *Monthly Labor Review,* U.S. Dept. of Labor, Nov. 1983.

[20]Dorothy P. Rice and Jacob Feldman, "Living Longer in the United States: Demographic Changes and Health Needs for the Elderly," *Milbank Memorial Fund Quarterly/Health and Society,* Summer 1983.

[21]Jacob J. Feldman, "Work Ability of the Aged under Conditions of Improving Mortality," *Milbank Memorial Fund Quarterly/Health and Society,* Summer 1983.

[22]Morrison and Betty H. Roberts, "Interim Report to Congress on Age Discrimination in Employment Act Studies" (Washington, D.C.: U.S. Department of Labor, 1982).

[23]Morrison, "Flexible Distribution of Work and Leisure: Potentials for the Aging," in B. Herzog, ed., *Aging and Income* (New York: Human Sciences Press, 1978).

[24]Best, op · cit.

[25]Charles Reich, *The Greening of America.* (New York: Random House, 1970).

[26]Robert Lawrence, "Sectoral Shifts and the Size of the Middle Class," *The Brooking Review,* The Brookings Institution, Fall 1984.

[27]Morrison, "The Transition to Retirement," (Washington, D.C.: Bureau of Social Science Research, Inc., 1985).

John L. Palmer and Stephanie G. Gould

Economic Consequences of
Population Aging

THE IMPLICATION OF THE aging of our society for our long-term economic health has been a topic of some concern in recent years, and has stimulated numerous suggestions for relatively far-reaching (and often inconsistent) changes in current public policies. In this chapter, we argue that much of the necessary economic adjustment to our aging society will occur automatically in the private economy, and that much of what does not occur automatically would be sensible public policy in any event. If there is a case to be made for changing our politics toward the aged—and we think there is, although we are not primarily concerned with making one here—the case would rest more on the grounds of present inequity and inefficiency than on any probable ill effects of demographic developments. In offering such a comparatively sanguine view of the effects of demographic change, we do not pretend to guarantee smooth sailing into the future, but only to suggest that, among all the potential issues clouding the economic and fiscal horizon, societal aging is likely to be much *less* problematic than many forecasts have suggested.

In support of these contentions, we first assess the probable impact of demographic changes on our general economic prospects and on the structural functioning of our economy; we then evaluate both the future fiscal burden that will result from the aging of our society if current policies are continued, and the future economic capability of the aged themselves for sharing that burden; and, finally, we con-

367

clude with a brief survey of some federal policy alternatives for shouldering the burden.

ECONOMIC GROWTH

Assessing the impact of our changing demographic profile on our prospects for economic growth necessarily involves conjecture, since "economic growth" is itself something of a mysterious phenomenon. We know that, apart from cyclical fluctuations of the economy, growth over the long term will be determined by two factors: increases in the effective size of the labor force (including both changes in the number of workers and in average hours worked) and increases in the output per person-hour of work ("productivity"). Because, however, even a slight increase in the size of the population could increase the labor force and produce a jump in the GNP without anyone becoming better off as a result, what we are really interested in is not the size of the work force per se, but its size relative to the *total* population. It is this factor, in combination with productivity, that determines our standard of living (GNP per capita). And it is the ups and downs of productivity growth that constitute the "mystery" of economic growth and are the major source of difficulty in predicting our future prospects.

From the late 1940s through the early 1970s, productivity grew rapidly, averaging increases of 3 percent a year and far outweighing the dampening influence of a shrinking work force relative to population for much of this period (the latter, a result of both the baby boom and a decline in average hours per worker). In the 1970s, however, productivity collapsed, for reasons still not well understood, and only the extremely rapid growth in the labor force that began in the late 1960s prevented a total arrest of the rise of our standard of living. Nevertheless, on balance the economic history of the last forty years has been extremely positive: increases in the labor force and in its productivity have produced a continuously rising GNP and a doubling of living standards. The question before us now is whether demographic trends should lead us to hold less sanguine expectations of our economic future than would otherwise be justified by our economic past. Will the aging of our population so adversely affect the relative size of our labor force and/or its productivity as to slow economic growth and retard improvements in our standard of living?

The labor force is projected to continue to grow faster than the population until about 2010. Although this growth will be substantially slower than that of the very recent past, it nevertheless will be a marked contrast to the overall experience of the past four decades, during which the relative size of the labor force declined appreciably. Thus, the growth in labor force relative to population should have a strong positive effect on per-capita economic growth for the next twenty-five years, compared to its average effect to date for the post–World War II era. Once the baby-boom generation begins to retire, this pattern will reverse and act as a relative depressant on economic growth per capita through about the mid-2030s. At that point, the demographic information now available indicates that the growth of the labor force relative to the population will once again have a more favorable impact on standards of living than it has had during the past forty years.

Assessing the impact of population aging on productivity is problematic. Explanations for the past fluctuations in productivity growth have centered on three factors: the amount of capital that is available per worker; the quality and efficiency of the labor force— how educated and experienced it is and how well it is distributed across locations and occupations; and a hodge-podge of other considerations generally lumped together under the label "technological change." Economists have attributed a little more than one-third of the average annual growth in productivity since the late 1940s to continuous additions to the amount of capital per worker, as the country has annually elected to reserve a certain portion of the GNP (typically about 16 percent) for investment, rather than for current consumption. Roughly another quarter of the annual average growth in productivity has been attributed to improvements in the education and experience of the labor force and in its allocation among the various sectors of the economy. All these factors—the amount of capital per worker and the quality and efficiency of the work force— had some hand in the collapse of productivity in the 1970s. In the case of the former, investment did not decline significantly relative to GNP, but the size of the work force increased dramatically as the baby-boom generation and hitherto non-working women flooded the labor market with young and inexperienced workers. By far the lion's share of the productivity collapse, however, must be attributed to the "black box" of technological change—that component of productivity that has proved the most influential over time and the most elusive to quantification. Explanations for the collapse have centered on factors that may prove mercifully temporary in their long-term effects: for example, the technological difficulties of responding to the rapidly growing burden of environmental and health regulation and to the industrial strains of the energy crisis. But these are really more speculations than explanations. "Technological change" remains the big wild card in our past, as in our future, productivity.

Looking towards that future, we might expect that the rate of growth of capital per worker will contribute modestly to economic growth for the next twenty-five years relative to the past forty, as a result of demographic trends. Now that all the members of the baby-boom generation are over twenty, the growth of the labor force is slowing markedly in absolute terms (while still growing more rapidly than the population as a whole). This means that, even if our capital stock grew no more rapidly than it has in the past, we still would have a greater concentration of capital per worker and could therefore expect more output per worker. But we can also expect capital to grow more rapidly for demographic reasons, since the private savings necessary for investment should increase as the baby-boom generation moves out of early adulthood (a time when households typically borrow in anticipation of higher future incomes) and into middle age (a time when households typically save in anticipation of retirement). By 2010, labor-force growth will stabilize, and the household savings rate should decline because of the big increase in households headed by the aged, who tend to spend more of their income to sustain their standard of living in the absence of earnings.

As regards the second productivity factor we have cited—labor quality and efficiency—we can expect some mixed impacts. The quality of the labor force is improved mainly by providing higher levels of education and training to its members, both before and after their entry into working life. Despite the huge increases in the youth and then the working-age populations in the past several decades, we have experienced continuous growth in this kind of "human capital" investment per worker, and this growth has counted for sizeable average annual gains in worker productivity since World War II.

Looking ahead, we might expect slower growth in educational capital now that the proportion of young people who receive higher education is leveling off. But the decline in the school-age population and slower growth in the labor force also provide an excellent opportunity for increasing the quantity and quality of general education and training per worker, since relatively fewer resources will be required to sustain previous rates of growth. Thus, we assume that the contribution to productivity growth from investment in human capital will not diminish appreciably in the future.

Beyond education and other such investments in human capital, we must consider how labor quality may change "naturally," that is, how an individual worker's productivity will vary over the course of his or her work life as a result of physical aging and the accumulation of experience. Studies show that physical aging generally makes a positive contribution to worker productivity in earlier work years, then levels off and eventually becomes a negative factor, while increased job experience and maturity generally continue to exert a positive influence throughout one's employed lifetime. The specific age/productivity profile does, of course, vary with individuals and has been extensively studied across a wide range of occupations. In general, the results indicate that, for most workers and occupations, productivity does not peak until after age fifty, and often not until age sixty, and then declines very slowly. (Factors other than age usually turn out to be more important to productivity, which varies much more within an age group than does its average across age groups.) Looking ahead, we can therefore expect that the general aging of the labor force over a broad range of occupations will enhance its overall productivity, and that only once the average age of the labor force is quite high might its continued aging become detrimental.

Finally, we need to consider how the labor force is distributed over industries, occupations, and locations, for it does no economic good to have a potentially highly productive worker misemployed or unemployed. In a dynamic economy such as ours, the economically optimal distribution of labor is constantly changing as a result of shifting patterns of consumer demand, technological innovation, competition from foreign producers, and so on. Our economy has historically derived much of its strength from the speed and flexibility of its labor force adjustments, aided both by the willingness of current workers to make job changes and by a relatively large pool of new entrants, who can more easily be directed into appropriate jobs and areas. A labor force that is both aging and growing only slowly is less likely to adjust as fully or as rapidly.

This brings us back to the "black box"—technological change—about which, as we have already noted, little can be predicted. Studies of the impact of population changes on the pace of innovation and invention have focused on three hypotheses that relate to our concerns. The first is that growing population per se promotes innovation because it produces a larger pool of ideas and greater returns to scale; the second is that an aging population will experience slower technological change because the creativity that promotes breakthroughs is more characteristic of younger adult minds; and the third is that an aging population will be more conservative in risk taking because of greater concern for financial security. The first hypothesis appears to have been borne out in the earlier development of the American economy, but seems to have little relevance for the present or future, and the scant evidence on the latter two fails to support any clear conclusion.

Having made all these disparate observations about the probable impacts of demographic changes on our future economic growth, what can we say about their net effects? What about the implications of our societal aging for our future standard of living? Table 1 offers a rough approximation of the probable magnitude of impact of each of the four factors we have examined. The table cross-references each factor with the three time periods we specified earlier; each (+) represents the potential for a 5 to 10 percent increase in the slightly under 2-percent annual average rate of growth of per-capita income since World War II, and each (−) represents a similar decrease. A (o) indicates a likely negligible difference in effect.

As we can see from the totals, projected demographic change appears likely to be a strong positive influence on per-capita economic growth over the next twenty-five years—raising it by more than 15 percent per annum relative to past trends. This would mean that per-capita economic growth would average in excess of two-and-a-quarter percent per year, and the general standard of living would increase by about 80 percent by 2010, *other things being equal.* (Of course, other things may well not be equal; as we have noted, we are not trying to forecast a certain future here, but only to isolate the probable contribution of demographics to that future.) We

TABLE 1. Projected Impact of Demographic Change on Per-Capita Economic Growth Relative to 1947–1981 Trends

	1985–2010	2010–2035	2035 on
Labor force to population growth	+ +	–	+
Capital per worker	+	0	–
Labor quality and efficiency	+	–	–
Technological change	–	–	–
Total	+ + +	– – –	– –

SOURCE: Authors' estimates.
Each (+) represents the potential for a 5–10 percent increase in the annual average rate of growth of real GNP per capita relative to post World War II trends and each (–) an equivalent decrease.

place considerable confidence in this positive demographic impact, since it derives primarily from projections of the relatively favorable relationship between labor-force growth and population growth (something which only an immediate and large increase in fertility rates could forestall). As we move further into the next century, however, demographic factors are likely to become negative influences on economic growth, although the probable magnitude of this influence is uncertain, and more likely than not overstated in table 1 (intentionally conservative as it is). The point is that, even given the relative pessimism of the estimates in the table, demographic change should no more inhibit rising standards of living over the next fifty years than it has in the past. Surely, this point should dispel much of the economic foreboding that clouds much public discussion of our "aging society."

STRUCTURAL ECONOMIC CONSEQUENCES

Our attention so far has focused very broadly on the economy, and on the way in which its potential for growth might be affected by the aging of our society. Nevertheless, as can be inferred from the preceding discussion, the effects are by no means evenly spread among all segments of the economy. We have already noted two developments—the changing nature of the labor force and the growth in private savings—that have implications for the structure as well as the growth of our economy. To these, let us add two more developments as demographic-driven sources of potential structural problems: the changing structure of consumer demand and altered patterns of population distribution.

Labor Markets

As we noted earlier, unless current patterns of work or fertility change quite markedly, the U.S. labor force will be both much older and much more slowly growing (perhaps even declining) as we move into the next century. The changing labor market will entail considerable adaptation on the part of workers and employers. Faced with a relative scarcity of young workers, employers will have much stronger incentives to increase labor efficiency, to invest in workers of all ages, and to encourage older workers to remain in the labor force longer. Thus, entirely through private initiative, we would expect to see employers provide better information about job openings to potential employees, increased amounts of training and retraining, and more flexible working arrangements, especially for older workers. But private initiative alone may well not suffice. With the strong role the public sector plays in funding and administering many employment and training programs, in shaping incentives and disincentives for labor force participation, and in determining the quality of preparation for employment that our public educational system provides, changes in public policy may also be necessary.

Private Pensions

As the "middle-aging" of the baby-boom generation takes place during the next quarter of a century, and as its members prepare for retirement, the accompanying increase in private savings that is anticipated may be favorable for economic growth, but the rapidly growing share of these savings accounted for by private pension plans will exacerbate a number of existing structural economic strains. Just after World War II, private pensions covered only about one-seventh of the private wage and salary labor force. Their assets were quite small in relation to the economy as a whole, and they resulted in negligible tax revenue losses. Today, private pensions cover more than half of the private labor force. Their assets are approaching $1 trillion and account for one-third of all publicly traded equity and debt of the country; and they receive federal subsidies of about $60 billion annually, or over 15 percent of federal income-tax revenues. The likely increase in the coverage of private pensions over the next several decades is a matter of considerable dispute, but there is general agreement that pension assets will continue to grow substantially faster than the economy until the baby-boom generation retires.

The growing economic importance of private pensions has already raised many issues that will assume even greater force in the future. Among the most relevant for our concerns are the characteristics of employer-based private pensions that run counter to needed adjustments in labor-market practices. For example, because most plans lack "portability" and disproportionately weigh long years of service with the same employer, they effectively discourage job changes that might be efficient from the economy's point of view. And because they came into being at a time when employers were anxious to move out older workers to make room for the abundant supply of younger ones with lower wage requirements relative to their productivity, most plans also contain strong incentives for early and full retirement. Also, both the equity and the efficiency of the tax subsidies for private pensions are highly questionable. The bulk (probably more than two-thirds) of private pension savings simply substitute for other forms of private savings that would have occurred even in the absence of tax subsidies. And higher-income workers and their families are the overwhelming beneficiaries of private pensions and, therefore, of the tax subsidies that support them. (Lower-wage employment is typically uncovered by private pensions, and lower-income families generally cannot afford to put aside current income into IRAs.) Finally, the growing importance of pension funds as financial intermediaries, often managed by third parties, raises a number of troubling issues. When pension funds hold a significant share of equity in a company, what consequences do they pose for corporate governance? To what standards regarding rates of return, etc. should managers be held accountable? Are pension funds likely to have a detrimental impact on equities markets? Will they result in a declining share of high-risk capital?

Consumer Demand

Because of our society's changing age structure, the particular mix of goods and services that our population wants in the decades ahead will obviously be quite different from that at present. There will be, for example, relatively less demand for athletic equipment, pop music, and large multi-storied single-family dwellings; there will be greater demand for gardening equipment, long-term health care facilities, and group living facilities. Will this shift in demand seriously disrupt the functioning of our economy? Most probably not. Both the public and private sectors are continually adapting to changes in consumer wants and needs from all sorts of anticipated and unanticipated factors. The salient issue is whether the changes in demand caused by the aging of our society will be so abrupt, so significant, or so unanticipated as to make the adjustments unusually difficult. In fact, they will be relatively gradual, quite predictable, and no greater in magnitude than past shifts in demand caused by both demographic and non-demographic phenomena. Within a decade, the television set moved from the status of a neighborhood oddity to a universal household accessory. The baby-boom generation has already put extraordinary pressures on our educational system and housing markets, both of which have adjusted reasonably well. And almost every day the newspapers report the conversion by local communities of still more schools into centers for the aged and the rapid expansion of retirement communities and continuous-care residences by both commercial and non-commercial sponsors.

This is not to say that we should anticipate no problems in meeting the changing consumer needs of our aging society, but only that they will not be untoward in the context of our past experience, and that the normal mechanisms of adjustment in the public and private sector should be generally adequate to the task. Of course, the general availability of goods or services, such as home health care, does not necessarily mean that it is affordable by all, or even by most, of those who need it; but this is an issue of the distribution of fiscal resources—a subject to which we shall return.

Population Redistribution

The United States has always experienced considerable internal migration and shifting population distribution, but in the context of a rapidly growing overall population, population gains in some areas did not necessarily mean population losses in others. With the advent of lower birth rates and an aging society, one region now gains at another's expense, and often with considerable economic consequences, for a redistribution in population generally means a redistribution in dollars and markets.

Our current migration trends have two distinguishing characteristics: Americans are moving away from metropolitan areas, particularly from center cities, to smaller communities; and they are moving from the snow belt to the sun belt. Because the out-migration is concentrated among the more affluent (especially among the aged) and young adults, many large cities find themselves with shrinking tax bases and disproportionate numbers of low-income and elderly residents, who require special services cities can ill-afford. If these migration patterns continue, in concert with our aging population, they will pose increasingly difficult dilemmas for public policy.

THE DISTRIBUTION OF ECONOMIC RESOURCES

Although the overall health of our economy—and all the factors we have outlined that bear on that health—will ultimately prove the single most important determinant of the well-being of aged and non-aged alike, this is not the issue that arouses the most popular concern in discussions about the impact of our aging society. Rather, it is the distribution of resources *within* the economy: the fact that current workers must share the goods and services they are producing with a faster growing population of aged. The heightened concern stems not only from the demographic picture sketched at the beginning of this chapter, but also from three developments over the last fifty years that have profoundly changed the nature and the scale of the sharing. From being a largely private matter—the concern of families, businesses, and charities—the support of the aged has become more and more a public or collective one, underwritten by such programs as Social Security, Medicare, Medicaid, and public assistance. The vast bulk of all transfers of resources between the working and the aged populations now occurs through the public sector—in particular, through the federal government. (Federal outlays for the aged total about 8 percent of GNP, compared with less than 1 percent for state and local outlays.) And the programmatic nature of most of these transfers ensures their automatic growth. That is, almost all the programs are entitlements, for which all aged members in households with low incomes, or with ex-workers or their dependents, are eligible; and program benefit levels (in the case of the two behemoths, Social Security and Medicare) are automatically adjusted upward to reflect not only rising costs in health care and general price increases for all recipients, but also the higher earnings of each generation of new retirees. Finally, legislative changes over the years fostered still more growth by making the programs progressively more generous. These three developments, in concert with the changing demographic picture, have resulted in a massive diversion of resources from the working to the non-working aged and have contributed to the current federal budget crunch. And these developments ensure that, despite recent cutbacks, aggregate public expenditures for the aged under current law will once again grow faster than the economy as we move into the next century.

Awareness that simply maintaining the present degree of support will require a proportionately greater tax effort on the part of the working population in the future has prompted many to argue for cutbacks in the current federal commitment to the aged. It has also stimulated concern about heightened competition for dwindling public resources between the aged and other dependent groups, namely, children and the poor. At the same time, it appears likely that the aged as a group will actually increase their demand for public resources simply as a result of longevity—i.e., by outliving their private means. All of this potentially adds up to quite a strain on the public purse.

Current proposals for coping with the strain fall into three general categories: continuing or even increasing the existing degree of public support for the aged, letting the increased tax burden fall on the working population as the bills come due; reducing the transfer of resources implicit under current law so that the future aged will have to assume a larger share of responsibility for their own support; pursuing policies that might foster future economic growth, in effect curbing the consumption of the current working generation to lighten the economic burden of future ones.

Deciding among these possibilities requires, first, understanding what would happen if we were to continue current policies—that is, what kind of burden the future working population would have to assume—and second, understanding the current and prospective economic status of the aged, and how it might be affected by reductions in federal support.

Fiscal Implications of Current Policies

Table 2, next page, summarizes projections of the federal budget outlays that would be required to support existing pension and health-care programs under the policies reflected in the 1985 federal budget and the long-run economic and demographic assumptions generally used for the Social Security program. Obviously, these projections are not hard forecasts, since the assumptions on which they are based will undoubtedly change, but they at least give us some basis for evaluating the federal policy options sketched above.

Of particular concern for our purposes is the projected steady rise anticipated after the turn of the century in combined outlays for pension and health-care financing as a percentage of GNP. These programs account for the great preponderance of all benefits to the aged, and the demographic projections we outlined in the beginning of this chapter play a large role in pushing their outlays upward. But while the pension outlays fluctuate down and then up over the next fifty years, the health-care financing outlays climb steadily, greatly increasing their relative importance. The pattern for projected pension outlays is dominated by the Social Security program, which accounts for nearly three-quarters of total federal pension costs. Average benefits per recipient under Social Security will grow more slowly than the economy, both because the benefits are adjusted only for inflation, and not for rises in the GNP, after workers retire, and because 1983 amendments of the Social Security legislation provided for significant cuts in benefits to be phased in gradually (the most important of these was a reduction in benefits for those who retire before age sixty-seven). Other federal pension programs, such as veterans' pensions and Supplementary Security Income, are also projected to grow more slowly than the economy; therefore, even with the retirement of the baby-boom generation early in the next

TABLE 2. Long-Term Federal Outlay Trends as a Percentage of GNP

	Pension Programs	Health Care Financing Programs	Pension and Health Care Financing Programs	Other Non-Defense Programs[a]	Defense and Net Interest[a]	Total Budget	Other Non-Defense Programs Assuming Total Budget Stays at Projected Level From 1990 on of 24.6 Percent of GNP
1965	4.1	0.3	4.4	5.3	8.3	18.0	NA
1970	4.7	1.4	6.1	4.8	9.3	20.2	NA
1975	6.4	2.0	8.4	7.1	7.0	22.5	NA
1980	6.5	2.3	8.8	6.4	7.8	23.0	NA
1982[b]	(7.1)	(2.7)	(9.7)	(6.4)	(8.5)	(24.6)	NA
1985	6.6	2.7	9.3	5.1	9.9	24.3	NA
1990	6.1	3.0	9.1	3.8	11.7	24.6	NA
1995	6.0	3.6	9.6	3.8	11.7	25.1	3.3
2000	5.7	3.9	9.6	3.8	11.7	25.1	3.3
2005	5.6	4.2	9.8	3.8	11.7	25.3	3.1
2010	5.7	4.5	10.2	3.8	11.7	25.7	2.7
2015	6.1	4.7	10.8	3.8	11.7	26.3	2.1
2020	6.6	5.2	11.8	3.8	11.7	27.3	1.1
2025	7.0	5.6	12.6	3.8	11.7	28.1	0.3
2030	7.1	5.9	13.0	3.8	11.7	28.5	—
2035	7.1	6.1	13.2	3.8	11.7	28.8	—
2040	7.1	6.2	13.3	3.8	11.7	28.8	—
2045	7.0	6.1	13.1	3.8	11.7	29.6	—
2050	6.9	6.0	12.9	3.8	11.7	29.4	—

SOURCE: For years 1965–1982, Table 1 of John L. Palmer and Barbara B. Torrey, "Health Care Financing and Pension Programs," in Gregory B. Mills and John L. Palmer, *Federal Budget Policy in the 1980s*, The Urban Institute Press, Washington, D.C., 1984; for years 1985 and 1990, The Congressional Budget Office, *The Economic and Budget Outlook, Fiscal Years 1986–1990*, Government Printing Office, 1985; for years 1995–1050, *The Social Security Trustees Report*, April 1984 and Palmer and Torrey, back-up to Table 1.

a. Assumed constant from 1990 on.　b. 1982 is included because it is the peak year for Social Security and, therefore, pension programs.

century, total federal pension outlays are not expected to rise above their previous (1982) high, after actually falling off considerably during the next two decades.

The contrasting faster-than-GNP growth in health-care financing outlays is entirely attributable to the Medicare program, which currently accounts for about two-thirds of total health-care financing expenditures. Two phenomena are primarily responsible for driving up Medicare costs. The first, as noted above, is demographic; not only, however, attributable to the general increase in the aged population, but also to the increase within that population of the very old, who face much higher average medical expenses than the younger aged. More important, however, are increases in general health-care costs per capita, which have for years greatly exceeded the rate of increase in GNP per capita and can be assumed to continue to do so, unless some major policy change intervenes.

In fact, some such change is occurring, and more is likely. If per-capita health-care expenses were to continue to increase at anywhere near their past rates, the total (both public and private) health-care sector's share of GNP would more than double from its current level of 11 percent over the next fifty years. Some increase in this sector's share will no doubt be deemed desirable, to reflect not only the greater health-care needs of an aging society, but also greater affluence and more health consciousness at all age levels. Yet it seems unlikely that a society already worried about "runaway" health costs, as they are frequently termed, will accept such a disproportionate allocation of its resources. Thus, quite independent of the possibility of further cuts in public health-care benefits for the aged, the projections for federal health-care financing costs in table 2 may prove overstated. In fact, the recent tightening of federal reimbursement under Medicare for both hospitals and physicians has already begun to curb the growth in outlays.[1]

Yet another development—this one demographic—should serve to moderate the fiscal severity of the picture presented in table 2. Under the demographic assumptions presented earlier, while the over-65 population will more than double in the next fifty years, the population under age twenty will grow by less than 10 percent. Although per-capita public expenditures on the pre–working age population are considerably less than on the aged, and because of the way we finance education (which is much more concentrated at the state and local levels), the total tax burden on the working-age population and the strain on private resources should be relieved somewhat by this relative shrinkage of the youth population.

Even granting these mitigating developments, however, if our current commitment to care for the elderly is not scaled down, we would appear to be facing a major federal tax increase early in the next century. In order to pay for everything that current policy entails (and aside from any effort at reducing the existing federal budget deficit), federal tax revenues could have to rise by as much as 5 percent of GNP. What would this increase in tax burden imply for the tax-paying population in 2035, assuming future growth of GNP per capita parallels that of the past four decades? Roughly speaking, it would mean that the purchasing power of the average taxpayer's after-tax income would rise by 135 percent, rather than by 150 percent, over the next fifty years.

From our 1985 perspective, this hardly seems an onerous burden. Nevertheless, if such a tax increase were phased in from, say, 2010 to 2030 (when most of the projected increased spending would occur), it would entail an appreciable reduction in the rate of growth of taxpayers' purchasing power at just the time that demographic forces are expected to have a depressing effect on the rate of growth of per-capita pre-tax income. In addition, it may raise concerns that the increase in tax burdens, per se, could further slow general economic growth below the levels assumed in our projections. On balance, however, it appears that demographic concerns alone do not constitute cause for fiscal panic: barring economic calamity that it is outside the scope of this essay to predict, we should be able to shoulder the financial burden of an aging society without experiencing intolerable fiscal strains, even in the absence of major policy adjustments.

We have boiled the issue of "the economic consequences of an aging society" down to the more familiar question of whose ox is to be gored, and for the beginnings of an answer to that, we need to look at the present and future economic status of the aged.

The Relative Economic Status of the Aged

The economic status of the aged as a group has improved markedly over the past several decades, so that it is now roughly on a par with that of the non-aged.

In 1980, the average per-capita money income of the aged was about 90 percent of that for the non-aged, and just under 75 percent of that of those aged fifty-five to sixty-four. Although these facts would seem to imply a substantially lower standard of living for aged persons than they enjoyed in their immediate pre-retirement years, such does not turn out to be the case. To reflect accurately the economic status of the aged, we need to adjust these simple income measures to take into account numerous other differences in the circumstances of the aged and non-aged. For example, the aged receive greater amounts of in-kind assistance (such as Medicare), pay proportionately less in taxes, have lower consumption needs (because of lower caloric intake requirements and fewer work-related expenses), and have greater net worth (as a result of a lifetime of savings). On the other hand, the aged generally cannot take advantage of the economies of scale available to the non-aged, who typically live in larger households. Several studies, using various methodologies, have tried to adjust for these differences; all have concluded that the economic status of the aged as a group is now such that *they can more or less maintain in retirement the standard of living achieved in their middle-age working years.* That the incidence of poverty among the aged is actually significantly *less* than among the non-aged further attests to the achievement of parity.

In fact, gains in the relative economic status of the aged fail to capture the full extent of the improvement in well-being for this group, since these gains have been realized despite a major reduction in the labor-force participation of aged men (from 46 percent in 1950 to 16 percent in 1984) and a corresponding drop in the share of earnings in the total income of aged households (from over one-third in 1950 to less than one-fifth today). Rising pension and asset income and rapidly expanding Social Security benefits made retirement a more economically viable alternative to continued employment for the aged, and many responded by taking a large portion of their rising standard of living in the form of leisure. (The same phenomenon also occurred among men of age fifty-five to sixty-four, who have increasingly opted for early retirement.)

Although it is commonplace to present data on the aged as a group, as we have just done, averages by no means tell the whole story. In fact, they mask an extremely heterogeneous population, which spans more than thirty years of age and highly disparate economic conditions. For example, the effective per-capita income is considerably lower for those aged who live alone as opposed to couples, for the very aged as opposed to the young aged, and for minorities as opposed to whites. In general, the overall distribution of economic status among the aged is considerably more unequal than among the non-aged, and far more aged households have income levels that are considerably below average. These same low-income aged typically have little or no net worth, since aged persons with low income generally have been members of households with low earnings before retirement.

The aged are also more subject than the non-aged to economic insecurity, because of their great vulnerability to financial exigencies—most notably medical expenses—that can overstrain their resources. Medicare, despite its rapid past and projected growth, pays less than half of all the health-care costs of the aged and covers neither long-term care nor many acute-care needs. By and large, the households facing the greatest insecurity are those (numbering nearly half of all aged households) that have incomes between the poverty level and the average. Medicaid covers virtually all health-care costs, including nursing homes, for the poor aged; and the well-to-do generally have either sufficient income and assets or supplementary medical coverage to cover most contingencies. But those in between are generally dependent on Medicare alone, and for those people large medical expenses can be economically catastrophic.

What of the future? Is there any reason to believe that the overall relative economic status of the aged, or the distribution within the aged, will change over time, in the absence of major policy changes? Any answer to this question must, of course, be speculative, but we would venture a weak "yes" to the first part and a strong "yes" to the second. Past improvements in the overall relative economic status of the aged have largely been a result of public pensions and health-care financing programs, whose coverage greatly expanded and whose average benefits increased far more rapidly than earnings. Both of these trends have largely ceased. Indeed, the fact that average Social Security benefits for new retirees will grow more slowly than average earnings of the non-aged (for reasons described earlier) and that the aged will live longer, could exert significant downward pressure on the relative economic status of the aged as a group. This pressure will probably be offset to some extent by a more rapid (relative to average earnings) rise in private income for the newly aged, reflecting the expanded coverage of the labor force by private employer pensions in the 1970s, and the growing tax incentives being offered in the 1980s for investment in individual retirement savings. But it is unlikely that more rapidly rising private income will fully offset the sources of downward pressure. Whether the aged will choose/be able to increase their work effort in anticipation of relatively lower income from public sources and more remaining years of life remains the big unknown in any assessment of their future prospects.

Leaving aside the matter of averages, we need to note the strong likelihood of increased disparities in the future economic status of the aged. Unfortunately, the public sources of income that will be growing less rapidly than average earnings are far more important to the lower-income aged, while the private sources that will be growing more rapidly are far more important to the higher-income aged. By way of illustration, consider that Social Security and public assistance currently comprise nearly three-fourths of the income of those aged living below twice the poverty level, but only one-fifth for those with incomes in excess of three times the poverty level. In contrast, income from assets and private pensions is extremely highly concentrated among the well-to-do aged. As a result of these factors and the greater longevity of the aged, it appears highly likely that the economic status of those aged with less than average incomes will decline in the future relative to the non-aged, while the well-to-do aged will continue to realize relative gains.

NEEDED CHANGES IN PUBLIC POLICY

As we noted at the opening of this chapter, concern over the economic and fiscal developments that we have been examining has prompted a number of different and sometimes conflicting recommendations for change in current public policies. We have already touched on some of the possible changes in the preceding discussion; here, let us retrace our ground to see whether we have turned up compelling evidence for any one change over another.

As regards the first topic we examined, economic growth, we concluded that the projected demographic changes alone do not pose major obstacles to the continued growth of our economy and that, therefore, they make no urgent case for changes in policy to stimulate growth. But we did not consider the possibility that some such changes might still be deemed desirable, as a way of easing our society's adjustment to our demographic future. That is, it might be desirable to take steps to enlarge the future "economic pie" so that when we do come around to slicing it up—to making the necessary adjustments in the size of tax burdens relative to GNP and/or reducing the relative amount of per-capita transfers to the aged—everyone would end up with a bigger piece. Since this sounds terrific, one might well wonder: if public policy measures can further increase the long-run rate of economic growth, why shouldn't we adopt them? Or, more to the point, why haven't we already done so?

In fact, the "supply-side economics" of the Reagan administration has emphasized the promotion of long-run economic growth, primarily through decreasing government regulation and increasing private investment and capital formation. But such measures have their costs as well as their benefits, as the events of the past several years have shown. Relatively major changes in public policy that often compromise other public objectives are required to effect relatively minor and uncertain increases in the rate of long-term economic growth. Thus, it turned out that public concern over the environment curbed many of the administration's ambitions for the commercial development of our natural resources. And, similarly, while the large tax cuts intended to stimulate private investment may have paid off in the short run, they also contributed to huge trade and federal budget deficits, which pose potentially serious obstacles to longer-term economic growth.

The major philosophical issue with regard to growth-promotion policies in general, however, is most evident when they are successful: namely, that such policies entail sacrifices by current generations in order to provide a richer economic legacy to future ones. The higher productivity growth engendered by devoting a higher percentage of GNP to investment will eventually permit higher annual levels of both investment and consumption than would otherwise be possible, since the total national income will be higher. But in the interim (which may be several decades), the greater share of GNP being devoted to investment means that current generations must reduce their consumption. Whether this is desirable or not is obviously a question of values, the response to which our society is continuously defining and redefining. The issue for us here is the extent to which the particulars of our demographic future should bear on the question, and the answer seems to be "not much." Demographic changes should actually be contributing strongly to growth over the next several decades, and current law (the 1983 amendments to the Social Security Act) already provides for large future surpluses in the Social Security account, which may or may not further enhance growth.[2] Even after the baby-boomers retire, the strain on our resources should not be so great as to disadvantage future generations. On the contrary, likely rises in standards of living and the overall economic status of the aged should provide plenty of room to effect some combination of increased taxes on the working-age population and modification in public benefits for the aged, without necessitating any large reordering of public policy objectives.

One obvious thorn in this relatively rosy picture is the growing burden of health-care costs, but—as we have already noted—this issue would be on the policy agenda independent of any of the demographic phenomena we have been considering. Although some steps have been taken recently to slow health-care cost increases in public programs, far more public and private attention to cost restraint in the entire health-care system will be necessary in the future, regardless of our societal aging.

Large federal deficits are also a problem. They have temporarily created the illusion that we can eat more of our economic pie and augment it too. But if these deficits are not soon greatly reduced—in which case the necessary spending cuts and tax increases will restrict current consumption—they will shrink the pool of savings needed to finance private investment and, in turn, slow our long-term growth. Like health-care costs, this issue is already on the nation's agenda. It provides quite enough of a challenge to federal policy-makers concerned with the prospects for long-term economic growth, without need for reference to demographic concerns.

When we turn from the broad issue of long-term economic growth to the more particular issues of structural functioning, however, we find that demographic concerns serve as potentially powerful arguments for the need for policy changes. Of the four structural issues we have raised, only one—changes in consumer demand—can be regarded as self-correcting in any real sense. By and large, the issues posed by population distribution and the growth in private pensions are already on the federal policy agenda, and the demographic developments that we have been examining will undoubtedly raise their priority. Yet both issues are so intertwined with non-demographic policy concerns (urban policy, industrial policy, tax policy, etc.), we cannot here explore the merits of possible policy changes. Suffice it to note that our aging society will in itself argue strongly for some sort of change.

Of the last structural issue we have examined—the changing labor market—a little more can be said. We have already noted the general desirability of greater education and training for all future workers and of retaining older workers in the work force, in view of the relative scarcity of labor that will ensue in the next century. Increasing the labor-force participation on the part of older workers (or simply arresting its decline) would not only contribute to general economic growth; it would also reduce the need for the higher tax burdens that would otherwise be imposed on the non-aged working population to finance resource transfers to the aged. Older workers' increased participation might also be justified on the basis that the potential time spent in retirement has lengthened enormously in the past several decades (from 7 percent of adult life in 1940 to 25 percent today) and will continue to do so with greater life expectancy unless the trend toward earlier retirement is reversed.

Such an increase in labor-force participation and an accompanying reduction of resource transfers to older workers could occur either because the latter causes the former—that is, restrictions on eligibility or cuts in benefit levels compel older people to depend more on earnings—or because they might choose to work more of their own accord, which results in smaller transfers. The latter alternative would be an unambiguous good from any perspective. We argued earlier that, come the tight labor market early next century, employers will have incentives to encourage older workers to remain in the labor force, and will undoubtedly take steps to do so. But encouraging such a change—by the greater public funding of continuing education, by retraining older workers, or by promoting more flexible working arrangements—ought to be a priority for public policy in any case.

The issue of whether public policy should stop with this priority or whether it should effectively compel a postponement of retirement for able-bodied older workers brings us again to the question of the distribution of the fiscal burden created by the aging of our society.

As we have already noted, there will be some additional burden beyond what we are already carrying, even if the economy lives up to our most sanguine expectations, and even if a reasonable number of older workers in fact elect to postpone retirement. The question is: will our current policies for sharing resources prove equitable and practical in the face of this added burden?

On the one hand, it is difficult to argue that, on the whole, more generous policies toward the aged are warranted, since the aged as a group have achieved parity with the non-aged and should benefit nearly equally from future increases in standards of living. Indeed, for these same reasons, a creditable case can be made for some *reductions* in the generosity of current policies by early next century, in order to ease the growing fiscal pressures they will begin to place on public resources. On the other hand, it seems clear that there should be a substantial reorientation of public policies toward the aged with the object of continuing to improve the financial security of those with low and moderate incomes.

The core of the problem with current policies is that even the well-to-do aged come out far ahead when both taxes and public transfers are considered. The favorable treatment of the aged as a group may have made some sense in the past, when being aged was more or less synonymous with financial vulnerability, but it no longer does today. It is hard to justify the non-taxability of most Social Security benefits, or the additional tax exemption based solely on age, in the face of the general economic parity of today's elderly. Similarly, it is hard to justify huge Medicare subsidies for a person who will leave a million-dollar estate to his or her children. Consider too: tax incentives that heavily subsidize the retirement savings of upper-income households and provide meager help for moderate-income households serve only to deplete the tax revenues, while doing little to forestall the possibility of increased claims on those revenues. And what sense is there in urging tax subsidies for, and public expenditures on, generous pensions for early retirees, at a time when we want to encourage older workers to remain active in the labor force?

It seems to us that only after these obvious inequities and inefficiencies are dealt with does it make sense to consider across-the-board reductions in transfers—which would have the potential of increasing the labor-force participation of all the aged "involuntarily." In contrast to the "voluntary" increased labor-force participation of older workers, increases that result from reduced transfers have more ambiguous consequences and raise more difficult issues for public policy. The strong trend towards early retirement in the past several decades makes it clear that older persons place a high value on leisure when they feel they can afford it. The effective income of an older worker may not decline if he feels compelled to increase his hours of work to compensate for lower transfers, but his overall welfare surely does. Thus, while everyone benefits from "voluntary" participation, "involuntary" participation simply shifts the burden from the general tax-paying population to those whose benefits are cut. This is a political decision and, as such, we reserve it for future generations to make. Here let it suffice to note that there is considerable scope in our current system of public benefits to improve the prospective economic security of moderate- and lower-income aged, through such measures as catastrophic and long-term health care coverage, while still reducing the overall fiscal pressures posed by the demographic changes that lie ahead.

ENDNOTES

[1]The projections in Table 2 are based on the 1984 report of the actuaries for the Social Security and Medicare programs. The figures in this report already reflected a new and more restrictive prospective reimbursement system for hospital care under Medicare, which replaced the old "cost plus" reimbursement system in 1984. A more recent amendment has led to a freeze on physician fees and a further tightening of hospital reimbursement, which, when projected forward by the actuaries, show a significantly slower growth in Medicare outlays than reflected in Table 2. However, political support for this stringent reimbursement policy may not be sustainable.

[2]The issue here is a complicated one—too much so to explore in any depth here. In brief, the question hinges on the extent to which these Social Security trust fund surpluses—projected to accumulate to between 25 and 30 percent of GNP over the next thirty years—actually materialize, and to what degree they are offset by deficits in the remaining public accounts.

Alan Pifer

The Public Policy Response

T HINKING ABOUT THE AGING of our society is inevitably an exercise in creative conjecture. Although the impact of this phenomenon is already clearly evident, and much can be predicted about the future of societal aging from known demographic data, we cannot at this stage comprehend its full impact as it extends into the next century. Nor can we predict what the public policy response will be to the social and economic effects of population aging. It may be ungenerous, short-sighted, and blind to the human needs of an aging society, or it may be sensitive to those needs, ungrudging and carefully crafted with an eye to long-term effects. It may simply intensify our society's present faults, such as its mean-spiritedness toward the unfortunate and its improvidence in regard to children. Or perhaps in the response may be found the potential for a very much better society—a society that puts a high value on its children, is compassionate toward all of its members and fosters a sense of mutual obligation among them, as citizens in a national community. The future awaits our invention, to make of it what we will, aided by the powerful social and economic currents set in motion by the aging of the population.

The intent of this chapter is to outline the principal public policy issues that lie ahead for the nation as a consequence of population aging and then to speculate about the effect these issues may have both on the national process of public policy formation and on the public values that inform that process. What follows is more than pure guesswork, for well-established demographic trends tell us quite a bit about the future;

but it falls well short of being confident prediction, since the future is inevitably opaque and given to surprises.

Nor is this chapter prescriptive in nature. To set forth one's own views of what the public policy response *ought* to be is tempting. Nevertheless, the reader will have to decide for himself what that response should be after weighing the sum of the evidence, opinion, and speculation that has been presented in this entire volume.

Finally, although this chapter will deal essentially with responses in the public arena to the aging of the society, it should not be taken to suggest that there will not also be major private responses. The private sector, whether employers, voluntary and religious organizations, the family, or most of all, individuals, will play an important role. Indeed, since public policy is almost always deeply influenced by assumptions about anticipated non-governmental policies and actions, both in the business and non-profit sectors, its definition is necessarily somewhat broader than what government does through its laws, regulations, and so on. In regard to the financing of higher education, for example, public policy assumes substantial contributions by private philanthropy, parents, and students, engendering a comprehensive national policy under which any young person with the requisite ability can, theoretically, attend some sort of higher educational institution. It is this broader definition of public policy that I will use throughout this chapter, including in it even the matter of widely held values that undergird public policy and give it meaning.

PUBLIC POLICY FORMATION AND PUBLIC VALUES

As everyone knows, the process of public policy formation in the United States is an extraordinarily complex affair. Influenced by enduring American values, beliefs, prejudices, and myths, by the nation's economic, social, and governmental structures, by constitutional constraints, by the configuration of domestic and international problems and the social forces of the moment, by bureaucratic and "expert" cadres, by powerful interest groups motivated by self-interest or by passionate devotion to a cause, and even by random events or the chance appearance on, or disappearance from, the scene of charismatic political figures, public policy somehow gets argued out, traded out, and eventually formulated. Sometimes the results are good; it is inevitable that they are sometimes bad.

Naturally, this messy, haphazard, frequently tedious, often undemocratic, and at times seemingly mindless process leaves many Americans frustrated, irritated, and yearning for a tidier, speedier, more efficient, and more rational system. Yet only in periods of great emergency, such as during the Great Depression or World War II, when national purpose is clear to all and the citizenry is united to achieve that purpose, does the process of public policy formation operate with real dispatch and general effectiveness. In non-crisis periods it makes its laborious way onward, from time to time provoking calls for reform but little concrete action, partly because the balance of countervailing forces makes such action all but impossible, and partly because, as bad as the system can be, most Americans are skeptical that a better one can be found in a nation as large and diverse as this one.

A second characteristic of our public policy process is its short-sightedness—its general inability, because of annual budgetary cycles and the frequency of national elections, to look very far into the future, reckon with long-term economic and social trends, or anticipate the consequences for tomorrow of policies established to meet today's needs or political imperatives. Myopia in social-policy development has always been a problem in this country, and examples of it are legion. In an aging society, however, it is an even greater danger.

Public values, prejudices, and myths are embedded in the formation of public policy. One of the more interesting questions we can speculate about as we look into the future is what effect population aging will have on these cherished beliefs. During much of this century, there has been a tension between two very different sets of values in our public life. In the first, individual welfare is held to be essentially the responsibility of the individual: equality is defined as the opportunity for equal competition, however affected by prior advantage or disadvantage that opportunity may be; freedom entails freedom from governmental control, and the society that emerges from the neutral, unfettered workings of a free-market economy is deemed to be the best and most just. This set of values is firmly rooted in the work ethic and a belief that, except for the "deserving poor"—widows, orphans, and the disabled—need is *prima facie* evidence of moral delinquency.

The second set of values holds individual welfare to be the responsibility both of the individual and of the community at large.

Equality of opportunity is understood as requiring that competition be based on at least some degree of equality of condition at the starting post. By freedom is understood the provision by government of opportunities for self-realization through social and economic mobility. The good society is based on a restricted free-market economy in which government compensates for the market's failure to distribute goods and opportunities equitably and to provide uneconomic "public goods." This set of values assumes that the work ethic is valid only if opportunity for adequately paid work is available, and it understands that social and economic conditions are more likely to be the cause of need than is moral imperfection.

I have presented these value systems as polar opposites. In practice, however, especially since the 1930s, the debate has centered less on *whether* government should perform a social role at all than on the *nature* and *extent* of that role. Nonetheless, the two sets of values, the one associated with individual responsibility and a free-market economy, the other with collective responsibility and government intervention, are clearly there; and each is sufficiently distinct to produce different public policy outcomes when it dominates in government. Indeed, in the period since the New Deal, public policy has oscillated between these two value orientations in a kind of cyclical pattern as the public mood has shifted and as national administrations have come and gone. The past few years, for example, have seen an apparent swing of the pendulum to the right— an oscillation more extreme than any others of the past half-century—back to a type of nineteenth-century belief that a largely unrestricted market and individual self-reliance (supplemented in exceptional cases of need by public and private charity) are sufficient to guarantee a good society.

The issue, then, is how the social and economic forces generated by population aging may, in the years ahead, affect these current assumptions. Will they help to perpetuate the present individualistic, social Darwinian, distrust-of-government philosophy as an approach to social issues; or will they serve to move the nation back to a more collectivist approach based on faith in government and a recognition by all citizens of mutual obligation and responsibility to each other within a national community?

FOUR ISSUES

There are several ways to classify the public policy issues that will arise from the continuous aging of our population. The issues can be classified according to distinctive population groups—children, women, minorities, baby-boomers, the frail elderly. They can also be categorized by province—health-care system, labor force, economy, political arena, educational system. Each of these approaches is useful in fostering understanding of the total impact of population aging on the nation's life, and each is therefore valid.

An even more illuminating approach, perhaps, is to seek out some broad, cross-cutting themes that can encompass these more specific categories. Four such broad issues come to mind. The first is the question of how to achieve the wisest possible use of resources in an aging and resource-limited society. The second is the matter of how to use our growing numbers of older citizens productively. The third is the issue of who is responsible for meeting the new social needs population aging creates. The fourth is the issue of what, in an aging nation, constitutes equity among the generations, and how this equity can be achieved. These four themes—the use of resources, the productivity of older citizens, the locus of responsibility, and intergenerational equity—are related and to some degree overlap, but they are essentially different in their thrusts, and merit separate examination.

The Use of Resources

In a rapidly aging society, how can we make sure that we not spend so much in responding to the claims of the elderly that we are unable to meet the needs of other groups, such as children? As previous chapters in this volume have shown, there has already been in this country a substantial decline in public spending on children and a sharp increase in spending on older Americans. This reversal of priorities does not seem to have come about as a result of a deliberate public policy decision to benefit the elderly at the expense of children. Such a tradeoff is hardly necessary, since the few billions needed to broaden the support of children could, if the will were there, certainly be found in a wealthy nation such as ours, without seriously penalizing the elderly.

This shift in priority, rather, seems to reflect other factors: demographic change—we have more elderly people and far fewer families with a direct interest in children; racism—a steadily increasing proportion of those children who are being born are of minority background; political ideology—a decline of interest in social programs generally; and, finally, a general heedlessness of the longer-term effects any society will experience if it neglects its children.

There are, however, some signs that the nation may be on the verge of awakening to the consequences of the systematic neglect of children. Mounting concern in many states today about the relationship between poor education and low economic growth is evidence that at least one aspect of the development of children is being reconsidered. It is just possible that this concern may in time stimulate a more general interest in the overall welfare of children, since educational attainment and other factors such as poverty, health care, nutrition, and home environment are so closely linked.

There is also a growing public understanding that the costs to society of *not* investing in children are far greater than the costs of doing so. It presently costs about $40,000 per year to keep a person incarcerated in the New York State prison system and, presumably, comparable amounts in many other states. This translates into an expenditure, from tax revenues, of over a million dollars per head for prisoners serving long-term sentences or recidivists who are re-sentenced a number of times. A case could be made that funds of this magnitude spent on programs that would help young people get off to a better start in life would clearly reduce the costs of crime later, since many young people turn to crime for lack of other opportunity. The elderly, who have the greatest fear of crime and who are often its most vulnerable targets, should be particularly sensitive to this.

The most powerful case, however, for investing in children during the next couple of decades, is that the nation will be enormously dependent on them as prime-aged workers when the baby-boom generation begins leaving the work force two to three decades from now. Because of the demographic twist of a period of exceptionally high fertility being followed by a sustained period of low fertility, today's and tomorrow's children promise to be the most heavily burdened generation in the nation's history. On their small numbers will depend the vitality of the economy, the defense of the nation, and the support of the elderly and children of that time. While this pressure may be eased to some extent by immigration, increases in productivity due to changing technology, and longer working lives for older workers, the burden will nonetheless be heavy. Given these circumstances, it is simple common sense for the nation to do all in its power to prevent casualties among today's children, casualties that would be yet another burden on their own generation.

This is not to suggest that such failures cannot be salvaged later. We know that this is possible, sometimes through heroic individual effort. On the whole, however, such a salvage operation requires substantial public investment, and this is something the nation presently seems unwilling to make, at least in regard to the needs of minority youth who have never held a job and, unless circumstances change, probably never will. Given a choice, it is a far more efficient investment to prevent failure in the first place.

An interesting question, as one speculates about children in the aging society, is how they will be regarded by the maturing baby-boom generation. At present, the baby-boomers seem to be almost totally preoccupied with their own lives and welfare, but as they age and many of them begin to understand how very difficult it is to save enough to ensure their own security in old age, it seems possible that they may begin to take an interest in the generation behind them—the generation that will have to pay the taxes to keep Social Security viable and provide adequate medical protection for them in their old age. If this proves to be the case, we may perhaps see a substantial reversal in public attitudes—given the numbers and influence of the baby-boomers—toward governmental social programs designed to benefit children, even including support for more generous assistance to single-parent families with children growing up in dire poverty. It may be that pure self-interest on the part of a major sector of the population, rather than some sort of fortuitous rebirth of generosity of spirit, may become the instigator of a more humane, more caring society, and one that is more provident of its human resources.

There is not necessarily a trade-off between spending on the elderly and spending on children. Yet the general question of how much we can afford to spend on the elderly, in view of the sharp rise in the cost of their benefits and the present federal budget deficit, is certainly on the national agenda. This raises the politically sensitive question of whether benefits for the elderly should be based on age or need. It is an article of faith with many social-welfare advocates that, once programs for the elderly are put on a needs basis—that is, once they become welfare rather than general entitlement programs—they will deteriorate. Programs for the poor, it is said, automatically become poor programs, and evidence from the experience with AFDC and Medicaid is cited to confirm this.

To the left of these advocates are critics who believe that, with poverty still a serious national problem, need should be the primary criterion for all public benefits. To the right are other critics who hold the same view on the grounds that general entitlement programs represent unnecessary and wasteful public expenditure. There is still another group that believes that age alone should never be a criterion for the award of public benefits because we should be moving toward an "age irrelevant" society that recognizes the possibility of continuing human development over the lifespan. People in this group maintain that there is no organizing principle that necessarily causes programs to be good or bad. In a democracy, they say, quality is determined by what the people, by and large, want it to be.

Nonetheless, assuming a substantial federal budget deficit extending well into the future, and a continued rise in spending on the elderly due to their increasing numbers and lengthening lifespans, the age versus need issue does seem to be inescapable. And nowhere will this issue be sharper than in the health field, where Medicare costs have risen at a staggering rate and where long-term care benefits, under Medicaid, are already granted only on the basis of need. Although the nation could very well design an efficient, cost-controlled, humane health insurance program for itself if it chose to, one wonders, as things stand now, what Medicare, which treats the elderly with considerable decency and dignity, might be like if put on the same needs-based footing as Medicaid. If this were to happen, it seems probable that we would soon see the development of a two-tier system of health care for the elderly—a second-class version for those who depend on public benefits, and a first-class version for those with personal resources or private insurance. At the moment, however, it seems more likely that Medicare will be gradually modified, by a process of increased user charges, into a program that lower-income people will be unable to take advantage of. This process, in fact, seems already to have begun.

Aside from the specific issue of the future of Medicare, we face a broader question of whether the United States, with an aging society and limited resources, can afford to spend as much as it is now spending on health care of the elderly generally. This is a subset of the even larger issue of whether we can continue to spend about 11 percent of our GNP, or $387 billion (1984), on the health care of the entire population without inhibiting economic growth, especially when some other developed nations spend only half as much per capita while apparently enjoying equally good health.

It can, of course, be argued that spending on the health care of children—of which there is far too little, since some children receive no care at all—and, to a lesser extent, of prime-age workers, is an *investment* in human resource development. That is a cogent argument, and the only question then is whether the nation is getting full value for the amount spent. Spending on health care for the elderly, however, must be regarded primarily as *consumption*, and since this now represents a very considerable sum—about a third of total personal health-care expenditures—the issue is a serious one.

Limiting health expenditure on the elderly, however, raises some very sensitive issues. One obvious way to accomplish this would be to ration expensive therapies such as organ transplants, artificial organs, and replacement joints. But on what basis would this be done? Age alone? Some arbitrary number of anticipated years of a good quality of life? The value of the patient to society? The patient's ability to provide private payment? The availability of treatment? All present difficulties. Who, for example, is to say that a sixty-five year old is less deserving than a sixty-four year old, or that a janitor is less deserving than a corporation chairman? Can the future quality of life be accurately predicted? Is it right to allow the rich to live longer or to suffer less than the poor, or to provide treatment to a resident of a well-to-do suburb while denying it to someone who lives in a poverty-stricken, medically underserved inner-city or rural area?

Unless the issue of rationing is explicitly faced, however, the inequities and the moral dilemmas it presents can only become more acute as the numbers of elderly increase. Meanwhile, the de facto rationing system already in place, based on ability to pay, will surely grow and will constitute an ever greater compromise of the nation's moral integrity.

A second very sensitive issue is society's heavy expenditure on life-extending technologies for elderly patients who will die soon, in any case, or whose quality of life has deteriorated to a point where life itself has become meaningless. This issue will continue to grow until a patient's right to terminate his or her life by prior will is legally recognized, and until abuse-proof legal procedures are established under which a physician and a patient's family can arrange the death of a brain-dead patient.

More difficult is the issue of patients who, because of senility or other disease, have become totally incompetent but may live on for years in a long-term care facility at enormous expense, using up funds that may be needed by families for their children. There may be those who will propose that legal ways be found to terminate the lives of such patients, but such a course could set our society on a very undesirable slippery slope.

Finally, the question is sometimes raised of whether it is right for the nation to spend so much money on medical research whose sole object appears to be extending the lifespan of the elderly. The paradox here, of course, is that new kinds of treatment that emerge from such research may save the lives of people of all ages. The proper issue is whether to minister to declining elderly patients merely for the sake of keeping them alive, without regard for the quality of life they may subsequently enjoy.

The question of whether the United States spends too much on medical research generally is a wholly separate issue, relevant to a discussion of the aging society only if one believes that endeavoring to decrease mortality, because this adds to life expectancy, is in itself a wrong. In the past, increases in life expectancy were attributable largely to declining infant mortality; in the future, aside from the possibility of reducing the death rate of young males from accidents and homicide, such gains will be attributable more to the eradication of the major killers of the elderly—heart disease, stroke, and cancer. Here again the problem is that these conditions also affect younger people, and clearly we are a long way from wanting to limit their life spans in order to prevent breakthroughs that cause numbers of the elderly to live much longer.

When all these considerations are added up, the question of what is the optimal distribution of resources remains. Is the nation already spending so much on the health care of older people that other areas of vital national interest are being deprived? What of the future as the population ages further? And what will our lives be like if the major medical advances predicted by the Nobel prize–winning geneticist

Joshua Lederberg come about? In a speech in Philadelphia in 1983 he said:

> Will the knowledge result in the reduction of health care costs? Not at all. Not because the DNA-based technologies are going to be expensive—by and large, they will not. What will happen is simply the alleviation of one misery after another that we are eager to shed—we want to be cured, we don't want to die of cancer, we don't want our loved ones to suffer from psychiatric disease, we don't want to have heart attacks—and at the present time we will do almost anything individually to deal with any one of these circumstances. And we will be able to provide large answers to many of them. But we will go on living. And we will get older.

> The end result is that the nursing care of many individuals between their tenth and fifteenth decades is going to be the largest cost connected with the elaboration of health technology. There is no way around that.

The Productivity of Older Citizens

The startling increases in longevity that we have experienced in recent decades have forced us to develop wholly new perspectives on the human lifespan. A person at the age of fifty, instead of being close to the end of life, may have nearly half his life still to live, and can look forward to the likelihood of at least a quarter of a century more of vigor and good health. In many cases, a newly retired worker can anticipate half as many years again in retirement as he spent in employment. Four-generation families have become commonplace, and most children of living parents are now adults. These and other changes shed a totally new light on the planning of the life course.

Many prevailing attitudes, however, left over from earlier times, are totally out of kilter with these new realities. In the popular view, a person past sixty-five is still considered to be "over the hill," "past it," "ready to be put out to pasture," and so on—in short, already suffering from bad health, diminished physical vigor, and declining mental acuity. Such a person is also assumed, by the very fact of reaching the magic age of sixty-five, to have achieved the status of veteranship in the society, and therefore entitlement to various special dispensations and privileges. Finally, it is generally assumed that the older person, by the very act of retiring, has automatically become impoverished.

A person *may* be over the hill at sixty-five and *may* be poor. Some are. But for the vast majority of past–sixty-fives, this popular stereotype is obsolete and inappropriate: they are still vigorous, healthy, mentally alert, capable of learning new things, and far from impoverished. The conferring of veteranship on this group is patronizing, demeaning, even insulting, and certainly unwanted. Its members are no different from Americans generally, and they wish to be treated that way. What is needed is a fundamental change of popular attitudes to abolish the now-irrelevant mystique of age sixty-five. Until such a change of outlook takes place, it will be almost impossible to put into place new public policies appropriate to the changes that have taken place in the human life course.

A helpful start would be to establish in the public mind a simple new concept that embodies, even if only symbolically, the new situation. I have recently proposed such a concept, which I call the "third quarter of life"—the years from about fifty to seventy-five. This notion assumes that everyone is now going to live to the age of one hundred—a somewhat tongue-in-cheek suggestion, although more and more people are, in fact, going to reach that age. It rests also on empirical observation that significant changes take place in the lives of many people who are in their early fifties. Their children are likely to have grown up and left home. They have probably reached their maximum level of advancement in their employment and their highest level of real earnings. They may well be bored and restless and feel the need of a career change—a "repotting"—but feel trapped in their present employment because of a lack of financial resources to facilitate a change, or by the prospect of a pension if they hang on for a few more years. The result is dispirited workers (who gradually become embittered as younger colleagues overtake them), loss of productivity, and problems for employers who would like to ease such people out but fear age-discrimination suits. This picture is, of course, something of a sterotype in itself and obviously applies more to male and to white-collar than other types of workers. Nevertheless, one can see large numbers of people who fit the mold.

The upper end of the third-quarter concept is determined by the readily observable fact that most people today are vigorous, in good health, mentally alert, and capable of making a productive contribution until they are at least seventy-five. This may be a bit on the high side for some, but not for most.

A significant proportion of the population, about 20 percent, or some 50 million people, falls within the third quarter today. What is especially startling is that, by the year 2010—only twenty-five years from now—some *85 million Americans* will be in the third quarter, and they will comprise close to a third of the population! How the nation is going to deal with this large group of citizens, and what opportunities it will offer them to stay in the mainstream of its life therefore constitutes a public policy issue of immense magnitude.

One could, of course, simply let the present situation drift on, with the pool of older, discouraged workers gradually increasing over the next decade and very rapidly thereafter, as the leading edge of the baby boom reaches fifty, and with employers using every device at their disposal to induce as many of this group as possible to take early retirement. This is what may well happen, but the costs of such inaction will be high.

In the first place, a large number of experienced workers who could, in the right circumstances, continue to make a valuable contribution to the productivity of the nation and the quality of its life will disappear from the labor force. Second, substantial income- and Social Security–tax revenues on their earnings will be forfeited. And, third, those who retire at sixty-two will start using their Social Security benefits earlier than they otherwise would.

Remaining productive during the third quarter of life does not, of course, necessarily mean continuing in paid full-time employment over that entire span. The concept implies a new definition of productivity—one based on accomplishment rather than on monetary compensation, and one that includes full- and part-time volunteer work as well as full- and part-time paid employment. What is important is that all of the employment be *productive*—that is, that it contribute something significant to the economy or to the quality of life. This means that even volunteer work must be well-organized, serious, and consist of real, if unpaid, jobs.

If the third-quarter concept became publicly accepted, it would stimulate a wide range of public and private responses, all aimed at enabling third-quarter Americans to remain productive. These responses could include efforts by employers to retrain older workers so that they could be transferred into new jobs that would provide a fresh stimulus. Certainly, under the new concept, all retraining programs, whether in industry or government, would be opened up to workers past fifty. Another high-priority response would be to change both public and private pension programs to make partial retirement possible. Still a third possibility might be to allow people to borrow against their Social Security benefits in order to finance their retraining or enrollment in wholly new educational programs. Under such an arrangement, a person might borrow, say, two years of benefits, which would be repaid by deferring for a similar period the right to qualify for them. (Social Security tax would, of course, have to continue to be paid in order not to penalize other contributors to the system.) An alternative would be the building up of individual retraining reserves or accounts under Social Security, financed by joint employer/employee contributions—a development that would recognize the huge impact increased life expectancy has had, and will continue to have, on our economy and society.

It seems probable that if these or other changes one might envisage to loosen up the rigidities of our present system were instituted, there might be a considerable demand from third-quarter people, not only to seek short-term retraining opportunities, but to enroll in demanding higher educational programs, especially those that might provide a professional degree. Colleges and universities would then have to devise special programs to meet the needs of such students.

Finally, government at all levels might find it feasible to organize public-service employment programs for older workers along the lines of the present successful Federal Senior Community Service Employment Program. The intent of such efforts would be to provide modestly paid work to older unemployed workers, those who want to defer retirement, or those who need to supplement their retirement benefits. This work might consist of taking care of the frail elderly and helping disadvantaged children, since no end of such work is needed. In order for such programs to be instituted, the present prejudice against public-service employment would have to be overcome. This might be achieved if it could be shown that when the costs of forfeited unemployment compensation, disability insurance, and Social Security entitlements are added to the value of the Social Security and income taxes paid, as well as to the benefits of the work performed, and when all these "assets" are then balanced against the cost of the programs, the net result would be a highly favorable cost/benefit ratio.

A possible objection to the third-quarter concept is that it might be perceived to conflict with the urgent need to find work for unemployed youth. This is possible at the margins, but in the main the kind of work that third-quarter people would be seeking, and for which they would be best qualified, would well exceed the qualification range of entry-level workers. It is also the case, as has been pointed out in previous chapters of this book, that there is likely to be a severe shortage of entry-level workers as members of the baby-dearth generation begin to enter the labor force. If serious efforts are made to prepare unemployed young people for employment, this favorable labor market situation could ease this problem considerably.

The third-quarter-of-life concept is not a universal panacea. Like all social ideas, it has its faults. Its principal weakness, it has been pointed out to me, is that it introduces yet another age-based construct into what ought to be an age-irrelevant society. It does have the virtue, nevertheless, of being infinitely more flexible than our present rigid system based on a mystique of age sixty-five, and it opens up exciting possibilities for change. Immense social and economic pressures will arise in the early decades of the next century as a result of an unprecedented explosion in the numbers of energetic, healthy, well-educated, and self-confident older Americans, and these will require a major response in both the public and private sectors of our national life.

WHO IS RESPONSIBLE?

As the population ages further, questions of responsibility will become increasingly urgent. This situation is not peculiar to an aging society: the issue of who should be responsible for what kinds of social action exists in every society. Should it be government? Private employers? The voluntary sector? The family? The individual? All are possible candidates, and each of these groups has its advocates. There are still other people who suggest that responsibility does not have to be assigned—that if the market is allowed to operate in an unfettered manner, its workings will automatically produce a good society. At the opposite pole are those who have so little faith in the private sector and individual initiative they would leave everything to government.

An aging population does present some issues that are new, and others that have not previously been considered important. It raises, as well, some hard questions about the traditional processes of public policy formation in a democratic society. There is, for example, the question of who is responsible for children. In the past, the answer would clearly have been, first, the family; followed by the state, insomuch as it provides public education, protective care for the severely handicapped, and income support for those born into poor, single-parent families; and, finally, voluntary agencies, which provide supplementary welfare services.

In the aging society, however, growing numbers of elderly citizens and a steadily declining proportion of children (a decline that could become even more precipitous if the fertility rate continues to drop) could require government—especially the federal government—to assume a much greater degree of responsibility for the young. With any luck, children may come to be recognized as the nation's most valuable resource, and conservation and development of that resource may be seen as a high-priority *national* objective. Such a changed outlook could elicit measures such as a federal family allowance program along European lines, the instituting of comprehensive child health and nutrition programs, a vast expansion of federal aid to education, federally imposed standards for AFDC payments, and even, in the extreme, a system of public boarding schools for children from severely disadvantaged backgrounds.

The health-care field offers further examples of the ways population aging may pose—indeed is already posing—new questions about responsibility. Who, for instance, should be responsible for the costs of long-term care for those frail elderly who can no longer stay in their homes and must be institutionalized? Should not their children provide the necessary support rather than spending their money on vacations and other attributes of a comfortable lifestyle? But suppose "the children,"—as may well be the case—are widowed, divorced, or never-married single women in their sixties or even seventies who are themselves just barely keeping afloat financially? Or suppose "the children" are of an age where they are faced with a stark choice between aiding their elderly parents and sending their own children to college?

One could say that the long-term care responsibility issue has already been decided in the provision of Medicaid benefits, but that is indeed an inadequate answer, since it forces the recipients of such care to pauperize themselves before they can become eligible for benefits. It is a fairly safe conjecture that, as the numbers of institutionalized, very elderly citizens increases, pressure will grow to regard their support as a collective, communal effort to be made by government in a decent, humane, and dignified manner. The costs of such a change, however, will be enormous.

Another example arising in the health-care field is an issue I have already discussed in another context: the termination of life. This subject is presently in a state of considerable confusion: physicians and other health-care workers are liable in some situations to be prosecuted for manslaughter, but not in others where death is skillfully "negotiated" by families, physicians, and lawyers. State law is already beginning to penetrate into this area, and the possibility is likely that in different states, quite different standards will be established.

Now it is one thing to have differing state laws on, say, the minimum drinking age (although even there Congress has interceded to try to impose a national standard). But it is quite another matter to have differing state laws governing the termination of life. It seems inevitable that the federal government will, at some point, have to intervene, and to accept responsibility for the development of a nation-wide solution to the problem. In any event, the increasing urgency of the issue—due to the proliferation of new life-extending technologies and the increasing population of very old people—has forced the issue beyond the realm of purely private responsibility.

Three other examples are to be found in the area of preventive health care. In an aging society that is experiencing steadily rising health-care costs, the question of prevention assumes an importance it has never been accorded in the past. One issue is to what degree corporations should be held responsible for the health-care costs stemming from products that are damaging to public health. A second is the degree to which individuals should be held responsible for protecting their own health—for example, by not smoking. A third is the question of educating the public about health mainte-nance and disease prevention. Physicians are still being trained almost exclusively to treat disease, not to maintain health. But in an aging society, the emphasis will clearly need to shift to helping individuals to stay healthy as long as possible; this will require a different set of attitudes both on the part of the public and within the health-care professions.

Perhaps the most crucial question raised by this whole issue of responsibility is just who ought to be providing retirement security for the elderly generally. Should this responsibility be assumed entirely by government? Or, rather, should the responsibility fall on individuals, families, employers, or some combination of these? Before 1935, planning for retirement lay almost entirely in the hands of individuals and families. There was no Social Security, and few private pension plans. Even Social Security, when it was first instituted in 1935, provided only a partial answer to old-age security, and only for some workers. As the years have gone by, however, increases in both its benefit and inclusion levels have created a widespread understanding that the program's retirement benefits are meant to provide adequate income to everyone past retirement age.

Private pension plans have meanwhile, in the past twenty-five years or so, been expanding so rapidly that today some 31 percent of the work force has vested rights in such pensions. For many retirees, in fact, these private benefits are considered the primary form of old-age security, with Social Security regarded as simply supplementary. This new situation was formally acknowledged in 1984, when Social Security benefits were, for the first time, assessed as taxable income for single retirees with an adjusted income of over $25,000, and for couples with a combined income of over $32,000.

In recent years, the federal government has taken further measures to encourage individuals to take responsibility for themselves in their old age, by granting special tax incentives for personal savings. This option has great appeal to many young workers who, because of the Social Security reserve fund "crisis" in 1982, have had their faith in the system shaken. Some conservatives would like to see Social Security scrapped altogether and supplanted by private pensions and individual savings.

The question, then, is how further population aging, especially when it will start accelerating rapidly as the baby-boomers begin to retire in large numbers about the year 2010, will affect the question of responsibility for retirement security. Will the Social Security system remain intact and, indeed, be expanded to insure adequate retirement income for everyone? Or will it, despite the eloquent protestations of politicians of both parties, be allowed gradually to erode?

For the time being, we have been assured by the National Commission on Social Security Reform that the program will be sound financially well into the next century. If that prediction is wrong and there is another "crisis," steps might conceivably be taken that would make eligibility for benefits subject to a means test, which would change Social Security into a welfare program for the elderly poor while encouraging the balance of the population to seek its protection in private plans and individual savings. Many people will be sorry to see this happen, but the taxes required to keep the program on a universal footing may prove such a heavy burden on the small numbers of prime-age workers after the turn of the century that they will simply refuse to keep it adequately financed.

Until recently, improvements in Social Security benefits and coverage, the additions of Medicare, Medicaid, SSI, and services provided under the Older Americans Act seemed to have settled forever the question of responsibility for the elderly. It was clearly to be a collective responsibility of the entire population, exercised through the national government. It was to be protection to which every elderly citizen was *entitled,* simply by virtue of age. It is possible this basic national decision will continue to hold for the indefinite future, but one can no longer be absolutely sure of it. Over time, population aging will, along with other forces, unquestionably subject the decision to immense pressure.

INTERGENERATIONAL EQUITY

There has been a certain amount of talk recently about the issue of intergenerational equity, or more precisely, intergenerational inequity. The general tenor of the discussion, the thrust of which is that younger age groups have been unfairly treated by older groups, has been marked by language of conflict and retaliation, and the use of such terms as "intergenerational rivalry" or even "the war between the generations." The allegation is being made by some young people that older generations of Americans have initiated public policies that have greatly benefited themselves at the expense of successor generations, which are now left with a crushing future financial burden and much less favorable life prospects. One might cite in this regard the manner in which we are presently financing the huge federal budget deficit with foreign borrowing that will have to be paid off by our children. Or one could call attention to the change, in recent years, from the use of grants to loans as the principal way of financing the cost of higher education—a practice that passes the burden from the old to the young. In 1975, loans constituted just 20.7 percent of federal student aid; by 1983 they were 61.4 percent.

While there appears, therefore, to be some truth to the claim of intergenerational inequity, the general argument that one generation cynically makes decisions it knows will benefit itself at the expense of future generations would be difficult to sustain. Every age has its opportunities and its problems, and in a democracy such as ours elected officials generally make the best decisions they can, given the knowledge available to them at the time. Some decisions turn out to be dreadful mistakes, but this is more often a result of lack of forethought in our process of public policy formation than deliberate exploitation of one generation by another.

There is, however, a legitimate concern about whether public officials, because of the voting strength of the elderly, may not divert too much public money in their direction, and too little towards other groups that lack voting strength—especially children. While it is appropriate to consider this issue in the context of wise use of resources, as we have done earlier in this chapter, it is also an equity issue that has several sharp edges to it.

There is a question, for example, of whether minorities are being fairly treated in our aging society. While it is true that some blacks live long enough to take advantage of Medicare and Social Security retirement benefits, many do not because their life expectancy at birth is some five years less than that of whites. In spite of this, black workers contribute payroll taxes to the financing of these programs at the same rate as whites. Partially offsetting this inequity is the fact that, proportionately, blacks benefit more than whites from Medicaid and disability insurance.

Obviously, the solution to this problem is not to establish separate, lower contribution rates for blacks, as this would raise the same equity problem in reverse that bedeviled the many private pension programs that paid lower benefits to women because of their greater longevity. The best answer in this case would be for the elderly, who as a group are predominantly middle-class and white, to give their support to public programs that disproportionately benefit low-income blacks, especially to urban school systems that have large minority populations. Such visible support for something of great matter to most blacks—good education for their children—might serve to head off a rising perception in the community of unfairness in the regressive Social Security payroll tax, which is far more of a burden to low-income workers than the partially progressive income tax. Thus, an implicit "deal" might be struck between young workers of minority background and the white elderly, in which support for the retirement benefits of one group is exchanged for support of schools for the other.

In the case of Hispanics, where there is no evidence that life expectancy is less than it is for the majority white population, the equity issue arises from the demographic characteristics of the several different Hispanic groups. Since, except for Cubans, these groups are predominantly composed of young people, their interest is heavily in programs that benefit children, especially adequate financing for good education in inner-city schools. Here again the white elderly would be well advised to offer their support for such expenditures as a *quid pro quo* for continued Hispanic support for heavy public spending in programs for the elderly.

The most far-reaching intergenerational equity issue, however, may arise in the early decades of the next century, when the large baby-boom generation retires and must have its Social Security retirement and Medicare benefits provided by the very small baby-dearth generation that will then be in their prime working years. The question then will be whether the young workers who will constitute that generation will rebel against the traditional unwritten compact under which each generation supports the one above it in exchange for support in its own old age by the generation below it. Such a decision would, of course, sound the death knell of Social Security.

THE IMPACT OF POPULATION AGING ON PUBLIC VALUES AND PUBLIC POLICY

This new demographic phenomenon we are discussing is creating an enormous social agenda for the nation that will occupy its attention for the balance of this century and well into the next, and will involve every American and virtually every public and private institution. As suggested at the outset of this chapter, the public policy response may largely take the form of reliance on individual initiative and the operation of the free market. If this occurs, I would predict an intensification of the problems caused by population aging, economic hardship for large numbers, growing social unrest, and a serious decline in the nation's inner strength. These consequences would stem from the disintegration of a sense of national community, a sense by which all groups in a society are aware of their responsibilities to each other and are willing to make the sacrifices necessary to meet those responsibilities.

I believe a more likely response will involve heavy reliance on the institutions of government, based on a growing understanding on the part of the citizenry that in a society as complex as ours, there are many problems that simply lie beyond the reach either of individual institutions or of the market.

Such a conclusion does not indicate any denial of the importance of individual responsibility in a free society or of a modified free market as the basis of the economic system. These will surely be necessary to maintain the economic strength required to provide a decent standard of living for everyone. But they cannot be counted on either to guarantee a sufficient degree of fairness to ensure social cohesion or to tackle many of the nation's most urgent problems. For these purposes, collective action will be obligatory, and the challenge will be to make the powerful instrument we possess in the institutions of government, especially in our federal government, serve the nation's purposes efficiently and effectively.

I raised the question at the outset of how the social and economic forces attendant on population aging may affect the process by which public policy is formed in this country. It would be optimistic, indeed, to predict that the impact will necessarily compel the emergence of some new and better system. And yet the impact will be so great, and the problems involved so novel, that the public policy response may well inspire major opportunities for reform.

It is possible that new types of advisory, quasi-judicial, or arbitrative bodies may develop to provide protected environments for the nonpartisan, disinterested exploration of sensitive new issues arising from population aging—issues that would only be exacerbated if subjected too early to the rough and tumble of the traditional process of public policy formation. The President's Panel on Medical Ethics might, perhaps, be considered a forerunner of such bodies. Another example, at the state level, may be the Advisory Committee on Life and the Law recently set up by the governor of New York to study and make recommendations in regard to such controversial issues as the termination of life.

It is clear at any event that the rapid pace of population aging has already made some of our existing social and political structures largely obsolete and is creating a need for the invention of new, more flexible, structures capable of developing new public policies and facilitating their implementation. Social engineering of this kind deserves our highest attention.

Despite the many complex and serious problems that will follow in the train of population aging, it is by no means certain that the considerably more aged American society of the future will be a less vigorous, less imaginative, less courageous society than our present one. On the contrary, it may have all of these attributes in equal measure and, in addition, be a much better society in other respects— more humane, more reflective, more far-sighted, more mature in its outlook, more concerned about the welfare of the entire community, even, perhaps, about the welfare of the world community.

We must not lose sight of two realities as we contemplate the future. First, we have to remember that future Americans of all ages, but especially older ones, will be different people—people with *different* capabilities and *different* outlooks from their predecessors. Second, we must never forget that the shape of what lies ahead is not preordained. We have the power both to invent the future we would like for our aging society and to bring that creation into being. In these two respects, the making of new public policy to respond to population aging now offers us as demanding a challenge as any we have faced since the founding of the Republic. It is an exciting prospect.

Notes on Contributors

W. Andrew Achenbaum, born in 1947 in Philadelphia, Pennsylvania, is professor of history at Carnegie-Mellon University and senior scholar at the University of Michigan's Institute of Gerontology. He is the author of *Old Age in the New Land* (1978), and *Shades of Gray* (1983), and co-editor, with Walter I. Trattner, of *Social Welfare in America: An Annotated Bibliography* (1983).

Jerome L. Avorn, born in 1948 in New York City, is associate professor of social medicine and health policy at the Harvard Medical School and attending physician at Beth Israel Hospital. He is the author of *Up Against the Ivy Wall: A History of the Columbia Crisis* (1968), co-author, with S.B. Soumerai, of *Social Medicine in the Developing World: An Introduction* (1983), and co-editor, with A. Caplan, of *Case Studies in Ethics and Geriatric Practices* (forthcoming).

James E. Birren, born in 1918 in Chicago, Illinois, is executive director and dean of the Andrus Gerontology Center, University of Southern California (Los Angeles). He is the author of *Psychology of Aging* (1964) and co-editor of the *Handbook of Mental Health and Aging* (1980), and *Handbook of the Psychology of Aging* (1985).

Lydia Bronte, born in 1938 in Memphis, Tennessee, is a consultant and staff director for the Aging Society Project at the Carnegie Corporation of New York. She is the author of two working papers for the Rockefeller Foundation, and eleven National Humanities Series Bibliographies.

Daniel Callahan, born in 1930 in Washington, D.C., is director of the Hastings Center in New York. His primary research is in biomedical ethics. He is the author of *The Tyranny of Survival* (1974), *Ethics, The Social Sciences, and Policy Analysis* (1983), and *Abortion: Understanding Difference* (1984).

Karen Davis, born in 1942 in Blackwell, Oklahoma, is chairman of the Department of Health Policy and Management at the Johns Hopkins School of Hygiene and Public Health, where she is professor of political economy. She is the author of numerous articles on health economics and policy analysis, and of a forthcoming book, with Diane Rowland, *Medicare Policy: New Directions for Health and Long-Term Care.*

Rose Campbell Gibson, born in 1925 in Detroit, Michigan, is associate professor at the University of Michigan. A former U.S. Public Health Fellow (1980), she is the author of numerous articles and monographs, including "Blacks at Mid and Late Life," in the *Annals of the American Academy of Political and Social Science* (1982) and "Work and Retirement Among the Black Elderly in Zena Blau," in *Current Perspectives on Aging* (1985).

Stephanie G. Gould, born in 1945 in Madison, Wisconsin, is an independent consultant for the World Bank and the Urban Institute. She is former director of Case and Curriculum Development at the Kennedy School of Government at Harvard University and has published numerous articles on public policy and management.

Gunhild O. Hagestad, born in 1942 in Herefoss, Norway, is assistant professor of human development at Pennsylvania State University and associate fellow at the Institute for Social Research, Oslo, Norway. A member of the program committee for the 13th World Congress of Gerontology, she has written on the role of influence in three-generation families and the impact of divorce on intergenerational relations.

Harry R. Moody, born in 1945 in Boca Raton, Florida, is deputy director of the Brookdale Center on Aging, Hunter College. He is the author of the forthcoming book, *The Abundance of Life: Human Development Policies for an Aging Society.*

Malcolm H. Morrison, born in 1943 in Cambridge, Massachusetts, is director of the Office of Vocational Rehabilitation Demonstration Projects at the Social Security Administration. An expert on retirement and age discrimination in employment, Dr. Morrison is the author of *Economics of Aging: The Future of Retirement* (1982).

Bernice L. Neugarten, born in 1916 in Norfolk, Nebraska, is professor of education and sociology at Northwestern University. Her principal books include *Society and Education* (1957), *Personality in Middle and Late Life* (1964), *Middle Age and Aging* (1968), *Social Status in the City* (1971), and *Age Or Need? Public Policies for Older People* (1982). She is recipient of the Brookdale Award for outstanding contributions to gerontology awarded by the Gerontological Society of America.

Dail A. Neugarten, born in 1945 in Chicago, Illinois, is associate professor at the Graduate School of Public Affairs, University of Colorado at

Denver, where she is on leave to participate in the U.S. Office of Personnel Management's Western Executive Seminar Center. She is the author of the forthcoming book *Careers in Public Management.*

John L. Palmer, born in 1943 in Darby, Pennsylvania, is a senior fellow at the Urban Institute, in Washington, DC. A former assistant secretary of the Department of Health and Human Services, he is the author of *Jobs for Disadvantaged Workers* (1982), *Federal Budget Policy in the 1980s,* (1984). He is also co-author of *The Deficit Dilemma* (1983) and editor of *The Reagan Record* (1984).

Alan Pifer, born in 1921 in Boston, Massachusetts, is president emeritus and senior consultant at Carnegie Corporation of New York and chairman of the Carnegie Corporation Project on the Aging Society and the National Conference on Social Welfare Project on the Federal Social Role. He has published articles on a wide variety of educational and public-policy issues in the *New York Times, Change, Foundation News,* and elsewhere.

Harold A. Richman, born in 1937 in Chicago, Illinois, is Hermon Dunlap Smith Professor at the School of Social Service Administrations, University of Chicago, and director of the Chapin Hall Center for Children at the University of Chicago. He is co-author, with F. Farrow and J. Meltzer, of *Policy Options in Long-Term Care* (1981), and of *State of the Child, 1985* (1985), with M. Testa and E. Lawlor.

John W. Riley, Jr., born in 1908 in Brunswick, Maine, is a consulting sociologist with the International Federation on Aging and senior consultant of the *International Glossary of Social Gerontology* (forthcoming). He is former president of the Sociological Research Association and the American Association for Public Opinion Research and has written in the fields of mass communications, research methods, and the sociology of death and dying.

Matilda White Riley, born in 1911, in Boston, Massachusetts, is associate director of the National Institute on Aging, National Institutes of Health, and president of the American Sociological Association (1985–1986). Her major publications include: *Aging and Society,* 3 vols. (1968–1972), *Aging from Birth to Death,* 2 vols. (1979–1982), and *Perspectives on Behavioral Medicine: The Aging Dimension* (forthcoming).

Alice S. Rossi, born in 1922 in New York City, is Harriet Martineau Professor of Sociology at the University of Massachusetts (Amherst). Former president of the American Sociological Association (1982–1983) and a founder and member of the governing board of the National

Organization for Women (1966–1970), she is the author of *Academic Women on the Move* (1973), *The Feminist Papers* (1974), *The Family* (1978), *Feminists in Politics* (1982), and *Gender and the Life Course* (1985).

Jacob S. Siegel is a professorial lecturer at the department of demography, and senior research associate at the Center for Population Research, Georgetown University. In addition to many monographs and papers on international population, aging, and evaluation of census data, he is co-author of the two-volume study *Methods and Materials of Demography* (1980).

Matthew W. Stagner, born in 1959 in Hutchinson, Kansas, is senior program associate at the Chapin Hall Center for Children, University of Chicago, and a doctoral candidate in public policy studies at the University of Chicago.

Cynthia M. Taeuber, born in 1947 in Conneaut, Ohio, is chief of the Select Populations Staff at the Population Division, Bureau of the Census. The author of numerous articles on the demography of aging, her other areas of interest include the status of women, the quality of census data, and data compilation and retrieval.

Fernando Torres-Gil, born in 1948 in Salinas, California, is staff director of the U.S. House of Representatives' Select Committee on Aging and assistant professor of gerontology and public administration at the University of Southern California, where he is on leave. He is the author of *The Politics of Aging Among Elder Hispanics* (1982).

Edward A. Wynne, born in 1928 in Brooklyn, New York, is professor at the College of Education, University of Illinois (Chicago) and editor of *Character II*, a newsletter on youth issues. He is the author of *Social Security: A Reciprocity System Under Stress* (1980), and principal editor of *Developing Character: Transmiting Knowledge* (1984).

Index